BELGIUM AND LUXEMBOURG 1976/77

Belgium and Luxembourg 1976/77

Illustrated edition with city plans

EUGENE FODOR
editor

ROBERT C. FISHER
executive editor

BETTY GLAUERT
RICHARD MOORE
associate editors

NINA NELSON
area editor

Drawings by Keith West

HODDER AND STOUGHTON

ISBN 0 340 20334 X

The following travel books edited by Eugene Fodor are current in 1976*:*

AREA GUIDES:

EUROPE
CARIBBEAN, BAHAMAS AND BERMUDA
INDIA
ISLAMIC ASIA
JAPAN AND KOREA
MEXICO
SCANDINAVIA
SOUTH AMERICA
SOUTH-EAST ASIA
SOVIET UNION

COUNTRY GUIDES:

AUSTRIA
BELGIUM AND LUXEMBOURG
CZECHOSLOVAKIA
FRANCE
GERMANY
GREAT BRITAIN
GREECE
HOLLAND
HUNGARY
IRELAND
ISRAEL
ITALY
MOROCCO
PORTUGAL
SPAIN
SWITZERLAND
TUNISIA
TURKEY
YUGOSLAVIA

REGIONAL GUIDES:

NEW ENGLAND
NEW YORK AND NEW JERSEY
MID-ATLANTIC
THE SOUTH
THE MID-WEST
THE SOUTH-WEST
ROCKIES AND PLAINS
THE FAR WEST
HAWAII
INDIAN AMERICA

CITY GUIDES:

LONDON
ROME
PARIS
VENICE
PEKING
VIENNA

LANGUAGE GUIDE:

EUROPE TALKING

LATEST ADDITION TO THE SERIES:

HOLIDAY U.S.A. (1 vol.)

Travel books edited by Eugene Fodor, now out of print:

1936 ON THE CONTINENT; 1937 IN EUROPE; EUROPE IN 1938; MEN'S GUIDE TO EUROPE; WOMAN'S GUIDE TO EUROPE

Printed in the Netherlands by Mouton & Co., The Hague

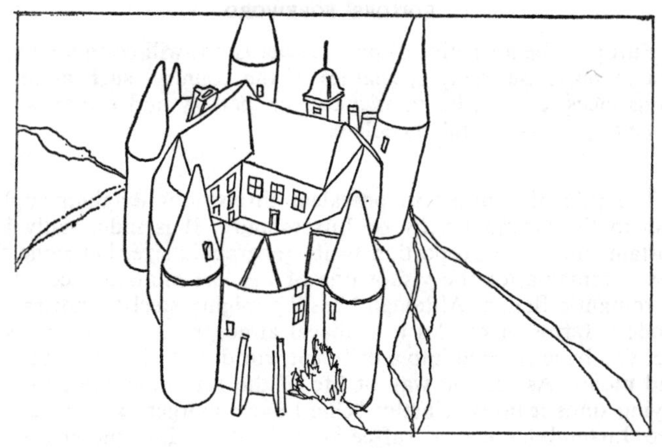

EDITORS' FOREWORD

Belgium and Luxembourg are among the smallest countries on the continent of Europe in area, yet the sum total of their tourist assets ranks them with the biggest. There are few areas of comparable size in the world where so much can be seen with so little expenditure of time and travel. You can go through centuries in a matter of hours: from prehistoric relics to visionary town-planning, from placid farmlands to throbbing powerhouses of technological progress.

Belgium possesses one of Europe's largest ports, Antwerp. It has cities, fabulously endowed with artistic treasures, such as Bruges and Ghent. Cultural centers, like Leuven (Louvain), Tournai and Mechelen (Malines), are spectacular monuments to a culture and way of life indigenous to this corner of Europe. Its capital, Brussels, also capital of the EEC and headquarters of the Atlantic Alliance, is one of the busiest spots on the continent and offers some of the finest food in the world.

This is the country of robust living, of joyous fun-fairs, uninhibited religious processions, and brassy nightclubs. It has also produced some of the subtlest artists, writers, and musicians, such as Memling, Van Eyck, Maeterlinck, César Franck.

Belgium also has two excellent holiday areas to offer: on its endless string of popular beaches, from De Panne through Ostend to Knokke-Heist, and in the pastoral, restful valleys of the Ardennes hills.

Belgium's wealth makes it one of the finest shopping-grounds in Europe. The attractive displays in her shops will certainly tempt you to purchase many specialties of the country, such as its famous laces, crystal, hammered copper, pottery and ceramics, not forgetting its guns and chocolate.

★

The rule of contrast so prevalent throughout Belgium applies also to the Grand Duchy of Luxembourg. It is industrially important out of all proportion to its geographic size, but none the less it remains for the visitor one of the last miniature countries of romantic fiction. Although boasting mighty steel foundries and modern farms, it exudes a medieval atmosphere that makes you feel you have stepped into a different world, full of castles, turrets, and moats. As for the way of life of the Luxembourger, the old saying sums it up succinctly: "One Luxembourger, a rose garden; two Luxembourgers, a kaffee-klatsch; three Luxembourgers, a band." This, too is a country of parades and processions, of good cheer and a hearty capacity to absorb beer and Moselle wine.

★

We wish to offer our sincere thanks to all those who helped us in the preparation of the book.

Mr. Arthur Haulot, Director of the Belgian National Tourist Office and Chairman of the European Travel Commission, extended all possible help through his organization with customary efficiency. Our particular thanks go to Mr. L. Mainil, deputy, Mr. Jean Gyory, Press and Public Relations Officer and to Mrs. Cecile Pierard of the same organization, to Mr. Pierre Claus, director of the Belgian National Tourist Office in London and to Miss Virginia Spruyt. Also to Mrs. Nina Nelson for updating the chapters on Belgium.

We are equally grateful to Mr. Georges Hausemer, Director of the Luxembourg National Tourist Office, for the advice and aid rendered us on his country. Mr. J. Uhres, secretary of the same organization, was also extremely helpful, as was Mr. Th. Pescatore, director of the Luxembourg National Tourist Office in London. Our thanks go, also, to Mr. D. Ned Blackmer, who revised the Luxembourg section of this edition.

★

Color photographs: Feature-Pix and the Luxembourg National Tourist Office.

★

In a book of this size, a few errors are bound to creep in, and when a hotel closes down suddenly, or a restaurant's chef produces an inferior meal, our comments seem suddenly out of place. Let us know, and we will redouble our efforts to investigate the establishment and the complaint. Your letters will help our correspondents throughout the world to pinpoint trouble spots, and may help them in evaluating the results of their own research. Our two addresses: **In the U.S.A.,** Fodor's Modern Guides, Box. 784, Litchfield, Conn. 06759; **In Europe,** Fodor's Modern Guides, 27b Old Gloucester St., London WC1N 3AF.

★

As faithful readers of the Fodor series know, merely listing an establishment in one of our books is sufficient recommendation. Needless to say, establishments will not know if they *are* listed, or dropped, until the book is published.

★

Although we accept advertising in some books, this does not affect the editors' recommendations in any way. We include advertising for two reasons: first, the revenue obtained helps defray the extremely high cost of producing this series yearly, something which we are the only guide book series in the world to do; and second, the advertisements themselves provide useful information (which would otherwise not be included) for our readers.

[illegible]

CONTENTS

THE LUXEMBOURG SCENE

THE FACE OF LUXEMBOURG

SUPPLEMENTS

FACTS AT YOUR FINGERTIPS

FACTS AT YOUR FINGERTIPS

Additional practical hints about hotels, restaurants, transportation, etc., not contained in this section, will be found in the chapters *Prelude to Belgium, Prelude to Luxembourg,* and in the regional chapters throughout this guide.

HOW TO PLAN YOUR TRIP

WHAT WILL IT COST? Budgeting is much simplified if you take a prepackaged trip paid for before you leave. The only extra expenses then are those you allow yourself for drinks, gifts, postcards and postage, extra entertainments, etc. Freelance travel (see "How to Go") usually works out to be more expensive than your estimate, so best take a reserve fund with you. Whether on a prepackage or freelance trip, the cheapest holiday is that spent at one or two centers, staying for several days in one hotel where you can have pension or semi-pension terms, and making day excursions.

If you are on a freelance tour, according to your personal tastes, you can figure out from the approximate prices below what you are likely to spend per day extra to travel costs.

In Belgium: *deluxe,* from 4,000 francs; *comfortably,* 2,000 frcs.; *economically,* 1,200 frcs.

In Luxembourg: *comfortably,* 1,700 francs (there are few deluxe hotels); *economically,* 1,200 frcs.

De luxe, as here used, means staying in the best rooms of the best hotels; traveling by chauffeur-driven car and first class on trains; and paying a reasonable amount of attention to nightclubs—in Belgium, the customary champagne type. *Comfortable* travel involves staying at good hotels, with private bath; eating in good restaurants, but not always at the most expensive ones; indulging in moderate doses of nightlife. *Economical* travel still lets you into clean comfortable hotels, but without style or much service; you can eat good food, but in crowded restaurants, since places both cheap and good are bound to be crowded; you'll patronize more theaters and concerts, not in the best seats, than nightclubs; you will travel second class in trains, comfortable in Belgium and Luxembourg.

For your further guidance, we give below some cost tables for hotels and restaurants in the two countries. Exchange rates, see under "Money" later in this chapter.

BELGIAN HOTEL ROOM PER NIGHT
(in Belgian francs)

	Brussels	*Prov. Capital*	*Major Coast resort*	*Small town, Country*
Deluxe Single	1400 up	-	900-1100	-
Double	1700 up	-	1150-2300	-
First cl. superior	1000-1400	700-900	450-600	-
	1400-1700	1000-1300	900-1200	-
First cl. reasonable	700-900	450-600	230-600	450-700
	1000-1400	800-1000	700-900	550-800
Moderate	450-680	340-450	230-450	230-340
	800-1000	580-800	580-680	450-580
Inexpensive	340-580	340-450	230-340	230-340
	340-800	580-680	340-580	340-450

Prices are for room with bath or shower, and include VAT and 16% service charge, but sojourn tax (where payable) not included.

PENSIONS. Belgium: A single room with bath or shower and full board will run from 580 to 680 francs in Brussels, a double from 1000 to 1150 francs. In other places, charges are from 340-450 francs single, 580 to 680 double. These terms are usually for a minimum stay of 3 days.

HOTEL MEALS
(in Belgium francs)

Main meal (set menu)	*Brussels*	*Prov. Capital*	*Major coast resort*	*Small town, Country*
Deluxe	500 up	400 up	-	-
First class sup.	290	230	230	-
First class reas.	290	230	170	190
Moderate	120-230	200	210	170
Inexpensive	140	80	140-170	150

Belgium, with its larger cities, greater amenities and reputation for gourmet dining, is obviously more expensive than Luxembourg. Also the cost of living is rising faster, and prices will probably rise in 1976.

A TYPICAL DAY IN BRUSSELS
(or Antwerp)

Hotel, moderate, breakfast, one meal	900 Frcs.
Lunch or dinner at moderate restaurant	300-400
Transportation (say 2 taxis)	300
Opera or concert	200
Coffee, beer, cigarettes	250

Roughly around 2,000 frcs. In small provincial places, this budget might decrease by 20-25%.

Luxembourg, being smaller, can limit rising costs more effectively than its larger neighbors: it is more likely that the Grand Duchy will stay close to its prediction of a 9% rise in the cost-of-living index by 1976 than that France, for instance, can keep to its officially announced level of inflation.

Finding a bargain vacation spot in Luxembourg is less a problem of geography than of selection, due to its compact size. In the capital city itself, it is possible to make a week's vacation on 4,000 francs per person, or to spend that much in a day — and half of that if you are camping or hostelling.

LUXEMBOURG HOTEL ROOM PER NIGHT
(in Luxembourg francs)

		*Luxembourg City**	*Major town**	*Small town*	*Village*
Deluxe	Single	850-1740	-	-	-
	Double	1290-2230			
First cl. superior	S	720-990	500-800	400-500	-
	D	850-1520	800-1400	700-800	-
First cl. reasonable	S	640-950	500-600	300-400	225-350
	D	840-1200	700-800	560-650	400-600
Moderate	S	370-640	350-400	230-270	200-300
	D	430-750	400-600	390-450	300-450
Inexpensive	S	230-350	170-200	170-200	200-250
	D	300-500	250-350	250-350	250-350

* Price is for room with bath. Rooms without bath, 15-40 % less

RESTAURANT PRICES
(in Luxembourg francs)

	Luxembourg City	*Major Town*	*Small Town*	*Village*
Main meal				
Deluxe	350-750	250-600	250-400	200-300
First class	250-350	200-400	180-300	150-280
Moderate	90-200	100-250	100-200	90-200
Inexpensive	50-125	60-150	60-150	50-125

Drinks not included; prices range from 12 frcs. for a bottle of mineral water to 250 frcs. for a top vintage wine.

PENSIONS. Luxembourg: A single room with bath or shower and full board will cost from 350-400 francs in Luxembourg City, from 300 to 350 in other places. Pensions offer half-pension (room, breakfast and one other meal) at about 8% less, and prices out of high season are about 10% less. Longer stays than the 3-day minimum usually bring reduced prices, by arrangement with the proprietor.

A TYPICAL DAY IN LUXEMBOURG

Hotel, moderate, with breakfast	350 Frcs.
Lunch at a moderate restaurant	150
Dinner at a moderate restaurant	275
Transportation (say 1 taxi, 1 bus)	127
Theater	200
Cigarettes, coffee, beer	53
Miscellaneous	115

Or around 1,270 francs. You are likely to pay more for meals and miscellaneous in Luxembourg City.

For further information on hotels, restaurants, and the cost of living, see "Prelude to Belgium" and "Prelude to Luxembourg" chapters later in this guide.

WHEN TO GO? The main tourist season in *Belgium* and *Luxembourg* runs from about the beginning of May to the end of September; the peak comes in July and August. This is when the weather is best and it is when most Britishers and Americans take their vacations. However, these two countries do not stage as many big festivals designed largely for foreigners as various other countries put on in the peak travel months. Therefore, if you are making an extended tour of Europe, you may, without missing much, go to the standard spectacles in some of the other countries, and explore Belgium and Luxembourg in the earlier or latter part of your vacation. The most charming features of these countries are just as lovely in May, June, and September as in July and August: the old buildings and canals of Belgian Flanders and the lovely scenery of the hills of Luxembourg and Belgium's Ardennes.

Off-Season Travel. This has become more popular in recent years as tourists have come to appreciate the advantages of avoiding the crowded periods.

Transatlantic sea and air fares are cheaper and so are hotel rates. Even where prices remain the same, available accommodations are better; the choicest rooms in the hotels, the best tables in the restaurants have not been pre-empted, nor are train compartments packed full. And if you really want to get under the skin of the country, the time to do it is when its inhabitants are going about their regular daily routines, not when they are putting on special shows for visiting foreigners.

DEVALUATION—REVALUATION—INFLATION

Devaluation of the U.S. dollar and fluctuating exchange rates in some European countries make accurate budgeting long in advance an impossibility. Prices mentioned throughout this title are indicative only of costs at time of going to press. Check with your travel agent near the time of your trip.

WHERE TO GO? Unless you travel on a packaged tour, with a fixed itinerary and schedule which you can't modify, it's most unlikely that you will follow unchanged any detailed plans you make in advance. Nevertheless it is advantageous to rough out your trip. This gives you an opportunity to decide how much you can comfortably cover in the time at your disposal. If you travel in the peak season, you will often have to make reservations. Finally, poring over the folders any travel agency will give you in profusion is as much fun as the winter gallop through the seed catalogs. The best places to get them are the National Tourist Offices. In *New York:* Belgium, 589 Fifth Ave. N.Y. 10017 (Information). Luxembourg, 1 Dag Hammerskjold Place. In *Montreal*: 1176 Sherbrooks St. West. In *London*: Belgium and Luxembourg, 66 Haymarket, SW1 4RB.

Seasonal Events. Special attractions that might influence you in your choice of itinerary or time of visit are:

In Belgium: *January,* the parades of the Magi, which occur especially in Flanders on Jan. 6. The Brussels Automobile and Motorcycle Show opens in January; end of *February* the carnival season commences, elaborately celebrated in many parts of Belgium, with particular liveliness at Malmédy and Eupen, where the entry of King Carnival sets off four days of fun. Most of the other carnival cities begin celebrating a day later, e.g. Binche, where the famous procession of the "Gilles," with their elaborate costumes, takes place during three days, through mardi-gras, while the wind-up of the open season on fun occurs at Stavelot, near Liège, with its renowned procession of the "Blancs Moussis." The Brussels International Trade Fair is held in *April.* The magnificent display of tulips in the French gardens of Annevoie Castle (Meuse Valley) opens around the middle of April and, weather obliging, remains open until mid-*May* or later. In May also, Ypres holds its unique Cat Festivities. The Queen Elisabeth Music Competition for young soloists runs usually through the month of May into June. But May's chief event is probably the famous Procession of the Holy Blood, in the medieval city of Bruges, on the first Monday after May 2.

The procession at Mons, ending with the mock slaughter of a dragon, takes place on Trinity Sunday. The St. Evermeire mystery play is staged at Rutten, and Kortrijk celebrates with the Procession of the Holy Hair. On the third Sunday in *June* a great carnival procession is held at Verviers. *July* contains Belgium's national holiday, on the 21st, celebrated with gusto throughout the country, and many other observances coming under the head of folklore. Probably the most famous is the Procession of the Penitents at Furnes on the last Sunday of the month, a solemn religious spectacle. If you are in Ostend on the Sunday after the day of Sts. Peter and Paul you can witness the rite of the blessing of the sea. Ghent's begonia fields blossom (to end September). *Son et Lumière* pageant at Beloeil Castle and Tournai Cathedral (through August).

Brussels' Planting of the May-Tree takes place in *August*. David renews his struggle against Goliath during the "ducasse" of Ath on the last Sunday of the same month. Bruges stages a passion play, Sanguis Christi, derived from the story of the Holy Blood (in years that end in 2 or 7); also every five years (years ending in 5 or 0), the Feast of the Golden Tree, re-enacting the historic marriage of Charles the Rash, Duke of Burgundy, and Margaret of York. Last weekend in the month, Lochristi (6 miles from Ghent) holds its Begonia Festival (the Begonia is Belgium's national flower). The Plague Procession, which has been held in Tournai on the first Sunday of *September* every year since 1052 is the chief event of that month.

In Luxembourg: On Easter Monday, usually in *April,* the Emmaus Fair takes place in Luxembourg City. The pilgrimage to Our Lady of Luxembourg occurs in the capital on the fifth Sunday after Easter, and the famous dancing procession of Echternach on Whit Tuesday. *June* 23 is Luxembourg's national day, opening the evening before with a torchlight procession and fireworks, and there all manner of festivities in Luxembourg City.

The end of June sees Rembrance Day celebrated in Ettelbruck, with a military review, fly-by, parachute drop, and gala ball in honor of General Patton and the World War II liberation of Luxembourg.

Bridging June and the beginning of *July* is the annual Tour of Ancient Automobiles, when entries from all Europe make their stately way through the countryside, with many stops for spectators to admire the vintage cars. At Mondorf-les-Bains you may have your automobile blessed on St. Christopher's Day. At Wiltz, from mid-July to early *August,* there is an open-air festival of theater and music which attracts international artists. *September* is the month of the wine festivals in the Moselle Valley.

HOW TO GO? When you have decided where you want to go, your next step is to consult a good travel agent. If you haven't one, the American Society of Travel Agents, 360 Lexington Avenue, New York, N.Y. 10017 and 130 Albert St., Suite 1207, Ottawa, Ontario KIP 5G4, or the Association of British Travel Agents, 50-57 Newman St., London WIP 4AH, will advise you. *Maupintour Associates, American Express, Thomas Cook* all have branch offices or correspondents in the larger European cities. The *American Automobile Association,* 28 East 78th St., New York, N.Y. 10021 (tel.: 212 286-1166) can arrange any type of foreign tours from package or excursion to individually escorted.

Travel abroad today, although it is steadily becoming easier and more comfortable, is also growing more complex in its details. As the choice of things to do, places to visit, ways of getting there, increases, so does the problem of *knowing* about all these questions. A reputable, experienced travel agent is a specialist in details, and because of his importance to the success of your trip, you should inquire in your community to find out which organization has the finest reputation.

If you wish your agent to book you on a package tour, reserve your transportation and even your first overnight hotel accommodation, his services should cost you nothing. Most carriers and tour operators grant him a fixed commission for saving them the expense of having to open individual offices in every town and city.

If, on the other hand, you wish him to plan for you an individual itinerary and make all arrangements down to hotel reservations and transfers to and from rail and air terminals, you are drawing upon his skill and knowledge of travel as well as asking him to shoulder a great mass of correspondence and detail. His commissions from carriers won't come close to covering his expenses, and thus he will make a service charge on the total cost of your planned itinerary. This charge may amount to 10 or 15 per cent, but it will more than like *save* your money on balance. A good travel agent can help you find rail reductions and generally save time and money.

There are four principal ways of traveling:

The **group tour,** in which you travel with others, following a prearranged itinerary hitting all the high spots, and paying a single all-inclusive price that covers everything—transportation, meals, lodging, sightseeing tours, guides. And here your travel agent can book you with a *special interest* group, thus you needn't spend a high proportion of your tour trotting round museums if you would much rather be wandering round botanical gardens, and you will be among people with similar interests to yourself.

The **prearranged individual tour,** following a set itinerary planned for you by the travel agent, with all costs paid in advance.

The **individual tour** where you work out the itinerary for yourself, according to your own interests, but have your agent make transportation and hotel reservations, transfers, sightseeing plans.

The **freelance tour,** in which you pay as you go, change your mind if you want to, and do your own planning. You'll still find a travel agent handy to make your initial transport reservation and book you for any special event where long advance booking is essential.

Travel for the handicapped person: Travel Companions Inc., P. O. Box 107, Cochranville, Pa. 19330, offers a companion/escort service in Europe. Other agencies in this field include: Flying Wheel Tours, 148 West Bridge St., Box 382, Owatonna, Minn. 55060; Evergreen Travel Service, 19429 44th St., Lynnwood, Washington 98036; Handy-Cap Horizons, 3250 East Loretta Drive, Indianapolis, Ind. 46227; and Kasheta Travel Inc., 139 Main St., East Rockaway, L.I. 11518.

Americans can arrange with one of the travel credit organizations for a European charge account that enables them to sign for hotel and restaurant bills, car rentals, purchase, and so forth, and pay the resulting total at one time on a monthly bill. This is particularly advantageous for businessmen traveling on an expense account or on business trips whose cost is deductible for income tax. Offering this service are the *American Express,* with branch offices in all major cities, *The Diners Club,* 10 Columbus Circle, New York, Hilton's *Carte Blanche, Eurocard International,* and many others.

YOUTH HOSTELS. Of late years, encouraged particularly by the extension of the Youth Hostel system, foreign visitors to the two countries, especially those under 25, have been participating in increasing numbers in the cheapest and ruggedest form of traveling, formerly confined pretty much to natives. This means moving about the country on bicycles, in boats or on foot, or hitch-hiking (German or Scandinavian number plates are the best bet). If you elect to travel in bourgeois fashion by train or bus, you can often get reduced rates through the Youth Hostel organizations.

In Belgium hostels are numerous and inexpensive, but locker space is often inadequate. For information write to *Fédération Belge des Auberges de la*

Jeunesse, 52 Rue Van Oost, 1030-Brussels.

Luxembourg has many hostels. Plentiful and rewarding, they are often parts of ancient fortresss and castles. You will find them at Clervaux, Echternach, Hollenfels, Luxembourg City, Vianden, and a number of other places. Full particulars can be had from *Centrale des Auberges de Jeunesse,* 18a, Place d'Armes, Luxembourg.

It is also possible to get information in England and the United States at the following addresses: American Youth Hostels, Inc., 132 Spring St., N.Y. 10012; Camping Club of Great Britain and Ireland, 11 Lower Grosvenor Pl., London S.W.1; Youth Hostels Association International Travel Bureau, 29 John Adam St., Strand, London W.C.2; Cyclists' Touring Club, 69 Meadrow, Godalming, Surrey.

CAMPING AND CARAVANING. In both Belgium and Luxembourg this is well organized, with both authorized campsites and other facilities. Information may be obtained from the National Tourist Office of the respective country and (for Belgium) from the *Royal Camping and Caravaning Club of Belgium,* 51 Rue de Namur, 1000-Brussels. For Luxembourg, consult the Fédération Luxembourgeoise de Camping et de Caravaning, 94 rue Jean-Pierre Michels, Esch-sur-Alzette. An excellent and very detailed list of camping and caravan sites is issued by the National Tourist Office of each country.

The Grand Duchy is probably the best organized country in Europe for camping. Specially arranged camping grounds with full amenities abound. There are some 120 sites, but camping is permitted practically anywhere, provided the consent of the owner of the ground is obtained.

FOR STUDENTS. In Belgium students should go to the Federation of Belgian Students at 60 Rue de l'Association in *Brussels,* or to the Secretary's office of the Université de Bruxelles, Ave. Franklin Roosevelt. *Louvain (Leuven),* Université Catholique de Louvain, Craecenstraat. *Ghent;* Universiteit van Gent, Voldersstraat 9. *Liège,* Université de Liège, Pl. du 30 Août.

A joint-relations office for educational and group travel has been set up in *Brussels*: Rencontres Internationales de Jeunes, Cité Administrative de l'Etat, Arcades, Niveau 2/3. Information in Britain may be obtained from the National Union of Students, 3 Endsleigh St., London W.C.1.

Student package tours of Europe, gaining in popularity, are organized by several American companies including American Express.

FAMILY STAY. The American Field Service, 313 East 43rd St., New York, N.Y. 10017 offers young people (ages 16-18) a chance to stay with families in 58 countries. The Summer Program lasts about 11 weeks and costs $1100; the full year School Program 11 to 13 months. Participants attend high school in the host country and live with a family with similar interests.

Other low-budget visitors can get useful information from the Y.M.C.A., 31 Rue Duquenoy, Brussels, or the Y.W.C.A., 43 Rue St. Bernard, Brussels.

WHAT TO TAKE? Travel light: If you plan to fly, the high excess baggage rates give you a real incentive to stay within the first transatlantic limit of 66 pounds, or the economy class limit of 44 pounds. Moreover, most bus lines and some of the crack international trains limit the weight (usually 55 pounds) or bulk of your luggage. The principle is not to take more than you can carry yourself (unless you travel by car). Motorists will find it advisable to be frugal as well. You should limit your luggage to what can be locked into the trunk or boot of your car when making daytime stops.

Clothing. At the head of your list should be a raincoat. It rarely rains hard in the Low Countries (Belgium is more dangerous than Luxembourg for this), but it drizzles a lot, all year round, and a clear blue sky in the morning is no guarantee that it won't be raining half an hour later. No one ever goes out for more than an hour without a raincoat, no matter what the sky looks like. Better follow suit. Otherwise, wear just what you would wear at home. If you plan to go to expensive restaurants or nightclubs, bring evening dress.

Women. You can achieve variety thanks to standard favorites: mix-and-match separates, sweater sets, accessories, etc. Crush-resistant blouses and dresses are ideal: dacron and orlon and the dripdry materials.

Practical shoes may be less flattering but they're better suited to wet weather, cobbled streets, and long hours on your feet. A pair of slippers may be a lifesaver during long plane or train rides.

Handbags are another problem. It's wise to select a handbag with enough interior pockets (or at least one with a zipper closing for your money) to keep things in order. A good way to keep foreign currency from mingling with your own is to relegate each to its own small change purse.

Men. A dark business suit is adequate for most functions; lightweight suit, sport jacket, and two or three pairs of slacks to wear with it will complete your outer wardrobe. Synthetic fibers are ideal because of their crease-resistance and washability (hotel laundering and dry cleaning services are expensive). Make sure the jackets have *two* inside pockets: one for your wallet, tickets, etc., and the other for your passport, travelers checks, and valuables.

Shirts of dacron, orlon, etc., are convenient for traveling light or one-night stops, but they do prevent proper airing of the body. You may prefer to pack two wash-and-wear shirts and six cotton shirts. You can have the latter laundered every few days, and you'll have the former for emergencies. A lightweight dressing gown is useful, as is a pair of folding slippers.

Travelers checks are the best way to safeguard travel funds. They are sold by various banks and companies in terms of American and Canadian dollars and pounds sterling. Most universally accepted are those of *American Express,* while those issued by *First National Bank of New York* and *Bank of America* are also widely used. Best known and easily exchanged British travelers checks are those issued by *Thos. Cook & Son* and the banks: *Barclay, Lloyds, Midland,* and *National-Westminster.* Banks now often charge a sizeable fee for changing them so do inquire before making the transaction. It is now possible for British travelers to cash checks abroad for up to £30 each transaction, on production of a Barclaycard (or one of many bank check cards participating in the scheme) in over 19 countries, including Belgium and Luxembourg (but only in European banks).

PASSPORTS. Generally there is some delay so apply several months in advance. **U.S. residents** must apply in person to the U.S. Passport Agency in New York, Boston, Philadelphia, Washington D.C., Miami, Chicago, New Orleans, Seattle, San Francisco, Los Angeles or Honolulu, or to their local county courthouse. In some areas selected post offices are also able to handle passport applications. If your latest passport was issued within the past eight years use this to apply by mail. Otherwise, take with you: 1) a birth certificate or certified copy thereof, or other proof of citizenship; 2) two identical photographs 2½ inches square, full face, black and white or color and taken within the past six months; 3) $13 ($10 if you apply by mail); 4) proof of identity such as a driver's license, previous passport, any governmental ID card. Social Security and credit cards are NOT acceptable. US passports are valid for five years.

If a non-citizen, you need a Treasury Sailing Permit, Form 1040 D, certifying that all Federal taxes have been paid: apply to your District Director of Internal Revenue. You will have to present: 1) blue or green alien registration card; 2) passport; 3) travel tickets; 4) most recently filed Form 1040; 5) W-2 forms for the most recent full year; 6) most recent current payroll stubs or letter; 7) check to be sure this is all! To return to the United States, you need a re-entry permit if you plan to stay abroad more than 1 year. Apply for it at least six weeks before departure in person at the nearest office of the Immigration and Naturalization Service, or by mail to the Immigration and Naturalization Service, Washington, D.C.

British subjects must apply for passports on special forms obtainable from your travel agency or a main Post Office. The application should be sent to the Passport Office for your area (as indicated on the guidance form) or taken personally to your travel agent. Apply at least 3 weeks before the passport is required. The regional Passport Offices are located in London, Liverpool, Peterborough, Glasgow, Newport (Mon.), and Belfast. The application must be countersigned by your bank manager or a solicitor, barrister, doctor, clergyman or Justice of the Peace who knows you personally. You will need two photos. Fee £5.

VISAS. Not required by either country for nationals of the United Kingdom, United States, Ireland, Canada, Australia or New Zealand. Visas are required from nationals of these countries, however, if a stay of more than three months is to be made in Belgium or Luxembourg. Nationals of Great Britain and Ireland are admitted also on presentation of a valid identity card.

HEALTH CERTIFICATES. Not required for entry to the Benelux countries. Neither the United States nor Canada requires a certificate of vaccination prior to reentry (unless an outbreak occurred during your European visit). But because of frequent changes in law, we suggest you be vaccinated anyway, before you leave. Have your doctor fill in the standard form which comes with your passport, or obtain one from a steamship company, airline, or travel agent. Take the form with you to present on re-entering.

How To Reach Belgium and Luxembourg

FROM NORTH AMERICA

BY AIR. *To Belgium:* From New York to Brussels is an easy overnight flight, and with jet services cutting the flying time to 7 hours, Belgium comes closer than ever to the New World. *Sabena* and *PAA* airlines offer daily non-stop services to Brussels from New York; *Sabena* and *Air Canada* have flights from Montreal. Other airlines flying this route are: *El Al* (New York, via London); *Pan American* (Detroit, Philadelphia, and Boston, via London); *British Airways* (New York, and other U.S. and Canadian cities, via London). *Air Canada* flies from Montreal and Toronto, direct.

To Luxembourg: Icelandic Airlines flies from New York and Chicago to Luxembourg via Reykjavik. *International Air Bahamas* links Nassau with Luxembourg, with connections from the American continent. Another scheduled, non-IATA carrier which connects with the U.S.A. is *International Caribbean Airways.* See your travel agent for the latest schedules of all carriers.

Another drawback is the luggage allowance, limited to 66 pounds (30 kilos) for first-class flights and 44 pounds (20 kilos) for economy flights. If you are the kind that travels light as a matter of principle, this will be no hardship, especially since you can carry a camera, a pair of binoculars, an umbrella, a laprobe, an overcoat, and a couple of books in addition to the luggage that is weighed. If you are not, then you'll be paying 1% of the standard first-class one-way fare for every kilo (2.2 pounds) of overweight.

BONUS STOPOVERS TO BELGIUM AND LUXEMBOURG

If you are going to Belgium and Luxembourg with a ticket to Brussels, why not stopover en route at Glasgow or Dublin, London or Paris? These and many other European points may be visited without extra charge when you buy a ticket from New York to the Belgian city.

You'll be pleasantly surprised at the way an ordinary roundtrip can be broadened in scope into a very comprehensive circle trip. When you buy a ticket to Brussels, you are entitled to 4,394 miles of transportation in each direction. This allows you to add many cities which lie off the direct route and saves you paying for separate side trips.

Stopovers are, of course, entirely optional. You can fly nonstop from New York to Brussels. However, if you wish to add a number of countries en route these stopovers are certainly useful.

Let's examine some of the available routings to Brussels. These are only a sampling of the total number offered and you should discuss the complete range of possibilities with your travel agent.

Leaving New York you may fly to Shannon (Eire) and then into Dublin. After a stopover in this country you can cross the Irish Sea to Liverpool, a fine jumping off point for trips to Southport and Blackpool (two English resort towns) and the nearby Lake District.

Then comes a short trip to Manchester, an industrial city of considerable importance and a good center for sightseeing trips to Yorkshire and the north-east of England.

Birmingham is the next stopover which you are entitled to make en route to Brussels. This is a fine base for trips to nearby Coventry with its new cathedral, Stratford-on-Avon with its Shakespeare plays and Leamington Spa. After these stopovers you can continue into London before crossing the English Channel to the Continent.

You also can fly from New York to Glasgow and make a stopover in Scotland before continuing to Brussels. Making Glasgow your headquarters for sightseeing, fine steamer and motor coach excursions to the Highlands and nearby lochs can be arranged.

Continuing to London, you may fly via Manchester and Birmingham or Edinburgh. The latter city is noted for its music festival and fine shopping.

Yet another possibility is to fly from Glasgow to Belfast (N. Ireland). Between Belfast and London you may make additional stops in Liverpool, Manchester and Birmingham.

Should you enter Europe via Shannon and Dublin, Glasgow and Edinburgh also may be included in your itinerary at no extra fare. You can fly to either Scottish city from Dublin then continue to London. Between London and Brussels, you may add in either Paris or Amsterdam.

If you prefer, you can fly from New York to London and then continue to the Continent. For that matter you can make Manchester, Paris or Amsterdam your initial gateway although this somewhat reduces the number of stopovers.

If you wish to bypass London, you can fly from New York to Glasgow and then direct to Amsterdam before making the short hop to Brussels.

What about circle trip possibilities for passengers wishing to travel to Belgium in one direction and return via another. You can fly from New York to

Shannon, Dublin, Liverpool, Manchester, Birmingham, London and Paris. Return via Amsterdam and Glasgow to New York. Thus you broaden your ordinary roundtrip into a very comprehensive circle trip.

Fares from New York to Brussels are about $612 winter economy, $1206 first class; both roundtrip jet. Check with your travel agent for details of special excursion fares available during certain times of the year. (Higher at weekends and peak periods.)

For travel to Luxembourg the same routings apply as from New York to Brussels. However, the fares are slightly higher. Add approximately $24 to the Brussels economy class ticket and $25 first class.

These fares and routings apply to members of IATA the International Air Transport Association. However, non-IATA Icelandic Airlines also can take you from New York to Luxembourg at substantially lower cost. IAL also throws in a stopover at Reykjavik, Iceland, which is well worth visiting for its waterfalls, hot springs and interesting scenery.

AIR FARES. Transatlantic airlines have first and economy class only, and a wide range of "group" fares through travel agents. From New York or Montreal to Brussels the oneway jet fare is about $603 first class, $412 economy, peak. Round trip is double the single rate. Fares and accommodations are subject to change and regulation by the International Air Transport Association and the above rates are only indicative of the maximum. A complicated structure of reduced air fares obtains at this writing, based on the dates of departure and the length of stay. Consult your travel agent on this in order to achieve the minimum rate. He will supply information about group rates, charter flights, credit facilities, and special excursion rates. Some of these are true bargains, such as the winter group affinity round trip, $341, or the 22-to-45-day individual excursion fare, $374 to $507.

With one exception, all North Atlantic air carriers charge the same fares, established by the International Air Transport Associations. As a non-member of IATA, and because its flights take a few hours longer, *Icelandic Airlines* is able to provide average Economy standards of comfort at a lower fare, with special youth fare (12-25 yrs.).

Children between the ages of 2 and 12 travel at half the adult tariff, but are entitled to a full luggage allowance. Infants under 2 not occupying a seat and accompanied by an adult are charged only 10% of the full fare. Although they are not entitled to a free luggage allowance, their food, clothing, and other supplies needed in flight are not weighed. Most airlines provide special bassinets if notified in advance. Students and military personnel are entitled to certain additional reductions.

Airline tickets can be bought on the instalment plan. A down payment of as little as 10% secures the reservations, and the balance can be paid off, after your trip, during the next 12 months. Hotel accommodations and other expenses of a trip can be added to the same instalment account, if desired. Interest charges make this arrangement more expensive.

> Brussels and Luxembourg airports operate tax-free shops for the benefit of passengers departing for destinations outside the Benelux Economic Union. Wide choice of goods. But for economic selection of goods, see "Customs" below.

BY SHIP. Regularly-scheduled transatlantic sailings are disappearing fast, however, it is still possible to cross the Atlantic by sea, if you choose your time. Crossing time takes 5 to 11 days, depending on the route and destination of the vessel.

The only major shipping line with regular transatlantic crossings, April to November, is the Cunard. The Baltic Shipping Co., c/o March Shipping Services, 1 World Trade Center, 52nd Floor, N.Y. 10048, and 400 Craig Street West, Montreal, P.Q., Canada, has a May, Aug., Sept., Oct., service from New York and Montreal to Cobh, Le Havre, London, Rotterdam, Bremerhaven and Leningrad. Rates are from $305 to $775; the ships, *Alexander Pushkin* and *Mikhail Lermontov* are both 20,000 tons.

The Gdynia America Line, 115 Broadway, N.Y. 10006 has 3 or 4 freighter sailings a month to northern Europe; one-way fares are around $275 and you should reserve 5-6 months in advance. Lislind International Inc., 5 World Trade Center, N.Y. 10048 are general agents for Nedlloyd, Royal Interocean Lines, and KNSM Royal Netherlands Steamship Co. and also have passenger service to northern Europe. For other shipping lines, consult your travel agent.

Two-class accommodation, first and tourist, is usual on the newer ships, which are now constructed so as to adapt for cruising. Life on board is usually less formal than in past years: you need not be any more dressy than you plan to be during your European trip, but may wish to include informal evening wear, though first class can be dressy. Remember, evening dress is not worn the first and last nights at sea. Entertainment may include cabaret, movie shows, a casino, dances; some ships have youth bars, discothèques, and nurseries.

Which brings up the subject of *mal-de-mer*. Some authorities claim that seasickness is all a matter of the imagination. This may be true of a few high-strung individuals, but for most travelers it's a question of unaccustomed motion. If you're apprehensive, *Dramamine, Marzine,* and several other well known motion-sickness pills are amazingly effective.

FARES. These vary according to route and season: there are currently three categories—on-season, off-season (thrift), and intermediate (between) season. In addition to the fare and tipping (which may add on $15 to $75), you are almost certain to spend at least an equivalent amount on incidentals during your time on board. On a top class ship the oneway fare can be from $880 first class, $505 second class, according to season and berth. Fares on passenger-carrying freigthers, which are single-class, run around $275-$325. This is much cheaper and explains their popularity. There are discounts on roundtrip fares of from 5-20%, also special excursion rates, and reductions for off-season travel and group travel. There are also possibilities to sail one way and fly the other. Consult your travel agent.

FROM BRITAIN OR IRELAND

BY AIR. *To* **Belgium.** *British Airways, British Caledonian* and *Sabena* link London with Brussels several times daily. There are also direct flights from Manchester. *Sabena* also has twice-daily services between Gatwick and Ostend. *BIA (British Island Airways)* operates 3 flights daily to Antwerp from Heathrow, once daily from Gatwick. *Aer Lingus* has flights from Dublin to Brussels. Other flights, from Birmingham, Derby, Bristol, Cardiff, Manchester, Glasgow and other northern towns, serve Middelkerke-Ostend. *Northeast Airlines* flies from Newcastle and Leeds-Bradford to Ostend in July and August.

Flying time from London airport to Brussels airport is under an hour. Fares: London to Brussels about £60 return, tourist class; and about £31 for a "night-before" booking. British Air Ferries have a rail-air-service at low rates.

Because of the short distance between London and Brussels, no stopovers are available for this trip. However, a passenger originating in Glasgow for Brussels can stop en route in Manchester, Birmingham and London.

To **Luxembourg.** *Luxair* and *Northeast* fly from London to Luxembourg direct. Tourist-class rates are about £40 one way. The special night excursion rate is about £70 return (round trip).

BY TRAIN. Two trains leave Victoria Station daily on the Dover-Ostend-Brussels-Luxembourg run and in summer high season there are also night, early morning and extra afternoon trains. Through Ostend the London-Brussels trip may be made in 7-8 hours. The Channel crossing takes about 3½ hours. The earlier train from Victoria brings you to Luxembourg City about 9 p.m. It is also possible to take the Dover-Calais route, with an hour and a half on the Channel, reaching Brussels in 8¾ hours via Lille and Tournai. Fares from London to Brussels are about £10 first class, £8 second class, via Ostend, one way. Children between 4 and 12 pay half-fare; children under 4 travel free.

Every evening a night train-ferry, with single and 2-berth sleeping cars, links London-Brussels via the Dover-Dunkirk crossing. It arrives either end about breakfast time. The extra cost of the sleeper avoids changing at the ports.

BY CAR. Car ferry routes across the Channel increase steadily to keep pace with the increasing numbers of tourists who take their car along.

Belgian Marine operates frequent daily-Dover-Ostend services, and *British Rail Sealink* has similar frequencies from Folkestone, and the two combine with a nightly service. (The E5, Ostend-Brussels route, is occasionally one-way on summer Sundays and holidays: drivers proceeding against the prevailing flow must use the old, slower N10 route alongside.) Single adult fares, about £4.50, cars from £4.50 according to length.

From Harwich, the *Harwich-Ostend Line* has frequent daily services to Ostend; single fare £5.30, cars from £4.

Townsend-Thoresen Car Ferries have daily drive-on-and-off services between Dover and Zeebrugge or Calais, and Felixstowe and Zeebrugge. Also long weekends in Belgium at £13.50 a head at their holiday village at De Haan, half-price 36-hour trips, and discounts on hire of caravans and camping equipment if travelling on their services.

Transport Ferry Service operates daily from Felixstowe to Rotterdam. Drive-on-and-off.

Complete tariff information from Continental Car Ferry Centre, 52 Grosvenor Gnds, London, S.W.1; from the AA, RAC and London office of the AAA; from Belgian House, 167 Regent St., London W.1.

BAF (British Air Ferries) operates several daily air ferry routes from Southend, Essex to Ostend. One way passengers fare is about £9 to Ostend, car tariffs from £15 up, according to length. *London office:* Liverpool St. station; *Ostend,* Airport.

Also Coventry-Ostend at about £17 and £29 respectively. Cheaper rates return and mid-week.

FROM THE CONTINENT, AUSTRALIA AND SOUTH AFRICA

BY PLANE. Sabena, the Belgian airline, has regular connections with most of the main European centers. Luxembourg may be reached by air from Brussels, Frankfurt, Scandinavia, Paris, Nice, Malaga, Athens, Rome, etc.

Australians and South Africans flying from their respective countries to London may include Brussels at no extra charge on their tickets providing they fly by IATA carrier. Leaving Sydney, for instance, for London it is possible to fly in one direction via Djakarta, Singapore, Bangkok, Delhi, Moscow and Brussels. Returning, you can stop at Rome, Beirut, Teheran, Karachi, Colombo, Singapore again and Darwin or Perth.

A *South African* can fly in one direction via Luanda (Angola), Las Palmas (Canary Islands) and Lisbon; returning, he can stop at Tel Aviv and Teheran.

BY SHIP. *Chandris Lines* runs a service between South Africa (Capetown), Australia (Fremantle, Melbourne, Sydney), New Zealand (Wellington), Southampton and Rotterdam with the 24,351-ton *Ellinis,* which cruises during four months of the year. A one-class ship.

BY TRAIN. In additions to regular electric trains, there are a number of all-first-class services between Brussels and other European cities that are part of the TEE (Trans-Europe-Express) network. Seats must be reserved in advance and a surcharge paid. Passenger cars are very comfortable, meals and refreshments are available in transit. From Brussels there are several fast electric trains to Luxembourg daily and the Holland-Switzerland expresses, via Liège, stop at Luxembourg City. Luxembourg is also tied into the German inter-city express system.

Etoile du Nord and **Ile de France** run between Paris and Amsterdam, via Brussels (about 3 hrs. from Paris; 2½ hrs. from Amsterdam).

Oiseau Bleu *and* **Brabant** run non-stop between Paris and Brussels (about 3 hrs.).

Saphir runs between Brussels and Frankfurt (Germany), via Liège (about 5 hrs. from Frankfurt).

Edelweiss runs between Amsterdam and Zürich (Switzerland) via Brussels and Luxembourg City. Respectively about 2½ and 5 hrs. from Amsterdam, 5 and 7½ hrs. from Zürich.

MOTOR ROUTES TO BRUSSELS. For the motorist whose goal is Belgium's capital, here are a number of suggested routes from neighboring countries. Points of departure are indicated in *italics.*

From **France:** *Paris* on the motorway direct to Brussels or via Soissons-Laon-Vervins-Avesnes-Maubeuge-Mons; *Calais* to St. Omer-Hazebrouck-Armentières-Lille-Tournai-Ath; *Dunkirk* to Poperinghe-Ypres (Ieper)-Courtrai (Kortrijk)-Oudenaarde (or Renaix)-Ninove; *Reims* to Rethel-Rocroi-Philippeville-Charleroi; *Nancy* to Metz-Thionville-Luxembourg-Namur.

From **Germany:** *Karlruhe* to Saarbrücken-Merzig-Luxembourg; *Trier* to Wasserbillig-Luxembourg-Arlon-Bastogne-Marche-Namur; *Cologne* by autobahn bypassing Aachen-Liège-St. Truiden bypass-Leuven (or direct Aachen-Antwerp by the Baudouin motorway): Aachen to Maastricht (Holland)-Hasselt-motorway to Antwerp-express highway to Brussels; *Ruhr region* to München-Gladbach-Roermond (Holland)-motorway to Liège.

From **Holland:** *Nijmegen* to Tilburg-Turnhout-motorway bypassing Antwerp-Mechelen-Brussels; *Amsterdam* to Rotterdam-Breda bypass-Wuustwezel-motorway bypassing Antwerp-express highway to Brussels; *Amsterdam*-express highway bypassing Utrecht, then right turn after Waal bridge to Gorinchem, Breda and Antwerp (this is the shortest route).

Arriving in Belgium and Luxembourg

CUSTOMS. *Belgium* and *Luxembourg* are members of the European Common Market, part of which is a customs union between them and Holland, Germany, France, Italy, Gt. Britain, Eire and Denmark. With a few exceptions, their customs regulations are the same; and anything lawfully landed in any of the Common Market countries can pass duty-free into any of the other countries. The only major exception are excisable articles, such as tobacco and alcohol; but customs still have the technical right to charge the local purchase (or transactions) tax on the value goods in the visitor's luggage. In practice, this right is very rarely exercised against the luggage of visitors from outside the Common Market crossing the frontiers non-commercially. For visitors from overseas, there is an agreed tolerance of 400 cigarettes, 500 g. of tobacco or 100 cigars (half these amounts for visitors from European countries). One or more bottles of spirits (to a total of 1 liter) may be brought in, even with the seals unbroken. There are no restrictions on bringing money into or out of Belgium. Luxembourg regulations are the same.

MONEY. In Luxembourg and Belgium the monetary unit is the franc. 100 centimes make one franc. In Luxembourg, Belgian money is legal tender, but the reverse is not true. This otherwise good currency having no official rating outside the Grand Duchy, you are advised to change your remaining banknotes before leaving the country.

Belgium issues notes in denominations of 20, 50, 100, 500, 1,000 and 5,000 francs. Luxembourg issues notes in denominations of 10, 20, 50 and 100 francs. Belgian coins are issued in denominations of 1, 5, and 10 francs and 25 and 50 centimes, with 20, 50 and 100 francs pieces for numismatists.

Note! At this writing, there were approximately 35 francs to the U.S.$, 85 to the pound sterling. But due to continuing worldwide currency crises, it is not possible to estimate what the exchange rate will be in 1976, so check with your travel agent before your trip.

LANGUAGE. *Belgium* has two national languages. Flemish, a variation of Dutch, is spoken in the north by over half of Belgium's population. To the south, French is spoken by the Walloons, who are of Gallic stock. Brussels is officially bilingual but French gets you almost anywhere. The language frontier runs roughly from north of the Tournai-Brussels road to south of the Brussels-Liège road. Each ethnic group teaches the other's language at school but that is soon forgotten. While educated Flemings all speak French more or less fluently, this cannot be said of their opposite numbers among Walloons. A German-speaking minority lives along the east border.

The learning of English comes easily to the Flemish and, if you speak to him in your halting French, the chances are he will answer you in English. He resents, however, any apparent assumption that French is or ought to be his language. If your French is really good, this is a point worth remembering. It even pays to acquire a few set phrases in his language, with which you can begin the conversation, and which will put your own tourist status on an understood footing.

Another point about touring in Flanders is the naming of towns and streets. The Flemish have names of their own even for towns outside their own borders, but this need not concern you very much. You will have roadsigns enough, with the names you know, to avoid any difficulty. (See the list of place names in the *"Prelude to Belgium"* chapter.

Far more acute is the crucial trouble with streetnames. In Brussels these are posted in French and Flemish, but no such concession is made in Flemish towns. Nevertheless, people who give you directions in French nearly always translate the streetnames. From instructions to walk down the Rue des Pierres till you came to the Grand' Place, you would probably manage to recognize the way to the Grote Markt down Steenstraat. Often, however, it is much less easy than this, and you may have difficulty in finding somebody who knows the streets by their French names. Be sure, then, that you know the Flemish versions of any streetnames that come into the directions.

In *Luxembourg,* French is official, but the people are bilingual, or even trilingual: *Letzeburgesch* is the everyday language, while French and German are spoken by everyone, and many people speak English.

Staying in Belgium and Luxembourg

Airport-City Transport: From Brussels Airport to city center there are bus services, also frequent direct rail services (16 mins.); this is quicker and much cheaper than by taxi, which takes about half an hour. Also bus services between Antwerp Airport and city center, every 10 mins., and from Liège Airport to center; also between Antwerp and Brussels Airport. In *Luxembourg,* regular airport and city bus services assure your making connections.

HOTELS. For detailed information on costs, see the beginning of this section. Neither of the two countries has officially classified its hotels. Their tourist offices, however, issue booklets with the addresses, telephone numbers and prices of a large number of hotels. In *Belgium,* breakfast is often included, but not always. The breakfast room is a habit here also, but the expensive hotels are likely to serve breakfast in rooms. In *Luxembourg,* the price of breakfast is ordinarily not included, but all taxes and services are.

TIPPING. In *Belgium* hotels and restaurants will usually add 15 percent to the bill; frequently people will give a bit more than the required sum. In *Luxembourg* hotels and restaurants, taxes and service charges are included in the charge. Cinema theater and concert ushers definitely expect a small tip. Café waiters expect about 15 to 20 percent, but you should ask whether the price they name includes the tip ("avec ou sans service?"). Porters in railway stations have a fixed priced per suitcase. The minimum is 20 francs.

A warning is in order about taxi drivers (especially in Brussels), who can be quite rude to foreigners if they consider the tip inadequate. Often their interpretation of an appropriate sum is ridiculously high and is accompanied by intimidation tactics. A request for a policeman is the swiftest way to end the conversation. The nicer drivers might even say "thank you" on receiving 20%. The minimum tip is 10 frs., and the basic hire rate 15 frs., plus 8 frs. per km, higher in *Luxembourg.*

CLOSING DAYS AND HOURS. Legal holidays in *Belgium* are: New Year's Day (Jan. 1), Easter Monday, May Day (May 1), Ascension Day, Whit Monday, National Holiday (July 21)), Assumption Day (Aug. 15), All Saints Day (Nov. 1), All Souls Day (Nov. 2), Armistice Day (Nov. 11), King's Birthday (schools, Nov. 15), Christmas Holidays (Dec. 25, 26); in *Luxembourg:* same, but National Holiday June 23, and Nov. 11 and 15 are not holidays.

The *Belgian* small businessman spends most of his life in his shop and usually lives in the same building where it is located. Grocers, butchers, and bakers may open as early as 7 a.m. and close between 7 p.m. and 8 p.m. In provincial towns there is a 2-hour lunch break between 12-2. The large department stores and shops in larger towns are open weekdays from 9-6, in some cases staying open in the evening one day a week (usually Wednesdays); and a number of supermarkets are open 9 a.m.-9 p.m. daily. Shopping centers usually make it a condition that the shops stay open from 9 a.m. to 9 p.m., six days a week. In holiday resorts (on the coast and in the Ardennes, tradesmen keep open until 9 p.m. or 10 p.m.). On Sundays bakers, butchers, grocers, fruit dealers, etc., keep open in the morning from 8-12; patisseries and flower shops the whole day. Belgian law limits employees' working hours to 40 hours per week, but since these are small family business, the authorities cannot interfere if they prefer to keep open—and the public has yet to complain. To prevent unfair competition the Government has imposed a compulsory closing day once a week—at shopkeeper's choice.

In general, the same hours are observed in *Luxembourg*. On Monday mornings nearly everything is closed, including banks. Most museums close for the 12-2 lunch break.

MEDICAL TREATMENT. The *IAMAT* (International Assoc. for Medical Assistance to Travelers), offers you a list of approved English-speaking doctors who have had postgraduate training in the U.S., Canada or Gt. Britain. Membership is free; the scheme is world-wide with many European countries participating. An office call costs about $8, though subject to change. Hotel and night calls, of course, higher. For information apply in the U.S. to Suite 5620, 350 Fifth Ave., New York 10001; in Canada, 1268 St. Clair Ave. W., Toronto.

A similar service to travelers, but charging $5 for membership, is *Intermedic*, 777 Third Avenue, New York, N.Y. 10017, which has 345 correspondent physicians in 82 countries, four of them in Belgium, one in Luxembourg.

Europ Assistance Ltd., offers unlimited help to its members. There are two plans: one for travelers using package tours or making their own trip arrangements, the second for motorists taking their car abroad. Multilingual personnel staff a 24-hr. telephone service which brings the aid of a network of medical and other advisors with everything needful for solving emergency difficulties. Special medical insurance is included. For details, write to Europ Assistance Ltd., 269 High St., Croydon, Surrey, CRO 1QH, England.

ELECTRIC CURRENT. In *Belgium*, newer sections and larger cities usually have A.C. Voltage is always 220, but check to make sure. Plugs and sockets usually fit American appliances. *Luxembourg* is different on this point. Voltage in Luxembourg is 110 in some parts of Luxembourg City, 220 everywhere else. Some circuits are 60-cycle, the majority 50-cycle. American appliances must have transformers to convert them to 220-volt operation (some travel irons are equipped with a simple switch, which converts them to the proper current). Best take along a battery-operated razor.

WEATHER. In general, seasonal averages are similar to those of New York or Montreal, without the extremes of heat or cold. They may be compared best with those of southern England, with perhaps less rain. Luxembourg's weather is more Continental: slightly colder in winter and less rain in summer.

Temperatures.

Average maximum daily temperatures in degrees Fahrenheit and centigrade:

Brussels	Jan.	Feb.	Mar.	Apr.	May	June	July	Aug.	Sept.	Oct.	Nov.	Dec.
F°	39	45	50	57	64	72	73	72	70	58	48	43
C°	4	7	10	14	18	22	23	22	21	15	9	6

WATER. The water is drinkable everywhere. The coastal areas obtain their supplies from inland sources.

Pollution Report: Visitors to *Luxembourg* will not encounter pollution in any of the severe forms suffered elsewhere. Luxembourgers all have a practical, immediate concern for the physical well-being of their country. Tourists, too, can help, particularly by not scattering litter after picnics, and should they find any form of pollution, a telephone call to the National Tourism Office, 48-79-99, or directly to the general emergency number of the Protection Civile, 012 (no charge), will be appreciated and will bring a prompt response.

MAIL. The communications services are government administered, but in *Belgium* post and telegraph are kept apart, though the telegraph offices are often close to the bigger post offices. *Airmail* letters to the U.S.A. cost 10 francs for the first 5 grams, 2½ frcs. for each additional 5 grs.; postcards with 5 words and signature cost 9½ frcs., more than 5 words, 12½ frcs. *Surface* mail letters are 10 frcs. for the first 20 gr., and 10 frcs. for each additional 20 grs.; postcards as above, 7 and 10 frcs.

Letters and postcards to Britain and European countries go *airmail* without surcharge or label. Letters cost 10 frcs. for the first 20 gr., 10 frcs. for each additional 20 gr.; postcards, 5 words and signature 5 frcs., more than 5 words, 7 frcs.

Belgium's red post boxes are easy to spot.

In *Luxembourg* post boxes are blue. Airmail to U.S. and Canada is 10 frs. for first 5 gr. (one airmail sheet and envelope), 2 frs. each additional 2 gr. To England (automatically by airmail), 8 frs. for first 20 gr. Postcards 5 frs.

TELEPHONES. There is an automatic direct dialing system in operation between all *Belgian* localities, to Luxembourg, Holland, France, West Germany, Austria, Spain, Scandinavia, Switzerland and Gt. Britain (but not to Ireland). Also to selected localities in East Germany, Greece, Italy, Japan and the U.S.A. Dialing instructions and code numbers are listed in the Brussels, Antwerp etc. telephone directories. To make such a call, dial the exchange number (prefix) of the locality and then the number desired. In case of difficulty, dial 991 for international calls or 909 for inter-city calls, then ask the operator for the number. A local telephone call from an automatic pay telephone costs 5 francs.

All Belgian police ambulance departments have switched over to the uniform emergency number of 900. The 900 service, which is free, is not restricted to road accidents—it may be used for any kind of disaster, such as fire or drowning. For the anti-poison service telephone (02) 45-45-45.

Luxembourg has direct automatic connections with Austria, Belgium, Denmark, West Germany, Gt. Britain and N. Ireland, Italy, Holland, Norway, Portugal, Sweden, Switzerland, Greece, the United States, and other countries. The Luxembourg emergency number is 012.

TOBACCO. Both American and British cigarettes are readily obtainable in Belgium and Luxembourg; local varieties are quite acceptable and cheaper.

Pipe smokers might want to try the local tobacco, raised in the Semois, Appelterre, Harelbeke and Roisin districts. Belgium is noted for its briar pipes.

PHOTOGRAPHY. Photographers would be well advised to bring color film, if their preference is for British or American makes. Both are more expensive here than the excellent Belgian-made Gevaert brand which is now amalgamated with the German Agfa. Processing is handled as a general rule through camera shops, which collect the film and send it, usually, to the Gevaert plant; charges are slightly higher than at home. Your Kodak color films are developed by Kodak's, Ave. de la Toison d'Or, Brussels.

SHOPPING. Good buys in *Belgium* are leather goods, guns, linen, crystal and lace. You can see a representative selection of the best of Belgian products at the permanent Design Center, 51 Ravenstein Gallery, near the central station and Sabena air terminal. There are no particular shopping specialties or bargains in *Luxembourg,* although prices are often some 20 percent cheaper than in Brussels.

SPORT. Both Belgium and Luxembourg are ideal for river enthusiasts, whether for fishing, boating or swimming. Then there is the fine coastline with its wide, sandy beaches. There are possibilities for golf and for hunting (shooting). For hiking or for leisurely rambles, both countries are ideal. For details, see "Prelude to Belgium" and "Prelude to Luxembourg" later in this volume.

INFORMATION AND GUIDES. Local authorities have more often than not organized tourist information services of their own. In Wallony (French speaking part of Belgium) and in the Grand Duchy they are known as *Syndicat d'Initiative,* in Flanders as *Dienst voor Toerisme.* Their addresses are indicated in our regional Practical Information sections.

Information of various kinds about Brussels and Belgium can also be obtained from the "Hostesses of Brussels" at the airport transit-hall, in the futuristic pavilion of Place Brouckère and from the no less charming ladies at the Belgian National Tourist Office Information Bureau which is at the Central Station (Gare Centrale), on the Blvd. de l'Impératrice side. The larger tourist centers have officially accredited guides to assist visitors; apply to municipal tourist bureaus.

Visitors to Belgium desiring the services of a guide should contact an enterprising organization in Brussels, called L. R. Gregg Associates, Place Rogier Skyscraper, which will provide cultivated, knowledgeable escorts for daytime or evening sightseeing, shopping, theatergoing, dining, or nightclubbing. The escorts are carefully screened for proper social background, fluent English, good conversational ability, and flair for interpreting Belgium to visitors. Another organization providing escort for sightseeing and shopping is "A Friend in Brussels", 14 Rue des Deux-Eglises, Brussels.

In Luxembourg, guides and tours can be arranged through the Syndicat d'Initiative, Place d'Armes, Luxembourg City, or any major tourist centers.

USEFUL ADDRESSES. Embassies: *American,* 27 Blvd. du Régent, Brussels, and 22 Blvd E. Servais, Luxembourg City; *British,* 28 Rue Joseph II, Brussels, and 28/IV Blvd. Royal, Luxembourg City; *Canadian,* 35 Rue de la Science, Brussels.

Tourist information: *Belgian National Tourist Office,* Central Station (Gare Centrale), Brussels, and Place de Paris, Luxembourg. *Luxembourg National Tourist Office,* Air Terminal, Place de la Gare, Luxembourg City, and in Brussels: ground-floor of skyscraper in Place Rogier, facing Hotel Albert I. All Belgian tourist offices are specially familiar with details concerning Luxembourg. *American Express* has offices in Antwerp and Brussels, and *Wagons-Lits/Cooks* has offices in all the principal cities; for addresses, see the Practical Information in the regional chapters.

Cultural exchanges: Association *Belgo-Américaine,* 13 Rue de Bréderode. *Belgo-British Union,* 166 Ave. Louise. *British Council,* 166 Ave. Louise. *U.S. Information Service,* 1c Square du Bastion. *Y.W.C.A.,* corner of Rue St. Bernard and Rue de Bordeaux. *Y.M.C.A.,* 31 Rue Duquenoy. All in Brussels. In Luxembourg City: *American-Luxembourg Society,* 28 Ave. Monterey; *British-Luxembourg Society,* 17 Rue Alphonse Munchen.

Traveling in Belgium and Luxembourg

BY TRAIN. The Belgium and Luxembourg rail networks are good, services being frequent and swift. They are augmented by bus services to villages, thus the whole area can be covered easily. For further information, see "Prelude to Belgium" and "Prelude to Luxembourg" later.

A *Eurailpass* is a convenient, all-inclusive ticket that can save you money on over 100,000 miles of railroads, railroad-operated buses, ferries, river and lake steamers, hydrofoils, and some Mediterranean crossings in 13 countries of Western Europe. It provides unlimited travel at rates of: 15 days for $130; 21 days for $160; 1 month for $200; 2 months for $270; and 2nd-class student (up to age 25) fare of 2 months for $180. Children under 12 go half-fare, under 4 go free. These prices cover first-class passage, reservation fees, and surcharges, for the Trans Europe Express services. Available to US, Canadian and South American residents only, the pass must be bought from an authorized agent in the western hemisphere *before* you leave for Europe. Apply through your travel agent; or the general agents for North America, French National Railroads, Eurailpass Division, 610 Fifth Avenue, N.Y. 10020; or the German Federal Railroad, 11 West 42nd Street, N.Y. 10036 and 45 Richmond Street, W., Toronto M5H 1Z2, Ontario, Canada.

BY CAR. Roads in Luxembourg are excellent but occasionally narrow. In Belgium they are now good and a system of express highways is being extended. See "Motoring" in the "Prelude to Belgium" chapter later.

Car documents: Similarly to the majority of Western European countries neither Belgium nor Luxembourg require from private motorists international documents: your national driving licence and your vehicle registration certificate will do. But be sure to carry third party insurance (green card) and a letter-plate indicating the country in which your car is registered (which you attach to the rear). Your automobile club can arrange these details for you. Once you have entered the Benelux countries, there are few formalities.

Fuel: In *Belgium* gasoline (petrol) costs about 15 frs. a liter for the super or extra grade. In *Luxembourg* the cost is less.

Winter Road Conditions. Dial 991 or 971.

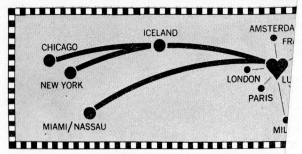

Highway Code. *Belgium:* The storming out from a side street—providing it lies to the right of the flow of traffic—is legal (*priorité à droite*). Streetcars, however, continue to have priority over all traffic. All this is a bit confusing; the best advice we can give you is to drive slowly in built-up areas and watch the side streets to your right. Absolute priority on the highways is indicated by the usual black arrow in a red triangle—nevertheless, use your horn generously when approaching a T-road or a crossing. When entering a first class road from a secondary one, an inverted red-framed white triangle warns you to slow down. Speed limits are posted where applicable, but a limit of 37 mph operates in Brussels, and all urban districts. On motorways a *minimum* speed of 70 km. per hour (43 mph) is required, and there is a maximum limit of 90 km. per hour (55 mph) on all roads of less than four lanes.

Tire mouldings must not be less than 1 mm. deep over the whole surface in contact with the road.

Dipped lights must be used in all areas when driving between nightfall and dawn, as well as in unfavorable weather conditions.

Red triangle for use following breakdown or accident is obligatory, and the car and car driver's identification papers must be carried in the car.

The *Luxembourg* highway code differs in some important ways from the Belgian. The use of horns, for instance, is reserved for cases of *imminent danger*. The speed limit is fixed at 60 km. per hour (37 mph) in built-up areas, 90 km. per hour (55 mph) outside the agglomerations except for 3-lane roads, where 120 km. per hr. (75 mph) is permitted. Areas of exception to these speeds are marked. A parking disc (available free in many stores and banks) properly displayed is required for blue zones in the Luxembourg City town center and railway areas, Esch-sur-Alzette, Dudelange, Remich and Wiltz. This is supplemented by parking meters and a system of ticket dispensers which allows motorists to buy any time period desired for parking at 1 fr. for 6 minutes.

Automobile Clubs. In Belgium (all in Brussels): *Royal Automobile Club de Belgique,* 53 Rue d'Arlon; *Touring Club de Belgique,* 44 Rue de la Loi; *Fédération Motocycliste de Belgique,* 18 Rue Capouillet; *American Automobile Association,* 48 Rue d'Arenberg.

British *AA* and *RAC* port representatives assist members at the Antwerp, Ostend, and Zeebrugge marine piers.

In Luxembourg: *Automobile Club du Grand Duché de Luxembourg,* 13 Rte. de Longwy, Luxembourg-Helfenkerbruck.

CAR HIRE. A stock of cars, Volkswagen and Porsche, with U.S. specifications is kept expressly for deliveries to American and British tourists, by *Avis,* 145 Rue Américaine, Brussels, tel. 37-12-80, and Brussels Airport (Avis also at Antwerp, Charleroi, Courtrai, Liège, Mons and Ostend.) The firm will also take care of the home shipment of your car. *Hertz,* 8 Blvd Maurice Lemonnier, Brussels (tel. 13-28-86), at Brussels Airport. *ABC Rent-a-car,* 63 Rue Dautzenberg, near Ave. Louise, Brussels (tel. 49-90-05).

A complete service for all of Western Europe is offered by Godfrey Davis Ltd. with two offices in Luxembourg and 21 offices in and around Brussels, Antwerp, Liège and Ostend. Or make all arrangements before you leave through their office at 574 Fifth Avenue, N.Y. 10036.

If you arrive in *Belgium* by train, you can arrange through the Belgian Railroads to have a self-drive Volkswagen meet you at the following stations: Antwerp, Brussels, Dinant, Ghent, Liège, Mons, Namur, Ostend. A deposit of 5,000 francs is required. Rental for the first day is about 200 francs, including 50 free kilometers (31 miles). If you arrive in Brussels via Sabena Airlines, you may arrange (at the time of purchasing your ticket) to have a self-drive car meet you at the airport. Cars with or without chauffeur may also be hired from garages in the large towns.

In *Luxembourg,* Volkswagen rentals and arrangements, 88 Rte. de Thionville, tel. 48-81-21. *Avis,* 13 Rue Duchscher, tel. 48-95-95, *Hertz,* 25 Ave. de Liberté, tel. 48-54-85. All in Luxembourg City.

ON THE ROAD. One of the most confusing experiences for many motorists is their first encounter with the metric system. The following quick conversion tables may help to speed you on your way.

Distances: 1 kilometer is 0.623 of a mile; or roughly, 8 kilometers equals 5 miles.

Kms.	Miles	Kms.	Miles
1	⅝	16	10
2	1¼	30	18⅝
3	1⅞	50	31⅛
4	2½	100	62⅛
5	3⅛	500	310¼
10	6¼	1,000	621⅜

Motor fuel: an Imperial gallon is approximately 4½ liters; a U.S. gallon about 3¾ liters.

Liters	Imp. gals.	U.S. gals
1	0.22	0.26
5	1.10	1.32
10	2.20	2.64
20	4.40	5.28
40	8.80	10.56
100	22.01	26.42

Tire pressure: measured in kilograms per square centimeter instead of pounds per square inch; the ratio is approximately 14.2 pounds to 1 kilogram.

Lbs. per sq. in.	Kgs. per sq. cm.	Lbs. per sq. in.	Kgs. per sq. cm.
20	1.406	23	1.828
22	1.547	28	1.969
24	1.678	30	2.109

Leaving Belgium and Luxembourg

CUSTOMS RETURNING HOME. If you propose to take on your holiday any *foreignmade* articles, such as cameras, binoculars, expensive timepieces and the like, it is wise to put with your travel documents the receipt from the retailer or some other evidence that the item was bought in your home country. If you bought the article on a previous holiday abroad and have already paid duty on it, carry with you the receipt for this. Otherwise, on returning home, you may be charged duty (for British residents, VAT as well).

Americans who are out of the United States at least 48 hours and have claimed no exemption during the previous 30 days are entitled to bring in duty-free up to $100 worth of articles for bona fide gifts or for their own personal use. The value of each item is determined by the price actually paid (so save your receipts). Every member of a family is entitled to this same exemption, regardless of age, and families can pool their exemptions. All goods purchased must accompany the passenger on his return, and a list of them should be kept handy.

Not more than 100 cigars may be imported duty-free per person, nor more than a quart of wine or liquor (none at all if under 21 years old or you are from a "dry" state). Only one bottle of perfume that is trademarked in the United States may be brought in, plus a reasonable quantity of other brands.

Do not bring home foreign meats, fruits, plants, soil, or other agricultural items when you return to the United States. To do so will delay you at the port of entry. It is illegal to bring in foreign agricultural items without permission, because they can spread destructive plant or animal pests and diseases. For more information, read the pamphlet "Customs Hints", or write to: "Quarantines", U.S. Department of Agriculture, Washington, D.C. 20250 and ask for Program Aid No. 1083, "Traveler's Tips on Bringing Food, Plant and Animal Products into the United States".

Antiques are defined, for customs purposes, as articles over 100 years old and are admitted duty-free. If there's any question of age, you may be asked to supply proof.

A foreign-made automobile that was ordered before your departure is subject to duty even though delivered abroad. This same rule applies to any purchase initiated in advance of your trip .

Small gifts may be mailed to friends in the United States (but not to your own address) and be sent with a written notation on the package: "Gift, value less than $10".

British residents. There is now a two-tier allowance for duty-free goods brought into the U.K., due to Britain's Common Market membership. *Note:* The Customs and Excise Board warn that it is not advisable to mix the two allowances.

If you return from an EEC country (Belgium, Luxembourg, Denmark, France, W. Germany, Holland, Eire, Italy) and goods were bought in one of those countries, the duty-free allowances are:

300 cigarettes (or 150 cigarillos, or 75 cigars, or 400 gr. tobacco); 1.5 liters of strong spirits (or 3 liters of other spirits or fortified wines) plus 3 liters of still table wine; 75 gr. perfume and ⅜ liter toilet water; gifts to a value of £50.

If you return from a country outside the EEC *or if the goods were bought in a duty-free shop, or on ship or plane* the allowances are less:

200 cigarettes (or 100 cigarillos, or 50 cigars, or 250 gr. tobacco); 1 liter of strong spirits (or 2 liters of other spirits or fortified wines) plus 2 liters of still table wine; 50 gr. perfume and ¼ liter toilet water; gifts to a value of £10.

Canadian residents. Residents of Canada may, after 7 days out of the country, and upon written declaration, claim an exemption of $150 a year plus an allowance of 40 ounces of liquor, 50 cigars, 200 cigarettes and 2 lbs. of tobacco. Personal gifts should be mailed as "Unsolicited Gift—Value Under $10". For details, ask for the Canada Customs brochure "I Declare". Regulations are strictly enforced: you are recommended to check what your allowances are and to make sure that you have kept receipts for whatever you may have bought abroad.

THE BELGIAN SCENE

THE BELGIAN WAY OF LIFE

Zest for Work and Play

You must always shake hands with a Belgian. In all social observances, he is one of the politest people on earth; but handshaking is his specialty. They say the handshake is by origin your assurance that your right hand carries no weapon; and maybe, through many centuries of foreign occupation, Belgians have learned to need such assurance. However this may be, wherever you meet a Belgian, shake hands with him.

By the same token, no nation is more meticulous in the minor politenesses. There is a special postage rate for courtesy postcards containing nothing but your signature and five words of greeting; when you go from Brussels to Bruges or Bastogne, don't forget to send them to all your Brussels acquaintances. If you meet an acquaintance, don't forget the courtesy enquiries for all his family and, if you have ever met his wife, be sure to slide in "*mes hommages à madame*" with the second or third farewell handshake.

For all the Belgian's courtesy, it used to be hard to get to know him. Visits to private houses, and even from one private house to another, were always formal. Young folk were sometimes betrothed after long courtship before seeing the inside of one another's homes. Today, however, many of these customs have broken down among the younger generation which, over the last couple of decades, has adopted the more familiar and casual social life that is standard among its British and American contemporaries.

You'll gather from this that familes are rather self-contained and their unity is strong. You'll often find a widowed mother and some of her married children living on separate floors on the same house. This is not—at least not primarily—tender solicitude of child for parent. It is because Ma has a lawful right to the use of the house while she lives, and afterwards it will be sold and the proceeds split among the children. Dad couldn't cut his children, or his widow, out of his will. He didn't have to make a will, for the law settles what becomes of his property after his death. You'll see signs of this in the Flemish farm country, where the laws of succession have resulted in fields being split and split again, till one man's farm consists of half a dozen narrow strips several miles apart, with all the kindred bickerings about access and drainage, and the utter impossibility of getting a tractor onto the land.

One of the first things you'll notice is the narrowness of many of the older houses. Even in the countryside you'll see houses standing by themselves, presenting to the road a frontage barely a quarter of their back-to-front depth. This is a town-man's fancy, for street frontage has always been expensive and a responsibility. You'll find each floor consisting of three, or even four rooms leading out of one another from the front of the house to the back, and with windows only in the front room and the back. When it comes to frontage, the householder is responsible to his commune for the sidewalk outside his house.

A Horror of Draughts

Another thing you'll notice about the Belgian is that he hates cold and draughts. Fears of grippe and trouble in the sinus haunt him, and he likes his office, café, restaurant, and living room elaborately heated. (His bedroom may be freezing.) He seldom keeps his windows open. Even on a hot summer day, a dispute about windows among the 20 passengers in a railroad carriage may be ended by the guard, not by a counting of votes, but by a firm ruling that open windows are "abnormal" and the normal man wins. In private houses there are casement windows (opening inwards) rather than sash windows. They can only be completely open or completely shut, and most often they are the latter. Slatted wooden shutters complete the illusion of unoccupancy.

In Brussels the town trams, which used to have end platforms open to the street on one side, have been replaced by closed, up-to-date versions into which unwelcome drafts can creep only rarely. Only a few years ago you could travel the whole length and breadth of Belgium by tram. The *Vicinaux* service, now almost totally replaced by buses, runs from town to town, and from town to suburb. Take a few trips in these trams or buses, especially in the Flemish country, and note how little the faces have changed since the days when they were painted by Pieter Breughel.

In the same way, amusements have changed little. The people of Belgium are great lovers of fairs, and even in big towns like Brussels you will find roundabouts and swings taking up their stations week by week in different city squares the summer through. Attached to each there is the nougat stall, the fresh doughnut stall and the inevitable fried potato stall. The Belgians, be it in the home, the restaurant or the street, are great eaters of *frites*—potatoes cut long and fried in deep fat oil. The English eat them with fried fish, but the Belgians eat them by themselves, or with mayonnaise. There are stalls at many street corners, and the evening smell of Brussels is the smell of chips—just as, at eight in the morning, it is the smell of coffee. The latter is Belgium's biggest love. By the time a Belgian is five years old he is a confirmed coffee drinker.

Fondness for Sports and Cockfighting

Belgium is a country on everybody's way everywhere. This means that Belgians are very conscious of foreigners and foreign thought. Their women copy their fashions preferably from Paris, to which the wealthier resort for their shopping. The sporting fraternity has taken up football (or soccer) in a big way, and holds its own valiantly in international company. Their football heroes are not professionals in the British sense, but "independents", with separate jobs of their own, receiving match-money from their clubs but no regular salary. There is little sport in the schools, and Belgian boyhood finds most of its outlet by graduating through the many junior teams of the big league clubs, the humblest scholar keeping the target of the national team (the "Red Devils") firmly before him from the start.

The Belgians devote plenty of time to sports which are characteristically their own. One of these is the *jeu de balle* or *pelote,* of which there are two distinct versions, and which is played (mostly in Wallony) in the wider streets and squares on weekend afternoons, often to the confusion of the motorist. Apart from the championships, attracting even royal patronage, this singular mixture of lawn tennis and handball is a players' game, ending in a friendly café atmosphere.

Far more intense are the passions surrounding cycling, which is the national sport *par excellence*. It is a country in which everybody cycles—when you've seen two nuns on a tandem machine riding across a golf-course in a snowstorm, you'll realise how true this is—and every right-minded boy starts life with the idea he'll one day win the *Tour de France*. The summer roadracing has more fans than the covered-track events of the winter, and the heroes of the road are the true national idols. Arguments on their form play the same part in the schoolboy's life as batting and bowling averages in England, or baseball form in America. If you take a motor ride on a Sunday, you will run across a cycle race every few villages.

Other sports for Mr. Everyman are pigeon-racing and cockfighting. Every Sunday morning the radio gives five minutes of every hour to weather reports from the routes of the day's big races, which may start from as far afield as Southern France or Spain. Immense care and skill go into the pigeon loft, and high values attach to the doughty birds with good winning records. Cockfighting is in a different class, since its many thousand fans have never succeeded in having it made lawful. It is played, more or less *sub rosa*, under two quite different sets of rules in Flanders and the Walloon provinces in the south, but it is not a sport that forces itself on the tourist's attention.

Of Ethnic Differences, Food and Work

The difference between Flanders and Wallony goes much deeper than a mere difference of language. By tradition Flanders is the land of the big family and the small enterprise, usually family-run; and Wallony is the area of the big factory, of the blast furnace, the glassworks, the machine, the making of fire-arms and, in general, massive employment which results in small families. All this has changed, and is still changing fast—in favor of Flanders.

In the language upheavals, which every so often make the international headlines, two factors play a part—population pressure and economic change. The Flemish now outnumber the Walloons; and though many of them speak French, they see no reason for giving it precedence. Universal education is not only ironing out the local differences in peasant-Flemish; it has strengthened the pride of the Flemings in a cultural tradition which dates back many centuries, has contributed much to history and the arts, and is very much their own. It is no longer true that "the Flemish is a cultivator, the Walloon is cultivated"; some people even say it is the other way round. While it is true that everybody in Belgium is within easy reach of the local town, this is more true in crowded Flanders, so that the Fleming is the more urban and often the more urbane. He has, however, had to fight down the traditional assumption that French was culturally superior, and this accounts for occasional excesses. It is no longer true, outside the Brussels area, that Belgium is bi-lingual. It consists of two one-language communities; and the language of the region prevails, and is expected, in the schoolroom, the boardroom, the officers' mess, the law courts, the tax office and in church.

The change has been helped by the fact that, since World War II, the economic tide has been running strongly in favor of Flanders, which contains the whole of Belgium's coastline. Access to seaports is a condition of modern industry, especially in a country so necessarily export-conscious. The great bulk of American investment in recent years has been in the Flemish provinces, and even Belgium's own steel industry is moving seawards and has set up its biggest unit in the port of Ghent. This has made a deep-seated change in the occupational structure in Flanders and produced a sizeable rise in income levels. It also threatened to starve Wallony. It is only recently that purposeful development (roads, waterways etc.) in southern Belgium, coupled with substantial "inducements", has attracted big employers to absorb the manpower which was being pushed out of the collieries and other jobs.

A thing all Belgians have in common is a fondness for their food. They speak of looking after their interests as "defending their beefsteak", and it is indeed true that the working-class Belgian hates having his food messed up". He likes to eat an honest beefsteak—which may indeed be a pork or veal chop but is very seldom mutton—at least once a day. He is a hard worker and most people wonder how good manual work can be supported without such nourishment. Where the household budget is cramped, the manual worker has the largest share of the meat, which may cost as much as a third of the family's spending. Vegetable soup, often enriched with meat, is universal. And mayonnaise—made in the classical way, very patiently, stirring good-quality oil into egg yolks, is a staple at all social levels and is even eaten with *frites*. It is quite usual, in middle-class as well as working-class households, for only one meal per day to contain hot meat. The other meal will consist of *charcuterie*, of which the variety is enormous.

The Belgian is a hard worker. If you take a before-dawn bus journey across farming country, you will see the little lanterns of the farm workers bobbing across the fields to be ready for the dawn. In shops and offices the nine o'clock contingent are the late starters. The lunch hour, however, has ceased to be two hours, except for those executives who still prefer to go home to lunch. Employees eat sandwiches in their offices or in one of the many cafés and milk bar type of establishments that have sprung up during the last few years.

A Nation of Shopkeepers

An enormous proportion of Belgium's shops are family businesses. This is the great middle class, and the usual pattern is for the wife to mind the shop in the daytime while the husband goes to the real bread-winning job.

This unprofessional system served, and still serves, a very useful purpose; for you can shop early or Late, and you can shop round the corner without parking problems. These tiny businesses, however, have in recent years seen the writing on the wall: they have been brought within the social legislation, which means a fortnight's holiday closure and 24 consecutive hours closure each week; and finally, the legislation which had curbed the development of multiple retailing was repealed.

You can still do quite a bit of your household shopping at 8 o'clock in the evening; but the little retailer is often only an emergency solution. First came the self-service stores; then both the popular counter stores and the department stores launched into an energetic supermarket development with enormous car parks. In 1968 came the first of the shopping centers, with shop leases which stipulate minimum opening hours from 9 a.m. to 9 p.m. six days a week; and now the hypermarket is established. For all this, the little shops have kept a brave front, and many of them still do a useful business. Still more unflagging are the street markets, mostly for fruit and vegetables, which are colorful, attractive and cheap, and seem likely to remain one of the main features of Brussels shopping.

Dodging the Tax Collector

The fear of the tax collector is part of a distrust of all things official, which Belgium has learned during periodical foreign occupations over many centuries. It has formed a robust no-nonsense spirit which is the nation's strength. One result is that the Belgian has been late in learning to use a bank, whether for savings or check purposes. He uses a Postal Giro Account for current transactions, and wage and salary earners also have postal savings; but the great bank of the *petit bourgeois* may be a hole in the floor of the back kitchen! Even the smallest households can, if the absolute need arises, produce surprising sums at a moment's notice. The knowledge that they can do this is the basis for the amusing game the Belgians play of asking one another for large sums as "guarantee" in all sorts of transactions. These are most noticeable in all matters connected with renting a house, installing gas or electric light, or hiring a car. If anybody asks you for money on account, by way of *garantie,* don't think it's because you're a foreigner.

In the same way, don't be aggrieved if you find your hotel bill contains a daily item for *taxe de séjour*. This is not Belgium soaking the foreigner, but Belgium teaching the foreigner to feel like a native. The Belgian's resentment of the tax collector, in all the normal channels of taxation, has led their government to raise revenue in all the by-ways it can find. The result is, the tax collector is at everybody's elbow all the time. Belgians sometimes spend the best part of half a day on the process of paying a tax, registering their change of address or getting the essential papers of their car. Value-added taxation was introduced in 1971. Its impact on prices can be called disastrous, but it may have killed the more popular forms of tax evasion which, in the past, has strengthened the robust independence of which the Belgians are justly proud. It has also created in them a desire to be themselves claimants for money wherever they can see a chance of raising it. Legislation supports this tendency. Many Belgians have pensions and an enormous proportion have means of claiming reduced fares on the railroads. There are many other advantages for which each seeks to qualify in his own way. Many of these originate under the social security schemes, notably the family allowances which are worth more than $50 per month to a man with a wife and five children.

The Belgium Catholicism

By religion, Belgium is deeply and universally Roman Catholic, so much so in fact that, where we should use the word "Catholic" the Belgians say "Christian". To them, the word "Catholic" has a significance that is political rather than religious, standing for the deep cleavage of opinion that runs right through Belgian political life. You cannot talk to any Belgian without becoming conscious of this. There is a very strong body of opinion which would separate the functions of state and church, giving the latter no real or moral voice in determining the political behavior of the citizen. As might be expected, this school of thought is at its strongest in the great industrial areas, most notably in the south of Belgium. Against this, there is the catholic school of thought which, in its religious loyalty, accepts the church's authority as a moral (and therefore as a very real) guide in all matters of the citizen's behavior. Convictions on both sides are very deeply held, and it is a matter on which it ill behoves the foreigner to have opinions. All this has somewhat abated since the Pope decreed more innovations, and the Belgians are certainly not lagging in this respect. The effects of the division used to be found everywhere. Even the new-born baby, when he was taken to the weekly clinic, had to go either to a Catholic clinic under the care of the devoted sisters of a religious order, or to a secular clinic—often run by a variety of trade unions—stigmatized as *légèrement socialiste*. When it comes to schooling, the youngster may go to one of the "public" schools run by his commune, or he may go to one of the many church-run schools—the *enseignement libre*—which the Catholic interests have at long last acquired the right to subsidize from public funds. Finally, when the young man goes out to work, he will have to choose between the socialist trade unions, grouped in the General Federation of Belgian Labor, and the unions belonging to the Confederation of Christian Unions.

The real strength of the Belgian is that he tackles his job with gusto and brings the same spirit into his play. Many of his enjoyments are simple, but you have only to see the zest with which the men of Mons slaughter their traditional dragon on Trinity Sunday to realise that it is the spirit which matters. The Belgian is a realist in all things, and as such he has firmly taught himself that what matters most in life is food. He has consistently gibed at all manner of political schemes whereby a tight belt for the present would be offset by advantages later on. The same approach has kept his attitude intact through many foreign invasions of his country, and it has created a hard core of realism which has a very useful part to play as a test-bench for the idealisms of modern international life.

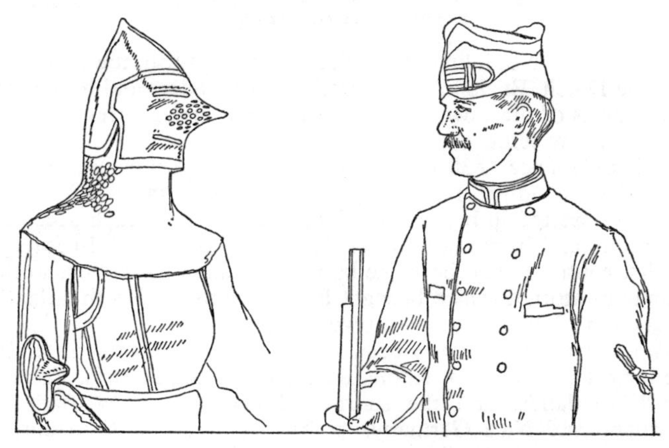

BELGIAN HISTORY

Perennial Butt of Power Politics

by

GAVIN GORDON

(Gavin Gordon's knowledge of Belgium and Flanders dates back well over a quarter-century. He has lived in Brussels for many years, and, as correspondent for British and American newspapers, he has strengthened his thorough knowledge of everything in the country from kings to cockfighting.)

A glance at the map will show you the importance of the Low Countries. Glistening with the estuaries of international waterways (Rhine, Scheldt and Meuse), they are the obvious trans-shipment point for goods and passengers seeking to avoid longer sea routes through the Baltic and the Mediterranean.

The Low Countries are in some ways still a single unit, for in 1921 Belgium and Luxembourg signed a customs and economic treaty, and in 1944, Belgium, Luxembourg and Holland formed the Benelux customs union (though it did not become fully effective until 1960).

With little natural defence against Europe's embattled armies, the Low Countries—especially Belgium—have provided a perennial battlefield. The ports have been the butt of power politics in the rival empire-building of the French, the Spanish, the Austrians and the Dutch. England's wool trade with Flanders and her access to the ports of the Low Countries have been undercurrents of history for many centuries.

It is only since 1830 that Belgium has been a separate and independent country. Naturally, therefore, her independence is strongly asserted in her constitution, in the oath of each acceding sovereign, and in the attitude of the man in the street. In foreign affairs, neutrality had been the basis of her national policy; so the change of attitude which brought Belgium into the North Atlantic Council in 1949 was akin to a revolution.

Another deep mark has been scored in Belgium's character by the long dominations of Rome, Burgundy, Spain, Austria, France, the Netherlands, and the short-lived occupations by Imperial Germany and Nazi Germany. A skill has been built up during many centuries in finding ways round rationing systems, regulations and impositions forced on the country by alien governors. This cannot be forgotten in two or three generations, or lightly laid aside even when taxes and regulations come from a parliament democratically elected.

From Roman Times to the Middle Ages

The Gaul of the *Belgae* tribes was primitive, but already productive, when Julius Caesar pushed his conquest to the North Sea. When Mark Anthony reminded the Romans, at Caesar's funeral, of "the day he overcame the Nervii", he was speaking of a battle fought against Belgians on Belgian soil. Soon the matrons of Rome learned to prize the Menapian cloth made in the Flemish coastal district; and, for nearly five centuries, Belgian Gaul had the protection of the *pax romana.* Great roads were built, radiating from Bavai, itself joined to Cologne by the Via Agrippa, passing through Tongres and Maastricht. Other roads passed through Tournai, linked Arlon with Trèves (Trier) and, in what is now Dutch territory, joined Leiden with the Rhine at Utrecht.

When the last Roman legion was withdrawn, in the first half of the 5th century, Belgian Gaul became part of the Frankish kingdom of the Merovingian kings, established from Tournai and stretching from the Weser to the Pyrenees. This, however, did not hold together; and two centuries later Belgium herself became a nursery of kings, and knew a period of early splendour.

Towards the end of the 7th century, the astute Hesbaye family of Pepin reunited the kingdom and, through the victories of Charles Martel, pushed it farther eastward. With the Pope's con-

sent, Pepin the Short was crowned King of the Franks at Soissons in 751; and in the year 800 his son, known to history as Charlemagne, was invested by Pope Leo III as Emperor of the West. His vast domain extended from Jutland to Naples and from the Ebro to the Oder.

The emperor's agricultural reforms were put into thriving practice on his Belgian personal domains at Herstal and Jupille. Roads were built and waterways put into use, notably the Scheldt up to and beyond Tournai. Charlemagne, apart from his military victories, was a great organiser and a civilising king; but his administrative feats did not long outlive him. After his death in 814 the Carolingian empire started to disintegrate under the rule of his son, Louis the Pious, and the Treaty of Verdun in 843 divided the empire in three. A boundary along the Scheldt separated Flanders, faithful to France, from Belgium's southern (Walloon) provinces, which belonged to Lotharingia. This meant strength for Flanders, comparative feebleness for the south.

In the northern half, Baudouin Iron-Arm, by his resistance to the Norse invasions, established himself as the first Count of Flanders, in 862. The confines of Flanders were enlarged south of the Scheldt, into France and the Netherlands. By the middle of the 11th century Robert I, with his sister married to William the Conqueror of England and a daughter to the King of Denmark, was becoming too strong a vassal for France.

Meantime the southern kingdom had had trouble with its own nobility. Its northern Duchy of Lothier, which covered what is now southern Belgium, became involved in quarrels between the empire and the papacy. With Godefroy de Bouillon's absorption in the First Crusade, the ducal authority dwindled. The duchy became little more than a collection of feudal domains, themselves a prey to a series of masterful prince-bishops of Liège.

Against this background commerce was growing, and with it came the rise of the towns. Even the supreme power of the Counts of Flanders began to wane. By the time (1256) Black Margot, as reigning countess, had set all Europe by the ears to determine which of her families was legitimate, the city of Bruges had already secured the English cloth monopoly. Most of the towns date from this period for, apart from Tongres and Tournai, the Norsemen's ravages had left little trace of earlier settlements. The cities demanded privileges. Under loose princely supervision they became states within the state, their citizens enfranchised from feudal serfdom, assuming their own responsibilities in education, justice, administration, even defence. Strong local patriotisms sprang up, trade and manufacture were regulated by guilds, rich merchants spent fortunes on public buildings and endowments. Liège prospered with its iron forges and its already flourishing arms manufacture. Bruges, with its fine port on the now vanished Zwin, became the central clearing house of Europe's trade, enriched by the counting-houses of German and Lombard bankers. The other "Members of Flanders", Ghent and Ypres, grew wealthy on fine cloth made from English wool.

It is small wonder that these prosperous and proud communities developed an autonomy unheard of at the time elsewhere in Europe. This autonomy, adapted to modern requirements, still exists in the administration of Belgian *communes.*

Battles and Revolts

France was naturally alarmed. Philippe le Bel, having made a truce with Edward I of England, was emboldened to "confiscate" Flanders. The answer was the "Matines of Bruges", when Pieter de Coninck, a master-weaver, led the Men of the Claw in the merciless butchering of the Men of the Lily, whose French tongues boggled at a Flemish catch-phrase. The commons of Flanders rallied and, in 1302, routed the might of French chivalry near Courtrai in the Battle of the Golden Spurs. Their triumph was short-lived, and the resistance was wiped out by 1328, except that in Ghent, Van Artevelde led a revolt against the victimization of Flanders by both France and England at the beginning of the Hundred Years' War. The result was a strengthened friendship between Flanders and England, cemented by Edward III's sojourn in Ghent, where John of Gaunt was born.

The spirit of the communes was still strong, and was the background to the next great period, the ascendancy of the four Dukes of Burgundy. The first two dukes meddled little in Flemish affairs, but the long reign of Philip the Good (1419-67) was Belgium's cultural high-point. Allying himself with the victorious Henry V of England and out-intriguing his brother-in-law, Duke Humphrey of Gloucester, Philip gained ascendancy over Hainaut. He bought the lordships of Namur and Luxembourg and, for lack of an entitled rival, was proclaimed heir to the Duchies of Limburg and Brabant and the Marquisate of Antwerp. With his domains stretching into Holland as far as Texel, he was nicknamed Grand Duke of the West, and he united his nobles and princelings in the Order of the Golden Fleece.

His fabulous reign is the period of the Van Eycks and Hans Memling in painting, of the architects Jan van Ruysbroek and Mathieu de Layens, of the De Limbourg brothers in miniature painting and of sculptors such as Claus Sluter and the Borremans. Politically there were troubles—firmly dealt with—between Philip and the communes of Ghent and Bruges: and there was strife which led to the sacking of Dinant and the razing to the ground of Liège. When Philip died, his son, Charles the Rash, was too keen a soldier and too impatient a politician to hold the situation Philip had so sumptuously built up. His death at the siege of Nancy (1477) left his 19-year-old daughter, Mary of Burgundy, to face a revolt of the communes and the intrigues of Louis XI, the "eternal spider", to bring Burgundy under the French crown. A statesman-like marriage with Maximilian of Austria, the defeat of the French at Guinegatte and the birth of a son, Philip, and a daughter, Margaret, seemed to consolidate the Duchy of Burgundy, when Mary's sudden death removed the king-pin.

Three Hundred Years of Spanish Ascendancy

Maximilian, who was soon to become emperor, was faced with the union of Spain under Ferdinand and Isabella. Power politics had taken a new turn and, as an act of political prudence, he married both his children to children of the Spanish sovereigns. Young Philip's wife, Juana the Mad, later became heiress-presumptive; and, though Philip died before he could succeed, he left an infant son, Charles of Luxembourg, born in 1500. This lad was to be enfranchised as reigning Prince of the Low Countries in 1515, crowned King of Spain a year later, and anointed as Emperor in 1520 under the title of Charles Quint.

The Low Countries, now under Spanish ascendancy, were to be the plaything of power politics for the next 300 years. Charles embarked on long and costly wars with France; and, when he abdicated in Brussels in 1555, his son Philip II, determined not to be a king of heretics, installed the Duke of Alba as governor and began the worst persecution these troubled countries have known. In the Belgian provinces the Catholic confession was more widely accepted than in the Netherlands. Reformed churchmen fled to the England of Elizabeth and, with the fall of Antwerp in 1585, resistance in Belgium was at an end. In the Netherlands a stubborn resistance had been started by William the Silent, Prince of Orange. It continued after his death and finally, in 1648, the Treaty of Munster recognised the independence of the (Dutch) United Provinces.

The currents of power politics were changing. Spain was falling out of the picture and the France of Mazarin and Louis XIV was now the rising sun. The United Provinces were masters of the sea in the north, and shared with England an interest in preventing French dominance in the Spanish Lowlands—effectively the Belgium of today. The Anglo-Dutch community of interest was strengthened by the accession to the English throne of Wiliam III of Orange in 1689. In the next quarter-century five major wars rolled over Belgian soil, with Marlborough's victories at Ramillies, Oudenaarde and Malplaquet featuring the later stages. In 1713, by the Treaty of Utrecht, the Spanish Lowlands—still dominated by the Dutch and retaining Dutch garrisons in eight towns—were handed over to Austria.

French ambitions were not killed. When the young Empress Maria Theresa was faced with the rise of Prussia and the War of the Austrian Succession, a French-Irish force beat the Anglo-Austrian-Dutch allies at Fontenoy, near Tournai, in 1745. Having invested and occupied Brussels, they conquered the country; but, finding it war-scarred and the people illiterate and riddled with pauperism, handed it back to Austria.

Two attempts to imitate the French Revolution, in Brussels and Liège, failed ingloriously for lack of popular support. Five regiments of Belgian volunteers were formed to aid the Austro-Prussian support of the French monarchy against the new Republic, and there was a Belgian Legion on the opposing side under General Dumouriez, who crushed the coalition at Jemappes. Belgium changed hands several times and was annexed to France in 1795 at the price of a Peasants' Revolt against compulsory military service and a firm refusal by the English to allow the French to occupy the Flemish ports.

After Bonaparte's first exile, the powers decided the fate of Belgium by handing her over to the newly-formed Kingdom of the Netherlands. The Congress of Vienna was busy approving this when news came of Bonaparte's return. His romantic march northward was halted only a dozen miles short of Brussels and, when Waterloo had been fought, the Netherlands were re-established. The Bishop of Ghent at once led an outcry against the liberty of conscience to which William I of Orange was committed, and the king rather provocatively adopted various anti-Catholic measures and others appearing to favour the Dutch against the Belgians. Attempts by the Dutch to quell riots in Brussels (September 1830) were abandoned after some bloodshed, a provisional government was formed and a National Congress elected. French intrigues secured the election as king of the second son of King Louis-Philippe, but British opposition was so strong that the final choice fell on Prince Leopold of Saxe-Coburg-Saalfeld, an uncle of Queen Victoria.

Emergence of Modern Belgium

For 110 years, until 1940, the main aim of Belgian policy was to keep her territory intact, to defend it if necessary and to avoid being drawn into European quarrels. There were difficulties about the latter, especially in the early stages of the nation's independence, but they were successfully surmounted. The nation prospered on the basis of its ports and a dense rail network; its coal mines, stretching across southern Belgium and also farther north in the Campine basin; its great steel industry centred on Liège and the important metal manufacturing industries; the diamond cutting industry in Antwerp; the quarries; the glass industry, the leather industry; and the traditional textile industry centred on Ghent, Courtrai and Verviers.

Her far-sighted sovereign, Léopold II, acquired personal control of the Congo basin in central Africa, and the Belgian State accepted it from him on condition it should cost them nothing. In fact, it produced incalculable wealth but the tide of African nationalism did not spare it, and today it is running its own affairs.

Twice in the present century treaties have been violated and Belgium has been invaded. In the 1914-18 war a small piece of Belgian territory was defended throughout, thanks to Albert the Soldier King, the heroic Belgian army, and at the cost of nearly a quarter-million British lives. No such defence was possible in 1940-45, which made the years of enemy occupation infinitely more painful for the many patriots, exposed as they were to the claim, urged by advocates of the "new order", that the war was over. That Belgium emerged from the dark years with her spirit unimpaired is shown by the speed of her recovery.

The attempted return of Léopold III to the throne nearly sparked off a civil war in 1950 and to obviate the constitutional crisis he abdicated in 1951 in favour of his son Baudouin who, together with his wife Fabiola, enjoys universal popularity among his subjects.

Most recently of all, Belgium has re-discovered its international vocation. Brussels is the capital of the EEC (European Economic Community), of which Belgium is a founder member. Belgium also houses SHAPE and NATO, besides a host of smaller European and international bodies. Three separate diplomatic corps are accredited to Brussels, which thus has every right to rank as the "Capital of Europe".

A GLIMPSE OF THE ARTS

A Melting Pot of Diverse Origins

Belgium, as a national unit, is quite a new affair and its artistic traditions, therefore, are far from being national. The country which is now Belgium has, at various times, been part of much larger units, and dominant influences have come from the Netherlands, from France, from Spain and Germany and, of course, from Italy in the crucial revolutions of Romanesque architecture and later in the painting, decoration and building influences of the Renaissance and the period which followed. It would, however, be untrue to say that the arts of Belgium are derivative. Artistic trends know no frontiers, and work done in Belgium has always been as much a compound of local conditions and the trends of its period as that of any other country. If it is true that Thierry Bouts and Hieronymus Bosch were Dutchmen and James Ensor of English origin, it is equally true that Sir Anthony van Dyck was a native of Antwerp, and that Jean Lhome—who built the famous tomb of Charles III at Pamplona—was from Tournai.

The history of all art is tied up with the history of its patrons. There is little enough surviving in Belgium which dates from before the 10th and 11th centuries, by which time the land was ready to reconstruct after the depredations of the Norsemen and, the two phases of Christian evangelization having taken a firm root, the abbey communities were ready to build. The new idea in architecture was the Romanesque, which was reaching the Meuse valley by way of the Rhine and not without Germanic influence. The main patron was the church and the abbeys, and if Notger as Prince-Bishop gave us the fortifications of Thuin (of which a tower still stands), he also gave us the octagonal plan of the Liège Church of Saint John, which clearly owes its inspiration to Aix-la-Chapelle and hence to eastern influences. A great deal of the pure Romanesque has been lost or swamped by the additions and embellishments of later centuries, but there are unspoiled cloisters at Tongres and Nivelles. The Church of Saint Vincent at Soignies is a fine example of well preserved work of the 10th and 11th centuries, though it was built under French influence which is lacking at Xhignisse and Condroz. This is explained by the fact that the Bishopric of Tournai came under the jurisdiction of Rheims, while that of Liège was under Cologne. At Tournai itself, the five towers of the cathedral show unmistakable German influence, though the interior, with its Norman *triforium*, owes so much to France that it begins to define the Scaldean Gothic which was to play so large a part in the later architecture of the Flemish plain.

Early Art and Sculpture

Meantime the art of sculpture was developing in line with architecture, and it was early in the 12th century that Renier de Huy designed and Lambert Patras of Dinant cast the font in Saint Bartholomew's in Liège. There are a number of other early works, including especially those at Tournai and Nivelles and a Madonna in the Archeological Museum (Curtius Mansion) at Liège. The big developments in sculpture were, however, to come later. They were preceded by sculpture in its smaller forms, the arts of the ivory worker, the coppersmith and the silversmith. The ivory workers seem to have been the first to reach eminence, and you will see works of special interest in the Archeological Museum at Liège—again dating from Notger—at Tongres and in the Museum of Art and History in Brussels. The coppersmiths of Dinant had been famous from a very early period, but their work in church decoration was a later development. It was in *champlevé* enamel that Godefroid de Huy brought renewed fame to the Meuse craftsmen, and for examples of his work you must again go to the Museum of Art and History. The next stage was the development of the silversmith's work, largely through Nicolas of Verdun, late in the 12th century, and his pupil, Hugo d'Oignies, whose wonderful work is best seen in the convent at Namur, though an example of it stands side by side with one of his master's at Tournai. Hugo marked the peak of the Meuse silversmith tradition. The reliquary at Nivelles, all but destroyed in 1940, dates from later in the 13th century and was noticeably of French inspiration, for the Belgian work thenceforth seems to have lacked its native force.

Sculptors in this period were dominated by French influences, and architecture was passing from the Romanesque to the Gothic. Churches were now built under the severe discipline of the crossed ogive, and the Gothic majesty of the Ile de France achieved an early triumph in the choir of Tournai Cathedral. Churches such as those of Notre Dame in Oudenaarde and Bruges were setting the stage for the more heavily decorated Gothic of the flamboyant phase that was to characterize the next century, which, as good luck would have it, was to be a time of mighty patronage. Sculptors such as Pépin de Huy, André Bonneveu and Jean de Marville were preparing the ground for the time when Claus Sluter should come from Haarlem into Brabant and accomplish great works for the Dukes of Burgundy.

The Burgundian Period

This was the state of things when Belgium entered the first of her two great periods of artistic creation, periods separated indeed by only half a century but basically different. The first begins with the accession of Philip the Good in 1419, and lasts through the early Spanish period though perhaps not quite until the abdication of Charles Quint (1555). By this time the communes were in the ascendancy and, with the acquisition of trading wealth and the granting of civil liberties, there was a big demand for social architecture, town halls, town belfries, cloth halls, and other commercial edifices, as well as for churches. At the same time, the sovereign of the Low Countries was a prince who had learned the language of Flanders, who maintained a sumptuous court and whose English alliance had effectively sealed off the fear of French aggression for the next 40 years. It was a time of great opportunities for all the arts, and ended only when the religious troubles of the 16th century took precedence over the achievements of the arts. There was then a period of small achievement, to be followed by another great period after Belgian resistance to the Inquisition had collapsed, and Antwerp was ready for the immense decorative activity which centred round Rubens. The great man died in 1640 and Van Dyck, who had already gone to England, lived only another year. With the loss of Antwerp's prosperity through the closing of the Scheldt a few years later, the force of Rubens' personality no longer dominated the world of painting and achievement (as seen in the work of Jordaens) was less noteworthy for some time to come. Building, in the baroque style which was by then in vogue, and which is sometimes in Belgium confused with the Renaissance influence, still continued.

It is in the Burgundian period that Belgian painting seems suddenly to come to life. There had indeed been painters before 1400, as well as some admirable illuminated manuscripts, but many people think of Belgian painting as having suddenly come into existence with the Van Eycks (if there were indeed two of them) whose masterwork in Saint Bavo's at Ghent was finished in 1432. It does not, indeed, seem that Jan van Eyck had nearly so elaborate an artistic pedigree as, for example, Fra Angelico, who was his approximate contemporary; but, though Belgian painting is often referred to simply as Flemish, it is worth remembering that Robert Campin was painting in Tournai at the same time, that he and Van Eyck came from no common stock, and they died within three years of one another. It is important to remember this when comparing the Campin at Westerlo with the Van Eyck altarpiece at Ghent.

Research tends to prove that the existence of Hubert van Eyck, supposedly Jan's senior, may have been invented about the middle of the 16th century to justify the presence of the *Mystery of the Lamb* (started by Jan but finished after his death by his brother) in Ghent—and Jan van Eyck was master of the Bruges school. This rivalry between Ghent and Bruges was manifested in every field.

The Age of Creative Giants

Neither master created a school. Van Eyck died in Bruges; and Campin's chief pupil, Roger de le Pasture, translated his name into Flemish (Rogier van der Weyden), and worked for a time in Bruges before visiting Italy and returning to settle down as official portraitist to the city of Brussels, where he died in 1464. Thierry Bouts held a similar job in Louvain (Leuven) about the same time. That wandering anonymous artist of the period, the Master of Flémalle, created a sensation in the art world in 1957, when his *Annunciation* was sold for a fabulous sum to the Metropolitan Museum of Art in New York amidst an outcry of protest from Belgian public opinion. Bruges, in full flower with the Burgundian court and its own merchant prosperity, was the natural meeting place of painters. Hugo van der Goes was here for a time, and Hans Memling depicted the great Bruges of the closing decades of the century, though the clouds already forming on the city's horizon may have determined the beginnings of a mysticism notable in his *Marriage of Saint Catherine.* This seems to have prepared the ground for the more disturbed work of Gerard David and the rather terrifying achievements of Hieronymus Bosch. Lancelot Blondeel, a man of many talents, is best known for the fireplace of the Frank at Bruges, though he gave much attention to the problem of linking Bruges with the sea by a canal. Like Leonardo da Vinci, to whom he was almost a counterpart in versatility, Blondeel seems to have created no intimate artistic following. Had he done so, Belgium might have had a bigger share in the glories of the Renaissance, which she seems rather to have missed. There were indeed Italian influences at work in Antwerp, where Quentin Metsys (died 1530), a friend of Erasmus, achieved a mastery of tactile values and of figure perspective well in advance of his time; but it was rather lost on his contemporaries and followers such as Patenier, Josse Vanderbeek and Mabuse. In Brussels about the same time the chief effect of the facile paintings of the over-prolific Bernard van Orley was an impulse towards classicism, carried on by such painters as Michel Coxcie and Pieter Pourbus the Elder.

During this period François de Vriendt (alias Frans Floris) essayed in Antwerp some Michelangelesque ideas in figure composition that give him a place in the spiritual pedigree of Rubens; but the only painter of mark in the middle and late 16th century was Pieter Breughel. This Campinois, who made Brussels his home, owed more to Hieronymus Bosch than to any other master. He was the creator of a new style which gave painting an entirely fresh significance. Though he could, and did, produce pictures of the conventional religious subjects, he was essentially an artist in the human angle, in the direct line of succession between Homer and man-bites-dog. He was poet enough to assess the eternal in things temporal, and he painted the Flemish peasant as he was and is and always will be. If Belgium has made any great contribution to the arts, it is in the work of this intensely individual master whose contemporaries could make nothing of his spirit and technique and of whom Teniers the Elder and Brouwer—born after Breughel's death—were little more than imitators.

The Flowering of Architecture

In the period of the Dukes of Burgundy, the art of the silversmith seems to have been translated into that of the cook, in the fantastic table decoration which characterised this court. Some of the architecture, which had been following a line of its own, was in this period called upon to satisfy an immense secular demand upon an art which had hitherto had a strong religious bias. Matthew de Layens in the masterly Hôtel de Ville at Louvain, created a building which could be a saint's reliquary. The same cannot be said of the Hôtel de Ville in Brussels, which indeed owed much to ecclesiastical design when it was begun in 1402, though the mid-century addition and the spire have given it civic character at its very best, so that it ranks as Jan van Ruysbroek's masterpiece. Works such as these were the precursors of much else, and above all those of the great Kelderman family. This family included Antoine, who worked with Layens at Louvain; Jan, who was one of the major artisans of Saint Peter's; and Rombaut, who died in 1531, the last of the dynasty. Rombaut was a partner of the two De Waghemakers (Herman and Dominique), and thus among the first planners of the Hôtel de Ville at Ghent, as well as joint designer of a number of other masterpieces in Belgium, including the cathedral at Antwerp. Other names appear in this period of intense creativity, such as the Brussels master van Pede whose most brilliant work is at Oudenaarde, and Aert van Mulcken who was responsible for the Palace of the Prince-Bishops in Liège and helped finish the late Flamboyant Gothic churches of Saint Martin and Saint James in the same city.

Appearance of the Baroque

The religious troubles interrupted art, and the excesses of the iconoclasts destroyed a great deal, especially in the field of sculpture. In this field, magnificent work had been done in Tournai; and in Brussels there were masters such as Nicolas de Bruyn and the father-and-son Bormans (Jan and Paschier). Already, however, in the 16th century, it was becoming evident that the humanised splendour of the Renaissance was outside the scope of the Belgian spirit, and decorative exuberance was degenerating into the over-decorated Baroque. Nevertheless, the time produced great craftsmen in several departments of art, notably such men as Cornelis Floris, the painter's sculptor brother, and Jacques de Broeucq, who was the master of Giovanni da Bologna. Alexander Colins, sometimes compared with Ghiberti, was another great master of this period, and so are the three members of the Dusquenoy family, of whom the elder, François, was better known in Italy as Francesco Fiamingo. There was Matthew de Wayer and the Verbruggen family. There was Artus Quellin the elder. There were master architects such as Brother Pieter Huyssens,

Wenceslas Coeberger and Father William Hessius. The Baroque style was well suited to conditions in which there was rivalry in decoration. It was now that the beautiful gable-ended construction which had been characteristic of so much house-building in Flanders was improved into the over-ornamented roof-ends of which there are so many. By this time the high tradition of discriminating patronage had lost ground in favour of a taste for the ornate, and it says much for the mastery of Pieter Paul Rubens that he achieved so much against a background so filled with artistic decay. The glory of the 17th century is to be found in Rubens' work, with that of the astonishing Van Dyck, who, in the 42 years of his life, found time for five years as Rubens' assistant, seven years in Italy, another five years in Antwerp when Rubens' absence brought him many of the orders he might otherwise have missed, and nine years in England, where he received the honour of knighthood, and died there. Beside these great names the work of their contemporaries and followers pales into insignificance but in this period were also Jan Breughel (son of Pieter), the two Jacques van Oost, Theodore van Loon, Daniel Seghers, and Jan Siberechts.

The 18th century brought "*le temps des équipages*", and with it a great deal of attractive building in which the names of Montoyer, 't Kindt, and Dewez stand out. Good examples of the period are the *hôtels* of Jean de Coninck: the d'Hane Steenhuys in Ghent, and the Ansembourg in Liège. The painters, however, do not seem to have found the period congenial, apart from Pierre Verhaegen and perhaps a few minor masters such as Garemyn and François de Marne.

The 19th and 20th Centuries

It is a great pity that so formative a period should have arisen only when the art of architecture was nearly dead. It is true that the Church of Notre Dame at Laeken, the foundation of which was laid by Leopold I in 1854, is a tomb of taste as well as of kings. The artist who designed it, Joseph Poelaert, achieved an impressive edifice (for size) in Brussels' Palais de Justice, though many cities in many periods have crowned their hilltops more elegantly. At least the 19th century achieved several buildings in Brussels that dominate without offence, notably the arch of the Cinquantenaire (reminiscent of Schönbrunn, but worked into a worthy context) and the hothouse at the back of the Jardin Botanique. The latter dates from early in the 19th century, as does the Palais des Académies on the corner of the Place des Palais. The main success of 19th-century construction, however, is the Beaux Arts Picture Gallery (Musée d'Art Ancien) by Balat, fronting on the Rue de la Régence.

Sculpture passed through a time of some difficulty in shaking off the Baroque influence which was still dominant in Verhaegen, but Jacques Bergé was already importing a French influence in the early 18th century and Godecharle was flourishing in the early 19th. With the independence of Belgium came a wave of statuary—it would be unkind to call it a plague—and many citizens have wondered whether their country owed so much to so many national heroes that all this street-decoration was desirable. There was undoubtedly a great deal of mediocre work, but some good pieces have emerged. Paul de Vigne created the Breydel de Coninck statue in Bruges, Lambeaux produced the Brabo fountain at Antwerp, and Van der Stappen and Devigne did the bronze groups which flank the frontage of the Musée Ancien in Brussels. The major sculptor of the 19th century was Constantin Meunier, pupil of Fraikin, the artist of the Egmont and Hornes statue in the Petit Sablon in Brussels. Meunier was a dramatic interpreter of industrial scenes and emotions, whose work was strong and realistic. The aftermath of his work has been disappointing, in that so distinguished a sculptor as Georges Minne (the *Ephèbes* fountain at Ghent is his work) took refuge in symbolism, just as the literary symbolism of Maurice Maeterlinck seems to have been less a development of Guido Gezelle than a revolt against the peasant realities of Camile Lemonnier. The vigour of Meunier's work, however, may have influenced the less dramatic but equally vital paintings of Rik Wouters.

It is a pity that the destruction produced by the 1914-18 war was repaired by so many attempts to reconstruct what was old and by so few attempts to create. The fairly recent Albertinum, the national library, and its surroundings bring new ideas in civic architecture.

Painting, in the meantime, has pursued its course on quieter lines. The art has found fewer and less free-spending patrons than architecture and sculpture, and the 20th-century trend took the painters nearer to nature than they had been for some time. Jacob Smits was the leader of the Campine painters, while a school of rather mystic painters congregated at St. Martens Latem around the sculptor Georges Minne, producing *inter alia* such painters as Albert Servaes, Evenepoel, de Saedeleer, and Constant Permeke. Independently, James Ensor—of British descent—produced from his Ostend background a style and achievement which was never wholly impressionistic and may have left a permanent mark on the painting of the country in which he was born (1860) and in which he died in 1949. His home at Ostend has been made into a museum. Other masters of violent colour are Tytgat and Opsomer, a seascape painter of the Scheldt estuary. Joss Albert's work is strikingly reminiscent of the old masters. Two outstanding surrealists, Delvaux and Magritte enjoy wide international recognition and their works command on the art market prices approaching those of Salvador Dali's.

Music

It is not generally known that Roland de Lassus, born in Mons in 1532, was not an Italian. Before becoming "Master of Musick" at the Bavarian court, he spent many years in Italy and, in keeping with the fashion of those times, adopted the name of Orlando di Lasso. His elegantly phrased madrigals, jewels of vocal polyphony, were forerunners of the Italian opera, perfected a few decades later by Monteverdi.

Liège, cradle of Belgium's great musicians, produced Grétry, fashionable 18th-century composer of numerous intimate operas. One hundred years later, César Franck, better known for his symphonic and chamber music than for his magnificent organ works, contributed greatly to the rebirth of French music. From the same region came his most gifted pupil, Lekeu, in whose few works, completed before his death in 1894 at the age of 24, we have a measure of his genius.

Bériot and Henri Vieuxtemps initiated the famous Belgian school of violin playing; their concertos are still standard works with music schools throughout the world. Eugène Ysaye and his disciples perpetuated this virtuoso tradition, which finds its contemporary expression in the late Queen Elisabeth's Music Chapel, where promising young artists can devote their talent to polishing their technique work, free from everyday cares. The same foundation acts as patron of the annual music competition, which has now become an international institution.

Literature

Flemish, a variation of Dutch, is spoken by slightly more than half the population, while in Brussels and south of the capital, French is the predominant language. Thus two regional literatures have developed, following the trends of those of France and Holland.

Strangely enough it was Flanders that gave the French literature of Belgium its two most outstanding figures at the beginning of this century: the poet Verhaeren, and Maeterlinck, playwright and Nobel Prize winner in 1913, whose best known work is *Pelléas et Mélisande*. Among contemporary Belgian writers, Georges Simenon has acquired world fame with his psychological thrillers. The novelist Françoise Mallet-Joris has brought a mature depth of characterization and cool, spare style to bear on a wide-range of plots. She is rapidly becoming one of the leading writers of the day.

TRADITIONAL EVENTS

A Timetable of Legends

There is nothing the Belgian likes better than a festival. In the spirit of this people there is an engaging simplicity which accepts local legends and even amplifies them so that celebrations continue long after their origin is lost in obscurity. Moreover, though the nation is young, the countryside is old; and it has had an adventurous past which is naturally a great legend producer. In all this there is abundant raw material, to which must be added the fact that the church, as ever adapting ritual observance to the older ceremonies associated with the seasons of nature and the frailties of man, has lent its ready support. There are quite a number of places where you can have your automobile blessed, at appropriate times, in the name of Saint Christopher, the patron of transport; and, though the automobile has no basis in folklore, there is no reason why the Cadillac should be less favoured than the ox-cart.

Folklore observances have a very real place in the cultural life of the country, for they remind the people of their traditions. Most of the festivities are timed to fall on Sundays or public holidays, not for the sake of foreign holidaymakers for whom one day is as good as another, but for the sake of the Belgians themselves, who will gladly go long distances to assist at spectacles of this kind.

The calendar is full of *manifestations folkloriques,* nearly all of which have religious connotations and some of which have their roots in the remote past. It is interesting, for example, that in the Lumeçon carnival at Mons on Trinity Sunday, the story of Saint George has become confused with the local legend of Gilles de Chin. (Gilles' legend survives in its pure form at Wasmes in the neighbouring countryside.) This, however, is less surprising when it is remembered that the desire to celebrate the victory of the shining armour of spring over the sinister aspect of all-devouring winter is much older than Gilles de Chin or even than George of Cappadocia himself.

Of the three other major spectacles which attract many foreign visitors, two are purely religious and one purely secular.

The Procession of Penitents at Furnes is Spanish in origin and in the ecstatic attitude of the crowd. There is a less devotional atmosphere in the Bruges Pageant of the Holy Blood, though the event is religious in both its origin and intentions. By contrast, the Dance of the Gilles at Binche contains not a shred of Christian observance. It is said to have originated with the festivities Mary of Hungary gave for her nephew, Philip II of Spain, to commemorate the Spanish conquest of Peru during the first half of the 16th century. The oranges so boisterously flung by the exotically plumed and dressed Gilles are supposed to represent the gold of the defeated Incas.

Other Outstanding Spectacles

On the other hand, there are a great many celebrations in which the Christian and pagan elements are indissolubly mixed. This is the case at Mons, but it is still more noticeable elsewhere. For example, both priest and burgomaster attend the marriage of the giant Goliath and his bride at Ath, and the *marches militaires* of the country between Sambre and Meuse are astonishingly pagan and noisy for celebrations that are primarily devoted to the procession of saintly relics. The church has evidently taken the view that religious faith has the greater meaning for being allowed to enter into the joyous phases of the people's life. This is especially true of the biggest *marche* of all, that of Saint Feuillen at Fosse, where the once-in-seven-years ceremony begins with the blessing of the arms of the many thousands of warriors, arrayed in the uniforms of all manner of troops who have at various times been seen in the Low Countries. The legend of Saint Feuillen relates the miraculous separation of the waters of the Sambre, a curious reminder of the Israelites' passages of the Red Sea.

An ancient origin can often be claimed for ceremonies in which trees play an important part. One of these is the planting (in

August) of the May tree, a rite in connection with which there is a curious, though not so antique, story of rivalry between the universities of Brussels and Louvain. In another of the tree-legends, around which there centres an observance on Trinity Sunday at Walcourt, the basic legend tells of the miraculous escape from fire of a Madonna statue which refused to leave its tree-refuge until the local chevalier (13th century) had promised to endow an abbey in its honour. After the yearly re-enactment of the scene, the tree is torn down and dismembered, and the lucky possessor of a fragment is insured against ill fortune for the ensuing year. A tree, too, plays a vital part in the *dénouement* of the Cracknel Festival at Geraardsbergen, beginning with the burgomaster and aldermen swallowing live fish in their cup of wine. This takes place in daylight on top of a small hill up which, at nightfall, the population wends, again to witness the ceremonial burning of a tree, which is the signal for the lighting of a number of beacon fires across the Flemish plain below.

The motif of many bonfires finds its echo on Saint John's night (24 June), when fires burn across the Walloon countryside in a sort of modern Walpurgis in which the spirits of good and evil are locked in their endless battle. Good children stay at home on this night, for strange beings are abroad and there is ill luck in the kiss of the werewolf or the very sight of a headless horse. This fear of the terror which walks by night has a pleasing and less terrifying counterpart when the bells of the church are returning from Rome, whither they repair on Holy Thursday. They are supposed to fly close to the ground, and no good can befall the child who obstructs them. On Good Friday, the children not only hear the bells are back, again pealing from the belfry, but will find they have brought along their little brothers and sisters—some made of chocolate or marzipan—with which their bedrooms are hung.

A historic procession of pomp and circumstance, the Ommegang, takes place nearly every year in July at the Grand' Place in Brussels. Its origins go back to the 14th century when, according to legend, the Virgin appeared to a young girl of Antwerp, Beatrice Soetkens, and complained about the inconstant devotion of the Antwerp people. On the spot where the vision occurred, the girl found a statue, which she placed in the Church of Notre Dame du Sablon in Brussels. The procession's religious significance disappeared over the centuries, and it became a sumptuous cortege in which nobles, the guilds, and the common folk took equal part. Nowadays, Emperor Charles Quint and his court (represented by members of the Belgian aristocracy) head the procession; the emperor then mounts a dais to receive the homage of his subjects. The richness of the costumes and the historic décor of the Grand' Place make the Ommegang a unique spectacle.

Rural Celebrations

Naturally enough, a very large part of the folklore ceremonies is in some way connected with the hazards of a farmer's life. The farmer's year is dotted with small associations with the days of saints, beginning with the hope of a still night on the eve of the Annunciation (March 25). Saint George's Day, 23 April, is particularly important because of Saint George's patronage of horses; and, since he is also patron of the little Brabant commune of Grez-Doiceau, it is here that the drafthorse is the centre of special celebration. All the horses from the farms around are ridden in procession on this day, after which they receive the blessing of a priest standing before an altar especially erected in a farm cart. This is a simple ceremony, but typical of many in which divine blessing is sought for human activities. It has a parallel in the blessing of the sea, which, although the tourist attraction of the spectacle has been somewhat overplayed, is a stern reality of the Flemish fishermen.

Another parallel, though without the farming interest, is the procession of the Virgins at lower Wavre. For this, which is wholly religious and attracts the very highest church patronage, Madonna statues are sent from all over Belgium. The procession ends with the local Virgin who, legend asserts, refused to have her church built on a hilltop because she had chosen this valley to be the valley of peace. There is in Wavre, however, another festival, the religious origin of which is more doubtful, though the church enters into it. This is the Wastia procession in June, the feature of which is the parading of a 55-pound loaf of bread, heavily garlanded with flowers. The loaf, after a sojourn in the church, is cut up and distributed to those who require protection against hydrophobia, though the good luck brought by possession of the flowers is of a more general character.

The highlight of the farming year is the procession to the tomb of Saint Guidon at Anderlecht, now a suburb of Brussels. This happens twice a year, on Whit Monday and on the Sunday that follows 12 September. The cab-drivers' pilgrimage, which used to be part of the Whitsun homage to Saint Guidon, is of course no longer a reality; but the sincerity of the peasantry is no less real, for Saint Guidon is especially sovereign against all contagious diseases and especially against the illnesses of animals. A small number of pilgrims still arrive on horseback, and the offerings of the pious in cash and kind are large. Another case in which the offertory is a central feature is that of the black chickens, which are laid in their cages on Saint Giles's day before the church door at Rumsdorp (Landen) and sold off by the priest after the celebration of Mass.

There are a number of observances which are in reality references to historical incidents. Among these is the Plague Procession in Tournai, and the campaigns of the Duke of Marlborough (who, it will be remembered, goes to war in a popular song) earned him an annual burial during the Kermesse at Kessenich. In the same class must be reckoned the annual homages paid on 3 November to Saint Hubert, both in his own town in the Ardennes and in Liège (Sainte Croix) and Brussels (Grand Sablon). These scenes, with all the colour of early November in forest country, are picturesque enough; but their connection with Saint Hubert is a trifle tenuous when it is remembered that his main association with hunting was that he foresook it when he found the stag he was stalking carried an illuminated cross between the antlers.

Santa Claus, Belgian Version

From the children's standpoint, the great festival of the year is Saint Nicholas' Day (6 December). The festivity of Christmas has been encouraged by the shopkeepers and restaurateurs and others who cater for grownups, but at the popular level Christmas is essentially religious, whereas Saint Nicholas' Day is the time for which every child is taught to long. In the big cities, of course, even this kindly saint has been commercialised, arriving by all types of transport (we've seen him step out of a helicopter), and spending his time parading the streets in a cart with advertising slogans or sitting in the window or the gift department of a store. Such unsaintly goings-on are destructive of the beliefs of childhood, but this, unfortunately, has not been made a criminal offence in Belgium or anywhere else. When you really get down to the Saint Nicholas whom children believe in, you will find his routine is very strict. His entry is always made on a white horse, and he is always accompanied by a black-visaged page in medieval attire, who carries his sack.

A calendar of folklore events which can be seen by the interested visitor is available through the National Tourist Office. They offer a field of great interest, whether it be casual or whether it be concerned with sorting out the pagan from the Christian or the historical from the myth. Behind it all is the real and evident gusto with which the Belgians enter into these festivities, a factor which prevents their degenerating into drab pseudo-authentic revivals. If you tell a Belgian to kill a dragon, he goes out and kills it with skill and daring. He enjoys the deed as much as you do, and will enjoy the chance to talk it over with you in the café afterwards. This, perhaps, is the unifying key to the whole thing, for all observances, be they pious, sportive or traditional, end at the café table. The Belgians are great traditionalists, and on 1 and 2 November they honor their ancestors by their annual trip with white chrysanthemums to the local cemetery. But, when all is over and the little *Zielekoekjes* ("soul cakes") have been eaten, the café radio in all the villages will be playing fortissimo, and the cafés will be full of bright-faced women of all ages, all dressed in mourning weeds and all spoiling for a dance.

A SATIRICAL GLANCE

The Belgians without Tears

by

GEORGE MIKES

(Mr. Mikes, author of How to be an Alien, How to Scrape Skies, Wisdom for Others, *and* Milk and Honey *is, of course, the well known debunker of peoples. In the short commentary below, he makes his first attempt at alienating the Belgians.)*

The British should love Belgium, because it is a country of compromise. To the superficial observer it would seem partly French, partly Dutch, but Belgium is neither. It is one of the Low Countries, but the Ardennes rise on its territory. It is one of the smallest countries in Europe and one of the most densely populated. Its soil is neither rich nor poor. It is full of chimneys and blast furnaces, but the countryside is mild, green and charming.

Further, the English should love Belgium because it used to be Britain's little protégé. For centuries Belgium was governed by Spanish, French and Austrian princes, but in the 19th century Britian decided otherwise. Britain did not want Belgium but was determined that no one else should have her. This policy—which may sound selfish by purely personal standards—was called the balance of power. What the balance of power really meant was that Britain—as far as it could be helped—allowed no real power to anyone else. In 1914 Britain went to war mainly to safeguard Belgian independence and honor its word, given after the Belgian revolution of 1830, and true to ancient British traditions, fought for right and justice, mainly for selfish reasons.

The Americans, too, should love Belgium because it is very small, and Americans love everything very small or very big. Belgium is only slightly larger than Maryland, and Austria is three times larger than Belgium. Texas is 25 times as large. The Americans should love Belgium again because it is—as I have already mentioned—the most overcrowded spot on earth and the Americans adore overcrowding. (This overcrowding should not be taken too literally. It is not a slum country; on the contrary, it bears no resemblance at all to Coney Island on a really lively Sunday afternoon.) And the Americans have another good reason for loving Belgium. It was for long a matter of dispute whether the Belgians formed a distinct nation, just as some ignorant people used to question the right of the Americans to be regarded as a distinct nation. In the case of the Belgians, however, it was mostly the Belgians themselves who maintained that Belgium was not a country, but only a geographical expression. By now they have resigned themselves to the fact that they are a distinct and individual nation. They would not dream of regarding themselves either as Dutch or as French. They have their own dynasty, great love for their country and—I should not go so far as to state that they have their own "way of life"—but they certainly have their own mentality. While there are no cultural frontiers to the south—many Belgians read French newspapers, periodicals and books, and are within France's spiritual orbit—they are conservative, sedate and temperate; consequently less romantic and exciting than the French. I was struck and amused reading a remark, reported to have been uttered by the Austrian Joseph II, then ruler of Belgium. The emperor gave Belgium some modern institutions, freedom of belief, modern courts, etc. In consequence of his reforms he found himself in 1781 in great trouble and bitterly remarked to the Count of Ségur: "The people of Brabant have revolted against me because I wished to give them what the people of France are clamouring for." (I should stop here for full effect. But I must add that the Belgian people were right and the emperor—this son of the "age of enlightenment"—wrong, because forcing freedom down a people's throat is just a form of enslaving them.)

Belgium And The Grand Duchy

People quite wrongly believe that Luxembourg is a part of Belgium. It is not. Luxembourg is an independent Grand Duchy—a charming and idyllic place. But Luxembourg has such close political, financial, and economic ties with Belgium that the belief in Luxembourg's dependence on Belgium was certain to arise and spread. Why does Belgium keep up these close ties with Luxembourg? For scores of very excellent reasons. But for a long time, however, I believed that Belgium's case was parallel to that of Mr. Balogh, who a few decades ago was editor-in-chief of a Budapest daily paper. Mr. Balogh was an excellent editor, a brilliant writer, but an extremely tiny fellow, and this worried him to no small extent. So he kept in his immediate entourage a Mr. Moller, who was a most amusing companion but far from an epoch-making journalist. Mr. Moller, however, had one great merit. He was about five inches shorter than Balogh. Next to Moller even Balogh looked a giant,—one of the modest, undersized giants it is true, but still a giant. Luxembourg is Belgium's Moller.

Politics And The Church

In England, people are either religious or they are not. They either go to church or they do not. Religion, as a rule, is not a central problem of their lives. In Belgium, however, Catholicism is the central political, social and moral force and this should not be forgotten by anyone who tries to understand Belgian mentality and politics. All this does not mean that everybody is a good and practising Catholic; but it does mean that nobody can afford to remain neutral and that everybody is forced to take up either a positive or a negative attitude to Catholicism. Anti-Catholic feeling, too, is much stronger in certain groups in Brussels and other parts of the country than in other lands where religion does not rule almost supreme. A Belgian friend once explained to me that in Belgium the most important division between people does not run on political lines. It is less important, he said, whether people are Flemish or Walloons, than whether they are Catholics or anti-Catholics. I am not sure that my friend was right. It seems to me that a Catholic and anti-Catholic undercurrent further complicates the waves of the Flemish-Walloon scene.

I cannot dwell on all the subjects I should like to. I should have liked to say a few words on Belgian art; and I should have liked to give a detailed description of Bruges—my favourite of all the cities in the world, after Florence. Time stopped over Bruges: once in the 15th and then again in the 18th century. You take a walk in the city and in five minutes you can cover 300 years. You walk in its narrow streets, intersected by canals, you listen to the lovely chimes of the famous bells, and when you are quite enthralled by the spirit of a bygone age, you enter one of the old houses with high, pointed gables and red roofs—to find yourself in the hubbub of a modern department store. In Bruges the spirit of Michelangelo embraces the spirit of Woolworth's.

Better Cooks Than Drivers

I wish to add now a few remarks on my personal impressions of Belgium. For me, Belgium is, first of all, the "Country of Peculiar Car Drivers". I have driven through Belgium many times and have often been painfully surprised by the individual style of the country's drivers. Of course, there are as many good drivers in Belgium as anywhere else, but there are also far more bad ones. In Belgium only new drivers have to pass a test before obtaining a driving license. Others may get into a car and drive away at their own risk. This is all right as regards the driver's risk; I am not so sure that is all right as regards the pedestrian's risk. If a man is run over and has ten bones broken—well, it is the driver's responsibility. I am a lawyer myself and can tell you that this is absolutely right from a legal point of view. I am not certain that it is right from a medical point of view, as well—but, again, I am no doctor.

The English visitor will find it surprising that the Belgians know how to cook. In the last few years the English have become aware of the fact that their cooking is the object of worldwide admiration. Their food, indeed, is just on the verge of edibility. The English, however, are extremely touchy about this subject. Criticise their food and they all become ardent nationalists. They are proud of their food; but if they want a really good meal, they go over to France or Belgium.

The second surprising phenomenon for the English visitor is the fact that the Belgians work. Even the Americans will be taken aback by the Belgians' zeal. I know, that in New York, too, one can buy a piano or a set of Zane Gray's collected works between 2 and 4 in the morning, but New York is a vast metropolis. And New York is only one town in the United States; you cannot buy any pianos in Washington or Tucson after 7 p.m.

Shops in Belgium used to keep open until incredibly late hours. Once in Knokke my wife decided to buy shoes at 1:30 a.m. Not that they sell any better shoes at 1:30 a.m. than at noon, but she wanted to be able to remark casually to her friends: "I bought these shoes at half past one in the morning." We did get the shoes at the appointed hour—we stayed up specially to go over to the shop—but she has never been able to wear them. She was half asleep when she bought them and the shoes were two sizes too big. Alas, times are changing, even in Belgium.

Breaking the Bank at Belgian Casinos

Finally, for me and for thousands of English and American visitors, Belgium is a wonderful place for gambling. Gambling does not go on at the Monte Carlo level—which is an advantage for many people—but there are a number of casinos at various Belgian resorts and they are extremely popular.

I am not a gambler myself—or at least, I am deeply convinced that I am not. My wife is more honest than I am and she openly admits that she likes gambling in a mild fashion and within reasonable limits. Whenever we arrive in Belgium, I always explain to her in a paternal and somewhat haughty manner that gambling is a low kind of passion and the basest of all pastimes. Fortunately or unfortunately, however, I picture myself not only as a wise anti-gambler but also as a kind and obliging husband with a heart of gold, so on the second day of our *séjour* I graciously consent to visit the casino—naturally, for her sake only. On the third day I am urging her to hurry up not to miss the first ten minute after the opening of the casino and on the fourth day I am queueing up in front of the establishment, waiting for the doors to open.

Belgian casinos are the only ones in the world (as far as I know and I know one or two casinos) where you have to pay tax on each winning stake, with the result that you may ultimately lose all your money on roulette, but still, you have the gratifying feeling of having given up quite a round little sum in the form of winners' taxes, on the few occasions when you made some lucky shots. Psychologically this is a great help because when you have not a penny or a franc left in your pocket, it is extremely relieving to remember that at least from the point of view of the Collector of Taxes you were occasionally regarded as a winner.

FOOD AND DRINK

Accent on Quality

The tourist will enjoy finding out for himself that Belgian cooking, while based on the French, is different in many ways and certainly no less a *tour de force.* There are more restaurants in Brussels per head of the population than in Paris. The Belgian gourmet associations maintain every bit as high a standard as their French counterparts and such organizations as the *Club des 33, Club des Gastronomes* and *La Ligue des Amis du Vin* bestow their diplomas only sparingly.

International haute cuisine tends to be the same the world over but Belgians contrive to add their own distinctive touches by the use of more of the expensive ingredients, with emphasis on the fatty ones. At the popular levels they do not try to make much out of little as the French do: instead they concentrate on quantity *and* quality (as indeed they do throughout) and, while food is expensive, you will find excellent value for money everywhere.

Most Typical Dishes

As befits a nation which likes its food well presented, the most characteristic of their dishes is colourful. This is the *tomates aux crevettes,* a tomato stuffed with shrimps impregnated with mayonnaise. They are, of course, served cold, but have a warmer brother, the delicious *croquette aux crevettes.* You will be surprised to see how popular these miniature shrimps have become, and to hear the acrimonies that are bandied about in Ostend and Zeebruge when for a fleeting moment, it is found Dutch shrimps are getting cheaper on the Brussels market than the Belgian.

A dish to be found all over the country is *anguiles au vert*, baby eels served hot or cold. It owes its charms to the delicate aroma of the shredded herbs—sorrel, mint, sage, verbena—used in its preparation.

When the Belgian looks after his own interests he is said to be "defending his beefsteak". Very true this is, for his most accustomed dish is *bifteck et frites*. The steak varies in size and quality with the price, but it normally comes to table with a lump of butter coyly melting on the summit. The alternative is pork chop or veal chop; lamb is seldom eaten. The *frites,* are, of course, the familiar English "chips" or American "French fries". You can buy them, without fish or other accompaniment, in paper bags at strategic streetcorners. They are a national dish of the first water, normally served with salt, though the discerning often eat them with mayonnaise. The latter is also a national dish, prepared fresh, abundantly and with religious thoroughness at all social levels. The conception of mayonnaise bought readymade in a bottle is a supermarket innovation, still mainly for foreigners.

The pride of the Belgian dinner table is Brussels' own vegetable, the chicory, locally known as *witloof* (white leaf), which the French perversely call *endive* and the English perversely boil in water. The Belgians know the cult, as well as the culture, of this delicious vegetable and serve it *poêlé,* or garnish it to make a number of main dishes in which it has pride of place. It produces crops from October to March, and we can think of no more solid reason for a winter visit. The other great vegetable culture is the hothouse grape. It is the industry's pride to be able to produce good grapes all the year round; but, to see them at their best you should come in late September to the grape festival at Hoeilaart, on the fringe of the forest of Soignes.

We almost forgot asparagus. Reared with care in the sandy soil of the Malines region, it is at its best in May and June. *Asperges à la flamande* is a preparation of hardboiled eggs crushed in melted butter. You may take the asparagus with your fingers and dunk—absolutely delicious!

Sausages and Fish

Another national dish is the *boudin* sausage. All Belgian sausages have their very full quota of meat, and their flavours are distinctive. The *boudin de Liège* is made with herbs and is particularly savoury. The *boudin noir* appeals most to connoisseurs; the *boudin blanc* is more popular. The latter is a separate sausage and is served hot with varied accompaniments. Apple sauce goes well with it, but in the Ardennes it is served with grapes and is unusually delicious. Another Ardennes speciality is ham, and you can get *jambon d'Ardennes* in almost any restaurant; accompanied by *saucisson d'Ardennes* (salami) it makes a most appetizing hors d'oeuvre.

Unless you are an early-summer visitor, delicacies you will not want to miss are mussels (*moules*), which can be eaten during the months with an R in them. Though products of the seaside, you will find them at their best in Brussels: several popular restaurants in the Soho of Brussels, the Rue des Bouchers quarter, serve them in many guises. Remember, you don't order mussels as part of a general meal; you either eat mussels or other things and you will be surprised, not to say appalled, at the size of the bowl set before you. You can, indeed you usually do, eat them with *frites,* but by the time you have mastered the dish you will be far from hungry. Belgium has a number of other fish specialities to offer, notably *bisque de homard* (a very rich lobster soup), *écrevisses à la Liègeoise* (crayfish cooked in white wine sauce with butter of cream), and fillet of sole *Saint Arnould,* dressed with hops and bits of toast. You will also find fried eel very commendable and, at Namur especially, you will have them served *à l'escavèche*. The essential of this dish is that your eel is first pickled. Later it is fried and served cold in jelly. The practice of serving fish *à l'escavèche* is largely local, though it is found too in the Chimay region. Down by the Ourthe and the well-stocked Semois, they will serve your trout *meunière,* fetching it for you not from a tank but from the river, or even inviting you to do so yourself.

Fish Soup and Other Specialities

A dish that is a "must" in any visit to Belgium is the *waterzooi*, a variety of fresh or seawater fish boiled with herbs, as good as the vaunted *bouillabaisse* of which Thackeray wrote. You will get the best *waterzooi* at Ghent, but both Brussels and Antwerp can serve them very creditably. In Brussels, especially, you should try the *waterzooi* version that contains chicken instead of fish. Chicken is a Brussels speciality, but you can eat broilers off the spit everywhere.

Even for that poultry masterpiece (in a good cook's hands), *oie à l'instar de Visé*, the goose is first boiled before it is cut up and fried. Here, however, the boiling has a special function, for it is from this that the flesh takes on the savour of the vegetables and, most especially, of the garlic which reappears in the cream sauce. *Oie à l'instar de Visé* is certainly a thing to try. Gourmet historians, incidentally, say the recipe probably survives from the days of the Roman conquest of Gaul, though there is a legend which attributes it to a much later *Commissaire de Police* who ingeniously acquired a boiled goose in settling a dispute among his fellow-townsmen. Pride of place on a good restaurant's menu belongs to *rognon de veau à la Liègeoise*, a heavyweight affair of roast kidney, prepared with shredded juniper and a dash of gin.

During the hunting season there are some very fine dishes prepared with wine-soaked roebuck (*chevreuil*), hare (*lièvre*), and *marcassin* (young wild boar of the Ardennes). These dishes are called *civet*, not unlike the "jugging" of hare in the West of England.

There are, of course far more sophisticated ways of serving game, including game birds, especially partridge and quail. Many of them are specialities of individual inns in the Ardennes region. The same applies to trout, which are also natives of the region. You may well regret you can try so few.

It is a pity that modern tendencies are destroying much of the character of local cooking. You may find *carbonnades flamandes* (a type of goulash, more sweet than hot), that is very good indeed, and you may find one that is not; and either or both may be in or out of Flanders. In the same way, the practice of serving prunes with hare, a dish known as *civet de lièvre à la flamande,* is ceasing to be characteristically Flemish. You will find it everywhere in Belgium. Another Flemish speciality is *choesel au Madère*, small slices of various meats prepared with Madeira wine-sauce and garnished with mushrooms. In general, the characteristic of most Belgian food is its richness. The cooks use a great deal of fat, and fat bacon (or, puristically, a cut-up pig's ear and a trotter) is almost always one of the ingredients of the soup. You should not, by the way, neglect the soups. Every restaurant serves a *potage du jour*, which is nearly always very much cheaper than the special soups. Many cafés, too, though they do not cater for meals, serve soup cheaply and you can take it with your own sandwiches. This is one of the ways of getting a meal quickly, apart from in self-service restaurants, and snack bars.

Cakes and Sweets

There exist, too, a great number of typical biscuits and cookies, some of which have become associated with certain towns. Among these are the *kletskoppen* of Bruges, the Beaumont macaroons, and the *couques de Dinant* (gingerbread). *Tarte al djote,* a speciality of Nivelles, is made with beet leaves and cheese. *Pain à la grecque* is found throughout Belgium, but has nothing to do with Greece. It was named after the bread which the Augustinian monks of Brussels used to distribute to the poor. As their abbey was in the "fossé aux loups" (wolves' ditch), the Flemish called the bread "wolf gracht brood", later simply "gracht brood", which became "pain a la grecque" in French. The Greeks, of course, have never heard of it!

Gaufres, baked in front of you in cast-iron moulds at streetstalls, are delicious when warm. The teashops contain great quantities of cream cakes and you will notice that these are made on the same models from one shop to another, though they differ in excellence and in the richness of the buttercream (*crème de beurre*). You will notice, too, that there is seldom among the cakes anything made with pastry. The *tarte au sucre* (sugar tart) is another Belgian specialty which really should be tried by anyone with a gourmet's sweet tooth.

Sweets and candies follow traditional lines, though you will see a great deal of nougat and special stalls of it at fairs. Marzipan has a place of its own, for all the cakeshops are filled with marzipan animals and fruits in preparation for Saint Nicolas' Day (6 December). Once that day is over, they seem to vanish from the shop windows as mysteriously as the saint himself. "Custom-made" Brussels chocolate sweets, *pralines* are the last word in refinement, and among the best in the world, but you have to buy them in the specialized luxury shops (see regional chapters).

Wines and Liqueurs

So far as wine is concerned, the last of the Meuse-side vineyards disappeared during World War I. Belgian buying has helped the Moselle wines of Luxembourg get onto their feet and, because the wines are imported duty-free under the customs union arrangements, they are very good value as beverage wines. At the more precious levels it used to be a tradition that the pick of the Burgundies came overland to Charleroi and the pick of the clarets by sea to Antwerp. Nowadays, you will find the best of either in any city; for though time has broken down the exclusiveness of the main consignment centres it has not altered the fact that Belgium gets much of the best wine France has to offer. The Belgian palate is discriminating; and you will find really excellent cheap wines even in the self-service stores. The great growths and the prime vintages are, of course, bound to be expensive here as elsewhere. An attempt was made recently to introduce (under the trademark *Isca*) wine and champagne made from the renowned Belgian hot-house grapes.

Topnotch restaurants usually don't stock national liqueurs, though three of them are excellent. *Elixir de Spa* successfully captures the scent of the Ardennes pinewoods, while *Walzin* and *Elixir d'Anvers* are of the Benedictine type.

Belgians are not allowed to drink spirits in cafés. If you want a gin drink, therefore, you must go into a café labelled as a private club (*cercle privé*) and sign a membership form. The usual apéritifs are vermouth (which is curiously expensive) and light port (*porto*) which may be either red or white.

Beer, the Belgian Beverage

The national drink of the Belgians, however, is beer. For an ordinary glass of beer, the Belgian equivalent to "a half of bitter" is *un export* or *un pils,* a light, palatable drink, sweeter than the English bitter. Though standardization and large-scale brewing is winning the market on grounds of cheapness and wide distribution, Belgium has, by an ingenious tax structure, managed to keep alive quite a number of the small-scale and individual brewers. Their products, by their very nature, are not very widely distributed but there are a number of old and amusing cafés where you can find many of the less popularised beers.

Beer has, in Belgium, a very respectable history, mixed up with such eminent figures as Van Artevelde and Charles Quint. There is still brewed the wheat-based beer called *Faro*, which celebrated its 1,000th birthday a few years ago. It is now brewed in a modern brewery, and may have lost some of its character since the days when the Sire of Cantersteen, unable to choose between two beers contending for his favour, left it to a crow to be the judge. The high-density drink that you should certainly try is *Geuze* (so called when it is bottled, but *Lambic* when it is on tap), a strong beer based on half wheat and half barley, and slightly vinous in flavour. A similar drink is *Kriek-Lambic,* which is essentially *Geuze* but with a flavouring of cherries added after the brew. The old-style *Peetermans* have almost disappeared, but there are still strong, frothy white beers to be drunk at Louvain and Hoegaarde. The golden beer of Diest is still very individual, but you will not find a great deal of *Uitzet* and *Doppel-Uitzet* even around Oudenaarde, which is its home country. In a country with so many abbeys and

monasteries, it is surprising that there are so few monastic brews on the market, but two outstanding ones are *Orval* (made by the Trappists) and the still stronger "triple" from the abbey at Westmalle near Antwerp.

Most of the Belgian beers are of the lager type. Though the Belgians are great brewers, their market is not closed to foreign brews, and you will find abundant supplies of beers from Germany, France, Denmark, the Netherlands and, most of all, Great Britain and Ireland. The Guinness, incidentally, is imported from Dublin, and most connoisseurs agree that it is superior to the counterpart in England. Several British brews are bottled in Belgium; and, more recently, investments by the big British brewery companies have resulted in the British beers (which require a special type of fermentation) being actually brewed here. In recent years, British brewers—mainly Watneys—have introduced the Belgians, not only to British beer, but to the British way of drinking it—standing at the bar rather than sitting at the café table, with all this implies in friendliness and bonhomie.

The general impression emerges that the Belgians eat well and drink well. Moreover, they eat copiously, and it may be well to utter a word of warning against attempting to cope with two full-scale meals in one day. At all levels, the amount of fat used in the cooking is very large by Anglo-Saxon standards; and, though it is good to the taste, it often takes a day or two to get used to it. A bottle of Vichy water in your hotel bedroom is a wise, and almost universal, corrective.

SHOPPING

Common Market Show Window

by

GAVIN GORDON

Whatever you want, you can get it. Belgium, and Brussels especially, is the world's shop-window and one of Europe's great shopping centres. Since early postwar days, her market has been open to all comers; and now that Brussels is the centre of the Common Market, the shops there are even more tempting, with speciality goods from the United States, Great Britain, France, Switzerland, Scandinavia and other countries in profusion. Belgium buys abroad, and the immense choice of goods in the shops is the result. Another result, unfortunately, is that goods are expensive.

However, you will certainly wish to take home with you some of Belgium's specialities, which are described below (Shops are listed in the regional chapters.)

Linen and Lace

From the growing of flax to the weaving of the finished goods, linen is a Belgian trade. It has passed through various difficult periods from which it has learned much, and many of the articles offered are quite inexpensive.

For household linen you will probably find it easiest to go to the department stores where the choice is abundant and the layout puts most of the stock well in sight and within reach. If you are buying sets, remember that Belgian pillowcases are made to fit Belgian pillows, which are usually square.

Smaller household articles, such as afternoon teacloths, can be found in attractive colour designs in the chain-stores. For the less wealthy visitor, these are one of the most worthwhile souvenir purchases.

Lace-making was once an "accomplishment" of all nicely-reared young ladies. It is less fashionable today, but both point (or "needle") lace and spindle (or "bobbin") lace are still important products in Belgium. There is no limit to what you can spend and, once you are under its spell, no limit to what you will want to spend. If you are in this class, shun souvenir shops and be sure to learn something about lace beforehand.

Shotguns

Of all fine crafts, the making of firearms is one of Belgium's best claims to world renown. It has been her speciality since the days of the arbalest and the culverin, and a gun carrying the "Perron Liègeois" bears a mark of real distinction. It is a Liège industry, hand-wrought and hand-perfected to the last chiselling on the ornamented lock. Though it is possible to buy a gun straight off the rack, the gunsmiths would far prefer that the gun be made to fit you.

Glass and Wrought Iron

Fine products in glass and crystal-glass are another speciality of long standing. Apart from mirrorware, there is exceptionally good hollow glassware, and cut and engraved crystal. The most famous products come from the Val St. Lambert. These include massive glass ashtrays and bowls, as well as vases and pots in a variety of original designs. Of more general interest are the tableware sets, both in glass and in fine cut crystal, and the unique cut vases in coloured crystal made by a process which is still a secret.

Attractive souvenir items in wrought iron can be found in many department stores, for this is another old Belgian craft.

Chocolates and Flowers

Belgium is a maker of chocolate in all forms, and her filled-centre chocolates are justly famous. They are collectively known as "pralines", and you do not know Belgium if you have not eaten them—often.

You do not, as in England, buy "a box of chocolates". This is the mark of the tasteless and indiscriminating, for whom choice and freshness mean nothing. You buy by weight—250 grams (about half a pound) is a convenient and conventional buy—from counters luxuriously and lovingly stacked, enquiring carefully as to the centres and choosing your favourites. You may take them away in a paper bag, for your own consumption, or in a carton box which, if it is *pour offrir,* will be fondly wrapped in white paper in elaborate pleats and cunningly gold-corded without extra charge.

Belgians give one another flowers on the slightest provocation. Such a gift is never amiss, and its omission may be. The first time you visit a private house they are a must.

If you are in doubt as to whether flowers are appropriate—as when your hostess has her own flower garden—pralines will be equally as acceptable and appreciated.

Antiques and Jewelry

Brussels is a rich hunting-ground for lovers of old furniture and her antique dealers are among the most competent in Europe. They are also quite expert at asking high prices—if they can get them—and here a little bargaining is not out of place. If you want to acquire a valuable piece, state *your* price and leave your hotel address and see what happens.

And at the numerous auctions held in Brussels, you may make a "find" of an old Flemish master or a French impressionist.

Belgian women are particularly fond of well-designed jewelry, and there is a good display at shops in Brussels and Antwerp—which, of course, is a world centre for diamond-cutting.

Gallery Shopping

Apart from the department stores and growing numbers of hypermarkets and supermarkets for general shopping, there is a re-introduction of the 19th-century shopping arcades, called *Galeries,* particularly in Brussels.

These galleries are smart, and cover wide areas. They contain facilities such as tea shops, cafés, snack bars, nightclubs and even an "automatic banker" which delivers up to 5,000 francs on insertion of a coded account card. They contain, too, a great number of small shops and boutiques, among which the shopper can wander without weather worries. They are thus the ideal hunting ground for something different to wear, or for presents to take home. Moreover, though their rents are high, competition is keen enough to keep prices within reasonable limits. For individual shopping, especially if you hope for personal service, you must not neglect the galleries.

For inexpensive shopping, look out for branches of the counter-store chains *Priba, Sarma* and *Delhaize*. You will be amazed at the range of goods offered.

A multitude of shops offer ornamental novelties and dress accessories. Apart, however, from a few branches of Paris shops, they seldom seek to make their effects "striking" by the fashionable trampling on the borderline of the absurd. Belgian tastes are quieter, and more firmly based on design and workmanship—except in some of the pottery household ornaments.

THE FACE OF BELGIUM

PRELUDE TO BELGIUM

Practical Information

WHAT WILL IT COST? See the *Facts at Your Fingertips* section at the beginning of this volume for general information and specific hotel rates.

In a top restaurant you will pay 1,000 to 1,200 francs for a meal, depending upon the wines you choose. In a less lavish place the menu will be about 400-600 frcs., and you won't be looked down upon if you order beer or mineral water with your meal. In a *bourgeois* restaurant a 3-course meal will cost as little as 200-300 frcs.; and in a department store or other self-service restaurant or a snack bar, about 150 frcs.

Some local costs: An evening out means spending about 100 frcs. for a movie seat and 200 or more for theater or opera. In a nightclub you will spend 150 frcs. or more if you nurse along your only drink at the bar; if you want the best tables you will have to order champagne, 1,500 frcs. or so a bottle, on which four people can thrive without dishonor. A bottle of wine at the other tables will cost roughly 1,000 frcs.

American or British cigarettes are 30 frcs. or more for a pack of 20; man's haircut 50-70 frcs., a woman's shampoo and set around 175-250.

Package Savers: "Belgium's Bonus Days" is a facility offered to passengers from the USA and Canada traveling on *Sabena, PanAm* or *Air Canada.* Get your travel agent to validate the bonus certificate before leaving, and exchange this at Brussels Airport for a book of coupons. These can be used as part or complete payment for hotel bills, meals, tours and visits, and can save you up to $70 if used intelligently. A number of hotels and restaurants, from the expensive to the cheap, take part in the scheme, as does *Avis* car hire and *Belgian Rail.* At present, the scheme applies only to Brussels, and is partially limited to weekends.

For travelers from Britain, *Townsend-Thoresen Car Ferries* offer a "Long weekend in Belgium" at £13.50 per head for motorized tourists crossing from Dover to Zeebrugge or Calais. The weekend starts Fri., returning Mon., with a 3-night stay at the company's Holiday Village at De Haan, and the cost includes travel fares. Accommodation is in fully-equipped chalets.

WHEN TO GO? July-August is the high season, when accommodation in coastal hotels is at a premium, but the season runs from the beginning of May to end-September, and the Belgian countryside is particularly lovely in May and June. Brussels is attractive in any month, and here it is well to remember that on any weekend it is possible to find accommodation (often at a reduced rate), because the city is now a commuting center for people concerned with the Common Market activities.

For seasonal events throughout the year, see *Facts at your Fingertips* at the front of this title.

WHAT TO SEE? The Highlights of Belgium. Foremost are the two biggest cities: Brussels, a lively capital, a great but rather expensive, shopping center, a place of gay nightlife, and the site of several fine museums, and Antwerp, a tremendous port that is also a notable museum city. Probably the two most visited cities aside from these are the so-called "picture-book towns," Ghent and Bruges, gems of medieval reminiscence. If you like reminders of past wars, you have your choice, from Waterloo (where there is a very good Wellington museum which will interest Napoleonic specialists) to Dixmude (World War I) and Bastogne (World War II). There are any number of other cities with picturesque qualities worth visiting—Liège, Leuven, Ypres, Namur, Mechelen, Tournai, Lier, Furnes. The ancestor of all watering places is Spa, in Belgium. On the seacoast, Ostend is big, but the most fashionable beach area is Knokke-Heist. To get away from the teeming life of Belgium's cities, journey into the rolling hills, dark woods and green fields of the Ardennes, where you will find Belgium's greatest natural curiosity, the grottos of Han-sur-Lesse and of neighboring Rochefort.

HOW TO GET ABOUT? By Rail: The very modern Belgian railroads are a bit more expensive than most European trains. On trips of 100 kilometers or more, one should count on the following average rates per kilometer: 1st class, 2 frcs.; second class 1.50 frcs.

Various reduced-rate plans, however, are available. Commutation tickets for 5, 10, or 15 days, allowing unlimited travel during each period, become cheaper than ordinary fares for people who plan to travel 240-300 miles, 360-420 miles, 540-660 miles within those periods. Fares range from 60 frcs. (5 days, second class) to about 1,700 frcs. (15 days, first class). There are also special group rates. Children under 4 years of age travel free; those between 4-10 years pay half fare.

By Bus: Europabus (combined with the Belgian State Railroads) operates a number of tours lasting from half a day to a Grand Tour of ten days, and showing you most of what Belgium has to offer (which is a good deal). Particulars from travel agents.

MOTORING. A system of express highways is being extended, and the new motorways are the Wallonie (E41), the Brussels-Paris (E10), the Brussels-Liège (E5), and the Antwerp-Lille (E3). Unfortunately, some roads rebuilt since the war show signs of wear, some badly. A few roads in country districts may be cobbled and narrow. The hillier nature of southern Belgium means, of course, more curves and slower average speeds. In Brussels the traffic growth is a continuous challenge. The system of over- and underpasses is being extended; and, with more paying car parks, the tolerance of street parking is growing less.

Although cyclists have separate paths alongside major routes, motorists must exercise extreme caution everywhere else, particularly at night, to avoid collisions with slow-moving traffic.

Except in the Ardennes and on the motor highways (A-roads), there is not a mile of principal roadway in Belgium without a gasoline station. Main highways are patroled by Touring Secours (Wegenhulp), who are expert mechanics. They attend to the needs of foreign drivers just as willingly as to their paying members. Their tool-carrying vehicles are painted yellow, and their uniforms resembles those of the British AA patrols, which actually served as a model for this organization.

One-day Sightseeing Itineraries for Belgium

CATHOLIC BASTIONS (Leuven and Mechelen). Depart Brussels-Tervuren (Congo Museum and park)-Leuven (Town Hall, St. Peter's University)-Mechelen) (St. Rombaut's Cathedral, Grand'Place, old and new Town Halls, churches, quaint streets)-return to Brussels via Vilvoorde; in good weather break your journey at Hofstade Lake for bathing and sailing: 2 miles after leaving Mechelen take turning to the left (railway viaduct). Total, approximately 47 miles.

FOUR ART TOWNS. Depart Brussels. Take road via Leuven. Tienen-Zoutleeuw, turn left at Dormaal-St. Truiden-Diest-return via Aarschot and Leuven. Total, approximately 90 miles.

CASTLES AND BATTLEFIELDS. Depart Brussels via Uccle-Beersel Castle-Huizingen Manor-Gaasbeek Castle and museum-Notre Dame de Hal-Nivelles-return via Waterloo. Total, approximately 48 miles.

FLANDERS ART TOWNS. Depart Ghent-Laarne Castle-Overmeire Lake-St. Niklaas-Dendermonde-Aalst-Oudenaarde-Kortrijk (Courtrai)- Deinze from there along the River Leie back to Ghent. Total, approximately 100 miles.

FLANDERS ART TOWNS AND COAST. Depart Bruges-Damme-Knokke-Heist-Zeebrugge-Blankenberge-De Haan-Ostend-Nieuwpoort- Furnes (Veurne)-Ypres (Ieper)-Dijksmuide-Torhout-Bruges. Total, approximately 110 miles.

THE CAMPINE AND ITS ABBEYS. Depart Brussels via Leuven-Aarschot-Scherpenheuvel-Averbode-Westerlo-Tongerlo-Herentals-Lier-Brussels. Total, approximately 85 miles .

HAINAUT AND ITS CASTLES. Depart Tournai-Antoing-Peruwelz-Beloeil-Mons-Binche, Mariemont Castle-Roeulx-Ecaussines d'Enghien and Lalaing-Ath-Cambron Casteau-Lens-Chièvres-Attre-Moulbaix-Leuze-Tournai. Total, approximately 115 miles.

BETWEEN SAMBRE AND MEUSE. Depart Namur-Fosse-Charleroi-Aulne and Lobbes Abbeys-Thuin-Beaumont-Rance-Chimay-Lake of Virelles-Couvin-follow Viroin Valley into France-Givet-cross into Belgium at Heer-Agimont to Dinant-Profondeville-Namur. Total, approximately 125 miles.

CIRCUIT OF THE 5 VALLEYS. Depart Namur-Meuse Valley-Annevoie Castle and park-Molignée Valley-Maredsous Abbey-Dinant-Anseremme-Lesse Valley-Yvoir via Dinant-Bocq Valley-Spontin Castle-Crupet Manor-Assesse-Gesves-Samson Valley-Marche les Dames via Namèche-Namur. Total, approximately 75 miles.

ARDENNES PLATEAU AND GROTTOS. Depart Namur-Marche-Rochefort Grottos-Han Grottos-St. Hubert-Barrière de Champion-Bastogne-Mardasson Memorial-La Roche-Ourthe Valley to Hotton-Marche-Namur. Total, approximately 155 miles.

SEMOIS VALLEY. Depart Arlon-Florenville-make boat excursion Chiny to Lacuisine-Bouillon-Corbion-Membre-return via Vresse-Rochehaut-Noirefontaine-Dohan-Cugnon-Herbeumont-Florenville-Orval Abbey-Virton-Arlon. Total, approximately 135 miles.

SPA AND EASTERN ARDENNES. Depart Spa-Theux and Franchimont-Verviers-Gileppe Dam-Eupen and Vesdre Dam-Baroque Michel-Robertsville-St. Vith-return via Malmédy-Stavelot-Coo Cascades-Remouchamps Grottos-Spa. Total, approximately 90 miles.

OURTHE VALLEY AND SOUTHERN ARDENNES. Depart Liège-Tillfs-Esneux-Comblain au Pont-Hamoir-Durbuy-Hotton-La Roche-Nadrin-Hérou Defile-Houffalize-Baroque Fraiture-Salmchâteau-Trois Points-Coo Cascades-Ramouchamps Grottos-Louveigné-Gomzé-Chaudfontaine-Liège. Total, approximately 120 miles.

LIMBURG ART TOWNS. Depart Liège-St. Truiden-Zoutleeuw-St. Truiden-Hasselt-Bokrijk-Genk-Bilzen-Rijckhoven (Château Ouden Biessen)-Tongeren-Liège. Total, approximately 85 miles.

SPORT. *Sailing* enthusiasts find ample opportunity to spend their days on the water while in Belgium. Ostend, Zeebrugge, Nieuwpoort, and Blankenberge all offer good yachting. There are many navigable rivers and canals.

The most picturesque for small craft and canoes are the upper Meuse, the Semois, the Lesse and the Ourthe. For further information contact *Fédération Belge de Canoë* (Mr. Holemans). 21 Bogaardenlaan, Aarschot, *Fédération Belge de Yachting* 5 Rue du Chêne, Brussels. *Land-yachting* is a favorite activity on Belgian beaches, chiefly along the west coast from La Panne to Middelkerke.

In Belgium hunting (shooting) is allowed to holders of temporary licenses. Write to the *Société Royale St. Hubert,* 25 Ave. de l'Armée, 1040-Brussels. You also need a license for *fishing.* Full information regarding deepsea or freshwater fishing may be obtained from the Belgian National Tourist Office, Central Station, Brussels.

Golf: Among the many golf clubs, there are the following: Royal Antwerp Golf Club course, at Kappellenbos, 22 km from Antwerp; Royal Golf Club de Belgique course in Tervuren, close to Brussels; Waterloo Golf Club at Ohain, near Waterloo; Royal Zoute Golf Club; Golf Club d'Ostende. There are also courses at Klemskerke (Le Coq), Ghent, Liège, Mons and—the finest—Spa (Golf Club des Fagnes).

Tennis facilities are very good, especially on the coast. *Billiards* is a popular game, with tables in many cafés throughout the country. In the form played in Belgium there are no pockets and one scores by getting "cannons".

SPAS AND CASINOS. Spa, which has given its name to similar establishments around the world, produces a well known mineral water of high iron content. The waters of The Queen's Spring are particularly beneficial for all forms of arthritis, and various mud, turf, and carbonized water baths are also available. Chaudfontaine possesses the only warm springs in Belgium. Ostend offers mineral waters and thermal baths.

Ostend's casino, Europe's biggest, is open all the year round, usually from 2 p.m. onwards. The casino at *Blankenberge* is open from 11 a.m. on Sundays and from 2 p.m. on weekdays; at *Dinant,* daily from 3 p.m., Sundays one hour earlier; *Knokke-Heist* opens at 4 p.m. on Sundays; *Namur,* weekdays at 2 p.m., Sundays and holidays at noon; *Spa,* 4 p.m. on weekdays, one hour earlier on Sundays; *Chaudfontaine,* 3.30 p.m. daily. *Middelkerke,* near Ostend, has a small casino (in season 4 p.m. daily—weekends only in winter). All these casinos open year round. For information on admission, etc., apply directly to the casinos; formalities are simple, membership fees reasonable.

CARILLONS. One of the outstanding features of Belgium are the carillons, which usually play automatically on the hour and half-hour; a few also play every quarter-hour. Chief places to hear the carillons are: Aalst (belfry), Antwerp (Notre Dame Cathedral), Oudenaarde (St. Walburga's Church), Binche (belfry), Bruges (belfry), Charleroi (belfry), Courtrai (St. Martin's Church), Ghent (belfry), Huy (Notre Dame), Liège (St. Paul's Cathedral), Lier (St. Gummaris), Mechelen (St. Rombaut's Cathedral), Dendermonde (Town Hall), Tongeren (Notre Dame), Tournai (belfry). For times of the principal concerts given by the carilloneurs at Bruges, Ghent, and Mechelen, see the Practical Information sections for these cities.

BEGUINAGES. These distinctive communities, less secluded than convents, were started in the 13th century for lay sisters of humble origin (*béguines).* Most characteristic in Flanders (in Flemish called *begijnhof*), a few are also found elsewhere. The most important ones are located in: Bruges, Courtrai, Diest, Ghent, Lier; others in: Aalst, Antwerp, Brussels (Anderlecht), Dendermonde, Dixmude, Leuven, Mechelen, Tongeren, etc.

BELGIAN PLACE NAMES

You may see *Antwerpen* (Flemish) and *Anvers* (French) on signs posted along the highway, even though both names refer to the same city, *Antwerp.* This is because roadsigns normally reflect the language spoken by the people living nearby, even though the city in question may be located in the other language area. We give, first, the local version of certain towns, and, second, what the other language-group calls them.

Local version	*Alternate version*	*Local version*	*Alternate version*
Aalst	Alost	Huy	Hoei
Arlon	Aarlen	Ieper	Ypres
Aat	Ath	Koksijde	Coxyde
Antwerpen	Anvers	Leuven	Louvain
Oudenaarde	Audenarde	Liège	Luik
Baarle-Hertog	Baer-le-Duc	Mechelen	Malines
Mons	Bergen	Menen	Menin
Beauvechain	Bevekom	Mouscron	Moeskroen
Bassenge	Bitsingen	Namur	Namen
Waremme	Borgworm	Nieuwpoort	Nieuport
Leopoldsburg	Bourg-Léopold	Nivelles	Nijvel
Braine-Le-Château	Kasteelbrakel	Oostende	Ostende
		De Panne	La Panne
Braine-Le-Comte	's-Gravenbrakel	Ronse	Renaix
Brugge	Bruges	Roeselare	Roulers
Bruxelles	Brussel	Scherpenheuvel	Montaigu
Kortrijk	Courtrai	Sint-Niklaas	Saint-Nicolas
Diksmuide	Dixmude	Sint-Truiden	Saint-Trond
Tournai	Doornik	L'Ecluse	Sluizen
Drongen	Tronchienne	Soignies	Zinnik
Enghien	Edingen	Temse	Tamise
Braine-L'Alleud	Eigenbrakel	La Hulpe	Terhulpen
Veurne	Furnes	Dendermonde	Termonde
Gent	Gand	Tienen	Tirlemont
Geraardsbergen	Grammont	Tongeren	Tongres
Jodoigne	Geldenaken	Vilvoorde	Vilvorde
Genappe	Genepiën	Visé	Wezet
Halle	Hal	Zoutleeuw	Léau
Hannut	Hannuit	Het Zoute	Le Zoute

BRUSSELS, HEART OF BRABANT

City of Arts and Neon-Lit Bustle

by

GAVIN GORDON

However you come into Belgium, you will find that all ways lead you into Brabant, fertile and industrious, green and smiling, with waterways, roads, railways and airlines leading inevitably to Brussels. The province is the epitome of Belgium. As a duchy it was once the buffer state between the Lotharingian empire and the marauding counts of Flanders; it contains enough both of north and south to be typical of neither.

While Antwerp is for Belgium *La Métropole,* centre of all things commercial and the real hub of economic life, Brussels is *La Capitale.* It sits at the centre of a star of roads, on everybody's way everywhere, and as such is accustomed to sorting out the tangled skeins of international thought and acquainting itself with destinies greater than its own. In buses and cafés you will hear every language of Europe.

Brussels will strike you first as a modern city, in the sense that your first impression is of shops, cafés, taverns, and entertainment generally. Equally impressive is the network of express roadways and tunnels to lead traffic around bottlenecks. But unless you know the one-way streets, and exactly where you are going, you may have difficulty in finding your way. You will find a wide choice of hotels, and all the amenities of modern life. Only some of the remaining cobbled streets and the tramways will remind you that Brussels has grown from an eventful and romantic past.

Cavalcade of History

You will not see much, if anything, of the River Senne, which now takes its unlovely course underground through the city, and which could be the origin of the capital's name—*broeck* (brook), *sele* (dwelling). It was an island on this stream which was the South's bastion against the Flemish a century before William of Normandy invaded England. Here, too, the Senne's course ceased to be navigable to craft coming up from the Schelde and the sea beyond. A merchant community grew round the discharge point of the barges, and for this community the Duke of Brabant—Graaf Jan, or Jean le Victorieux—fought and won the Battle of Woeringen (1288). In this he wrested from Renalt the Bellicose, not only the Duchy of Limburg, but also the safeguarding of the open road from flourishing Bruges to Maastricht and the Rhine at Cologne. This road ran through Brussels, and the battle consolidated the city's position as capital of the duchy.

This was the age when the merchant communes were struggling with feudal princes for their liberties. In 1356 the reigning Duchess Jeanne, and her husband, Wenceslas of Luxembourg, were forced into signing the *Joyeuse Entrée,* a declaration of rights as basic and as confusingly drawn as Magna Carta. A few months later, however, Duchess Jeanne was brought to book by the quarrelsome Count of Flanders who, having married her sister, came with an armed force to claim the dowry. At Anderlecht, now a suburb of Brussels, the Flemish swept the floor with the men of Brabant, and hoisted their standard in the Brussels Grand' Place.

The first of Brussels' many liberations came six months later, when Everard 't Serclaes led 70 patriots to a surprise assault on the occupying garrison. He became the first of Brussels' heroes and, living to be chief alderman, was assassinated 30 years later by order of the Lord of Gaasbeek, Sweder Abcoude, who coveted the city. This brought the citizens of Brussels to a vengeful storming and destruction of the Castle of Gaasbeek, a few miles away.

From 1430 onwards, Brussels became more and more the pivot of the Low Countries with their varying fortunes in the next five centuries. Both the dukes of Burgundy and, later on, the Spanish Habsburg kings made Brussels into an elegant centre of the arts. This was the golden age of Flemish painting, tapestry, and lacemaking.

Under Philip the Good, Brussels was on the crest of a wave. The Coudenberg Palace was enlarged and beautified, and was to be the court centre of Brussels life till it was burned down three centuries later. The nobility of the Golden Fleece built their stupendous mansions nearby. The foundations were laid of the collection of manuscripts which the Spaniards were later to centralise as the Bibliothèque Royale—now the great reference library of the Belgian state. Fountains decorated the streets, and Roger van der Weyden brought to Brussels the skill and fervour of the painter. The first, comparatively modest, wing of the Hôtel de Ville had been begun early in the century. It was the duke's 10-year-old son, later to reign as Charles the Rash, who laid the first stone of the new wing which, with its perfectly proportioned tower, was Jan van Ruysbroek's masterpiece.

Brussels passed through another period of splendour, 40 years after Philip's death, with the court of Charles Quint in the first phase of the Spanish ascendancy. It was Charles who enclosed the Parc de Bruxelles, at either end of which now lie the Royal Palace and the Palace of the Nation (Parliament). Contemporaries tell us the park then contained "valleys with vines and divers manner of fruit". Already, however, the Reformation was sweeping across Europe.

Charles had abdicated in Brussels in 1555. Persecution started in earnest under the Duke of Alba as governor for Philip II. Those who resisted were called the *gueux* (tramps) and the leaders of the revolt, the counts of Egmont and Hornes were brought from Ghent to Brussels for execution in the Grand' Place (1568). The central figure of the resistance was William the Silent, Prince of Orange, who was called to Brussels in 1577 and received by the people on bended knee as a liberating "angel from Heaven". William, however, was assassinated seven years later, and the Italian Prince Alexander Farnese re-liberated Brussels for the king of Spain, despite Olivier van den Tympel's brilliant defence.

The 17th century Occupations

Resistance was virtually over, and the Spanish Lowlands had comparative quiet during the first half of the 17th century. Brussels, indeed, became known as the hostel for exiled princes. But Spain was on the decline, and soon the France of Louis XIV was in the ascendant. In 1695 a 46-hour bombardment by the red cannon balls of Marshal Villeroy reminded Brussels of the French defiance of the Augsburg league. Four thousand houses were destroyed, including all the Grand' Place except the Hôtel de Ville itself.

The Austrians, who had been nominal masters of the Spanish Lowlands since 1713, had begun oppressively but, under Maria Theresia, were more accommodating when they recovered the country in 1748. Charles of Lorraine was a popular governor. Forty years after the disastrous fire of 1731, when the Coudenberg Palace was wholly destroyed, a new layout was given to this part of Brussels and the Parc de Bruxelles put more or less into its present form. Nevertheless, after all the trials Brussels had been through, it is small wonder that there was much poverty and illiteracy. Voltaire wrote, "In Brussels the arts no more live than the pleasures. A calm, retired life is the lot of private people, and this is so near akin to boredom that it is easy to call it so."

It was against this background that Joseph II, son of Maria Theresa, started constitutional reforms on too ambitious a scale, even going so far as to cancel the *Joyeuse Entrée*. Brabant led the uprising against this at the very time when the French Revolution was altering the main currents of European thought. Under the leadership of Henri van der Noot, the people of Brussels took arms, troops deserted *en masse* from the Austrian service, and the United States of Belgium were proclaimed in January 1790. The movement did not, however, outlast its sectional schisms, and the Austrians were back by the end of the year. Two years later revolutionary France was at the door. Brussels changed hands three times in as many years, and remained under French control till 1814. It was at Brussels that Napoleon's last thrust was aimed in 1815, to be halted at Waterloo.

William I made many mistakes, not least of which was the sending of an armed force under his son to suppress growing dissatisfaction. His 14,000 men converged in four lumbering columns, and a 4-day battle was fought in the Brussels streets and in the Parc de Bruxelles. The result was the evacuation of the Dutch, and the setting up of the kingdom of the Belgians, with Brussels as its capital (1830).

Modern Brussels

This is the background of the Brussels of the defiant burgomasters Adolphe Max in 1914 and Van der Meulebroeck in 1940. It is a city that has learned the hard way to adapt itself to varying circumstances, personalities and ideas. Now capital of the Common Market and NATO, Brussels has become a magnet for politicians, diplomats, reporters, bankers, brokers, and businessmen. More and more cars speed along the flyovers and underpasses. Yellow trams remain, but many have gone underground to form the city's first tube system whose clean, new stations greet you with soothing piped music.

Despite the creeping commercial takeover, much of old Brussels remains with its *fin de siècle* houses, monuments and unique Grand' Place—all so attractive to the visitor.

If you come to Brussels by air, you will land at Zaventem airport, begun by the Germans in World War II, which has jostled the old Château of Steenokerzeel almost off the map. A highway and a railway spur connect Zaventem Airport with Brussels. The railway takes 20 mins. to the Air Terminal, adjoining the underground Central Station.

Practical Information for Brussels

WHEN TO COME? Brussels is sometimes cool even in midsummer, though next day the heat can produce temperatures close to 90° Fahrenheit. You will want light clothes, sweaters and, in keeping with the climate, rainwear (which carry with you at all times).

Events: Heading the calendar is the *Jan./Feb.* International Motor Show. In *April* the musical season is in full swing and *May* sees the traditional Queen Elisabeth Musical Competition for young artists of all nationalities. Late April or early May heralds the 2-week Brussels International Samples Fair. Early *June* witnesses the pilgrimage to St. Guidon at Anderlecht. The Foire du Midi begins on 15 *July,* and the Maiboom is planted each year on 9 *August*, a traditional ceremony going back to 1311. On 3 *September,* Manneken Pis, oldest inhabitant of the city, dons the uniform of the Welsh Guards in commemoration of the capital's liberation by this regiment in 1944; on 27 *October* (Navy Day in the U.S.A.) he becomes an American sailor for the occasion. University students rule the city on 20 *November,* St. Verhaeghe, their patron's day.

HOTELS. The role of Brussels as capital of the European Community has enormously increased the pressure on hotel accommodation, especially during the week. So it is best to book ahead, except for weekends when business and official visitors leave; and as an inducement to weekend tourists, seven of the big hotels offer a booklet of vouchers for free visits to most of the sights of Brussels, including Boitsfort racecourse. Also, several hotels offer reduced weekend prices.

INTERNATIONAL DE LUXE

AMIGO, 1-3 Rue de l'Amigo. Tucked away behind the Hôtel de Ville (Town Hall), there are 180 rooms and suites in Empire and Directoire style, all with bath.

ASTORIA, 103 Rue Royale. A modernized but still somewhat old-fashioned hotel, quiet, dignified; 102 rooms, about 85 % with bath. Reasonable for its category.

ATLANTA, Blvd Adolphe Max, 200 rooms, most with bath. Friendly family hotel. Central.

BRUSSELS HILTON, Blvd. de Waterloo, opening on the gardens of Palais d'Egmont; 373 rooms with bath and shower, air-conditioned. Sauna. Restaurants: *Panorama,* and *Western* on ground floor.

BRUSSELS RESIDENCE, 319 Ave. Louise. (40 apartments with bath), first class throughout.

EUROPA, 107 Rue de la Loi, 254 rooms with bath. *Beefeater Restaurant* has English décor and French *haute cuisine. Dukes Restaurant* is open all day for meals.

HOLIDAY INN, next to the airport. Functionally deluxe. Indoor pool.

LENDI, Manhattan Center, Pl. Rogier. Recent high-rise hotel, two-thirds of rooms singles, 3 restaurants.

MACDONALD, 321 Ave. Louise, small but with superb amenities. Its 80 rooms have bath, champagne-stocked refrigerator, remote control TV. Supper club, *Rôtisserie* restaurant for lunch or dinner, and the *Causerie,* quick grill room.

METROPOLE, 31 Pl. de Brouckère. Central and a little old fashioned. 392 rooms, most with bath; good grill room and international club bar.

PALACE, 22 Pl. Rogier, backing on Botanical Gardens and facing the World Trade Center; 364 rooms with bath, a few suites. Good restaurant.

PLAZA, Blvd. Adolphe Max, 230 rooms. Comfortable, well-converted, good amenities and restaurant.

(Both the Plaza and the Palace are to be demolished for the new Manhattan Center buildings.)

RAMADA INN, 38 Chaussée de Charleroi. 202 rooms, garden restaurant.

ROYAL WINDSOR, Rue Duquesnoy; 300 rooms. Underground parking. *Duke of Wellington,* English style pub with Victorian décor. Near Grand'Place, Central Station and Air Terminal.

SHERATON, in the vast Manhattan Center, Pl. Rogier. Rooms have color TV, air-conditioning, mini-bar; 5 resturants, indoor pool.

WESTBURY, 6 Rue Cardinal Mercier, opposite the Air Terminal. 252 rooms with bath, air-conditioned. Panoramic restaurant.

HYATT REGENCY, Rue Royale, 350 deluxe rooms and suites. Opening 1976.

ARCADE STEPHANIE, 91 Ave. Louise. Small, comfortable flats.

FIRST CLASS SUPERIOR

ASCOT, 1 Pl. Lois, tucked away in an old quarter, is pleasant, recent.

MAYFAIR, Ave. Louise. Rebuilt, excellent décor and comfort. No restaurant.

NOVOTEL, Brussels Airport, Diegem. Air-conditioned, heated pool.

PARK, 21 Ave. de l'Yser, 46 rooms, most with bath. Comfortable and obliging, without grandeur.

PRESIDENT NORD, 107 Blvd. Adolphe Max, 63 rooms with bath. Clean and bright. No restaurant, but English bar.

PRESIDENT CENTRE, 160 Rue Royale. Same chain as above, slightly more expensive.

DIPLOMAT HOTEL, 32 Rue Jean Stas. New. 68 rooms with private baths.

FIRST CLASS REASONABLE

ALBERGO, Ave. de la Toison d'Or. Good value, 54 rooms, most with bath. Good Italian restaurant.

ARENBERG, a few steps from Grand' Place. 160 rooms. Garage.

BEDFORD, 135 Rue du Midi, quiet setting; 159 rooms, most with bath.

CHARLEMAGNE, next to EEC headquarters, 64 modernly appointed rooms. Garage.

QUEEN ANNE, 110 Blvd. Jacqmain. 57 rooms, most with bath or shower. Central, modern; has good rôtisserie restaurant.

VENDÔME, 98 Blvd. Adolphe Max. 38 rooms with bath, modern furnishings. Reader-recommended.

GB MOTOR HOTELS has opened its third property—at Brussels Airport. It is along the same delighftul lines as those at Aartselaar and Wepion. Facilities include 130 guest rooms with airconditioning and TV, an outdoor-indoor swimming pool, grill, coffee shop, bar. Parking for 250 cars.

MODERATE

CENTRAL-BOURSE, opposite the Bourse; 174 rooms, less than half with bath.

SCHEERS, 132-142 Blvd. Adolphe Max, 65 rooms, most with bath. Central. Has inexpensive restaurant.

INEXPENSIVE

There are many hotels in this category. *Cecil,* 13 Blvd. Jardin Botanique, is one of the largest and is centrally located. The *Canterbury,* 129-135 Blvd. Jacqmain, has comfortable rooms above an excellent and distinguished restaurant. *Residence Rembrandt,* 57 Rue de la Concorde, comfortable old town-house.

RESIDENTIAL HOTELS

More often than not, you will be expected to take one main meal at these small hotels, especially in peak season.

Among the first class establishments: *Résidence du Bois,* 12 Ave. Lloyd George. Magnificent location facing woods. Most rooms with bath.

Also good, *Résidence Osborne,* 67 Rue Bosquet, and *Résidence Richmond,* 21 Rue de la Concorde, half of rooms with bath. Mrs. Dewhurst will welcome you at her well-situated guest house, the *Lancaster Résidence,* 114 Rue du Cornet, near Common Market buildings. Breakfast only.

For Students: *Youth Hostel,* 124 Rue Verte; *Y.M.C.A.,* 36A Rue Jourdan; *Y.W.C.A.,* 43 Rue St. Bernard.

ON THE OUTSKIRTS

In the Bois de la Cambre is the *Châlet de la Forêt,* 43 Drève de Lorraine; only 7 rooms with bath, first

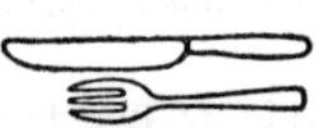

RESTAURANTS. Brussels has more than 600 restaurants of all classes of real Belgian cuisine (with French undertones). Foreign restaurants enjoy a certain popularity, and American-type snack bars are plentiful. You can eat in so many places, and in so many styles in Brussels that our listing can only be representative; and remember that the fashionable restaurant of one month may be *démodé* in the next. Hotel restaurants are not included.

A word of warning is necessary: do not expect quick service. Ingredients are plentiful and rich, the food is prepared to your order, and it can't come till it's cooked. Allow two hours for dinner and put all other thoughts aside.

Except for a very few deluxe establishments, even the best restaurants offer a fixed menu at a price substantially less than your bill is likely to come to if you order *à la carte*. The menu, however, does not cover wine or extras; so if you add wine, coffee, and so forth, by the time the 15% service charge and VAT (value added tax) are added, the price will be considerably augmented. At lunchtime you need not order a complete meal, but in the evening a full course dinner is almost an obligation, but a pleasant one—the cooking is excellent, even at the bottom of the price scale. Most high-class restaurants close on Sundays, so best telephone to check, and in any case, best reserve ahead.

A word about prices. You can eat modestly but well for about 150 francs at one of the impeccable department store restaurants, in pleasant surroundings. You will eat much better for 600 francs in one of Brussels' gastronomic temples, and you may pay almost as much elsewhere for the pleasure (or discomfort) of sitting on a barrel or some other "atmospheric" gimmick. To find the place that suits you, consult the bill of fare that is usually exhibited at the restaurant's entrance or in one of its windows. Finally, a *warning*: as Brussels is now the capital of Europe, the city is crawling with expense-account types who don't mind paying huge bills as it's usually your (the taxpayers') money. Accordingly, some restaurants have been inclined to jack their prices up more than inflation would warrant, and it is also hard to get reservations in many instances. So book well ahead and be prepared to pay, pay and pay.

For an evening in quest of culinary adventure, go to the Rue des Bouchers, a street of restaurants—mostly small—which climbs the hill between the Galerie du Roi and the Galerie de la Reine. Every restaurant here has its own style and its own specialties. Mussels, in season, are a subject in which several of these houses are expert.

TOPS IN CUISINE AND ELEGANCE

EPAULE DE MOUTON, Rue des Harengs. Unpretentious décor, small. All your concentration is directed towards the cuisine and wines, for you are on sacred ground and among the high priests of gastronomy. Sorry, we cannot quote here the 89-culinary creations. This has been a hostelry for nearly 300 years.

FILET DE BOEUF. Same street. Almost as good, almost as expensive. Cozy and intimate. Gastronomic experience worth paying for.

LA COURONNE. Same street and corner of Grand' Place. Food as opulent as interior. Old-fashioned grills are their specialty.

LA MAISON DU CYGNE, in Grand' Place (entrance under archway). Attractive décor, splendid food. Excellent for club dinners. Try Waterzooi de Homard.

CARLTON, 28 Blvd. de Waterloo. Very fashionable, very busy at lunchtime; dancing after dinner. Summer garden. You can eat lightly at its *Manhattan Bar*. Try pheasant in season, and baby chicken with tarragon sauce.

RAVENSTEIN, 1 Rue Ravenstein. A 16th-cent. nobleman's house, with summer terrace. Delicious seafood specialties such as Sole Albertine with white wine sauce, garnished with mushrooms, carrots and truffles; also noisettes of lamb cooked in wine, with tarragon sauce.

BERNARD, 93 Rue de Namur, a favorite for after-theater snacks of caviar, oysters or foie gras.

LONDRES, 23 Rue Ecuyer. The table d'hôte, with its alternative choices, is not very expensive, and excellent. Book for lunch, half empty in evening.

ECAILLER DU PALAIS ROYAL, in Rue Bodenbroek (Grand Sablon) is a top specialist in shellfish. Try the crab consommé and the crêpes Normande — delicious pancakes with apple rings and caramelized sugar. Small, so must reserve.

COMME CHEZ SOI, Place Rouppe. If it's not Sunday or Monday, visit Monsieur Wyant and try his sole done in Riesling.

MODERATELY EXPENSIVE

Central: Most of these restaurants are on or around the main artery, Blvd. Adolphe Max, leading from the Gare du Nord to the Bourse.

On Blvd. Jacqmain is the *Canterbury,* one of the best known places in town; almost opposite, *Rôtisserie d'Alsace* is the spot to sample foie gras.

From there it's a stone's throw to Quai aux Briques, formerly a famous fishmarket, hence the numerous seafood restaurants. Best are *L'Huitrière, François, La Marie Joseph* and *Cheval Marin* in an authentic 17th-cent. house. Try Turbot fines herbes. In the neighborhood: *Les Crustacés* and the *Rugbyman.*

Between the Opera House and the Bourse you will find in Rue Grétry, *Les Provençaux.* You will have to work your way through their procession of hors d'œvre before being allowed to touch the main course of the menu. *Bon Vieux Temps* is a charming old place in Rue Marché-aux-Herbes, tucked away in a blind alley opposite St. Nicholas' Church. Highly atmospheric, with a bar downstairs. Try Poulet poivre. *Eperon d'Or,* 8 Rue des Eponniers, classical cuisine in the French tradition. (Small, book ahead.)

We have now reached the Rue des Bouchers quarter, where almost every old building houses a seafood restaurant. Moving uptown, opposite Sablon Church in the Rue de la Régence, Marius takes us to sunny *En Provence* with his deliciously prepared specialties of the south of France. New York in Brussels is the recent *Harry M's,* where expatriate executives congregate for lunch.

La Balance, 6 Rue des Six Jeunes Hommes, near the Sablon has 16th-cent. décor, and specialty dishes.

Uptown: *Maggi,* Rue des Teinturiers and *Pimm's Grill,* Rue du Baudet are classic restaurants of the best order. For a late dinner, try *Chez Stans,* at 12 Rue des Dominicains.

For an authentic home-from-home American atmosphere, of several types and price levels, and from breakfast time onwards, go to *Tops,* in the skyscraper at 149 Ave. Louise.

You'll get excellent value and the friendliest service at *Henri I,* 181 Ave. de Messidor, which concentrates on grills rather than luxury setting; but book ahead. *Caroline,* 28 Rue Ten Bosch (by 275 Ave. Louise), has a good choice, but her specialty is the congolese chicken *moambe.* Small, book ahead.

MORE MODEST—STILL EXCELLENT

For lunch only, you can try the *Rôtisserie* of the Bon Marché department store on Place Rogier. *Coq au Vin,* 62 Marché-au-Charbon, is known for its French regional dishes; usually jampacked, book ahead.

Among the less expensive restaurants, *Chez Léon,* 18 Rue des Bouchers, has a good reputation; try moules au vin blanc. *Petite Auberge,* 14 Rue des Harengs, competes valiantly against neighboring gastronomic giants and has a faithful clientele that comes for its waterzooi, fondue and Brazilian vatapa.

INTERNATIONAL CUISINE

Four outstanding and fairly expensive restaurants head the long series of transalpine eating places. *Peppino,* 86 Rue du Marais near Gare du Nord, has an elegant interior and sometimes a pianist on his best behavior. *Old Mario* is uptown in Ixelles, at 8 Rue de Paris, and a maestro in the preparation of scampi fritti. *Myconos,* 18 Rue Jourdan, is a Greek restaurant with a *bouzouki* orchestra, and next door, at No. 20, the excellent *Meo-Patacca,* Italian.

If you recall nostalgically your Spanish or Portuguese holidays, *Casa Manuel's* singers and guitarists will put you in the mood (fairly expensive) at 15 Grand' Place, in a 15th-cent. cellar. The *Fado* is uptown, 58 Rue Bosquet, and *El Cortijo,* 26 Rue du Pont Neuf (Off Blvd. Adolphe Max). Portuguese dishes at *Mouton d'Or,* Petite Rue des Bouchers.

Speaking of guitars, this time Italian tunes, try *La Trattoria,* 58 Ave. de la Toison d'Or. Their pizza oven is the most spectacular one this side of the Alps.

Our choice among some 20 Yugoslav eating places is *Chez Stanimir,* Rue de la Roue (near Pl. Rouppe), an unpretentious and inexpensive spot.

Wine flows till the early hours to the sound of Viennese songs at *La Saucisse Joyeuse,* 20 Petite Rue des Bouchers. Try Côte de Veau Vallée d'Auge.

India and Bangladesh are represented by the *Taj Mahal,* 12 Ave. des Gaulois, elegant and expensive, and by *Bengale,* 72 Quai aux Briques, not much cheaper.

Swallow's nest and shark's fins at *Le Dragon,* 29 Rue de la Fourche, or at *Ming,* Rue du Grand Cerf (uptown).

Fish à la polonaise or wiener schnitzel are reasonably priced at *Nor-Club,* 86 Blvd. Adolphe Max. On the same street, *Cocorico* offers grilled steak at about 110 frs., half a chicken with chips at about 85 frs.

You can eat excellent couscous at the North African *Tizi Ouzou,* Rue de Moscou, near Porte de Hal. An expensive Italian restaurant with a pleasant terrace is *Sole d'Italia.*

In Rollebeeke, off Grand Sablon, *La Mandarine,* French and Indochinese, menu of the day 110 frs., and down a passage next to it *L'Estrille.*

At 1035 Chaussée de Waterloo, is *Swiss Grill*; first class Swiss cuisine. Also expensive is *Rôtisserie de L'Abreuvoir,* 682 Chausée de St. Job, Uccle. Good, with fashionable, farm-style setting.

Relais de Suède, 138 Rue de Flandre, has exceptional quality and location. Try the gravlax salmon. Expensive.

OUTSKIRTS OF BRUSSELS

BOENDAEL. Not far from Brussels University, *Auberge de Boendael,* 130 Ave. du Bois de la Cambre, is a slickly converted farmhouse, where slickly prepared food may be had expensively.

BOIS DE LA CAMBRE, vast park just southeast of Brussels. *Villa Lorraine* (E), reputed the best in Belgium; patrician atmosphere, impeccable service, superb food. *Pavillon de l'Horloge* (E), on Waterloo road, excellent.

BOITSFORT. At the far end of Ave. Roosevelt, within the precincts of Boitsfort Racecourse, the elegant *Orée du Bois* is moderately expensive.

LAEKEN. On the way to Antwerp, at 445 Ave. des Pagodes, *Pergola* is in the higher price group. Terrace. The restaurant of the *Atomium* overlooks the former site of the Brussels World Fair and part of the city. Dancing. Three minutes away, *Rôtisserie du Kam,* is an authentic 17th-cent. inn. All moderately expensive.

STROMBEEK. On the old Roman road. *Bon Accueil,* a small but pleasant manor house in a park, where superlative cooking awaits you. Tender Brussels chicken treated with champagne-brandy is *the* item on the menu card. Fairly expensive.

WOLUWE. As you descend Ave. de Tervuren, turn left at traffic lights into Ave de Woluwe. Opposite the parish church is an 18th-cent. inn, *Auberge des Maïeurs.* Almost opposite, close to the Woluwe shopping center, is *Mon Manège à Toi.* Both first class. On the other side of the ring road, the *Moulin de Lindekemale* is a converted water mill. Décor better than the food; moderately expensive.

NIGHT SPOTS. Brussels night life is growing in sophistication, and its level has risen markedly in recent years. There are still many *bôites de nuit,* especially down-town, where the doorman tries to pull you in and the lonely visitor may find it only too easy to meet a companion as lonely as himself whose job is "to make the lemonade flow". There is, however, a great deal more than this; and you can find a wide choice of atmosphere and entertainment. In the floorshow clubs you must expect to be asked about 1200 francs

AV. ROGIER
rue Josaphat
rue du Moulin
LIEGE
rue Marie-Thérèse
RUE DE LA LOI
CH. DE HAECHT
rue de la Limite
CH. DE LOUVAIN
rue du Méridien
AV. DE L'ASTRONOMIE
BOULV. BISCHOFFSHEIM
PL. MADOU
AV. DES ARTS
BOULV. DU REGENT
RUE ROYALE
PORTE DE SCHAERBEEK
rue Dupont
JARDIN BOTANIQUE
rue Verte
ANTWERP
PL. ST LAZARE
BOULV. ST LAZARE
BOULEVARD DU JARDIN BOTANIQUE
6
RUE ROYALE
RUE DE LA LOI
PARC DE BRUXELLES
12
GARE DU NORD
Boulv. Pacheco
Boulv. Berlaimont
rue des Colonies
rue du Progrès
PL. ROGIER
AV. DU BOULV.
3
rue de Loxum
C. MERCIER
rue Ravenstein
11
rue des Charbonniers
PL. DES MARTYRS
rue de l'Écuyer
BOULV. DE L'IMPÉRATRICE
CANTERSTEEN
MONT DES ARTS
BOULV. ADOLPHE MAX
rue Neuve
RUE
CH. D'ANVERS
BOULV. BAUDUIN
BOULV. D'ANVERS
Boulv. E. Jacqmain
2
Pl. de la Monnaie
rue de Fripiers
Pl. de Brouckère
1
rue du Lombard
9
rue de Laeken
BOURSE
BOULV. ANSPACH
rue du Midi
rue Van Artevelde
PL. SAINCTELETTE
rue Ullens
rue de l'Intendant
BOULV. LÉOPOLD II
BOULV. DU 9e DE LIGNE
Flandre
rue Antoine Dansaert
rue de
rue
rue d'Anderlecht
BOULV. DE NIEUPORT
rue de l'Avenir
PORTE DE FLANDRE
BOULV. BARTHELEMY
rue de Ribaucourt
OSTEND
rue de l'École
BOULV. DE L'ABATTOIR
CH. DE GAND
rue Ransfort
Ch. de Jette
rue Piers
rue des Quatre Vents
rue Delaunoy
CH. DE NINOVE
rue de Mariemont
rue Heyaert
rue de Liverpool

QUARTIER LÉOPOLD
rue Montoyer
rue du Luxembourg
RUE DU TRONE
CH. DE WAVRE
rue Malibran
PL. EUGÈNE FLAGEY
PL. H. CONSCIENCE
rue du Conseil
CH. D'IXELLES
CH. DE VLEURGAT
NAMUR
rue Lesbroussart
rue Mercelis
rue de Naples
rue d'Edimbourg
AV. MARNIX
PORTE DE NAMUR
rue du Prince Royal
AVENUE LOUISE
rue de Stassart
PL. STEPHANIE
rue Crespel
AV. DE LA TOISON D'OR
BOULV. DE WATERLOO
PORTE LOUISE
rue Blanche
rue Veydt
rue Defacqz
CH. DE CHARLEROI
RUE DE LA RÉGENCE
PL. DU GRAND SABLON
PL. POELAERT
rue Berckmans
rue Jourdan
rue d'Ecosse
AV. HENRI JASPAR
rue de la Victoire
rue Hôtel des Monnaies
rue de Parme
rue Haute
rue Blaes
CH. DE WATERLOO
PORTE DE HAL
CH. DE ALSEMBERG
AV. DU PARC
rue Th. Verhaegen
de Stalingrad
BOULV. DU MIDI
AV. DE LA PORTE DE HAL
Ch. de Forest
rue de l'Argonne
AV. FONSNY
rue de Suède
BOULV. JAMAR
PL. BARA
GARE DU MIDI
PARIS
rue de France
rue Bara
rue des Vétérinaires
BRUSSELS (Centre)
0
1/4 Mile
1 Grand'Place
2 Post Office and Opera
3 St. Michel Cathedral
4 Royal Palace
5 Palace of Justice
6 Unknown Soldier
7 Museum of Nat. Hist.
8 Royal Museum
9 Manneken Pis
10 South Station
11 Central Station and Sabena
12 North Station
13 Museum of Fine Arts

for a bottle of champagne, and find it compulsory at floor-side tables while lesser wines, at about half the price, are served at the others; in most cases, too, you can dally at the bar and see the show for about 100 francs in drink. In many cases the establishments are indeed clubs, but membership can be arranged at the door and costs little.

Among hotels, the Hilton has its roof-top restaurant *En Plein Ciel,* top in more ways than one, with a small dance floor; the Macdonald has *The Gong,* a valued addition to the nocturnal amenities, as is the *Club Room Dansant* at the Brussels Résidence.

For a floorshow the best downtown is *Chez Paul* (au Gaity) at 18, Rue Fossé-aux-Loups, with the *Moulin Rouge,* 18 Pl. de Brouckère a near competitor, and uptown is *Maxims,* Rue Crespel. You can dine, too, in a Spanish décor with dancing and a show at *Las Cuevas del Tio Pepe,* 3-9 Marché-aux-Fromages (off the Grand' Place), and you can find a good orchestra and floorshow at *Le Shako,* 25 Rue du Pépin. In the same street, the *Troika* for Russian cabaret. Weekend shows at *Chez Géraldine,* Rue des Dominicains.

For up-town dancing, the orchestra is good at *Les Anges Noirs,* 23 Rue de Stassart, and at the rather swankier *Les Enfants Terribles,* 44 Ave. de la Toison d'Or.

The Galerie Louise contains a nest of night spots, including the comfortable *New Key Club* and the *Golden Gate.* The New York type of bar is represented by nearby *Bunny's,* 14 Rue Jourdain. Downtown for disc dancing is *Seaclub,* on the corner of the Palace Hotel block, which has a good clièntèle.

For the younger set, those only a bit over the student age-groups, there is *Fashion,* Ave. Louise and *The Puzzle,* in Petite Rue des Bouchers, where there is often live group music. On the fringe of town is *Les Gemeaux,* Blvd. du Souverain.

Jazz clubs worthy of special mention are *New Pols Jazz Place,* Rue Stassart, *Sweet and Hot,* 40 Rue du Beriot, the *J-Club* in Marché-aux-Fromages, and the *Blue Note,* 5-11 Galeries des Princes.

There are a great number of other nighteries, some more to be recommended than others, and many over insistent on attracting the notice of the passer-by. *Charley's* in the Rue Jean Stas, with its soft music and boy-and-girl atmosphere, is by now an institution. The *Black Horse,* 3a Pl. du Bastion and, nearby, *Le Bastion,* are very much "in". You might also try *South Village* on Ave. Winston Churchill, or *Le Cinéma,* Ave. des Celts. Many of these haunts open, flourish and close so quickly that no listing can really keep up.

TEAROOMS. The smartest are within a 300-yard radius in the Porte Louise district: *Hostaria,* 57 Ave. de la Toison d'Or, an elegant Italian place; *Melrose,* first floor in Galerie Louise, the smart shopping arcade on Ave. Louise, and almost opposite, *Kies,* at No. 37. Five o'clock tea music is provided by all department store tearooms. Sabena *Air Terminal* has a pleasant gossip terrace.

Cheer and rhythm prevail at the open-air tea dances in the Bois: *La Laiterie,* more sophisticated; *Les Rossignols,* preferred by simpler folk. Summer only.

BOTTLE CLUBS AND PICTURESQUE BISTROS. Since hard liquor cannot be sold in cafés, there is a thriving branch of the catering industry that calls itself *club privé.* As soon as you comply with the statutes by becoming a member for a nominal fee, you are entitled to your well-earned drink.

Among those in the Galerie Louise is *Le Bivouac,* highly atmospheric, under a Napoleonic tent.

On the Grand' Place is *Le Cerf,* serving drinks in an appropriate setting. At the other end, *La Brouette,* and next to Town Hall, *le Cygne,* are very pleasant.

Next door to it is *Au Roi d'Espagne,* a truly Breughelian place with a no less picturesque beer cellar below. Not far from there, opposite St.

Nicholas' Church in the Rue de Tabora, is *La Bécasse,* where you can sample a real *geuze* beer, with a flavoring of cherries added to the brew. *Au Bon Vieux Temps,* just behind the same church, at 12 Rue Marché-aux-Herbes will give you an idea of what Brussels formerly was. A scant few houses away, at No. 6, *À l'Image de Notre-Dame* is also an old inn.

Other amusing bistros of olden times where you can find many of the less known "medieval beers:" *Vieux Spijtigen Duivel,* 621 Chaussée d'Alsemberg, at Uccle; and *Moeder Lambic,* 786 Chaussée de Waterloo, now enlarged as a restaurant (in the Orangery). All their beers, Geuze, Faro, Orval, Lambic should be drunk with a spot of caution–they're strong.

British-style pubs are growing popular, serving English beer and Irish Guinness. Downtown, near the Bourse, is the *Red Lion.* Popular.

ENTERTAINMENT. Opera and ballet may be seen at the *T.R.M.* (Théâtre Royal de la Monnaie). Founded by Bombarda in 1659 and rebuilt in 1855 by Poelaert, it produced the first performance of Meyerbeer's "L'Africaine", and today maintains a full international repertory for most of the year. June is traditionally devoted to operetta, and the famous Ballet Béjart also dances there from time to time.

All theaters, except the *Flemish,* play in French. The charming *Parc* has a good company presenting modern comedies and serious plays. The same applies to *Galeries,* where top Paris companies quite frequently try out their plays before presenting them in the French capital. *Théâtre National* is a troupe with a mission and has its home in the Place Rogier skyscraper. *Théâtre Cent-Quarante* has an avant-garde flavor, and so, too, does *Théâtre de Poche.* But the most original is the *Théâtre de Quat' Sous,* once a beer cellar, at 16 Grand' Place. *Théâtre de l'Esprit Frappeur,* 28 Rue Josaphat, is located in old cellars. Its shows are often outstandingly good, as are those of the *Théâtre Poème,* 30 Rue d'Ecosse. *Théâtre Molière* has reopened after long rebuilding works. There a number of other small theaters recently opened, bearing witness to the vitality of the city's theatrical revival.

Serious music is provided by two *Beaux Arts* concert halls. Other subscription concerts are held in the victorian *Conservatoire* in Rue Royale.

SHOPPING IN BRUSSELS. The main shopping areas are Blvd. Adolphe Max and Rue Neuve, running from Pl. Rogier, and their extensions as far as the Bourse, and turning left uphill, the Rue Marché-aux-Herbes; the Rue Royale, sedate and rather select, continuing through Pl. Royale, and uphill through the archway, Rue de Namur; both sides of the boulevard between Porte de Namur and Porte Louise, and the first part of the wider section of Ave. Louise. The latter are the best spots for fashionable shopping.

Among the shopping arcades are: the little *Passage du Nord* in the Metropole block and the more ambitious *Galeries Saint Hubert* which, besides its smart shops, shelters two theaters, a cinema and several cafés. Using the street levels of tall new buildings, there is the *Agora Gallery* near Grand' Place; the *Ravenstein Gallery* near the Central Station, adroitly using the differences of level; the ultra-smart *Galeries Louise,* almost opposite the Hilton; with a few hundred yards along the boulevard the *Galeries de la Toison d'Or.* Up the Ave. Louise, too, is a smaller and more individual version, the *Garden Stores,* an imaginative architectural venture, and the honeycomb of galleries in the Post Office Building (Place de la Monnaie). And there is now the *Manhattan Center* in Pl. Rogier.

ANTIQUES. *Regency,* 26 Ave. Louise, for 18th-cent. French and English furniture; *Le Brun,* 26 Blvd. de Waterloo and *van Hove,* 19 Rue de Namur and 132a Ave. Louise, for all periods; *Callens,* 4 Blvd. de Waterloo.

The area around Sablon Square is the main antique trade center. Perhaps the best in Brussels is *Costermans,* 5 Place du Grand Sablon. Open-air antique market at weekends at the foot of Sablon Church. The *Palais des Beaux-Arts* stages important winter auctions.

BOOKSHOPS. *Corman,* 28-30 Rue Ravenstein, large selection English books; has branches in Le Zoute and Ostend. *Libris,* 29 Ave. de la Toison d'Or. The *Paperback Shop,* Chaussée de Waterloo where it meets Ave. Winston Churchill.

CHOCOLATES. For really important occasions, *Mary,* 180 Rue Royale and *Neuhaus,* Galerie de la Reine and 27 Ave. de la Toison d'Or. Also *Godiva,* 22 Grand' Place and 37 Blvd. Adolphe Max (with a branch in New York, 701 5th Ave. and can be bought in Charleston, South Carolina), and *Daskalides,* 26 Ave. Louise. Lower prices, medium quality at *Leonidas* (open-air) chocolate counter, 46 Blvd. Anspach, and branches.

CLOTHING. *Hit Lapidus,* Pl. Louise, for latest youth fashions; *Butch,* Rue de l'Ecuyer, and in the *Garden Stores,* Ave. Louise. *Rampont,* 60 Rue des Colonies, has fine selections of men's and women's wear, expensive, as is *Séverin Frères,* 42 Rue de Namur. For raincoats and those wonderful Austrian "lodens", try *Frey & Bastian,* 14 Ave. de la Toison d'Or, or *Paris-Londres,* No. 28 on same street and at 106 Rue Neuve. For Swiss "Hanro" knitwear, *Hanchar,* 2 Rue de l'Ecuyer and 2 Blvd. de Waterloo.

DEPARTMENT STORES. On Rue Neuve, the main shopping center, *Innovation, Bon Marché, Marks & Spencer* and *C & A.*

FLORISTS. *Frouté,* 27 Ave Louise; *Janine,* 71 Rue Stallaerts; *Madeleine Lison,* 10 Blvd. Adolphe Max; *Isabelle de Backer,* 13 Rue Royale.

GLASS & CRYSTAL. *De Backer & Van Camp,* 73 Rue Royale; *Buss,* 84 Marché-aux-Herbes and 3 Galerie Louise (expensive). For Val St. Lambert crystal, see the stock at the official depository, 57 Rue des Chartreux.

GLOVES. In Rue des Fripiers, *Ganterie de Luxe* and *Schuermans,* the latter also in Galerie Louise. Also *Jean Coessens* and *Kent* (see under Leatherwork). *Fernand Sandam* and *Gaston Samdam,* with branches in main shopping streets, for a wide, less expensive selection.

JEWELRY. *Wolfers Frères,* 82 Ave. Louise; *Leysen Frères,* 28 Marché-aux-Poulets and 53 Blvd. de Waterloo; *Sturbelle,* 24 Blvd. de Waterloo. On fine evenings a street market for costume jewelry has sprung up on Rue des Petits Bouchers.

LACE. *Real Lace Manufactory (Louise Verschueren),* 16 Rue Watteeu; *Madame Foiret,* 29 Pl. de Brouckère; *Maria Loix,* 54 Rue d'Arenberg; *Maison Antoine,* 26 Grand' Place; *Manufacture Belge de Dentelles,* 6 Galerie de la Reine; *Lace Palace,* Rue de la Violette.

LEATHERWORK. *Delvaux,* Blvd. Adolphe Max, Ave. de la Toison d' Or, and in Galerie de la Reine; *Alligator,* 28 Rue Treurenberg; *Jean Coessens,* Pl. Stéphanie (Ave. Louise); *Fontaine,* 5 Ave. Louise; *Kent,* at No. 36. *Maroquinerie Delvaux,* 22 Blvd. Adolphe Max, for expensive handbags.

LINEN. *Tissages Réunis de Courtrai,* 107 Rue Royale, for a wide range of articles; *Biot-Belièvre,* 8 Rue de Naples, for exclusive trousseaux.

LINGERIE. Superb handmade undies at *Maison Marguerite,* 22a Chaussée de Charleroi and *Walewyk,* 113 Ave. Louise. Tempting items from shops on Ave. de la Toison d'Or: *Suzanne,* at No. 49; *Bavog,* No. 42; *Aux Champs-Elysées,* at No. 37.

SHOES. The Italian shoemaker

Tafferia, 2 Pl. Stéphanie (Ave. Louise) will make you a pair within 3 days, but you pay heavily. World-famous *Ferramoro* is at 48 Blvd. de Waterloo (has American-type lasts). *Walton,* 35 Ave. de la Toison d'Or, for handmade shoes for men. Numerous shops sell British shoes, such as *Brevitt Toison d'Or,* 16 Ave. de la Toison d'Or; and 36 Rue Neuve; *Walk-Over,* 128 Rue Neuve; *Church's English Shoes,* 2 Pl. Stéphanie; *Manfields,* with several outlets; *Old England,* Pl. Royale.

SHOTGUNS. *Christophe,* 3 Rue Washington; *Binet,* 17 Rue Royale; *Maison du Chasseur et Mahillon Réunis,* 413 Ave. Louise.

SILVERWARE. *Altenloh,* 14 Blvd. de Waterloo and *Georg Jensen,* 172 Ave. Louise, for Danish ware. *Wiskemann,* 20 Ave. Louise, with its own models.

SPORTSWEAR. You will admire the outfits at *Van Schelle,* 24 Rue d'Assault and in Galeries du Roi; *English House,* Rue Marché-aux-Herbes, and, almost next door, *Au Feu de Camp* which offers sports equipment. *Disy Sports,* 164 Ave. Louise, is distinctive.

WROUGHT IRON. *Les Fils Costermans,* 5 Pl. du Grand Sablon; *Le XIII-ème Siècle,* 62 Galerie Agora, *Ferronnerie d'Art,* 134 Rue Sans Source (take a taxi). For antique-style door handles or fireplaces, *Henry Mathieu,* 184 Chaussée d'Etterbeek.

MUSEUMS. Two important museums of fine arts are in close proximity to each other. The *Musée Royale d'Art Ancien* (Museum of Ancient Art), Rue de la Régence, contains renowned masterpieces of Belgian paintings. There are three sections: Flemish primitives (Van der Weyden, Bouts, Memling, etc.), Renaissance (H. Bosch, the Breughels, etc.), and Baroque (Rubens, Van Dyck, Jordaens, etc.); also remarkable collections of the great foreign schools. Qualified guides are available to show the most important works.

Nearby is the *Museum of Modern Art,* where you will find paintings of such 19th- and 20th-century masters as Lawrence, David, Gauguin, the French Impressionists, and an important collection of outstanding Belgian paintings by Ensor, Permeke, Rik Wouters, and others. Open daily (except Mon.) 10-5, Wed. 8-10 p.m.; closed Jan. 1, Nov. 1 and 11. Free entrance to Modern Art Museum. (Check opening times, as these sometimes change.)

Museum of Art and History, Parc du Cinquantenaire. Half the collections are shown on alternate days. In the same building are housed the *Army Museum* and the *Collection of Historical Coaches.* Open 9:30-5, closed Jan. 1, May 1, Nov. 11, also Fri. and an hour at lunchtime.

Institut Royal du Patrimoine Artistique, 1 Parc du Cinquantenaire, first of its kind in the world for scientific preservation and restoration of works of art; sponsored by UNESCO.

Museum of Natural Science, 31 Rue Vautier, and *Museum of Arms and Armor,* old city rampart tower, Porte de Hal, open same hours as Museum of Art and History.

Brussels City Museum, Maison du Roi, Grand' Place. Open 10-5, closed weekend afternoons and holidays.

Musical Instrument Museum at the Bellevue Palace, Place Royale; contains over 4,000 instruments, both European and Oriental. Open Tues., Thurs., Sat., 2:30-4:30, Wed. 8-10 p.m., with period concert (free) and Sun. 10:30-12:30.

Postal Museum, 162 Ave. Rogier; open Tues., Thurs., and Sat., 10-12 and 2-4. Guide by appointment.

Brewery Museum, 10 Grand' Place; open weekdays 9:30-12 and 2-5.

Applied Arts, Abbaye de la Chambre; open daily 2-5, except weekends.

Poor Law Administration, 298a Rue Haute; open 9-12 Mon., 1-5 Wed.

Albert I Library, Blvd. de l'Empereur; collection of manuscripts. Open daily 9-12 and 2-5, except Sun. and holidays.

General Record Office, 78 Galerie Ravenstein. Public room open weekdays 9-5.

Breughel Museum, 132 Rue Haute, in the house where the painter lived his last six years: private collection paintings.

Great 19th-century Belgian artists: *Musée Wiertz,* 62 Rue Vautier; 10-5 (closed Mon.); *Musée Charlier,* 16 Ave. des Arts, Sun. only, 9-12:30; *Constantin Meunier,* 59 Rue de l'Abbaye, 9-12 and 2-5 Sat.; 9:30-12:30 on Mon., Wed., Fri.

Maison Schott, 27 Rue du Chene. Home of the late artist-painter. Open Tues., Thurs., 2-5 p.m.

Important art exhibitions are held at the *Palais des Beaux Arts* (see newspaper announcements).

At *Galerie Helios Art,* 208 Ave. F. Roosevelt, there is a permanent exhibition of modern art from Cubism to the present day.

On the outskirts: At Anderlecht, *House of Erasmus* and *Folklore Museum,* 31 Rue du Chapitre. Open 10-12, 2-5 closed Tues. and Fri. Guided visit by advance request. At Laeken, in the Palace Park, the *Chinese Pagoda,* Oriental art, porcelain collections. Open 9:30-5, closed Fri. *Royal Greenhouses,* open for about a fortnight in May (time—see newspapers).

BUILDINGS AND MONUMENTS. *Town Hall* (Hôtel de Ville), Grand' Place. Open to the public 9-5 except Sat., Sun., and holiday afternoons. Famous tapestries and Assembly Hall. Ascension of the tower, 420 steps.

Cathedral (St. Michael). Visits: 11-5 (when no service). While repairs are in progress, the tower is closed to visitors.

Law Courts (Palais de Justice), Pl. Poelaert. Visit of Main Hall on weekdays 9-4. *Congress Column* (Colonne du Congrès), Rue Royale. A climb of 192 steps to the top. At foot of column is the tomb of Belgium's Unknown Soldier.

The *Royal Palace* is open from about 22 July (after the royal family goes on vacation) until the second Sun. in Sept. 9:30-4, daily exc. Mon.

TRANSPORTATION You must not allow your reactions to the transport system to spoil your enjoyment. Buy a street map (*Guide-Plan)* and plan your movements accordingly. Trams are a long-established feature of Brussels traffic, and they have absolute right of way. Recent road improvements have resulted in some trams being put on special sections of the road, and the noise problem has been partly solved by up-to-date equipment. Most recently, some key tram services are underground (this system is called the *Metro*). Communications between uptown and downtown have been improved enormously as a result.

The tram and buses run as part of the same service. A single ticket, anywhere in the city area, costs 8 frcs. and a transfer ticket (*correspondance)* 10 frcs. A card, valid for 10 rides, sells for 62 frcs. From the Brussels Information Center, 12 Rue de la Colline, near Grand' Place, you can buy for 75 frcs., a "rover" ticket, allowing unrestricted travel in the city for 3 days. (Prices due to rise.)

Tram and bus services are numbered, but the numbers have been changed and rechanged during the metro construction, and are almost certain to be changed again. Any attempt to suggest useful route numbers would therefore be misleading. You can get up-to-the minute leaflets from the Information Center.

Best get to know the names of destinations you are likely to want, such as Nord, Midi, Bourse, Bois, Place Royale, Cinquantenaire, Place Flagey, which are marked on the destination boards. If you are uncertain where to get out, ask a fellow passenger, not the conductor.

TAXIS. These are expensive and most cabmen are ill-humored and mercenary. Cabs have to be phoned for (your hotel will see to this) or hired from a rank. The fare is fixed on the meter. The drivers work on a small margin of profit and expect a tip of 20 to 25% of the fare.

SPORTS. *Football* (soccer) is the most popular sport. Important international games are held at Heysel Stadium and S.C. Anderlecht sports grounds (see newspaper announcements). *Athletic meets* are held at the Racing Club Stadium. Covered *swimming pools:* 28 Rue du Chevreuil; 25 Rue St. François; 38 Rue de la Perche; open-air pools, 121 Rue de Genève; Solarium Beausoleil; Solarium du Centenaire, Ave. de Meisse. *Water-skiing* at Genval and Hofstade lakes. *Tennis,* Lawn Tennis Federation, 164 Ave. Louise. *Horseback riding:* L'Etrier Belge, 19 Champ du Vert Chasseur; Country Riding Club, Welriekende dreef, Jezus Eik. Poffé, 872a Chaussée de Waterloo. Duwez, 55 Allée du Vivier d'Oie. *Sport flying* at Grimbergen Airfield. *Yachting:* Royal Yacht Club, Avant Port, Chaussée de Vilvorde. *Horseracing* at Boitsfort, Groenendaal, and Zellik racetracks (see newspaper announcements). *Bowling.* There are plenty of bowling alleys. A few: *Brunswick,* 43 Quai aux Foin downtown; *Crossly,* Blvd. de l'Empereur; uptown, the *Molière,* 115 Ave. Molière.

CHURCH SERVICES. *Catholic:* All parish churches. Especially convenient for visitors are St. Nicholas (Bourse); Notre-Dame au Sablon (Rue de la Régence); Ste. Marie (Rue Royale); Carmes, Ave. de la Toison d'Or. Weekday Mass at 6 p.m. at the first two and 6:15 p.m. at the others.

Anglican and American Episcopal, Christ Church, 29 Rue Capitaine Crespel. Sun., Holy Communion 8:30, Morning Prayer 10:30; Sung Eucharist 11:30, Sunday school and creche for infants; Evening Prayer 6:45.

American Protestant Church, Kattenberg, Boitsfort (in grounds of the International School). Sun. service and school, 10:30 a.m.

Christian Science, 98 Chaussée de Vleurgat, Wed. 8 p.m., Sun. 11:15 a.m.

Presbyterian, St. Andrew's Church of Scotland, 181 Chaussée de Vleurgat, Sun. 11 a.m..

Methodist Church, 5 Rue du Champs de Mars (service in English on Sun. 9:30 a.m.).

Jewish, 32 Rue de la Régence.

Seventh Day Adventists, 23 Rue Ernest Allard.

Mormon, 14 Rue Fraikin.

MAIL AND TELEGRAPH. The General Post Office, Pl. de la Monnaie (facing Opera House), is open weekdays 9-6; for express and airmail, 9-8. An office is open at 48 Ave. Fonsny (Midi Station) on Sun. and holidays; also for all-night express and airmail, 8 p.m. to 9 a.m. Stamps and postcards may be purchased, and correspondence mailed, at the Banque de Bruxelles, 2 Rue de la Régence; you may also send cables from their private telegraph office. General telegraph and telephone service in building next to Sabena Air Terminal.

USEFUL ADDRESSES. Embassies and Consulates: *American,* 27 Blvd. du Régent. *British,* 28 Rue Joseph II. *Canadian,* 35 Rue de la Science. *Australian,* 51-52 Ave. des Arts.

Travel Offices: *American Express,* Palace Hotel building, Pl. Rogier; *Wagons-Lits/Cook,* 17 Pl. de Brouckère, and 41 Ave. de la Toison d'Or, drive-in office at 68 Rue Belliard; *Havas-Exprinter,* 13 Blvd. Adolphe Max; *Generalcar,* 10 Rue de la Montagne.

Tourist Information: *Belgian State Tourist Office,* Central Station; *Brussels Information Center,* 12 Rue de la Colline, near Grand' Place. For current events see two English-language weeklies, *The Bulletin* and the *Brussels Times.*

Car hire: *Avis,* 145 Rue Américaine, and Sabena Air Terminal; *Hertz,* 8 Blvd. Maurice Lemonnier, and at Brussels Airport; *ABC Service Rent-a-car,* 63 Rue Dautzenberg.

EMERGENCIES. *Police,* dial 900; *Ambulance,* Red Cross, tel. 44-70-10.

Exploring Brussels

You can buy a map (*guide-plan*) of Brussels at any stationer's or bookstall. The central city is enclosed by a heartshaped boulevard (the line of the Ramparts), with the Nord station at one end and the Midi Station at the other. Its name changes every few hundred yards, so the practical Brussels people call it *petite ceinture* (small belt) in contrast to the outer boulevards (*grande ceinture*) that enclose several boroughs. Both "belts" were modernised for the 1958 World's Fair and, whenever the modernisations are not being re-modernised and amplified, they are models of their kind for fast-moving automobile traffic. The two stations are joined by a central boulevard (beginning at the north with the Boulevard Adolphe Max).

Taking the southward line, the streets on your left run uphill towards Saint Michel Cathedral, the administrative government area, and the Parc de Bruxelles. Farther on, the uphill streets lead towards the Palais de Justice, the high dome of which is the landmark you will have seen from many miles away. In doing so, they traverse the once poor but colorful quarter of the Marolles (gradually being replaced by new housing projects), with the Sunday flea market in the Place du Jeu de Balle. The streets on your right as you pass down the central boulevard lead into a more popular, and more populous shopping quarter, the highpoint of which is the street market in the Place Sainte Catherine, which you reach by turning right opposite the Bourse.

Typical Features of the City Streets

The first thing to strike you in the Brussels streets is the enormous number of cafés. The Belgians are, indeed, great coffee drinkers, great beer drinkers, and great drinkers of light port (*Porto*), which they take as an apéritif. These are the main trade of the small cafés, many of which, however, seem to do very little business. There are, of course, a large number of popular cafés, that do a good trade most of the day.

A second thing to notice is the great amount of very fine ornamental ironwork. The Belgians have for centuries been forgers of iron and, though their taste in house-furnishings is often cumbrous

Flemish art in painting is exemplified by Breughel, whose works hang in Antwerp's private, authentically-furnished Mayer van den Bergh Museum.

The Belgians are enthusiastic gourmets who pride themselves on the variety of their cuisine, whether it's a question of fresh shrimps from East Dunkirk, or game from the tempting display at one of Brussels' many food shops.

and heavy, they have managed to express themselves in iron in ways that deserve special admiration. You will find, especially in the streets around the Grand' Place, a number of shop signs, some of which are of considerable age and many that have histories of their own. You will also find wrought-iron park railings, balcony railings, and banisters of private stairways, of intricate and generally highly pleasing design. Though much of this work is old, wrought-iron work in general is far from being extinct. There are, for example, butchers' shops where the joints hang on hooks and from battens of exquisite design, but which are of recent execution.

There is nothing self-conscious or art-ridden in the way this work is brought into use, and it is seldom pointed out to the visitor. For this reason, as you walk through Brussels, it is wise to be observant of little things. This will also ensure your seeing the many streetcorner shrines, with their effigies of the Madonna and the saints let into the walls of houses, though often too high for detailed scrutiny.

On one of your walks you will undoubtedly have wandered from the Grand' Place along the Rue de l'Etuve, where you will come upon rather a self-conscious corner surrounded with lace-and-souvenir shops. On this corner you will find Brussels' "Oldest Inhabitant", the charmingly outrageous statue known as *Manneken Pis*. No apology is needed for bringing him in at the start of your visit. He is the most loved piece of the Brussels of the Bruxellois, and if you are capable of being shocked by him you must go away, for Brussels is not for you.

His origin is wrapped in mystery, though certain it is that a similar effigy, moulded in sugar and similarly occupied—though with rose water—garnished one of the banquets of Philip the Good. The figure is identified with the fortunes of Brussels. Many amusing legends surround it, the most persistent being his sprinkling of a Spanish sentry, passing under the windows of the little man's parents. The statue in bronze was ordered by the city from the 17th-century sculptor, Duquesnoy, to replace the one in stone, whose origin was unknown. Hidden during the 1695 bombardment, he was carried off by British soldiers before Fontenoy and later kidnapped by the French. On this occasion he was invested with a gold-embroidered suit by no less a dignitary than Louis XV of France. He has many other suits, which he dons on ceremonial occasions, including a number bestowed by American and British armed forces after World War II. His latest, a John Bull uniform, was presented in 1973 by Arthur Lowe (of *Dad's Army* fame), on the occasion of Britain's entry into the EEC.

Unique Landmark: Grand' Place

The Grand' Place is the noblest of market places, with ornate gold-scrolled façades making an irregular skyline of guildhouses which have been likened to theater scenery. They are, however, as solid and enduring as the flagstones in the square and much more sacrosanct; yet it is true that they are theatrical, especially so when you emerge from one of the dark, narrow side streets as from the wings of a stage at night when it is floodlit. The magic remains year after year.

You will see the Grand' Place to best advantage around dawn, when it is the great wholesale market of the farmers and market gardeners for many miles around the capital. On six mornings a week there is also a market for flowers and garden plants in the center of the Grand' Place. But the whole square is cleared and neat by the time people arrive for business in the offices around. Go on Sunday morning for the bird market, and at night to see its floodlit beauty. By a 1972 municipal ruling, the parking of cars in the Grand' Place has been prohibited, a most happy decision which gives the visitor a proper chance to contemplate at leisure this unique ensemble from one of the many sidewalk cafés.

By this time you will be a confirmed admirer of the Hôtel de Ville, with its Lion Stairway as entrance to the original building and the main gateway surmounted with the exquisite tower and its 16-foot statue of Saint Michael and the Devil. Over the gateway are statues of the prophets, and female figures representing Peace, Prudence, Justice, Strength, Temperance and Law, attributed to the 14th-century sculptor, Claus Sluter. Within the gateway the inner court, with its two fountains representing Scheldt and Meuse (Schelde and Maas), and its fine floral displays, is a most refreshing spot.

Inside the Hôtel de Ville, the burgomaster's antechamber contains an extremely interesting set of pictures—painted in the 19th century by Van Moer—of Brussels, before the Senne was taken underground. In the Council Chamber the brilliant ceiling (*Assembly of the Gods*, by Victor Janssens, early 18th century) is especially noteworthy, and there are three excellent 18th-century Brussels tapestries depicting historical scenes. There are other fine tapestries in the Maximilian Chamber, but more interest attaches to the more modern (about 1880) Mechelen (Malines) tapestry panels in the Gothic Chamber representing the crafts of Brussels.

In the Grand' Place itself, the buildings were erected soon after the French bombardment of 1695, and are a curious mixture of French and Italian Renaissance architecture, their façades decorated with gilded scrollwork and statues. The houses, which were built for the craft guilds, have been described by a Belgian author as "ostentation in opulence". One of the houses, No. 4, known as "The Sack", has still the ground and first floors of the original building which, however, dates from only 50 years before the bombardment. No 10, "The Golden Tree", was the meeting house of the Brewers' Guild and today is the Brewery Museum. On top of its ornate roof there is an equestrian statue of Charles of Lorraine. No. 26, "The Pigeon", was for a time the dwelling of Victor Hugo. Round the corner from No. 8, under the colonnade, is a memorial plaque for Everard 't Serclaes. By recent tradition, the touching of the shiny arm of the statue or the head of the little dog will bring a wish true. You will find not only tourists but local people waiting to do this.

Opposite the Hôtel de Ville a 16th-century Flamboyant Gothic palace known as Maison du Roi today houses the City Museum. It is said to have been the scene of Charles Quint's abdication in 1555 in favour of his son, Philip II of Spain. Arch enemy of the kings of France, master of an empire "over which the sun never set" (Austria to Peru), he spent the rest of his life as a simple monk at Juste, in Spain. The museum houses an important collection of 18th- and 19th- century porcelain and ceramics, together with some remarkable 14th-century rood-screens and sculptures from the façade of the Hôtel de Ville. Here, too, are the Manneken Pis wardrobes.

Other Sights

You should not miss the little Church of St. Nicholas, almost invisible because of the tiny houses plastered against its walls. It lies just behind the Bourse, which was decorated in part by Rodin. St. Nicholas is the traditional church of aspiring dancers, and hopeful ballerinas light candles in prayer for an engagement. There is a small *Virgin and Child* attributed to Rubens and, outside beside the porch, the exquisite *Milkmaid* by Marc Devos.

Leaving the Grand' Place on your right, you now climb the hill by the Marché-aux-Herbes and the Rue de la Madeleine, and come out with a view of the best of Brussels' new buildings. You are facing the equestrian statue of King Albert. To the left is the Central station and beyond it the Westbury Hotel and the Telecommunication building. To the right, flanking the formal gardens is the Albertine, Belgium's National Library. As you walk up through the gardens, do not neglect to look back at the clock over the lower archway. You should hear (and see) it strike the hour (preferably noon). The building in front of you at the top is the Palais des Congrès. Through the upper archway, in mellow brick, is one of the rare vestiges of the Burgundian period. This is the Ravenstein Palace, birthplace of Anne of Cleves, the "Flemish mare" who was fourth of the six wives of King Henry VIII of England.

The Place Royale

Climbing farther into the Place Royale, a Regency-style square of elegant proportions, you are on the site of the Coudenberg Palace. Behind the statue of the crusading Walloon hero, Godefroy de Bouillon, is the unlovely neo-classic façade of Saint-Jacques-sur-Coudenberg, which contains a number of sculptures worth seeing, including a *Moses* by de Marseille and a collection of pieces by Godecharle. Standing on the steps of the church, the redecorated Belle Vue Palace, former home of King Leopold III and Queen Astrid before their accession, is at the corner on your right. Beyond this stretches the Rue Royale, alongside the Parc de Bruxelles.

To your left, the Rue de la Régence runs up to the Palais de Justice, sometimes called the ugliest structure in Europe. The large building to the right contains the Musée Royal d'Art Ancien, with its magnificent collection of Flemish and Dutch paintings, among numerous other works of art. Down the side of this building runs the Rue du Musée, which luckily still preserves the fine façade of the former National Library building. The nearby Musée Moderne specialises in the more recent periods of painting, although it includes works by Ingres and Sir Thomas Lawrence.

Returning to the Place Royale, you may care to remember that Brussels is above all a city of music. You can get to the Palais des Beaux Arts, with its many art galleries, concert and lecture halls (not to forget its cinema), all located below street level, by the Rue Ravenstein or down a broad stairway from the Rue Royale. Even if you have little taste for music, it is always worthwhile finding out what there is at the Beaux Arts to be heard or seen. The *Orchestre Nationale de Belgique* has an excellent name, and is under the direction of the well-known conductor, Van der Noot. In the Rue de la Régence is the Conservatoire Royale.

Diagonally opposite the Petit Sablon museum is the Church of Our Lady of Victories (*Eglise du Sablon*), originally a small chapel built by crossbowmen in 1304. The church itself, which took a century to build, is a 15th-16th-century masterpiece. It is the church rather than any individual monuments or treasures that deserves a visit, though there is a delightful statue of St. Hubert just beyond the porch, with a stag at his side and between its horns is a hanging Christ, and there is some very fine work in the choir, though much of it is too high to see easily. Here is held the Mass of Saint Hubert, patron of huntsmen, on 3 November each year.

On the other side of the Rue de la Régence is the attractive little garden square, the Petit Sablon. You should notice the variety of railings, but above all the little statues representing Brussels' medieval guilds. There are 48 of these and it is easy to guess each trade for the furniture-maker holds a chair, the wine merchant a goblet and so on. At the far end of the garden is a large statue of the counts of Egmont and Hornes, surrounded by a semi-circle of statues of various Belgian scientists of the 16th and 17th centuries.

Immediately beyond the square is the Palais d'Egmont. It now houses the offices of numerous semi-public bodies, but there is nothing to stop your entering from this end, walking through what were once the stables and emerging into the gem of Brussels gardens. Here you will find a replica of Frampton's *Peter Pan* (the original is in Kensington Gardens), "given by the children of London to the children of Brussels", and come, rather to your surprise, to the outdoor terrace leading into the coffee shop of the Hilton.

The Palace of Justice to the Fashionable Boulevards

At the end of the Rue de la Régence is the Palais de Justice, in the big square called after the architect Poelaert. You cannot fail to notice the size and style of the building (the definition "Assyro-Babylonian" would fit it best). The impression of immensity as you mount the steps is well designed to impress you with the majesty of justice. If you climb the 500-odd steps to the cupola, you will get a view of the Brabant countryside worth remembering. This site is the former Gallows Hill.

The precipitous descent from the Palais de Justice brings you quickly into the quarter known as Les Marolles, and sometimes also called after Pieter Breughel the Elder who died here in 1569 and whose tomb is in the Eglise de la Chapelle, in Place de la Chapelle at the foot of the hill. Parts of this church date back to the 12th century, and it contains the beautiful statue, *Our Lady of Solitude,* wearing a black lace mantilla and attributed to the Spanish master Becerra. It is said to have been brought here by the Infanta Isabella, "light of the eyes" of her father, the cruel but pious Philip II, who ceded the Low Countries to his daughter a few months before he died of gout in 1598.

The puppet theatre of Toone VI, has been moved from this square down the hill, to a little blind alley called Schuddevelde, near the Rue des Bouchers. It is no longer in the father-to-son tradition, but its charms and fun have been maintained, and it has an attractive café. It is a good place to spend an evening.

To appreciate Les Marolles you should visit it during the fun of the Braderie Breughel in October. These autumn *braderies*, or shopkeepers' festivals, are held as a joint effort in all the shopping streets in Belgium. They are a time of fairy lights, amplified music at street corners, shopping surprises aimed to catch your goodwill, and stupendous shop-window decoration. In the Braderie Breughel you will see how little the faces, and the spiritual gusto, of these people have changed through the centuries since Breughel painted them—though the damsel elected "Miss Breughel" for the year habitually conforms to 20th-century standards of beauty. It is not true, as sometimes alleged, that this distinction is reserved for the winner of the sausage-eating contest.

Returning along the Rue Blaes, which runs parallel with the Rue Haute (both are one-way streets), you will pass the Place du Jeu de Balle, scene of the Sunday flea market (it also functions on weekday mornings), which is also the traditional centre of all the black markets in Belgium. It was, of course, a happy hunting ground for Hitler's scouts in quest of forced labour for deportation, and the Church of the Immaculate Conception opposite provided the citizens with emergency exits into adjoining roads with the ready connivance of the Capucin fathers. At the end of the street you are again on the ring boulevard; 50 yards higher up is the Porte de Hal, last survivor of the city's fortified gates, now an arms museum with unusual souvenirs of Isabella and Albert, including their horses.

Stretching downhill from this point, the boulevard for almost a mile is the scene of the Brussels Fair (sometimes called the Foire du Midi) from mid-July through August. The Belgians are devoted to fairs, and the preambulating amusement caterers are to be found running fairs on a small scale in almost all the city squares at various times during the spring and summer. The Foire du Midi is the meeting place for all of them, and you will find everything that is newest and most thrilling in this peculiarly Belgian form of amusement congregated here as a gathering of old friends.

Taking the uphill route, you quickly reach and pass the Porte Louise. The outer section of the Avenue de la Toison d'Or, between the Porte de Namur and the Rue des Chevaliers, has been transformed into a pedestrian zone. The pavement has been gaily colored in red and white stones in diamond shapes, evergreen bushes and shrubs have been laid out, benches installed and fountains play. It is a pleasant place for shopping and strolling in winter or summer. From the Porte de Namur you can best take a tramcar down the long and crowded Chaussée d'Ixelles to the Place Eugène Flagey (named after the former burgomaster of Ixelles). Here (until its outward move is completed this year or next) is the studio building of R.T.B. (Radio et Télévision Belge), the broadcasting and television authority. The square itself is a morning food market which often finds room for a fair and even a circus.

Beside it you find the start of the lovely Ixelles lakes. To see these at their best you should come in May, when the white and red chestnuts are in full bloom. Do not miss the delightful walk round these lakes (they are the centre for a firework display in June), and leave plenty of time for a visit at the far end to the Abbaye de la Cambre, the serene setting of which is somewhat spoilt by the new ITT office tower. The history of the Cistercian sisters, from the early 13th century to their dispersion after the French Revolution, epitomises the troubled story of the Low Countries. Here, too, lie the remains of Saint Boniface who died here in 1260.

Returning the length of one of the lakes, a bus will take you back through the Place Eugène Flagey, up Rue Malibran and into the Rue du Trône. Alighting at the Chaussée de Wavre crossing and turning downhill, you can fork up the Rue Vauthier to the Musée Wiertz—a collection of the works of a single powerful painter.

From this vantage point you walk round into the Parc Léopold, once a zoo. Here, among a number of institutional buildings, you will find the Natural History Museum with several extremely interesting prehistoric remains, including the Lierre Mammoth and the two human skeletons from Spy.

Leaving the park and walking up the Rue Belliard, you again come to the ring boulevard. Crossing it and taking the short Rue Lambermont, you will find yourself in the Parc de Bruxelles. Byron resided for a time on the Rue Ducale, a fine, late 18th-century street bordering the park. It was here that he wrote the third canto of *Childe Harold* on the Battle of Waterloo. The street now contains the residences of the United States and British ambassadors.

The City Park and Cathedral of Saint Michael

To your left is the Royal Palace with, at the farther end, the white block of the Belle Vue Palace. The Royal Palace owes its present appearance to Léopold II, who had it altered several times by architects who drew their inspiration from Versailles and the Tuileries; there are magnificent crystal chandeliers in the Throne Room and remarkable Gobelin tapestries in the Grand White Drawing Room. Opposite the centre of the palace, a wide avenue leads you across the park, past two lake-fountains to the Rue de la Loi where, surrounded by a row of government departments, stands the Palais de la Nation, housing the two chambers of the Belgian Parliament. It has an impressive frontage by Barnabé Guimard. The building is accessible to visitors when the chambers are not sitting. The government offices on either side of the Parliament building have a good deal of historical interest. No. 16, now the Prime Minister's office, was built by Montoyer for a religious community. No. 2, again the work of Guimard, has been a private house and a hotel and it housed the meetings of the revolutionary committee in 1792; it is now the Ministry of National Defence. At the farther end of the park, opposite the Royal Palace, is the Palais des Academies, home of the Academy of Sciences, Arts and Letters and other learned bodies, and the occasional meeting place for top-level international conferences.

Crossing the park to its corner on the Rue de la Loi, a hundred yards' walk downhill and a short turn to the right bring you before the Cathedral of Saint Michael. The church stands on the site of a Chapel of Saint Michael, to which were carried in the year 1047 the remains of Gudule, a saintly lady of Ham, near Alost, who had died 335 years earlier. As a young girl she had carried a lantern which was extinguished by the wind and, in answer to prayer, re-lit by divine power. Although known for years as the church of Ste. Gudule, it is now dedicated to St. Michael, and only recently became a cathedral (on the creation of the See of Mechelen-Brussels).

The church itself was begun in 1226, and there is 13th-century work (restored in the 19th century) in parts of the nave and choir. You will find a beautiful statue of the saint as Guardian of the City, but the chief treasure of the church is its stained-glass, designed by Bernard van Orley, early 16th-century painter at the court of Margaret of Austria, regent of the Lowlands during Charles Quint's infancy. Note in particular the two magnificent lights in the north and south transepts, and the windows in the Chapel of the Holy Sacrament showing the incidents connected with the Profanation of the Host, a Jewish-Christian episode of 1370 often used as a subject by Brussels artists. The chapel was in fact built in the 16th century to house the remains of the Host salvaged from its profaners. In summer, the great west window of the church is illuminated at night so that its colour values are strikingly apparent to people coming uphill into the Place Sainte Gudule.

On the north side of the church is the National Bank of Belgium. Again climbing the hill on this side, you emerge into the Rue Royale by the Column of the Congress commemorating the first National Assembly of independent Belgium in 1831. In front of it, flanked by two huge bronze lions, are the tombs of Belgium's Unknown Soldiers—one of the First World War and the other of the Second. The statue that crowns it is of Léopold I, the country's first king. Behind is the new Civil Service building (Cité Administrative), with a vast public terrace overlooking the lower town.

The Heart of the City

From here your way downhill is easily found, and you will be able to reach the Rue du Marais and the Rue aux Choux, to find the Place des Martyrs. This architecturally very attractive square is also a cemetery, since the Brussels citizens who lost their lives in expelling the Dutch in 1830 are buried here in a common grave. The monument is perhaps less worthy than the neo-classic square itself, which, despite its commercial importance, is curiously quiet and dignified.

Hence you emerge into the Rue Neuve, and a few yards to the right is the little Eglise du Finistère, a triumph of religion over circumstance: originally planned to be built from the proceeds of a lottery, the treasurer ran off with the funds. It houses the statue of *Our Lady of Good Success* (the *Aberdeen Madonna),* presented by Scottish Roman Catholics to the devout Infanta Isabella in 1625.

If you cross the Place de Brouckère diagonally and turn into the narrow busy streets behind Ste. Catherine's market, you will see on Place Sainte Catherine the Black Tower, part of the first fortifications of Brussels, dating from the mid-13th century, long before the fortified circle of the ring boulevard had defined the city's growth. This market quarter has existed since Brussels was founded.

Across the market square is the entrance to the Rue de Flandre. The side streets leading from it have a picturesqueness of their own. Wandering round to the right through the Marché-aux-Porcs and the Rue du Grand Hospice, another right turn takes you in front of the Eglise du Béguinage. This is all that is left of the Béguinage—hostel for the order of lay sisters named after the Liège monk, Lambert le Bègue (Lambert the Stammerer), who have been active since the 13th century. The 17th-century church is known as Brabant Baroque, a local version of the Italian form. It's furnishings are rich and there are paintings, carvings and a lovely ivory crucifix attributed to Duquesnoy.

Three Side Trips

There are three trips outside the center of Brussels which, if you have time, are worth the taking. The first is to Laeken, which can be reached by several tram routes. You can walk round the Royal domain (on some days in spring the greenhouses are open to the public) and see the Chinese Pavilion and Japanese Tower imported by King Léopold II from the Paris Exhibition of 1900, also the fine Neptune statue. The original (in Bologna) from which it was cast is by Giovanni da Bologna, who was of Flemish origin. Across the public park you will skirt the Atomium, with its nuclear museum, and arrive at the approaches to the Palais du Centenaire, site of the 1935 and 1958 Brussels World Fairs.

Another trip is a walk along the Rue de la Loi to a decorative archway (visible all the way), which is approached in the last lap through a small park and is in fact the Cinquantenaire Memorial. If you are driving, your route is along the (parallel) Rue Belliard and up to the left through a tunnel which emerges in the park. The buildings on either side house the Museum of Art and History and the Museum of the Army. The former is one of the richest and most complete in Europe and includes lace among its many collections. The latter, perhaps because of the amount of fighting that has taken place on Belgian soil at one time or another, also has a notable series of displays. From the Cinquantenaire Arch you can see the 13-storied building of the European Common Market on Place Schuman. It is shaped in the form of a cross and has over a thousand offices.

In Anderlecht you will find a colony of interest centered round the Church of Saint Peter and Saint Guidon. The latter is buried here and, as patron of farm animals, attracts devout throngs on given dates in spring and autumn. The lovely 15th-century church is marred by a hideous 19th-century spire, but its crypt, and the tomb of the saint, are of real interest. In the Rue du Chapelain, behind the church, is an old Béguinage (Begijnhof) dating from 1252. On the other side of the church is the Rue du Chapitre, where you will find (No. 31) the house where Erasmus, the great Dutch humanist and precursor of the Reformation, stayed when in Brussels in 1521. It is now a museum, highly evocative of the man. It's diamond-paned windows overlook a quiet walled garden and the library contains a fine collection of his works including *In Praise of Folly* in Latin, English and French, and a first edition with the date 1512 under its original title *Moriae Encomium*. Engravings show him on his many travels and in one he is having an animated talk with his great friend Sir Thomas More. Holbein's portrait of Erasmus hangs in the study and there are several other portraits of this unusual scholar.

Finally, after these town pilgrimages, it is good to know that it's only a 20-minute tram or bus ride to the Forêt de Soignes, via Ave. Louise to the gates of the Bois de la Cambre, a public park and forepart of the forest, with open-air cafés. Beyond this, the Drève de Lorraine plunges through the forest, the road running almost to Waterloo. On the fringe of the forest is the Boitsfort racecourse.

ENVIRONS OF BRUSSELS

Historic Places and Rural Calm

Excursions farther afield in the Brabant countryside are many. Brussels is one of the more fortunate capitals so far as the variety of its surroundings is concerned. Places of historic significance alternate with vast forests and sites of perfect rural peace. The size of Brussels presents no problem in getting out of the city, and good signposting will lead you on your way within a few minutes. An alternative to your car are the numerous Belgian Railways-operated buses and fast electric trains leaving the principal stations at reasonably short intervals.

Practical Information for Environs of Brussels

HOTELS AND RESTAURANTS. Most probably you will set up headquarters in Brussels and make an excursion or two into the Brabant countryside. If you want to put up at an hotel in the quiet green belt surrounding the capital, here are some addresses in attractive spots. There are too many restaurants and inns in the immediate vicinity of Brussels to be included in this list; we shall quote only a few selected ones. You can't go wrong by having a meal at the others.

Restaurants listed below are designated (E), (M), or (I)), for expensive, moderate, or inexpensive.

ASSE. Excellent lunch or dinner halt on the alternative road to Aalst: *Old Irish Inn* (M).

BEERSEL. Famous feudal castle. Restaurant: *Auberge du Chevalier* (M-E), medieval interior, highly atmospheric.

CHAUMONT-GISTOUX. Good weekend spot, 22 miles southeast of Brussels, beyond Wavre.

Hotels: best is *Auberge du Vieux Moulin,* small, moderate, good cuisine.

Two excellent restaurants: *Butte Chaumont* (M-E), and the somewhat cheaper *Moulin d'Inchebroux.*

ESSENE. Hotel: *Bellemolen,* 12 rooms, 9 with bath. Also has excellent restaurant (E). This is a converted 12th-cent. mill.

GENVAL. Charming lake. Hotels: *La Perle du Lac,* moderate, as is the *Argentine.* Both have good (M) restaurants. *Le Lido,* small, inexpensive.

Restaurants: *La Lagune* and *Chalet Normand,* both (M), good.

GROENENDAAL. Hotels: *Château de Groenendaal,* 7 rooms, first class reasonable, with topnotch restaurant (E) for gourmet dining.

Restaurants: *Romeyer* (E), outstanding; *La Père Mouillard* is justly famous though (M); Nearby *Tissens* is less expensive.

HOEILAART, in the Forêt de Soignes.

Restaurants: *Victoria* and *Fol Atre,* both (M).

HUIZINGEN. Hotel: Has 18th-cent. moated manor, converted into hotel. Vast park, small zoo, playing fields, swimming pool: *Domaine Provincial,* 20 rooms, moderate.

ITTRE. Hotel: *Hostellerie d'Arbois* (7 rooms) moderate.

MEISE. Ten miles from the city center, along the Brussels-Antwerp highway.

Restaurant: *Auberge Napoléon* (M), highly atmospheric.

NIVELLES. Historic city, full of good eating places. Hotels: *Aigle Noir,* small, moderate, good cuisine. *France,* inexpensive.

Restaurants: *Pascall* (M), prepares in season grouse in wine sauce: *La Gueulardière,* out of town on La Louvière road. Can be expensive; cooking superb. *Restaurant de la Collégiale* (M), noted for first class cuisine, pleasantly individual.

NOTRE DAME AU BOIS (Jezus Eik), 8 miles to southeast, on old Namur road. Restaurants: *Barbizon* (E), elegant, excellent. *Auberge Bretonne* (M).

TERVUREN. Hotels: *Beausoleil,* 18 rooms, half with bath, first class reasonable. *La Vignette,* Chaussée de Louvain, moderate.

TIENEN (TIRLEMONT). Hotel: *Monty,* Grand' Place, is good, inexpensive.

Restaurants: *Normandy* (M), on Grand' Place.

In the station square, *Nouveau Monde* (E), small, prepares delicious food: in season, woodcock (bécasse fine champagne).

VILLERS-LA-VILLE. *Restaurant des Ruines* (M).

WATERLOO. Hotel: *The Wellington,* near the Lion Monument, is inexpensive.

Restaurants: *Le Bivouac,* near Waterloo Lion. Historic setting, and grills on open fireplace. *Solarium Rossome,* fine swimming pool; on the Charleroi road. On the same side, *Auberge du Caillou,* converted farmhouse, next door to Napoleonic Museum, emperor's former H.Q. Specialty: Flaming kidney (rognons de mouton flambés). All (M).

At Plancenoit (road to Charleroi), *Auberge Plancenoit* (M).

WAVRE. Hotel: *Marchal,* 15 rooms, moderate.

Camping sites in this area are located at Beersel, Braine-l'Alleud, Evere, Huizingen, and Uccle ("Camping Europa" Ave. Carsoel), among many others.

MUSEUMS AND CASTLES. At **Beersel;** the *Castle* is open daily 10-6, from Mar. 1-Oct. 31; Nov. 1-Feb. 28 on Sat. and Sun. only, 2-5. At **Gaasbeek,** the *Castle,* home of the counts of Egmont, open Easter-Nov. 1 from 10-5 on Tues., Thurs., Sat., Sun. At **Nivelles,** the *Archeological and Folklore Museum,* closed Tues. At **Tervuren,** *the Central Africa Museum* contains collections from the Congo, open daily 9-5. At **Waterloo,** the *Wellington Museum,* open 10-12 and 2-7, except Mon; in winter, 4-6 only; *Battle Panorama,* near Lion Monument, open all year; *Musée du Caillou* (Napoleon's headquarters), on the Charleroi road, houses relics of historic interest; open 9-7 in summer, closes at 5 in winter and Tues.

Exploring the Environs of Brussels

Here are some of the interesting places you might visit in the Brabant countryside:

Hoeilaart-Overijse: You can reach Hoeilaart by train from the Gare de Luxembourg, or a good walk across the Forêt de Soignes will bring you into this fantastic capital of the glasshouse industry, which has 30,000 hothouses and boasts that it can produce you a bunch of grapes fit for the table on each day of the year. There is a "Grape Fair" every year, in August at Overijse, end-September at Hoeilaart. A bare 8 miles south of Brussels.

On the Charleroi Road

Bois de la Cambre—Forêt de Soignes: A delightful drive that takes you 10 miles or so to the southeast. This is the Bois de Boulogne of Brussels, studded with super-smart restaurants and modest inns. You can picnic here, under the centuries-old trees.

Waterloo Battlefield: Twelve miles to the south. Reached by the local "W" bus. Most tourists content themselves with climbing the lion memorial, which almost obliterates the battlefield. Nearby, a panorama gives you a tabloid idea of the battle, but you may grasp more of the tactics from the cinema reconstruction (opposite). To get a real knowledge of the battle, study the excellent phase-maps recently installed in Wellington's Headquarters in Waterloo, now a museum. Hougoumont farm is still privately owned, but you can visit the tiny mutilated chapel where the British wounded were brought. Inside its simple, whitewashed interior, you can still see the wooden statue of Christ against which the flames miraculously died when the French tried to set it on fire. Another farm, Le Caillou, has been transformed into an interesting museum. It is said that Napoleon spent a restless night there, before the battle.

In 1973 preservationists won a new battle at Waterloo. A motorway was to have passed a mere 15 feet away from Mont St. Jean farm which was used as a field hospital for British wounded during the famous battle. It will now be some 45 feet distant.

Genval: Thirteen miles to the southeast, between Waterloo and Wavre. There is a charming lake, several hotels, and a dozen lakeside restaurants. Overcrowded on Sundays.

Villers-la-Ville: Twenty-five miles southeast of Brussels. Best reached by road through Waterloo and Genappe. By train about 20 minutes from Ottignies. Quite astonishing remains of 12th-century Cistercian abbey. Also restored 10th-century church and a castle. Five miles away, at Gentinnes, is the memorial shrine to the missionary martyrs of the Congo, erected in 1967. It draws 50,000 pilgrims and visitors each year.

On the Ghent Road

At *Groot Bijgaarden,* five miles out of town on the Ghent motorway, is Grand-Bigard Castle, which dates back to the Frankish period, although its recorded history begins with Almeric de Bigard in 1100 and ends with the pillaging of the French Revolution. Its vestiges span several centuries. The manor house itself, with its long rows of windows and dormers is a good example of Brabantian 17th-century architecture, reminiscent of the French Louis XIII style. The entry-way, with its twin towers, and the moat covered with water lilies have a romantic air, and the interior decoration of the château in general is remarkably well preserved.

Asse, Hekelgem: You will pass through Asse as the first major town on the old road from Brussels to Ghent, which runs parallel to the Brussels-Ostend highway. The town, which lay on an important Roman road was, as late as 1829, the starting point for as many as 35 stage coaches per day. The church, which has a tower going back to the 13th century, contains one or two rather important paintings, including those by Otto Venius and the younger Breughel. A little farther on is Hekelgem, where several of the cafés proclaim *Zandtapijten* (sand carpets). These are well worth stopping to see. You pass into the back parlour of one of the cafés, where you find an artist busy preparing a picture with saucers of coloured sand. This is an art of the people, and its foremost representative, Roger de Boeck, was a few years ago invited to Florida to teach the technique. Unfortunately the motorway has resulted in so much traffic, with visitors bypassing Hekelgem, that it has lost some of its character as the center of this art.

Along the Mons Road

Beersel: Only six miles south of the capital. This 13th-century beautiful castle is surrounded by water-filled moats and is worth a visit in itself. During the summer, Shakespeare and outdoor folklore plays are given there. Nearby is the attractive 230-acre domain of Huizingen, where you can indulge in various sports. There is a restaurant, too.

Gaasbeek: Off the road to Mons, 8 miles out. Turn right while in the suburb of Anderlecht, or farther on where signposted. A castle of real historic and artistic interest, dating back many centuries. It has all the panoply of medieval gracious living: superb carved furniture, tapestries, and paintings. The rooms are so well arranged that you have the feeling people still live there. A copper-gilt icon, a gift from the Grand Duchess Marie of Russia, hangs in Count Jean Arrivabene's bedroom. In the richly panelled large gallery a 15th-century silver reliquary head of Isabella of Castille and some repoussé and engraved silver-gilt salvers and ewers are among the numerous objects d'art. Before each guided tour there is an eight minute introductory talk in a choice of 4 languages with projection of coloured slides. If some of the landscapes look familiar, it's because Breughel painted many scenes from here.

Hal (Halle): Ten miles to the southwest and on the Mons road. This curious town is devoted to the cult of the Virgin Mary, and there are processions of great devotion at Whitsun and early in September. The church, though nominally dedicated to Saint Martin, is known as Notre Dame because of the miracle-working statue, *La Vierge Noire,* which, according to the legend, played an active part in the defence of the town against the siege by Philip of Cleves. The church itself is especially interesting, not only as a comparatively unspoilt piece of 14th-century work, but because the sculpture gives an adequate show of the development of this art in the 13th-15th centuries. This is the more important for the student, because the triforium statues from the school of Claus Sluter will give him an idea of the work of this master whose own work, for the most part, contributed to the establishments of the dukes of Burgundy at Dijon. The font is a specially good example of Tournai (as opposed to Meuse-side) brassware, dated 1446, by Lefebvre; and the high altar is the only signed and recorded work of Jan Mone (1533), one of the few major works in Belgium to have caught the spirit of the Renaissance.

Hal was the birthplace of Adrien Servais, the master violin-cellist, and at his house here the guests included Liszt, Berlioz, Rubinstein, and even La Malibran, greatest operatic prima donna of the last century.

Braine-le-Château: Taking a southeastward byroad from Hal, you come to the little township of Braine-le-Château nestling in a hollow of the rolling country. This is the domain of the counts of Hornes, whose moated manor is here. The chief object of interest is the rather original pillory, set up by the count of the day in 1521. It is an unconventional design, consisting of a small caged platform mounted on a pillar, the cage being beautifully ornamented for a pillar of penance. Here, too, in a water mill seven centuries old, is an interesting Mill Museum (Musée de la Meunerie).

From Nivelles to Tienen

Nivelles: The same byroad brings you down to Nivelles, on the main road from Brussels to Thuin. The damage done to this town during World War II was a major tragedy. It included a fire that melted down all but a small part of the famous reliquary of Saint Gertrude. Still more, it destroyed hundreds of ancient dwellings, the Hôtel de Ville and, with it, the four town giants: Argayon, Argayone, Lola, and their horse Godet. These eminent citizens were, in their lifetime, privileged to follow the wholly devout procession of "Madame Sainte Gertrude", whose remains were annually taken from the reliquary and led on an 8-mile pilgrimage across fields and meadows. Saint Gertrude was a daughter of Pepin de Landen, great-grandfather of Charlemagne. She was born in Nivelles, and here she founded her abbey with becoming splendor, and it became one of the richest and most powerful in Christendom. The canonesses were carefully chosen as being "of good lineage and nation", a family tree of four quarterings on both the spear and distaff side being draconically demanded. These "white-surpliced young ladies" seem to have led a life of some luxury, under a regime that did not prohibit their visits to their homes and countries. It is, or till 1940 was, recorded on the tombstone of one of them, who died in 1558 in her 28th year as provost of the college, that "she lived decently and died virtuously; in paradise God owes her room and a seat."

The glory which had lasted a full thousand years had already gone out of Nivelles before the destruction of 1940. Bombs made away with much that was interesting and exciting in the town, but they left the lovely Romanesque cloister and much of the fabric and furnishings of the church. You can still admire the pulpits by Laurent Delvaux, a Nivelles man of the local woodworking revival of the 18th century who, in common with his pupil, Philippe Lelievre, achieved great renown. Nevertheless, you would scarcely suppose from the looks of the town today that an emperor (Henry III) attended the consecration of the church (1046), or that he would have written of the townsmen as "these fierce and hard-headed men of Nivelles, enraged by the nearness of the indomitable French."

The town has contributed much to the history of the arts. Jehan le Nivellois was the 12th-century troubadour and poet of the

Vengeance of Alexander; Gerard de Nivelles painted at Dijon for Philip the Brave, first of the Dukes of Burgundy; Jan Tinctoris, one of the first systematic explorers of counterpoint, and master-musician to the king of Naples in 1480, was a Nivelles man; and in the late 13th century, it was a Nivelles silversmith who worked with others from Douai and Anchin to break away from the Meuse-side tradition in the design of Saint Gertrude's reliquary.

Work is under way to restore the remains of Merovingian and Carolingian churches discovered after the town's bombing and during subsequent excavations after the war.

Chaumont-Gistoux: An enchanting commuters' countryside, with a 12th-century church, southeast of Wavre. Surrounding fir woods with pleasant walks. Several good hotels.

Wavre and Jodoigne: You reach Wavre from Nivelles through Genappe and Court-St.-Etienne with its 17th-century treasures. There is little enough to see in Wavre nowadays except the *Madonna of Peace and Concord* in the church at Basse-Wavre. It is the misfortune of Wavre, and the valley of the Dyle, to be always under fire when there is a war going on.

The road to Jodoigne leaves to the north Hamme-Mille, site of the ancient Valduc Castle of which there remains a farm and a mill. At Jodoigne you are in a hamlet of special interest to Welshmen because of the sojourns there of the Welsh Guards during World War II—an event which is commemorated by a tablet on the outer wall of the Hôtel de Ville under the shadow of the mighty lime that commemorates Belgium's independence. Apart from the Cambrian souvenir, the main point of interest in Jodoigne is the reliquary in the 12th-century Church of the Knights Templar, said to contain the jawbone of Saint Médard. This saint occupies in Belgium a position similar to Saint Swithin in England, in that rain on his day (June 8) is, according to tradition, followed by 40 more rainy days: a belief that leads to an agricultural-religious observance on the eve of the day in question.

Tienen (Tirlemont): Tienen, which you reach from Jodoigne through Hoegaarden, with its rival churches and its white beer, is another departed glory. It was a tourist town when it formed a stage on the Roman road that through the Middle Ages linked Cologne and Maastricht with the sea at the fabulously prosperous city of Bruges. It is known as the "White City", to commemorate the limewash which was one of the precautions taken during a cholera plague that once swept the area. The old glory of Tienen has given place to another, for it is now the capital of the sugar industry, as sugar beet has been grown on a large scale in Belgium since the continental blockade of the Napoleonic Wars. The

Church of Notre-Dame-au-Lac is more interesting outside than in, especially for the sculptured portal by Jean d'Oisy (1360).

Hakendover is three miles from Tienen on the road to Sint Truiden. It has a curious legend of three Frankish virgins who hired 12 workmen to build the church, duly meted out 12 pay-packets but always found there were 13 workers on the job. The site of the church had been miraculously revealed to them on the 13th night after Epiphany; and on this night there is nowadays the procession that honors the 13th worker, a procession that gets under way with prayers in the winter midnight and does not end till the hour appointed for the first Mass. The legend is fully illustrated in a remarkable carved reredos dating from 1430. The town has another procession, of a less religious kind, on Easter Monday. The participants come on horseback, and the cortege proceeds over the fields around the town, the field which is most trampled being that which will yield most abundantly at the coming harvest.

The Art City of Zoutleeuw

From Hakendover it is worth going a little farther on the Sint Truiden road before turning north to *Zoutleeuw* (or Léau), which lies near the farthest eastern boundary of Brabant province. This is another town that is no longer what it was, for in the 13th century it had a direct water route to Antwerp, which it fed with cloth as a part of the early competition against the Flemish cloth carried overseas from Bruges.

Zoutleeuw has a Hôtel de Ville carrying the arms of the empire, a building due to no less an architect than Rombaut Keldermans. Its greatest treasures, however, are in the Church of Saint Leonard, a building dating back to the 13th century and altogether out of proportion to the township's present population of only some 2,000 souls. All the more fashionable artists seem to have been commissioned, when the town was at its prime, to contribute to the decoration. Cornelis Floris made the 50-foot stone tabernacle in which the Gothic seems to be fading into the Italian style. Cornelis' brother Frans did the *Coronation of Christ* triptych, and Matthew de Layens one of the more heavily, though delicately, ornamental altarpieces. The great treasure, however, is the tall Pascal candlestick, by Renier de Tirlemont (1483), surmounted with its Crucifix around which are statues of the Madonna, Mary Magdalene and Saint John, and below which come the six branches of the candlestick supported by a wrought column on which there is an effigy of Saint Leonard. This is one of the finest pieces of brassware in Belgium. It came from Brussels, where

Renier was installed at the time, as did the gilded-wood reredos of Saint Leonard executed some five years earlier by Arnould to enshrine the painted and jewelled statue of the saint, which dates from about 1300.

Zoutleeuw shows little sign of eminent foreign residents or visitors, but it was one of the seven free towns of the Duchy of Brabant, and it has a 16th-century Renaissance Town Hall and a 14th-century Cloth Hall, now occupied by the local police.

On the Louvain Road

One of two roads from Brussels to Louvain (Leuven) continues through *Tervuren.* Follow route N. 3 to Tervuren, or take a No. 44 tram. The Central Africa Museum, beloved brain-child of King Léopold II in the days of colonialism, and today an active research center on African problems, is well worth visiting. There is a good swimming pool (Beausoleil). You should also visit the Bois des Capucins, vast and beautifully kept park, and admire the collection of tree species known as the Arboretum, covering 250 acres. The Ravenstein Golf Club's course is in the vicinity. Not more than a 30-minute ride from Brussels, exclusive and expensive.

CATHOLIC BASTIONS

Mechelen and Leuven

Two Flemish towns, though neither of them is in Flanders proper, are the centre of Belgium's Catholic faith today. Mechelen (Malines) lies in the province of Antwerp; and Leuven (Louvain) is in Brabant. The people of both towns speak Flemish, although French, as everywhere at a cultural level, has its due place in the Chapter at Mechelen and in the recently troubled Catholic University of Leuven.

On maps both cities have the look of fortresses, with their encircling boulevards that, in Leuven's case, mark the line of ancient fortifications. Leuven, indeed, has a military record of which to be proud. In 1925 it was decorated with the French *Croix de Guerre* at the hands of no less a hero than Marshal Foch and in the presence of Cardinal Mercier, the Cardinal-Archbishop of Mechelen, whose courageous attitude during World War I put to shame many self-conscious patriots.

Leuven was the domain of the dukes of Brabant. It grew around the fortress built by Arnold of Carinthia against the Normans, and it was in the 12th century that the Count of Louvain, Henry II, incorporated Brussels into his realm and took the title of Duke of Brabant. The town had the worst of the bargain after Duke Wenceslas' reprisals against the communal uprising led by Pieter Coutereel in the 14th century, when the nobles hid in the Hôtel de Ville and the populace threw them out upon the pikes of the mob below. Weavers (the town had a good business in the cloth trade) emigrated to England. Leuven fell out of consideration till the 15th century, when it was revived by the founding of the Catholic University, which is its chief glory today. This union of the Flemish element and the Catholic element is politically of the highest importance, and Leuven is now the nursery of much of the political and economic thought which governs the destiny of a country deeply Catholic at every level and predominantly Flemish.

Mechelen has two great names in its history. Besides Cardinal Mercier, there was, four centuries earlier, the court of Margaret of Austria. It was at Mechelen that this remarkable princess, as regent for her nephew (later to rule as Charles Quint), held her devout and cultured court. At 26 she was already twice a widow; having decided not to make a third attempt—after all, both she and her brother had been deprived of the throne of the newly united Spain, he by his own premature death and she by the death of her spouse—she was able to devote the whole of her thought and spirit to the affairs of the Low Countries. She it was who persuaded her father, Emperor Maximilian, into alliance with the Holy League against Louis XII and, having done so, saw that his forces and those of Henry VIII of England kept the Low Countries in a safe neutrality and even added to them the city of Tournai. Erasmus and Sir Thomas More visited her court, Michel Coxcie and the prolific Van Orley were among the painters who counted her as a patron; and her architect was Rombaut Keldermans, whose partnership with the younger De Waghemaker was to be so fruitful of results in Antwerp, Ghent, and Tongerloo.

Practical Information for Mechelen and Leuven Regions

WHEN TO COME? The usual tourist season, May through Sept., applies here. Not many special events are staged, but worth considering are: in Leuven, the festivities of the May Tree, early *June;* the Brabant Town's Day, early *September;* in Mechelen: the end-of-*May* farmers' pilgrimage to Onze Lieve Vrouw van Hanswijk is followed by carillon concerts from mid-*June* through *August* (Mon. at 8:30 p.m.).

HOW TO GET ABOUT? These two art cities are within a stone's-throw of Brussels and, in fact, constitute one big excursion from the capital, from which they are easily reached by good, paved roads and direct train service. Leuven may also be reached by direct trains from Ghent, Bruges, and Ostend; Mechelen from Ghent and Antwerp.

WHAT TO SEE? In **Mechelen:** St. Rombaut's Cathedral and carillon tower; Grote Markt; Begijnhof (Béguinage); St. John's Church with Rubens triptych; Palais de Justice. In **Leuven:** Stadhuis; St. Peter's Church with Thierry Bouts polyptych; Begijnhof, one of the largest and most important in the country, with 14th-cent. church; St. Gertrude's Abbey (open daily, except Tues., from 3 p.m.); Church, and 16th-cent. wine-press house (now a school for market gardening), on Wijnpersstraat; the late Gothic Van 't Sestich House and Baroque St. Michael's Church, both in Naamse Straat. The university library, with walls bearing the names of U.S. educational institutions which contributed to its reconstruction, is of special interest to American visitors.

HOTELS AND RESTAURANTS. Due perhaps to the proximity of Brussels and Antwerp, the region has relatively few hotels. There are several excellent restaurants.

KEERBERGEN is a good weekend spot, 20 miles from Brussels. Horseback riding in pinewoods.

Hotels: *Memling,* 10 rooms, is almost first class, some rooms with bath. A culinary specialty here is coucou de Malines à l'estragon. More modest establishments are: *Les Chanterelles,* 12 rooms, *Les Lierres,* and *Bois Fleuri* (closed Feb.), 8 rooms; tennis.

Two excellent restaurants: *Berkenhof* (with a few rooms), can be very expensive. On the road to Haecht, the *Paddock,* slightly cheaper.

KORTENBERG. Halfway between Leuven and Brussels. The *Hof te Linderghem* (E) invites the well-to-do motorist for a halt.

LEUVEN (LOUVAIN). Hotels: *Royale,* opposite station; 25 rooms, about half with bath, first class reasonable. Almost in the same class, *Majestic,* 14 rooms, some with showers. *Industrie,* in Royale's vicinity, also 14 rooms, but expensive. The adjoining *Aux Milles Colonnes,* is inexpensive but satisfactory.

At nearby Heverlee is the best of the Leuven hotels, *Hof Terbank,* 55 rooms with bath.

Restaurants: Leuven has more than a dozen restaurants, but none catering to the *fin gourmet* except at Heverlee, where the *Old Dutch* is first class. In town the best is *An de 7 Hoecken* (M to E), Layensplein, followed by *Maison des Brasseurs,* 1 Fochplein. For a simple meal, go to *Au Caveau,* 3 Layensplaats, or the big *Salons Georges.*

MECHELEN (MALINES). Hotels: *De Drie Paardekens* (Three Horses), 34 rooms, a few with bath. Its first class restaurant offers asparagus à la flamande (with butter sauce and crushed hardboiled egg). *Europe,* 10 rooms, some with bath, less expensive than the above, but both moderate. *Memling,* inexpensive, has 10 rooms. Its excellent restaurant keeps open until after midnight.

Restaurants: *Pekton* (M-E), 1 Van Beethovenstraat, excellent. Try peppered steak flambé fine champagne. *Bavaro* (M), Grote Markt, is excellent. *La Bécasse,* Medodestr., suits all pockets.

RIJMENAM, between Keerbergen and Mechelen, a good overnight stop when rooms are scarce in summer.

Hotel: *Bonten Os,* small but quite expensive, as is its restaurant. Remember that you are in asparargus country. (Season, May-June).

USEFUL ADDRESSES. City Tourist Offices: Town Hall, Mechelen; Stadhuis (Town Hall), Grote Markt, Leuven. *Camping sites:* Kessel-Lo, near Leuven, Hofstade and Hever, near Mechelen; also Aarschot and Kortenberg.

Exploring Mechelen

Mechelen, present population 70,000, was known to Margaret as the seat of the Grand Council, or Supreme Court of Justice, under the system created by her grandfather, Charles the Rash. The town itself, lying on the banks of the River Dyle, had been an appanage of the prince-bishops of Liège and a bargaining bait between the prince-bishops and the Berthout, the *sept* (7) in control of the free town lying on the left bank of the river. For a time Mechelen came under the See of Cambrai, and it was not until 1559 that it became an archbishopric.

You can look down from the heights of Saint Rombaut's tower over the white palace of the cardinal-archbishops and the dignified line of its trees in the refreshing green of its garden. Chiefly, however, you will have climbed the tower to see the bells and the manual of the *carillonneurs,* who carry on here the great tradition of Jef Denijn. It was in the last two decades of the 19th century that Denijn became conscious of the moribund tradition of the bells in the towers of Belgium, and set to work to create a musical idiom for this great art, to revive the craft and mystery of the *carillonneur* and, in short, to put belfries, and Belgian belfries most of all, firmly on the map. Denijn's life as a refugee during World War I gave him the chance to reawaken interest in bells —also in bell-founding—in other countries (notably at Loughborough and Croydon in England) and now there are carillons as far afield as Florida (Edward Bok's Singing Tower), New York (Riverside Church), Philadelphia, and Wellington (N.Z.) that owe much to his inspiration. Staf Nees worthily carried on the school (the only one in the world) founded by Denijn at the corner of Sint Janstraat and Mérodestraat; you will often find in the tower that the player is one of the school's young pupils, who has been through the arduous apprenticeship of the dummy keyboard.

The ancient art of tapestry weaving has pride of place among the surviving home-crafts in Mechelen. With improved methods and designs adapted to contemporary tastes, some firms not only weathered modern times, but made this art, applied to interior decoration, a paying proposition. The magnificent tapestry, offered by Belgium to the United Nations Building in New York was designed and executed in Mechelen.

Saint Rombaut's Cathedral

Half a millenium has passed since the raising of Saint Rombaut's tower, the work of Wauthier Coolmans in the 15th century. The original plans from which this structure was built are still in existence, so we know today, in spite of the lapse of five hundred years, how magnificent the tower would have been if it had risen to its full height. Even as it is, it is a fine example of late Gothic design. Parts of the cathedral church itself are in fact much older, dating back to the early 13th century. It contains the armorial bearings from a Chapter of the Golden Fleece held here in 1491, and also a Van Dyck *Crucifixion.*

The high altar is the work of Luc Fayd' Herbe in the 17th century, who was responsible for a good deal of work in his native town. He was a disciple of Rubens, and even if the Church of Onze Lieve Vrouw van Hanswijk is not an architectural masterpiece, there are highly original elements in its construction. The big high-reliefs inside the dome are also by Fayd' Herbe, and are in a class quite by themselves in Belgian decorative work, apart from that by the same hand in the Church of the Grand Begijnhof (Béguinage). Onze Lieve Vrouw van Hanswijk also contains a fine pulpit by another Mechelen craftsman, Theodore Verhaegen, but the confessionals by Boeckstuyns are half a century earlier.

The Grand Begijnhof itself, with its curious array of gables and turrets, is an interesting piece of 17th-century building. From here, passing the Church of Saint Catherine, you come to the museum of the archbishopric, which it is worth visiting if only for the sake of the souvenirs of Cardinal Mercier. The building itself is the former refuge of Tongerlo Abbey. It is not the only one of these abbatial refuge houses; that of the Abbey of Saint Trond lying as it does beside the Dyle, is one of the most charming sights in the town.

The Church of Saint John (St. Janskerk—closed between Easter and mid-September, call for doorman, from 2 to 4 p.m., at 57 Mérodestraat) contains on the high altar a triptych, an important work by Rubens, the *Adoration of the Magi,* and also some carving by Theodore Verhaegen. Mechelen has two other Rubens paintings, the more important of which is the *Miraculous Draft of Fishes,* in Onze Lieve Vrouw van Overdijl. The other is a *Crucifixion,* which you will find in the Busleyden Mansion (1503), now given over to the Communal Museum. This is a very absorbing small museum, and well worth an hour or two of your time.

The first courthouse of Charles the Rash's Grand Council was in the House of the Aldermen (Schepenhuis), separating the Grote Markt from the Square of the Iron Railings (IJzere Leen), beyond which, and past the houses reconstructed following the 1914-18 bombardments, you come to the 16th-century Fish Market building; thence to the Haverlei on the Dyle, where three very colourful houses of the same period are worth special attention. They are, in the usual way, named after the main features of their decoration. The corner building, known as Paradise because of the bas-reliefs of Adam and Eve, is specially characterized by the fine moldings in curve-patterns of a geometrical complexity (*anses de panier*), which was used in Mechelen in the late Gothic period but is not much found elsewhere in Flanders.

Go along the Haverlei, and to the left you will find the house of Beethoven's grandparents in the small street bearing this famous name. It is now used as a restaurant, the *Pekton*.

Walking up the Zoutwerf you come to a bridge, beyond which is the Botanical Garden, with its modern statue of the 16th-century botanist Dodoens, who was from Mechelen. On the farther side of the gardens you come, suitably enough, to the great present-day vegetable market. It is a forcible reminder that Mechelen is in the heart of the hard-working market-gardening country, which, founded as it largely is upon family enterprise, keeps Belgium so magnificently supplied with vegetables that she can afford to be choosy about the condition in which they come to market. Returning through the Botanical Gardens and turning right at the bridge, the street called Bruul takes you back to the Grote Markt past the Church of Onze Lieve Vrouw van Leliendal, a Baroque construction built for the Norbertines, another of the works of Luc Fayd' Herbe.

The old Stadhuis shows many signs of its patchwork history. It was begun in the early 14th century as a Cloth Hall, on the same lines as the belfry-topped market building at Bruges. The work was never finished, and two centuries later Charles Quint began its conversion into a palace, which was to be the seat of the Grand Council. The façade on the Befferstraat dates from this period, but once more the work hung fire, so that the building seems to taper into the Renaissance and shows little real unity, though the colonnaded street level is pleasing. Passing down Befferstraat, you come to another Baroque church, that of Saints Peter and Paul. Continuing to your right (Keizerstraat), you pass the theater, housed in the old building of the Imperial Court, opposite which is the Law Courts building.

The latter is perhaps the most interesting of the secular buildings in Mechelen, because it includes the most important contribution rendered by Rombaut Keldermans (though he also had a hand in the Stadhuis). The building was originally planned as a palace for Margaret of Austria, and she entrusted the work to Keldermans, who was responsible for the interior courtyard with its attractive galleries and porches. In 1517, however, Margaret imported the Savoyard architect, Guyot de Beauregard, who erected the façade on the Keizerstraat. This, with its dormers, its pediments, its balconies and gateways, is a Franco-Italian Renaissance achievement as different from Keldermans' late Gothic as chalk from cheese.

Three miles off, at Muizen, is the 90-acre Zoo, the estate of Planckendael, an outstanding collection where lions and bison live in semi-liberty. Open all the year round.

Exploring Leuven

Leuven (pop. 35,000) was more fortunate than Mechelen in its fine Stadhuis, the work of its own architectural master, Mathieu de Laeyens, who made a quick job of it by finishing it in 1459 after only 11 years work. If you know this astonishing building from photographs, you will be surprised to find that it is really life-size, for its crow's-nested pinnacles, its wealth of Gothic ornament, and its roof recall the art of the jeweller rather than the architect. The interior is less interesting than the exterior, though it contains some good 15th-century ceilings. The building itself, however, stands in the Grote Markt as a perpetual reminder to a religious people that miracles are not impossible. The miracle is not only in the building itself, but in the fact that it is still there after the vicissitudes of two world wars. The same could not be said of the Round Table building at the entrance to the same square, another de Laeyens masterpiece, which has, however, been restored.

The great Saint Peter's Church has the place of honor in the middle of the Grote Markt. Despite all that has been done, this fine edifice is little more than a memory. Mathieu de Laeyens had a hand in it and so, before him, had Sulpice van der Vorst from Diest, and Jan Keldermans, of the great Mechelen dynasty of architects. A shifting foundation led to the drastic shortening of the tower in the 17th century and the replacement of the spire by a cupola in the 18th. In 1914, cupola and roof were completely de- of houses in the town. The damage, in fact, proved repairable, but wanton burning of the city by the Germans in reprisal for the alleged firing of shots at the occupying Germans from the windows of houses in the town. The damage, in fact, proved repairable, but the bombardment of 1944 was more serious, and World War II left a large part of the church in ruins. It has now been repaired. In Saint Peter's you will find a remarkable polyptych, painted in 1464 by Thierry Bouts and representing the Last Supper.

A Great University

The important feature in Leuven, however, is always the Catholic University, which reached its apogee in the 16th century. It had among its alumni such men as Bishop Jansen of Ypres; Dodoens, the botanist of Mechelen; Mercator, the geographer; Erasmus; Juste Lipse (who was in the professoriate); and it housed the presses that first printed the *Utopia* of Sir Thomas More. There were some 50 colleges attached to the university at its most flourishing period, but the French suppressed the university altogether in 1797. Under the Dutch domination that followed the fall of Napoleon, William I founded here a Philosophical College, which was one of the grounds for protest by the clerical interests leading to the Belgian revolution of 1830. The bilingual university, in its present controversial form, dependent on the Catholic Church, was founded first at Mechelen in 1833, and transferred to Leuven two years later. Today it is one of the controlling influences in Belgian thought, especially in the politico-economic sciences, and its Board of Faculties is called upon to furnish the men who fill the highest places in public life. The buildings still surviving of colleges of the older university date mostly from the 18th century. They include the College of the Pope, the College of the King, that of the Premonstrants, of Viglius, Van Dalle (this dates from 1569), Arras, and the Haute Colline.

The fact that the Stadhuis escaped the 1914 fire was due to its occupation by the German staff, but the library of the university was less fortunate. Priceless manuscripts were lost with it, and the building opened in 1928 in the square named after Monsignor Ladeuze was the gift of American universities and was designed by the American architect, Whitney Warren. In 1940 it was again burned out and the Catholic University lost nearly a million volumes. Reconstruction proved possible, and has been completed; but libraries are more difficult to fill than to build, and the filling of the shelves is still going on.

It is difficult to do justice to the spirit of Leuven, which (like Oxford) has not escaped the inroads of modern industry, but in which the clerico-academic atmosphere still pervades the town and is obvious at the first contact. It is less in the buildings than in the spirit of the great Humanists that it holds treasures which will be dear to the human race as long as civilization survives. They have unfortunately suffered from the intolerances of the Belgian language disputes; but they are there all the same; and Ottignies, where the French-speaking faculties are being installed under the name of Louvain-la-Neuve, will have been the gainer.

Near the university is the Church of Saint Michael, a masterpiece of the Antwerp Jesuit, William Hessius, about 1666. This also suffered very badly in the 1944 bombardment, though a large part of the excellent 17th-century wood carving in the confessionals and the Communion rail was saved. This, however, is no consolation for the loss of the magnificent choir stalls in Saint Gertrude's Abbey, carved by Matthew de Wayer about 1543, and accounted the finest work of its type in Belgium. No amount of restoration, in the church and the Gothic cloisters, can replace a treasure of this kind.

Two churches that have been more fortunate are those of Saint Quentin and Saint James. The former contains early 13th-century work round the base of the tower, but the bulk of the church is the work of Mathieu de Laeyens in the Burgundy period. Nearby the Begijnhof, picturesque in itself and containing a church in very Brabançon style dating from 1305 and, rather surprisingly, containing some glass from about the same time, is now transformed into students' dormitories. Saint James's Church, which lies across the Dyle by the Brussels road, dates from a number of periods.

Outside Leuven, at Heverlee, a number of the University institutes are in less congested surroundings in the splendid park of the Renaissance-style Château d'Arenberg. At Heverlee, too, is the renowned Abbaye du Parc, founded in 1128, which may be visited by request.

Aarschot and Keerbergen

On the border of the Campine moorland country to the north-east lies Aarschot, sacked many times in its long history. The Church of Onze Lieve Vrouw has resisted the ravages of war, and its haughty, massive tower is visible from afar. It possesses a good Verhaegen painting, the *Disciples at Emmaus*. Asparagus is the livelihood of most of Aarschot's inhabitants—it is in Belgium that you should sample this delicacy—which they export all over Europe.

Keerbergen, with its dunes, pine woods, and heather has become lately a favourite weekend haunt of tired business executives. From there the road back to Brussels leads you through Haacht and along the side of Brussels airport. Just before reaching the latter, you cross the road from Waterloo to Mechelen. Along this, to the right, is Elewijt Castle, which belonged to Rubens and is now used for temporary exhibitions. Further on is the big pleasure-garden of Hofstade with its 70-acre lake, a favorite with the Brussels working classes.

ANTWERP

Commerce, Diamond Cutting and Art Collections

Wherever you go in Belgium, you cannot avoid being conscious of Antwerp. The mighty port has collected round itself so much of the commercial power of the country that it has become a great economic—and thus in large measure political—force. It is a large (pop. 650,000) and wealthy city, with a long history, but it did not establish its definite ascendancy until the silting up of the Zwin in the 15th century closed the seaport activities of Bruges. The prosperity of Antwerp has not been continuous, but she has had periods of such wealth and such cultural ascendancy that the traces of them are abundant; and she retains her port, and her vital diamond-cutting industry, source of a prosperity that never wholly deserts her, even in hard times.

Legend links Antwerp with a giant who would fling into the Schelde (Scheldt) the severed hands (*handwerpen)* of mariners who refused to pay his tolls. Two statues, indeed, commemorate his having suffered a like fate at the hands of the Roman soldier Salvius Brabo; but even the older one dates back less than four centuries, and scholars insist the city's name is less colorfully explained. In olden times the merchant brigantines could sail up into the central town which, therefore, was located "on the wharf" (*an het werp*).

Antwerp's Variegated History

Authenticated history begins in the 7th century, when Saint Eloi (best remembered in the early history of Bruges) and Saint Amand (who founded the two abbeys which were the beginning of Ghent) were joined by the Irish Saint Dymphne (whom we shall meet again at Geel) in their missionary work.

The Norsemen, of course, played havoc with the early civilization, but in the 11th century Antwerp was a marquisate belonging to the De Bouillon family from the south of Belgium, and during the 12th century Saint Norbert re-established doctrinal orthodoxy after Godfrey the Bearded had banished the heretic Tanchelin. After the marquisate passed to the dukes of Brabant, Antwerp was caught in the meshes of the anti-French policy of Edward III of England and, though this promised well for a time, Bruges got the best end of the bargain. This was confirmed when the astute Louis de Male, last of the counts of Flanders before the great dynasty of Burgundy, received the marquisate of Antwerp in fee (1357).

By the end of the 15th century, the strife between Bruges and Antwerp reached its crisis. Then it was the men of Bruges who struggled to re-establish their fortunes by holding Maximilian—Regent (or Mambour) of Flanders since the death of Mary of Burgundy—as a prisoner and hostage. He bought his escape by promises he had no intention of keeping, and proceeded to revenge himself on Bruges by giving more and more privileges to Antwerp, including the monopoly in alum and spices.

Thus began a period in which the power and commerce of Antwerp expanded rapidly. The Italians and Germans set up their trade from the port, leaving Bruges little beyond the Spanish wool monopoly. A commercial exchange had been founded in 1460, and Sir Thomas Gresham was so impressed that he took the idea back to London, which led to the founding of the Royal Exchange. The banking princes of Germany and Italy—the Fuggers, the Osteters, the Gualterottis, and others—set up their counting houses in Antwerp.

Following Amsterdam's example, Antwerp joined the powerful Hanseatic League that controlled the North Sea and the Baltic. With the arts also flourishing (this was the period of Quentin Metsys, Cornelis Floris and the younger De Waghemaker), Antwerp was already a city of world renown before the religious troubles began and vessels lay in the Schelde filled with the church statues and decorations saved from the iconoclasts. In the "Spanish Fury" (1576), more than 7,000 citizens were butchered by the

Spanish in a single night. Antwerp was the last citadel, and indeed the symbol, of resistance in Belgian territory to the Inquisition; and, when the defenses of Burgomaster Philippe de Marnix collapsed before the besieging armies of Italian general Allessandro Farnese, in the service of Philip II, that resistance ended (1585).

This sealed off a line of demarcation between what is now Belgium and the United Provinces (which became the Netherlands of today); it also brought Antwerp onto the Belgian side of the line, which is logical enough in view of the territory through which the Schelde flows, though it left the Dutch in control of the estuary. This was to have important consequences later. Meanwhile the ground was prepared for Antwerp's greatest period, the beginning of the 17th century, the reign of Albert and Isabella, the period of Rubens and his coterie, of Artus Quellin, Jacob Jordaens, Adriaen Brouwer, and Van Dyck. This was the time when Antwerp had the chance of building and decorating, possessed the money to do it, and had at hand the great artistic means by which it could be done. It is for this reason that much of Antwerp's architecture is colored by the rather heavy Baroque tendencies of the time.

Meantime, however, disaster was in store. While Belgian resistance to the Inquisition had collapsed, that in the Netherlands lived on, and the countrymen of William the Silent had their say in the framing of the Treaty of Munster (1648). Dutch ascendancy now reached its peak, through the final and definite closing of the Schelde. Trading from Antwerp became impossible, at the behest of the rich merchants of Amsterdam; and it was small consolation to the men of Antwerp that the Dutch had strengthened their position also against Bruges by closing what was left of the Zwin.

There followed nearly two hundred years of oblivion. There was indeed a period of hope when the French Revolutionary Convention reopened the Schelde in 1795, and later when Napoleon enlarged the port and built a naval arsenal as part of his campaign against England. The chance of a peaceful enjoyment of these benefits, however, came to very little owing to Belgium's incorporation in the Netherlands after 1815. After the Belgian revolution, so keen were the Dutch on maintaining their hold over Antwerp that they had to be turned out by force from the citadel (whence they had bombarded the town) by the French in 1832.

Since then Antwerp has been the chief port, and the second city of the Belgian kingdom. For a time in 1914 it was the seat of the government, then fell to the Germans after a short but intensive siege. In World War II it suffered most heavily after its liberation, when it was a constant target for V-1 and V-2 rocket attacks;

Although Belgian handmade lace is prized all over the world, few of the present generation are learning the art. The nimble fingers of this lace-maker from Bruges work the wooden bobbins according to age-old tradition.

Vital to the livelihood of countryside and city are the waterways of Flanders, flowing past an ancient windmill that looms from the level plain (above) or past medieval houses that line Ghent's busy Graslei.

some 20,000 buildings were destroyed or badly damaged and almost 3,000 civilians killed. Now, it is one of the water gateways to Europe, with its immense port installations, its pride in the quick turn-round of ships, and its diversified modern industries.

Modern Antwerp

In the past few years Antwerp has donned a new skin. The port has been pushed eight miles downstream to the new lock—the world's biggest—at Zandvliet. Big ships (though not supertankers) can now enter. Enormous tracts of land have been developed for industrial use and eagerly snapped up. As a motor assembly center, Antwerp's standing has greatly increased through the big second plant opened by General Motors and by the Ford tractor operation; and, based on the refineries, there is now a thriving petrochemical industry in which nearly all the great world companies in chemicals have important stakes. These huge investments, which have drawn most of the big American banks to open branches in the city, are now coming to fruition. Behind and among the romance of the port and the dignity of ancient buildings, Antwerp has become a boom town.

So great has been the expansion that Antwerp has spilled over from the right bank of the Schelde to the left, where great American and Canadian companies have set up production units. The development is mainly industrial and suburban and will soon lead to further port expansion; but meantime it has raised a communications problem. The brilliant solution is the Kennedy tunnel, opened in 1969, constructed by Swedish and Belgian engineers for both rail and road traffic. The five great concrete sections were pre-fabricated in a special dry dock on the left bank, towed to their sites, sunk into the river bed and joined up by a series of techniques never applied before and completing, incidentally, the motor highway between Antwerp and Ghent. The tunnel is a great monument to a great present, and no visit to Antwerp is complete without the sight of it.

Practical Information for Antwerp

WHEN TO COME? Subject to the whims of Belgian weather, all seasons of the year are suitable for a visit to this beautiful and stimulating city, giving natural preference to the summer months, when boat trips on the river and to Dutch Zeeland are more enjoyable, and when you can alternate sightseeing with an afternoon on the beach.

WHAT TO SEE? Antwerp is a notable art and museum city (see "Museums" below) and one of the largest ports in the world; its bustle and up-to-date installations are, without any doubt, one of its main attractions. You can take a roundtrip either in one of the *Flandria* excursion boats (which are allowed to enter the docks), or in a motorboat. The principal embarkation point is at the Steen.

A cruise to the mouth of the River Schelde and the Dutch "island" of Walcheren by fast pleasureboat is a unique experience. You'll have a wonderful time at little cost visiting one of the picturesque towns on the island: Vlissingen (Flushing) or Middelburg. On your outward journey you will notice that the *polders* are well below water level. On your return trip you will be impressed by the ancient city's skyline, dominated by the elegant tower of its cathedral.

Industrial visits: Modern industrial achievement can be studied in industrial visits to the General Motors (assembly), Ford Motors (tractor parts and assembly) and Chrysler (assembly) plants and, near Antwerp, in the Alto cigar factory at Turnhout, the Campine Foundry and the Egamo furniture factory at Herentals. Group visits are possible to a number of other establishments, including the SIBP refinery (Petrofina and BP) in the Kruisschans area of the port, Van Genechten (playing cards) and Anco (flour and cattle fodder) plants at Turnhout and the Materne (now controlled by W. R. Grace Inc.) canning and deep refrigeration unit at Grobbendonk. In all cases you must write or phone for an appointment some days ahead.

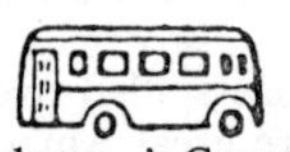

HOW TO GET ABOUT? The *Vicinaux,* narrow-gauge, long-distance tramcars have mostly been replaced by buses (terminal station, Roosevelt Plaats). They travel to such excursion spots as the picture-book town of Lier (Lierre), Schoten, 's-Gravenwezel, Brasschaat, and Lillo. Taxis are plentiful and all fitted with meters. Trips on the river Schelde or visits to the port can be made by the *Flandria,* at the Steen landing. (Dep. 10 a.m. and 2 p.m.).

MOTORING. The E3 motorway, which will eventually connect Stockholm with Lisbon, passes through Antwerp (this section was finished in 1971). Thus motorists using the circular road bypass the town center and reach the various highways leading out of Antwerp within a few minutes. On the Ghent route, the E3 passes through the J. F. Kennedy Tunnel under the Schelde. The old, more northerly tunnel, is now solely for car traffic to the far river bank.

SPORTS. The majestic Schelde estuary is a "natural" for the numerous clubs devoted to all sorts of water sport. *Yachting* is practised by the Royal Yacht Club of Belgium, 133 Thonetlaan; the Royal Sport Nautique, 29 Beatrijslaan, and the Liberty Yacht Club, 131 Thonetlaan (all on the left bank). Royal Antwerp Rowing Club, 84 Stokerijstraat and Antwerp Sculling Club at Wijnegem are the leading *rowing* clubs. Devotees of *water-skiing* should get in touch with Antwerp Waterski Club at 96 Elisabethlaan, Berchem, or Skianna Waterski Club, 6 Pothoekstraat. For *canoeing* fans, Red Star Canoe Club has its premises on the left bank of the river, at Antwerpen-Plage.

You can *swim* at several open-air establishments, such as Noordkasteel-Oost, or at St. Anne's Beach (Antwerp's Coney Island), reached by motorboat, by the excursion boat *Flandria,* or by bus from the Central Station. By car, through the Schelde tunnel. *Camping* at St. Anne's Beach (left bank), and at Le Grellelaan (near Wezenberg swimming pool).

From early Sept. through May you can cheer your favorites at *soccer* each Sunday afternoon at the home grounds of the leading Antwerp clubs: Beerschot F.C., De Geyterstraat; Antwerp F.C., Deurne Stadium; Berchem Sport, Stadionstraat.

INTERESTING BUILDINGS. The *Vleeshuis* (Butchers' Corporation), Vleeshouwerstraat, not far from the Steen, is a Gothic palace, built early in the 16th century by De Waghemaker; sumptuous assembly hall and a museum of applied arts. The *Brouwershuis* (Brewers' Corporation) 20 Brouwerstraat, of the same period. The council chamber is another example of opulent Antwerp decorative art. Its hydraulic installation provided local breweries with water; the distributive mechanism is still visible. Both buildings open daily, 10-5, except Mon. (Winter 10-4).

Town Hall and Guild Houses, Grote Markt. Gothic and Flemish Renaissance.

Oude Beurs (Commercial Exchange), 15 Hofstraat, near Grote Markt. Observe interior court and watchtower. Erected 1515.

Rockox Mansion, 10 Keizerstraat. Patrician mansion of Burgomaster Rockox, Rubens' intimate friend. Open daily, 10-6

The finest 18th-cent. buildings are the *King's Palace* and the *Osterrieth Mansion,* both in the Meir.

Among the modern edifices the *Torengebouw,* Antwerp's skyscraper and TV station, offers a fine panorama of the city from the 24th floor.

All notable churches are described in the main text. They can be visited in the morning, but access to the cathedral is in the afternoon.

MUSEUMS. The most representative collection among Antwerp's rich art museums is the *Museum voor Schone Kunsten* (Fine Arts Museum), Léopold de Waelplaats. Built in neo-classic style at the turn of the century, it houses on the first floor over a thousand works of old masters, mostly Flemish; but the Italian, French, Dutch, and German schools are also well represented. The ground floor contains paintings and sculptures of the 19th century and contemporary works, mostly by Belgians.

Most Antwerp museums close Jan. 1 and 2, May 1, Ascension Day, Nov. 1 and 2, Dec. 25 and 26. Unless otherwise stated, they open 10-5 daily (winter 10-4), but check locally.

The *Rubens House* is off Meir, at 9 Rubensstraat. The great master provided the plans for this opulent patrician dwelling, erected in 1610. Entrance and studio are in Italian Renaissance style, living quarters in the Flemish style of the period. The garden is a period piece. Paintings by Rubens and his pupils.

Plantin-Moretus Museum, 22 Vrijdagmarkt. An enchanting 16th-cent. patrician house with some later additions. The greatest and best equipped printing shop of the times, almost intact. Priceless manuscripts, first editions, engravings. Antique furniture and paintings (no less than 18 Rubens). Closed Mon.

Prentencabinet (Museum of Old Prints), next door to Plantin-Moretus Museum. Visits on request.

The *Mayer van den Bergh Museum,* 19 Lange Gasthuisstr.; works by Flemish masters Breughel the Elder, Jordaens, etc.; sculptures, fine furniture, china, and old lace. Open even-number days.

Smidt van Gelder Museum, 91 Belgiëlei. An 18th-cent. palace, beautifully furnished. Vast collections of China (Sèvres, Saxe, and Oriental). Open odd-number days.

Open-Air Museum of Sculpture, Middelheim Park. Over 200 sculptures by Rodin, Maillol, Zadkine, Moore, Gargallo, Meunier, and others. Open daily 10 a.m. to sunset. June-Sept.; odd-number years, there is an international Sculpture Exhibition.

Marine Museum (Steen). A 13th-cent. fragment of the city's fortifications, rebuilt under Charles Quint.

Old maps, navigation instruments, models of ancient ships, etc. Closed Mon.

Maagdenhuis, 33 Lange Gasthuisstr., a 16th-cent. girls' orphanage. Contains a small collection of paintings, furnitiure, 16th-cent. Antwerp ceramics, and household utensils of the period. Open daily except Sun. 8:30-4.

Museum of Regional Ethnology, 2-6 Gildekammerstr. (behind the Town Hall-Stadhuis), Flemish folklore collection. Closed Mon.

HOTELS. Antwerp hotels are less numerous, less luxurious, and, in corresponding categories, less expensive than those in Brussels. With very few exceptions, all have restaurants. Whether you stay at a superior or inexpensive establishment, you will be well looked after as a rule.

Quality Inns, with some 90 single rooms, should be open by the time this goes to press.

The *Plaza,* Charlottelei, is deluxe, 75 rooms, with all amenities. *Waldorf,* recent, Belgielei 36, 100 rooms with bath. The *Novotel*, 121 rooms, recent, is situated near the exit of the E 10 autoroute. *Eurotel*, 354 rooms, is in the business center.

First class superior: The modern *De Keyser* and older *Century,* 220 rooms with bath and a gourmet restaurant, are both on the Keyserlei, near station. The *Excelsior,* most rooms with bath, is connected by tunnel with the Century, but is not in quite the same class.

Others are the *City Park*, Plantin en Moretuslei 8, *Empire*, Appelmansstr. 31, *Theater*, Arenbergstr. 30, and *Congress*. All have comfortable rooms with TV, radio, frigobar; restaurants.

Recent are *Drugstore Inn,* Astridplein 43, small; and *Columbus,* Frankrijklei 4.

First class reasonable: Best are *Nautilus,* Scheldelaan, overlooking river, 20 rooms, huge restaurant; and *Waldorf,* Belgiëlei 36, 42 rooms, 26 with bath. *Tourist,* in Pelikaanstraat, has 146 rooms, most with bath, reasonable restaurant. *Terminus,* Rooseveltplein, 40 rooms.

The *Rivierenhof,* at Deurne, is a former château, in a beautiful park; only 15 rooms; tennis.

Moderate: *Billard Palace,* Astridplein 40, 70 rooms.

Inexpensive: *Florida,* De Keyserlei 59.

Motels: Best is the *GB Motor Hotel*, 136 double rooms, indoor and outdoor pool, at Artselaar, on the Brussels road; *Dennenhof,* at Brasschaat, on route to Breda (Holland); *Beveren*, road to St. Niklaas. New is the 312-room *Crest Hotel*, near airport.

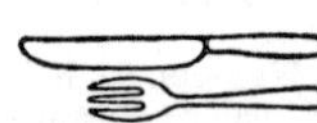

RESTAURANTS. If the choice of hotels—for Antwerp's size and importance—is somewhat restricted, we can't complain about restaurants. In addition to those in the hotels, there are over a hundred native, and nearly half as many exotic, eating places. You'll find everything from gastronomic temples to humble *fritures* in this city of good living.

From the estuary come the finest sea fish, eels, crayfish, and shrimp; excellent mussels from the nearby Zeeland area. Restaurants serve mussels in various ways: *au vin blanc, à la provençale* (with garlic in the tomato sauce), *marinière, à la crème,* etc. You can't go wrong by ordering *moules spéciales* with a *portion de frites.* Shrimps are served mostly as hors d'oeuvre, either cold, stuffed in tomato with mayonnaise (*tomates aux crevettes*) or hot, called *croquettes aux crevettes.*

Nearly all Antwerp gourmets agree that *La Rade,* Van Dyck Kaai 8, is the best and most expensive restaurant (specialties: chicken in the Antwerp fashion or prepared as *waterzooi).* Others mostly vote for the

Criterium, De Keyserlei 25, where we suggest an unforgettable caneton à l'orange (duckling). Still others prefer *La Pérouse,* near the Steen, on board ship pontoon (open Sept., May only), or *Cigogne d'Alsace,* Wiegstr. 9. All are (E).

Le Gourmet sans Chiqué, Vestingstr. 3, has Campine chicken on the spit as a specialty. At *Commerce,* Astridplein 30, grilled turbot with béarnaise sauce is recommended. Both (E).

In the heart of Antwerp port (gare maritime) is the atmospheric *Terminal,* Leopolddok 214. Gastronomy in a 16th-cent. setting at *St. Jacob en Galicie,* Braderijstr. 14.

If you like open-air dining, at the port, *Noordkasteel* (open Apr.-Oct.) offers good fare, with boating thrown in. *Rooden Hoed,* Oude Koornmarkt 25, near the cathedral, is Antwerp's most ancient restaurant and specializes in various preparations of eel and mussels. For a substantial meal, go to *Old Tom,* De Keyserlei 53. All (M). Next door, *Locarno* (I).

Best among the Chinese restaurants: *Dragon Vert,* Van Schoonhovenstr. 26, and *China-West,* Statiestr. 12. Indonesian food at *China,* Frankrijklei 18.

Ferri, Arsenalstr. 2, is considered the best Italian spot. For Yugoslav specialties go to *Dalmacija,* Vingerlingstr. 10. *Moszkowitz,* Pelikaanstr. 90, is Jewish. All (M).

Wienerwald, Frankrijklei 8, is not expensive for what it offers: hearty Austrian food, and music.

If you reserve at least 1 week ahead, you can take the one-day gourmet cruise from Antwerp to Rotterdam aboard the *Flandria,* and return by bus; *La Perouse* (above) supervises the one-menu meal. Apply: Flandria, Steenplein, Antwerp.

On the way to Holland, at Merksem-Schoten, *Ten Weyngaert* offers old-world atmosphere in a 17th-cent. setting, where you can sample such delicacies as Marmite Henri IV: best book. Two English-sounding spots outside central Antwerp: *Cromwell Pub and Restaurant,* 73 Heistr., at Wilrijk, and *Halewijn,* Ekeren Donk at Brasschaat. Both (M-I).

SHOPPING IN ANTWERP. Head for the main thoroughfare, De Keyserlei, which starts at the central rail station, and you are in the big shopping district. Side streets surrounding it are sometimes specialized—Léopoldstraat goes in for *haute couture,* lace shops are in the streets around the cathedral. And Meir has about everything.

CHOCOLATES. *Godiva,* De Keyserlei.

DIAMONDS. *Joaillerie du Club,* Pelikaanstr.; *International Diamond Sales,* Huidevetterstr. 51.

LEATHERWARE. *Ganterie Maroquinerie Select,* De Keyserlei 46 (also has scarves, accessories).

RAINWEAR. *Frey & Bastian; Weston; Paris-Londres.* All on Meir.

SHOES. *Brevitt Toison d'Or,* Meir 21.

WOMEN'S WEAR. *Lizzy,* on De Keyserlei.

CHURCH SERVICES. In all Catholic churches mentioned in the text, Sunday Mass is said hourly or half-hourly from 6 to noon. Anglican churches: St. Peter's, Van Schoonbekeplein, St. Boniface's, Grétrystraat. Methodist (in French), Gounodstraat. Synagogue, Oostenstraat.

THEATERS. Antwerp has ten theaters, but for those who don't understand Flemish (or Dutch) the choice narrows down to the *Oud-België,* Frankrijklei 3. There's no language difficulty at the *Ancienne Belgique,* Kipdorpvest 26 and *Billard Palace,* Astridplein, both music halls. Symphony concerts are held at Queen Elisabeth Concert Hall (near Zoo Gardens).

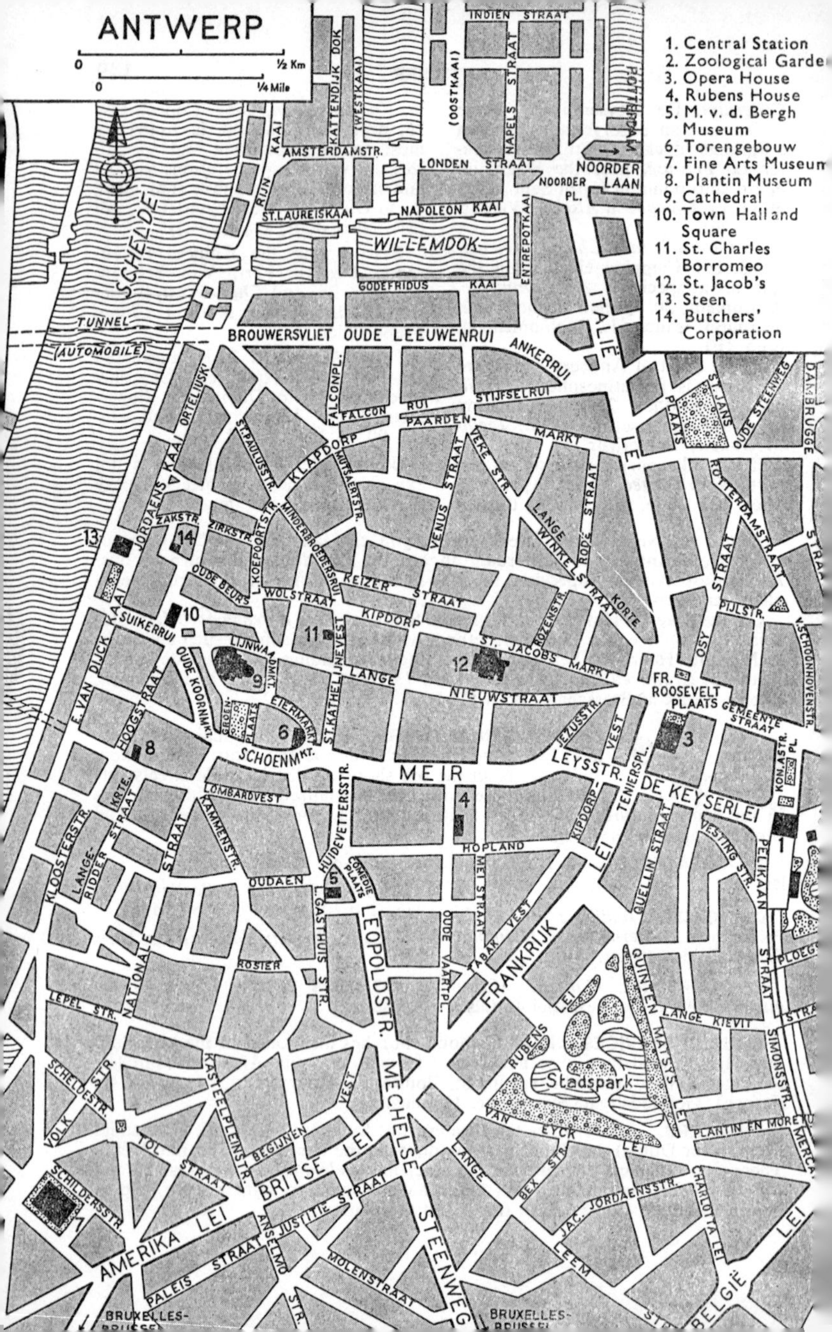
ANTWERP
0 ½ Km
0 ¼ Mile
1. Central Station
2. Zoological Garde
3. Opera House
4. Rubens House
5. M. v. d. Bergh Museum
6. Torengebouw
7. Fine Arts Museum
8. Plantin Museum
9. Cathedral
10. Town Hall and Square
11. St. Charles Borromeo
12. St. Jacob's
13. Steen
14. Butchers' Corporation

NIGHTCLUBS, DANCING. Like every self-respecting port, Antwerp is teeming with nightclubs and especially dance halls. Prices, with one or two exceptions, are not high, particularly if you have been through the Brussels wringer. Professional hostesses outnumber waiters.

In the neighborhood of Central Station, concentrated in Annessenstraat and vicinity: *Abbey* has the best striptease; in the same street, *Cactus* and *Chalet* are very popular. Others: *Luna,* Statiestr., *Cleo* and *Twiggy,* both in Van Schoonhovenstr. More select are *Bonaparte,* Grote Markt, and *Richelieu,* Britzel. *Scotch Inn,* Grote Markt, is the best dance spot. For a floorshow at little cost, *La Bamba,* Grote Markt. More like music-hall is *De Lachende Koe,* Statiestr. The *Bull Bar,* Frankrijklei, means what it says.

In the vicinity of the Flemish Theater are numerous bars and cabarets, others may be found in and around De Coninckplein. There are many dance spots and bars near the docks, especially in Londenstraat and Nassaustraat; better keep away.

USEFUL ADDRESSES. Consulates: *American,* Frankrijklei 64-68; *British,* Frankrijklei 105; Eire, Schermersstr. 14.

Information: *Tourist Office Pavilion,* facing Central Station.

Travel Agents: *American Express,* Meir 87; *Wagon-Lits/Cook,* Teniersplaats 5.

Emergency Calls: *Police* 906; *Ambulance* 900.

Practical Information for Environs of Antwerp

ARTSELAAR. Hotel: The *GB Motor Hotel* is recent, excellent.

Restaurant: *Lindenbos* (E), in former manor house, is outstanding.

BRASSCHAAT. Pleasant stop-over 7 miles to the northeast, on highway to Holland. Hotel: *Kasteel van Brasschaat,* first class, most of its 21 rooms with bath; large park, excellent restaurant, swimming, boating.

Restaurant: *Webb,* Bredelaan 538, is a very good garden-restaurant.

At Polygoon, *Dennenhof* is an attractive motel. Also at Polygoon, the *Withof* has 12 rooms, outstanding restaurant.

KALMHOUT. About 15 miles due north, favorite outing for weekends. Hotel: *Cecil,* 9 rooms.

Restaurants: *Buizerd* and *Cambuus.*

LILLO. Right on the banks of the Schelde, 7 miles north. Hotel: *Scaldis,* simple and inexpensive, 6 rooms, eel specialties.

RIJKEVORSEL. Between Antwerp and Turnhout, less than 4 miles north of Oostmalle. Worth a detour, excellent overnight halt: *Château de Gargantua,* 8 rooms, 2 baths. Its restaurant (E) specialty: roast chicken *flambé* with liqueur.

'S-GRAVENWEZEL. Wooded region, 8 miles east of Antwerp, via Schoten. Has three fine châteaux. Hotels: *Casablanca,* small excellent, fairly expensive; good restaurant, vast park. *'s-Gravenhof* is moderate in every respect.

SCHOTEN. Amid pleasant woodland, 5 miles east of Antwerp. Hotel: *Koningshof,* 10 rooms, good restaurant.

Exploring Antwerp

An important segment of Antwerp's economic background is the growth of the diamond-cutting industry. Here again the war left a number of problems, but Antwerp soon recovered her place as leader of the world's suppliers of finished diamonds. It is not an industry which, as such, thrusts itself upon the visitor's notice. Nevertheless, its products occupy little space for a large value, and this has given it a special importance in the postwar world of currency restrictions and clandestine flights of capital. Not every diamond that comes into Antwerp is the direct product of a diamond syndicate. Not every diamond that leaves Belgium does so through the authorized channels that give it its place in the trade returns. Until controls were tightened in September 1951, there were cafés around Pelikaanstraat where, if you watched carefully, you could see large values in stones and notes change hands.

Directly in front of the Central Rail Station is Koningin Astridplein, a large square surrounded by cafés and cinemas. Just east of the station is the 25-acre Dierentuin, one of Europe's most complete and modern zoological gardens. In one aviary the fronts of the cages are open, but ingenious use of bright lights dissuades the birds from flying away. In the reptile house, curtains of cold air prevent the pythons from roaming. Elsewhere, larger animals of the less dangerous sort wander about almost at will.

On the other side of the Central Station there stretches the broad, busy De Keyserlei, with Pelikaanstraat running down the side of the station on your left. The De Keyserlei goes to the main boulevard between the Frankrijklei and the Italiëlei, beyond which you are in the main shopping thoroughfare called Meir, which culminates in that modern achievement, the 24-floor Torengebouw (from the top there's a fine panoramic view). Continuing with this building on your right, you pass down the Schoenmarkt till you find yourself in the wide Groenplaats, containing a statue of Rubens, with the Cathedral of Our Lady occupying the opposite end of the square. Continuing your walk along the same line, you will come to the Schelde where, a hundred yards to your right, stands the fortress-like Steen, housing the Marine Museum.

The Steen is one of the few traces left of medieval Antwerp. It dates back to the 10th century, though of course it has been much altered through the centuries and much of it is no older than 1520. In the 13th century it was a prison, and one of the things you will see inside is the chapel where condemned men heard their last Mass. You are here upstream from the main port installations, but from these raised terraces you can watch the shipping on the busy Schelde.

The walk you have taken has led you along the boundary between the port and old Antwerp, which lie on your right, and modern Antwerp which, though it contains some survivals, is mainly the product of the city's 19th-century expansion and the growth of the residential area. Facing the river on the Steen, you are about midway between the under-river tunnels for foot passengers on your left, and for vehicles on your right, both about a couple of hundred yards distant, though the entrance to the latter is farther inland, in a square off the Italiëlei.

An Incomparable Cathedral

The chief architects in the first work on the cathedral, begun in 1352, were the Appelmans, father and son. At the end of the 15th century Hermann de Waghemaker made various additions, and about 1520 his son Dominique, an Antwerp man, in partnership with the Malinois Keldermans—a partnership responsible for the restoration of the Steen about the same time, as also for the original wing of the City Hall at Ghent–was at work on the tower. This single tower, on a structure evidently meant to carry two, gives the building an asymetrical look, but the tower itself is a masterpiece.

The interior of the cathedral needs some study before you realize how very large it is. There was indeed a scheme, in the days of Charles Quint, to make it about double its present size, but the work was abandoned. Philip II, maintaining the traditions of the House of Burgundy, revived the Order of the Golden Fleece by holding a chapter here in 1555. Ten years later the iconoclasts were smashing the statues, and in 1794 the best of the glass was removed, the church abstracted from religious use, and the Rubens masterpieces were carried off to Paris, whence they were not recovered till 1816, after the fall of Napoleon.

The great treasure of the church consists of the three works of Peter Paul Rubens, the two main ones—the *Elevation of the Cross* and the *Deposition*—being at the back of the two transepts. The former, painted just after the master's return from Italy, shows evident signs of Italian influence; but the latter, ordered very soon after, though not finished for three years (1614), defines Rubens' mature style and is generally considered the greater masterpiece. The painter's later manner is brought out by the treatment of light in his *Assumption*, which you will find in the choir (1626). Other works of outstanding interest in the cathedral include a *Last Supper* by Nicholas Rombouts (about 1503) and a white marble Communion table by Artus Quellin in the Chapel of the Holy Sacrament. Nearby there is a local antique market on Fridays between 8 a.m. and 1 p.m. Ask for the *Vrijdag Markt*.

The House of Rubens and Other Treasures

The Rubens pictures will probably have filled you with enthusiasm to see the house occupied by the artist from 1610 for the last quarter-century of his life. It is in a turning off Meir, partly a reconstruction, but a very conscientious one, and containing a wing with strong Italian influence, added by the painter himself. You will see here the studio in which the master worked, and the big studio for his pupils.

Van Dyck worked here for some time as well as Jordaens, Snyders, and many others. The house contains, besides souvenirs of the master, furniture and *objects d'art* of the 17th century. They help to recall the atmosphere of an Antwerp patrician's home.

Another period-reconstruction is the Plantin Museum, the house of the printer—himself a Frenchman by origin—whose name is remembered by a type-face and who was commissioned by Philip II and later made Archtypographer Royal. His famous printing business was continued by his son-in-law Moretus, and existed till the latter part of the 19th century, though it never regained its first eminence. The Renaissance courtyard and the gardens give the house a charm of its own, and the type-foundry and the typographical collection are of unique interest.

Plantin's was, in fact, Europe's most important printing shop in the 16th century. His 22 presses brought out no less than 50 to 60 volumes a year. His sumptuous patrician house was for many decades the meeting place of Humanist thinkers of all nationalities. Behind the latticed windows were produced books that were the admiration of all the universities. Through those doorways often passed the dashing Rubens and the courtly Van Dyck, gay in velvet. Dignitaries of all walks of life have been here: steeple-crowned Puritans, ecclesiastics from Rome, blackgowned professors from Leiden and—when in contemplative mood—the ferocious Duke of Alba himself.

Antwerp's Churches

Among the churches of Antwerp, the most interesting in itself is that of Saint Charles Borromeo, built in the early 17th century for the Jesuits and in the planning and decoration of which Rubens and his coterie had the lion's share. This is one of the few Flemish churches with a gallery construction. Unfortunately it has suffered very heavily through the centuries. The Rubens ceiling paintings were destroyed by fire in 1718, and the other chief paintings were taken to Vienna after the suppression of the Jesuits in 1773. Twenty years later the French turned the church into a Temple of Reason, after which it became a military hospital and then a Protestant church. It was at last restored to the Catholic confession, and contains an altar by Rubens and statues by Artus Quellin, besides a number of paintings by Scut, Seghers, and others, and an ivory Christ by Duquesnoy.

As you walk down Lange Nieuwstraat you will pass the restored Chapel of Saint Nicholas and the enticing little courtyard where a pillared statue of the saint himself is another link with a remoter past. Farther down the street is the Church of Saint James (Saint Jacob), begun by the elder De Waghemaker in 1491, and reopened in 1969 after the previous year's fire. Its treasures include more works of art than most others, especially a marble Communion table by Verbruggen and Kerricx, dating from the end of the 17th century, and an *Apotheosis of Saint James* by the latter. Artus Quellin was responsible for the fine carving in the choir stalls, one of the armorial bearings (of benefactors) being that of Rubens. In the fourth side-chapel is the tomb of Rubens himself with, on the altar, a *Holy Family,* one of the master's last works. It is scarcely necessary to list all the treasures in a church which has so many. You may be interested to compare the Rombouts *Mystic Marriage of Saint Catherine* with that by Memling at Bruges; and there is an intriguing *Temptation of Saint Anthony* by Martin de Vos, in which the painter's wife was model for the temptress.

There is, incidentally, a Rubens version of the *Mystic Marriage of Saint Catherine* in Saint Augustine's Church, in the southern part of the city, together with Van Dyck's *Saint Augustine in Ecstasy*. Not far away is the Church of Saint Andrew, largely of interest for the monument put up by the refugees Barbara Maubray and Elizabeth Curle for Mary Stuart, Queen of Scots, after her execution at the order of Elizabeth of England. The queen's portrait on copper above the monument is said to be a Pourbus.

Saint Paul's Church, close to the Butchers' Corporation, is now unhappily no more than a ruin, after the second of Antwerp's disastrous church fires in which the local hippies so distinguished themselves in saving the fine paintings—Rubens, Van Dyck, Quellin and others—which were among its possessions. It is feared the church may be beyond the possibility of meaningful restoration.

Magnificent Architectural Examples

Among the secular buildings of Antwerp you will find a fragment of the old Beurs, or Commercial Exchange, in the Hofstraat, near the Stadhuis (City Hall). The date of the building is 1564. It was not long before this building was replaced by another, on similar lines, which is still in use, in Twaalf Maandenstraat. The Stadhuis is the work, in the first instance, of Cornelis Floris (or de Vriendt), and it was still barely a dozen years old when the Spaniards burned it out in 1576. The galleried hall, with its 19th-century murals, is impressive rather than beautiful, but there are two rooms full of frescos by the 19th-century painter Leys which are worth seeing. In the room of the Burgomaster there is an interesting fireplace by Pieter Coecke of Aalst (1548). The Stadhuis is, in the usual manner, surrounded by the old houses of the corporations. These, for the most part, are opulent architectural examples of the early 16th century; as compared with the end of the 17th century when the corresponding houses in Brussels were built. They are of a more sober style than those in the Brussels Grand' Place. You will find a great number of old houses, of about the same period, in the surrounding streets. In the middle of the Grote Markt stands the Brabo fountain, which achieves an unusual effect by having no basin, the water running off through the rocks.

Passing down towards the Schelde by the Oude Beursstraat, you come to the Vleeshuis the house of the Butchers Corporation, built above the level of the street at the beginning of the 16th century. It is the biggest and best-preserved building in late Gothic style in Antwerp. In the stately hall on the ground floor meat was sold for many centuries. The most remarkable of the beautifully furnished first-floor rooms is the stately council chamber of the ancient Butchers' Corporation. It now houses one of the city's museums.

Proceeding along Vleeschouwerstraat you come to the ruins of Saint Paul's; on its farther side is the old Potagiepoort, a little closed-off square, which is an attractive survival. Reaching the Schelde and passing beyond the Loodshuis, the river pilots' building, you can turn down Brouwerstraat to find the Brouwershuis at No. 20. The work of the engineer Gilbert van Schoonbeke, this interesting relic is the remains of the system by which water was brought down from the Campine for the city, and more especially for the 20 or more breweries in this street. The system, started in 1552, was in service till less than a quarter-century ago. Quite apart from the house itself, which is a good example of the decoative art of the period, the study of the water system embodied here is of outstanding interest.

The Port and the Museums

Your visit to Antwerp will not be complete without a visit to the port, the world's third largest. The quays extend some 60 miles and the harbor and docks cover over an area of 40 square miles. You'll enjoy one of the boat excursions that start from the landing stage by the Steen. You can also visit the port by bus. Seats must be booked in advance from the Municipal Tourist Office, 19 Suikerrui, Antwerp 2000. Price 75 francs per person.

Another "must" in your visit to Antwerp is the Museum of Fine Arts. Even the uninitiated in matters of painting can hardly fail to realize how much Antwerp owes to Peter Paul Rubens and the painters of his circle; and there is no gallery in the world where the work of a painter can so easily be studied in its historical perspective. The collection of Dutch and Flemish masters is, indeed, formidable and covers nearly four centuries. A representative collection of all that is best in modern Belgian painting completes the circle.

Another outstanding museum which calls for a visit is the Mayer van den Bergh collection, housed in the testator's house and wonderfully presented. This collection is largely composed of primitives from a number of schools; but the furnishings and decorations are worth a visit, even if you are not a keen student of painting.

Smidt van Gelder bequeathed his 18th-century patrician dwelling to the city of Antwerp in 1949. It contains a unique collection of antique furniture, china, and some very fine paintings. What strikes the visitor is the totally different atmosphere from other museums: it is the richly furnished home of a refined art collector.

Those interested in folklore will find great pleasure in visiting the five restored corporation houses in the Gildenkamerstraat. The museum is a complete survey of Flemish popular activities, customs, and art.

The countryside around Antwerp lacks the picturesque quality possessed by the environs of Brussels. Thoughtful city fathers have been successfully trying to create a green belt and Antwerp can today boast a large number of beautiful parks on its outskirts. One of the finest is the Rivierenhof, which contains an 18th-century manor of fine proportions.

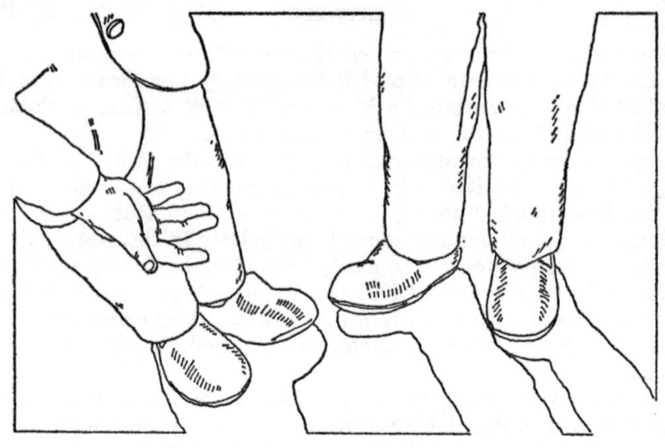

LIMBURG AND THE CAMPINE

Land of Strange Contrasts

The Campine is, in its native state, Belgium's desert, a lonely moorland alternating with sandy plains. It stretches from the Schelde to the Maas (Meuse) in the country north of Liège and Visé, where it becomes the Dutch frontier. The Campine includes the bulk of the provinces of Antwerp and Limburg, and it is a country of sandhills and scrub, where indeed most of the fertility —and there is much—is the product of human endeavor. Men and women in wooden *sabots* toil long hours on the land; it is here that one may still encounter such homely scenes as were painted by Breughel, Teniers, and latterday "realist" painters.

It is a Flemish-speaking country, full of strange contrasts between old and new and, above all, between a traditional simplicity of outlook and all the trimmings of modern mass-architecture. It was in the heart of this country that not long ago a woman was accused by her neighbors of witchcraft. Among her alleged accomplishments was the practice of turning herself after nightfall into a particularly ill-omened cat. This she was supposed to achieve in her ultra-modern kitchen, in a row of new redbrick residences which, apart from the pig-and-poultry backyards, would have done credit to any London suburb.

There are two great economic features in this country—the coalfield and the Albert Canal. The discovery of coal in the Campine basin dates back only about half a century, and the collieries are not only richer than their counterparts near Mons, Charleroi, and Liège, but they are also finely equipped, and the workers are housed and cared for on modern lines. The coalfield stretches east and west, roughly from Mechelen-aan-de-Maas to the big army establishments of Beverlo. The Albert Canal leaves the Maas just north of Liège, following much the same course as the river until, near Lanaken, it curves round to flow past Hasselt and carry the heavy Liège traffic to Antwerp.

Practical Information for Limburg and the Campine

WHEN TO COME? The main tourist season in this region is from May to Sept. It is worth seeing because it gives the visitor a good insight into the rhythm of country life that prevailed all over Belgium a hundred years ago. Pageants, as everywhere else in the country, abound.

Events: In *February* Hasselt stages its Annual Fair, complete with carnival and the election of a Carnival Prince. In early *May* the vast apple and cherry orchards in the St. Truiden region are in full bloom. On the first of that month, the Play of St. Evermeire, the only mystery play still performed in Belgium, is presented at Rutten. Also during the month of May occur a spectacular procession in honor of St. Dymphne at Geel and a Youth Music festival at Neerpelt. A folklore and carnival procession enlivens St. Truiden's Cherry Festival in *July*. In *October* there is a great procession of pilgrims at Lier.

WHAT TO SEE? Some of the country's oldest and finest art towns are in this region. In fact, Tongeren (Tongres) is the oldest Belgo-Roman settlement in Belgium. St. Truiden (St. Trond) was founded in the 17th century. The rare medieval charm of Lier (Lierre) and Diest will delight every visitor. There are Hasselt, Maaseik, the abbeys of Averbode and Tongerlo. You can admire the faithful reproduction of an ancient Campine village at Bokrijk, halfway between Hasselt and Genk, and visit the begijnhof (béguinage) at Diest, Lier, Tongeren, and Sint-Truiden. Galleries from Roman times have been discovered at Kanne. There is a museum with fossils and paintings of animals and plants.

SPORTS. If *fishing* is your favorite sport, you can try your luck in the valley of the Limburgse Maasstreek (Limburg section of the Meuse). The varied countryside of wood, heathland, and streams provides ideal ground for *camping* and *walking*. Camping sites in the region are located at Biest, Geel, Houthalen, Mol, Tongeren and elsewhere. There is plenty of *swimming*, notably in the provincial park at Zilvermeer, near Mol.

HOTELS AND RESTAURANTS. The Campine country is well provided with inexpensive medium-type hotels. They are, on the whole, cheaper than elsewhere in Belgium, probably because this region is touristically as yet "undiscovered". There are plenty of good restaurants.

AS. Five miles northwest of Genk. Hotel: *Mardaga,* 20 rooms, excellent but reasonable; so is the cuisine. Try one of their preparations of eel.

AVERBODE. Norbertine Abbey. Hotel: *Sint Norbertus*, inexpensive.

BOKRIJK. Model village of bygone days. Halfway between Hasselt and Genk, take a signposted private road to the left.

Restaurant: *Kasteel Bokrijk* (M), excellent.

DIEST. Charming old art town, home of good beer. All better establishments are in the main square. Hotels: *De Haan*, small and *Modern*, rather larger and with more amenities, both moderate.

Restaurant: *L'Empereur* (M-E), old Flemish atmosphere; try the lobster cocktail, and chicken in tarragon sauce.

GEEL. Hotel: *Het Lam*, 20 rooms, 4 baths, is best in town. Moderate to first class reasonable.

GENK. Hotel: *The Atlantis*, at nearby Sledderlo, is comfortable and moderate.

HASSELT. Chief city of province and art town. Hotels: *Park*, on Genk road; *Memling; Vogelsanck; Century*, good. All moderate to inexpensive. *Schoofs*, good, moderate, but some rooms inexpensive. Really inexpensive are *Pax* and *Europa*.

Best restaurants: *Van Dijck* (E), excellent, and *Memling*.

HECHTEL. Important crossroads north of Hasselt.

Hotel: *Miramar*, simple, moderate; has restaurant.

HERENTALS. Interesting town hall and church. Hotels: *Golf*, on the Lier road is moderate. *Rozenhof*, near station, inexpensive.

Excellent restaurant 2½ miles northeast, on Lichtaarsesteenweg: *Snepkenshoeve* (E).

LIER (LIERRE). Hotel: *Commerce*, small, inexpensive.

Restaurant: *Gasthof de Fortuin* (E), a gastronomic halt of the first order.

MAASEIK. Poor in hotels for a town its size. *Van Eyck* is best.

MOL. Road junction, nuclear center, overnight halt. Hotels: *Het Jagershof* and *Torenhuis*, both inexpensive. At Balen-Wezel, 5 miles northeast, *Casino*, inexpensive.

Restaurant: *Auberge Formentor*, excellent.

SINT-TRUIDEN. Hotel: *Astoria*, moderate, has good restaurant.

Restaurant: *Henri IV* (M), excellent. Specialty is veal steak Henri IV.

TONGEREN. The oldest (Belgo-Roman) city in the country and fine art town. Hotels are poor: *Lido* and *Casque* are a possible refuge.

TONGERLO. Famous abbey and château. Hotel. *Sint Antonius*, very small.

Restaurant: *Torenhof* (I).

TURNHOUT. Few hotels. Best are *Kempen, Terminus* and *Astoria*, all inexpensive.

WESTERLO. Fine châteaux, 15th-century church. Hotels: *Valkenhof* and *Geerts*, both inexpensive .

SHOPPING. Lier is the home and origin of beautiful beaded bags, one of the most popular gifts to take home. See them at *Custers*, Lipstr. 61; *G. Thomas*, Léopoldplein 1; and *Van Oekel*, Antwerpsestraat.

USEFUL ADDRESSES. Each Town Hall (Stadhuis) has its local tourist office.

Exploring the Campine Country

For the Brussels-based visitor, the best approach to the Campine country is the Liège road through Leuven, which brings you into Limburg province at Sint-Truiden (Saint Trond), in the very heart of the cherry country, of which you may have read in the works of Aldous Huxley. In blossom-time a drive round the neighborhood is an experience never to be forgotten; and every day while the crop is being marketed the streets are full of the brightly colored fruit. At Sint-Truiden you are still in the Hesbaye country, but the elegant little spire of the town hall belfry will prepare you for the fact that the Campinois are proud of their public buildings and have seldom disfigured them with bulbous growths such as those which mar the tower at Mons. This town, incidentally, was the center of an interesting outburst of civic consciousness in the middle 18th century, when the people took exception to the carillon cast for them in the first years of the century and were not satisfied until they got the bells—41 in number—that you hear today. The Grote Markt (Market Place), severe but elegant, is a jewel of medieval architecture.

This is the place to come to if you are interested in fresco work. In the Begijnhof there are 35 large frescos, varying in date, for some date from as early as the 13th century, while others are a full four centuries later. There is no indication of any outstanding artist having had a hand in this work, but the frescos are interesting in themselves for their simplicity and sincerity. A hundred yards from the church is an astronomical compensation clock, nearly 20 feet high and comprising 20,000 mechanical parts. The frescos at Zepperen, which lies three miles eastward, date back to the early 16th century; and in Sint-Truiden the fresco in Onze Lieve Vrouw is dated 1625.

Farther to the east, Borgloon is an attractive little town, ancient capital of the former county of Loon, which covered practically the whole of the present province of Limburg. Its principal curiosity is the Romanesque church with a 15th-century Gothic spire. The former residence of the counts of Loon was transformed into the present town hall in the 17th century.

Tongeren, Cradle of Resistance Movements

The road through Borgloon leads you on to Tongeren (pop. 20,000) at the intersection of seven roads, which serves to remind you that the town owes much of its importance to its location on the great Roman highway from Cologne to Bavai. This ancient town is the cattle market for the rich Hesbaye country, the country of Charlemagne; and heifers are bargained for under the statue of Ambiorix, who (even though his effigy is not yet a century old) is the father of all Belgium's resistance movements. It was he who rallied the tribes against the Roman invader in 54 B.C., and massacred the legions of Sabinus and Cotta, only to be frustrated by the treachery of the enemy's collaborators. He was finally driven underground by a top-speed counter-offensive led by Caesar himself. Tongeren was, by repute, the Aduatica Tungrorum of Roman Gaul. It reached its greatest size and eminence in the days of Tiberius Caesar so that, most surprisingly in view of normal trends in town life, the remains of the medieval 13th-century fortifications are well inside the towered Roman wall.

The Salian tribes destroyed Tongeren in the 4th century; and five hundred years later, Norsemen pillaged, sacked, and burned it. Duke Henry I of Brabant sacked it again in the early 13th century, and in 1677 it was burned by the French.

The outstanding Romanesque relic is the 12th-century cloister in the Vrouwbasiliek (Notre Dame), a church of some architectural interest with a very rich treasury containing, in particular, the 7th-century reliquary of Saint Remacle and also that of the martyrs of Trèves (Trier), early 13th century. The lectern and chandelier, both made by Jehan Josés in the latter half of the 14th century, are excellent examples of Dinant brassware. Near the south door of the church is an underground Roman tower, the sole remaining relic of the 4th-century fortification which took the place of the older Roman wall. If you walk along this rampart, starting out at the fortified gate (Moerepoort), you will soon reach the Begijnhof. Some fine glimpses of the old city make this short outing even more rewarding.

While you are at Tongeren, you should walk out to the Beukenberg, a manmade hill built—apparently as part of a regional fortification—at the order of Emperor Diocletian, and which now marks a conventional boundary between the valleys of the Maas and the Schelde. From here you can see the *tumuli* that cover the remains of the legionaries slaughtered by the ambush laid by Ambiorix; and you can pass on to the Fountain of Pliny, a spring that has not had the commercial success of Spa, with which it disputes the claim of being the spring mentioned for its invigorating qualities by Pliny the Elder.

There are a number of châteaux in this neighborhood, including the leafy 17th-century Betho and the very lovely 18th-century Château d'Hex, which stands in a large and stately park. It has a richly appointed and well preserved interior and may be visited on request. One you will not want to miss is some miles farther north, the Château des Vieux-Joncs (Ouden-Biessen) at Rijkhoven, which can be seen on Sunday afternoons except in winter. The commanders of the Vieux-Joncs, an order of knights, were still here until the last years of the 18th century. The château, which is quite intact, portraits, tombs and all, had Louis XIV and Louis

XV among its guests, as well as the young Duke of Cumberland, son of George II of England. Its present condition, however, could be improved.

From Tongeren you can go on to Liège or Visé, or by turning off the Maastricht road, you can see for yourself the famous bottleneck in the Belgian canal system at Lanaye (*le bouchon de Lanaye*) by which the big east-bound barges from Liège and Charleroi used to be prevented from sailing into the Dutch canals and—until 1962—forced northward.

Hasselt, Capital of Belgian Limburg

If, however, you are systematically touring the entire Limburg and the Campine country, you will strike northwestward to Hasselt (pop. 40,000), capital of the Belgian Limburg, a fragment of the old Duchy left on this side of the frontier by the events of 1830. Its principal curiosities are the tower of Saint Quintyn and a 17th-century patrician house in the market square, called Sweert (Sword). The Church of Our Lady has a fine altar by the Liège sculptor, Del Cour.

Hasselt is the gateway to the rather arid Campine and to its colliery district. You can come to the latter conveniently through Genk, a picturesque holiday resort with its lakes, woods, and open-air theater. It has grown rapidly, due to the Ford plant and other industrial ventures, and has an ultra-modern shopping center (park on the roof); many Italians and Turks work in the mines and factories.

Bokrijk, halfway between Hasselt and Genk, is a tourist "must". The administration of Limburg province inaugurated in 1958 a nature reserve which shows in all its unspoilt originality the Campine country of heather and pine, sand and broom, marshes and ponds visited by waterfowl. The farmhouses have been renovated and their interiors show old peasant furniture, ancient utensils and beaten copper-work, all familiar from paintings of the Flemish masters. Even a few mock peasants walk around in traditional garb. It is the largest open air museum in Europe.

Through As and Lanaken (in the latter you will find attractive holiday country similar to that of Genk), you can reach the Maas at lime-fringed Maaseik. As a pilgrimage to the birthplace of Hubert and Jan van Eyck, this attractive town is disappointing. The trip is, however, worthwhile for the visit to the church treasury to see the *Gospels of Aldeneik,* an illuminated version prepared by two Valenciennes nuns who came to Limburg in 730 A.D. This is one of the few examples of Carolingian art and craftsmanship to be found in Belgium.

The valley of the Maas (Limburgse Maasstreek) is a pleasant region stretching from Lanaken in the south to Lanklaar in the north. Many anglers practice here their favorite sport. The church at Eisden is an especially fine example of contemporary religious art.

Striking westward by the Beverlo road, you will pass through a country where the villages have once been towns and, having never recaptured their cloth-based prosperity of the 14th and 15th centuries, have (fortunately for us) never had money enough to replace their lovely Gothic churches by more pretentious edifices conforming to the tastes of later periods. Examples are at Bree and Opitter, though at Opoeteren the church is older (partly 9th century) and here, too, you will see the château that served as a hunting lodge to the prince-bishops of Liège. At Neeroeteren the church contains some fine statues.

Geel, Pilgrimage Center

For many centuries Geel was a center of pilgrimage for the light of head and, if they were not at once miraculously cured, they would often stay in the homes of the townsfolk. Their pilgrimage was to the shrine of Saint Dymphne who, about the year 600 A.D., fled here from the obsessions of her Irish father, who eventually caught her and split her skull open right in this very town. Her relics are in a wooden reliquary in the church which bears her name and which contains some beautiful stone and woodwork. In the northern part of the town, on the south side of the 16th-century tower, is the sickroom where pilgrims in search of cure were required to lodge during the nine days of their pilgrimage. The hospital has retained all the architectural features of its epoch (17th century) while the town hall has lost its original aspect through clumsy renovation.

Today, Geel is a byword among the Belgians for its main occupation, which is the care in private houses of non-dangerous mental cases. You will have to wander about Geel and the neighboring country to get an idea of the patients and the work this seeming freedom is doing for them. It is basically a religious work, though nowadays it is paid for by the families of the patients, or, more often, by the state. If you come by train you cannot avoid, at the station, the scrutiny of the male nurse who, in these modern times, will lead the patient to the infirmary where the non-dangerous cases are sorted out before they are placed with families.

From Geel it is barely 10 miles to Herentals, the Ypres of the north which, in the early days of the 14th-century cloth trade, was a serious rival to the Flemish industry. Its best buildings, the Stadhuis and the Church of St. Waudru, are early 15th century, and the latter contains a carved reredos by Pasquier Borremans, ranked as one of the masterpieces of Brabant wood carving. The countryside here is charming, dotted with ancient castles and mansions. Farther north, Turnhout offers little architectural interest. Its only outstanding building is the Gerechtshof (Law Court), formerly a hunting castle of the dukes of Brabant. Saint Peter's Church contains some fine Baroque furniture and paintings by Teniers. Since 1826 Turnhout has printed playing cards and has an unusual museum of them. It is open Saturdays and Sundays from 10 a.m. to noon and 2 p.m. to 5 p.m.

Passing southward through Olen, with its pre-Roman remains and its radium factory, you come to the two Norbertine abbeys of Tongerlo and Averbode. Both have had disastrous fires in recent years. Tongerlo has been restored, and the strikingly decorated church contains a particularly valuable copy (possibly by Andrea del Sarto) of Leonardo da Vinci's *Last Supper* which, in view of the restorations of the original in Milan, is thought to show the painter's own intentions.

Moated Tongerlo is one of the most active religious houses in Belgium. Its rich library has among its treasures a complete *Acta Sanctorum,* one volume of which was actually published from Tongerlo.

The buildings at Averbode, one of Europe's most important monasteries, are for the most part later than those of Tongerlo. Restored recently, it contains some magnificent Louis XV interiors and some old masters. In the Abbot's House there is an embossed plaque by Rubens, some four feet in diameter, depicting a man on a galloping horse, so lifelike that one recalls Reynolds saying, "His horses are perfect in their kind". The Baroque church, with its choir longer than its nave, contains a particularly fine sacristy decorated by Feuillen Houssart of Namur (18th century). Both abbeys have well appointed guesthouses.

Between Averbode and Tongerlo is Westerloo, with its two châteaux of the princely house of Mérode and the fine *Annunciation Triptych* by Robert Campin of Tournai, presumably the Maître de Flémalle who, because of this picture, has sometimes been referred to as the Maître de Mérode.

Diest and Lier, Prettiest Towns of Belgium

Continuing south to the main road, you can turn eastward to Diest, famed not only for its beer but also for its ramparts—one of the very few examples of a medieval fortification kept intact. For its size, it is Belgium's richest town in monuments of the past and in the absence of new buildings, one of the most unspoiled. Its principal attraction is the Grote Markt, where 17th-century houses present a fitting background to the town hall and the Church of Saint Sulpice. There is an unusual museum beneath the Town Hall, laid out in three cellars at different levels, but linked together: no cameras allowed, but there are excellent postcards on sale. A pleasant walk in the old town will delight you and take you to the Schaffen Gates, showing distinctly Diest's triple line of fortifications. Diest has a delightful begijnhof, where the church is dedicated to St. Catherine. There is also a park and open air theater.

In the opposite direction the road lies through Scherpenheuvel (Montaigu), a townlet created at the behest of the Archduke Albert and Isabella and to which a large-scale religious pilgrimage, known as the Procession of the Candles, comes on the Sunday after All Saints' Day each year.

Beyond this you come to Aarschot (both Diest and Aarschot are in northern Brabant), and so back into the province of Antwerp to Lier (pop. 30,000), a town you should on no account miss. Already described in the 13th century as a little paradise, it is still today (despite the damage done by the siege of Antwerp in 1914), outstandingly the prettiest town in Belgium. You will enter it over a bridge, and so perplexing is the course of the Nete that the town is almost all at the riverside, with willows leaning over the water. Everything in such a town is bound to be charming, and the 18th-century Stadhuis accords miraculously well with the belfry which stands at its side and is prominently dated 1369. There, each evening, the last medieval watchman in the country establishes himself until dawn, sounding a trumpet every hour. This is one of the more elegant towers of its kind in Belgium.

Lier is rich in history, political and cultural. If you want to know the time of day, the season of the year, the phase of the moon, or even the date of the next eclipse, you have only to climb the old (but rebuilt) tower to the much more modern studio of the astronomer Louis Zimmer, whose "Centenary Clock" was one of Belgium's exhibits at the New York World Exhibition, 1933. The Church of Sint Gummarus, 15th-century Gothic at its best, planned by Hendrik Mys, of Mechelen, and worked on by the De Waghemaker-Keldermans partnership, is rich in works of art. Particularly outstanding are its 15th- and 16th-century stained-glass windows. On the first Sunday after Trinity and after 10 October, the relics of the saint, in their massive silver *châsse*, are the center of a long procession through the streets. See the Wuyts Museum's fine paintings, and the Begijnhof, one of Belgium's most beautiful, with an outstanding monument of the Calvary in one of the courtyards. Lier is a miniature walled town of cobbled streets and houses ranging from the Renaissance to the last century.

Oddly enough, though Lier is pleased to see visitors and encourages them to come, it seems reluctant for them to stay long. Already in the 14th century its citizens were refusing John of Brabant's offer to found a university within their precincts. Today they have only one very small hotel listed by the Tourist Commissariat. However, the town is within a dozen miles of Antwerp and Mechelen, from either of which your way is cut and dried to return to the more sophisticated pleasures of Brussels.

HISTORIED FLANDERS—ITS ART TOWNS

Fabulous Ypres, Ghent and Bruges

Of all the age-long stories of strife, bloodshed and conflicting interest, that of Flanders is surely the most eventful. Remotest Gaul to the Romans, it was the buffer between the Capets and the Lotharingian emperors, and its sandy shore offered no obstacle to the depredation of the Norsemen. Struggling to independent existence under Baudouin Iron-Arm, its weaving industry became the big market for English wool and its independence of French or imperial domination became a key point of English policy. The alliance of the last count of Flanders with the first of the dukes of Burgundy was the cornerstone upon which Philip the Good built the Grand Dukedom of the West, by which time the strife between its patricians and the men of the loom had given place to the strife of the cities for their civil liberties. Ruined as it was by arrivals of cloth that refugee Flemish weavers had taught the English to weave, it lived to become a centre in the fight for religious tolerance and, in consequence, a butt for the Duke of Alba's persecutions. Fought over time and again, it was the scene of Marlborough's victory of Oudenaarde; and its northwestern corner, centred on Ypres (Ieper), was the final bastion on Belgian soil to stem the German advance on the channel ports in World War I.

The Flemish language is a variant of Dutch, but it is first and foremost a spoken language and varies crucially from place to place. "God made us Flemish; only politics made us Belgian" is still a much-quoted slogan from their poet, Guido Gezelle. Its people have resisted, with all the stubbornness they showed in the Middle Ages, the real or supposed French dominance in Belgian affairs. There is scarcely a Fleming who has no stories to tell of victimization of his people during the 143 years of Belgium's history as a nation; to be fair, it should be added that such stories are told also on the opposite side, now that the Flemings (grown to 60% of the population) are taking the upper hand, but the effect in Flanders has been a certain self-consciousness in the language, which suppresses the occasional Gallicisms classical Dutch allows, yet apes much of the Gallic phraseology.

Practical Information for Flanders

WHEN TO COME? The best time to visit Flanders is summer but, in this country of changing weather you are bound to have sunny and rainy days during any season, so you are almost as safe during spring or fall. Important events take place as early as March.

Events: A characteristic cortege can be seen at Aalst (Alost) on Shrove Sunday. On the following Sunday, Geraardsbergen holds its curious Cracknel Festival. Every 5 years (ending in a 5 or 0) in *April,* Ghent has its world-famous Floralies Gantoises flower show. *May's* outstanding event is the famous procession of the Holy Blood in Bruges, held annually on Ascension Day. At Ypres, the second Sunday inaugurates the Cat Festivities, which end the following Wednesday. The same month Kortrijk (Courtrai) celebrates the cortege of the Holy Hair. Also in May (weather permitting), international rowing regattas are held in Ghent's Aquatic Stadium. In the same city, from end May to early *June* annually, the Antiques Fair of Flanders is held in the restored St. Peter's Abbey. On the last Sunday in *July* you can witness the solemn spectacle of the Procession of the Penitents at Furnes (Veurne). St. Niklaas holds its traditional flower corso early in *August,* Ghent on the first Sunday in *September* and nearby Temse stages a water fantasy (alternate years) on the Schelde River.

The splendor of old Bruges is brought to life against floodlit canals and monuments during a few days in August. Scenes of bygone days are reenacted by several hundred costumed players, musicians, etc. This is the Reiefeest.

Two other *August* events are staged in Bruges every five years: *Sanguis Christi,* a modern passion play based on the story of the Holy Blood, performed before the Belfry (years ending in 2 or 7), and the Feast of the Golden Tree, re-enacting the wedding procession of Charles the Rash and his bride, Margaret of York (years ending in 0 or 5).

WHAT TO SEE? First of all, Bruges and Ghent, two outstanding art cities. Bruges' art and architectural treasures blend so well with its medieval charm that it is undoubtedly one of the most enchanting cities of old Europe. In its buildings Ghent reflects a stormy yet gracious past. After these two "musts," your own interests will decide which direction you will take. You may prefer to linger on the Leie or strike out westwards to Ypres, Furnes, or Oudenaarde. Bruges' latest attraction is the *Dolfinarium,* near the Boudewijn Park, where sea lions and dolphins perform several times daily from end March till end October.

The countryside around Ghent forms a colored carpet of flowers tended by horticulturists who have made the garden-fields of Ghent famous. The beauty of the Leie area (Afsnee, Drongen, Deurle, Astene) has made it a favorite weekend haunt of Ghent's nature lovers.

St. Amandsberg, just outside Ghent, is known for its great Beguines Convent. Two feudal castles, Laarne and Ooidonk, are open to the public on certain days.

Of interest to British visitors are the World War I battlefields and military cemeteries near Ypres and the Menin Gate. American memorials and cemeteries of World War I are located near Waregem (between Kortrijk and Ghent), Oudenaarde, and Kemmel (near Ypres).

HOW TO GO? The quickest way to see the two principal cities is to take the fast electric train from Brussels in the morning, returning in the evening—quickest but the least satisfactory. Bruges and Ghent merit at least a two-day visit unless you are pressed for time. There are numerous train and bus services to the smaller art towns, and you can easily do a round trip.

MOTORING. Via the Brussels-Ostend motorway (*Snelweg),* Ghent is 33 miles and Bruges 61 miles from the capital. From Brussels, St. Niklaas is about 30 miles (but is perhaps more easily reached from Ghent, 21 miles, via the motorway to Antwerp); Oudenaarde is 35 miles; Kortrijk, 54 miles; Ypres, 72 miles; Furnes, 91 miles.

BOAT EXCURSIONS. The most interesting excursion from *Bruges* is to historic Damme, on the canal that connects Bruges with Sluis, a small Dutch border town. For excursions from *Ghent* on the Leie and Schelde rivers, embark at Bartsoenkaai, near Verlorenkost (May-Sept.). To visit the port, apply to Port Authority, 1 Vliegtuiglaan. The M.S. *Groot-Brugge* takes you around the port of *Zeebrugge* with its supertankers, etc., in 45 min. Departure hourly (May-Oct.) from the fishing port.

MUSEUMS. Bruges, the purest of medieval towns in Northern Europe, has several art collections of the first importance. From Apr.-Oct., when not otherwise stated, Bruges museums and historic buildings are open to the public from 9:30-12 and from 2-6 (in winter 4 p.m.). The *Groeninge Museum* is open evenings from 8-10 p.m., June 1 to Sept. 30 for temporary exhibitions (enquire beforehand). A special lighting system strikingly sets off the paintings of the Flemish primitives. Transferable season tickets entitling one to visit all museums are obtainable at the City Tourist Office and at the museums.

BRUGES (BRUGGE). *Groeninge Museum*, on the Dyver Canal. Shows some of the best known masterpieces by Jan van Eyck, Van der Goes, Memling, Pourbus, Gerard David, and Hieronymus Bosch.

The adjoining *Brangwijn Museum* contains a collection by the English painter, Frank Brangwyn, who offered his works to the city of Bruges.

The *Gruuthuse Museum,* originally the palace of the lords whose name it bears today, was King Edward IV's refuge in 1471 during his exile from

England. It shows lace, pottery, goldsmith's art, etc.

Memling Museum, a onetime chapter-room in St. John Hospital's precincts. A unique collection of the master's paintings. Interesting old furniture and household utensils can be seen on the cloister premises next to the medieval pharmacy.

Museum of the Holy Blood. Contains the gold and silver reliquary made in 1617, wrought copperwork, and paintings.

A *Folklore Museum,* converted from 7 adjoining cottages, is found in the little street to the left of the Church of the Holy Sepulchre.

The *Archers Guild of St. Sebastian,* is a unique architectural complex in Carmerstraat and has a remarkable collection of paintings and silverware.

Storie Museum, Steenhouwersdijk 2. The story of lace, in a 12th-15th cent. house.

GHENT. *Fine Arts Museum* in the Citadel Park. Fine collection of paintings by Breughel, Rubens, Jordaens, Pourbus, Tintoretto, Reynolds, etc. Open 10-12 and 2-6.

Museum of Decorative Arts, Breydelstr. 7, the former De Coninck mansion (1752). Rich collection of furniture arranged so as to recall the atmosphere of domestic life in a patrician family of the period. Exhibitions of modern arts and crafts.

Byloke Museum, Godshuizenlaan 2. Officially archeological, by its contents more of a historical museum. Reproduction of late medieval Ghent homes, ironwork, weapons, costumes, etc. Open 10-12:30 and 1:30-6. (In winter: 1:30-5).

Folklore Museum, 41 Kraanlei, Commemorates customs and traditions in the city of Ghent. Interesting and entertaining. Open 10-12 and 1:30-5 (closed Tues.).

Michel Thiery Natural Science Museum, St. Pietersplein 12. Open 9-12 and 4-6:30, closed Mon. and afternoons of Sat. and Sun.

CARILLON CONCERTS. The principal concerts given by the carillonneurs take place in the following localities. *Bruges:* year round from 11:45 to 12:30 on Sun., Wed., and Sat.; from mid-June through Sept., 9-10 p.m., Mon., Wed., and Sat. *Ghent:* less regularly, enquire at City Tourist Office.

THEATERS. Ghent offers opera at the *Koninklijke Schouwburg,* plays in Flemish, puppet shows, and music-hall entertainment. In the *Belfry Cloth Hall,* an audio-visual spectacle, "Ghent in the 14th century".

HOTELS AND RESTAURANTS. The whole region is well supplied with hotels and restaurants. Flanders is too close to the rest of the country to have a distinctive cuisine of its own. You might find the *carbonnades flamandes* better here in Flanders than elsewhere, but that could be auto-suggestion. It is generally agreed, however, that you get the best *waterzooi* version at Ghent, so don't miss the opportunity while you are there. Another local dish is *gentse hutsepot,* containing all sorts of meats and all the vegetables Flanders produces.

AALST (ALOST). Best hotel: *Atlanta,* Stationsplein. Good restaurant in house dating from 1630, *Bourse d'Amsterdam.*

BEVEREN-WAAS. The *Beveren Motel,* on the cross-Flanders road from Ghent, is well-equipped but has only 18 chalets.

BRUGES (BRUGGE). Hotels: *Holiday Inn,* deluxe, the façade is designed to fit in with local architecture, all modern amenities. *Portinari,* Garenmarkt, is self-styled deluxe.

First class superior: *Park Hotel,* 6-8 Vrydagmarkt, 37 rooms each with bath, TV, radio, telephone and mini bar. *Au Duc de Bourgogne,* Huidevetterstr. (overlooking a waterway), 22 rooms with bath; inn-like atmosphere, has a justly famous restaurant. *Grand Hôtel du Sablon,* Noordzandstr. 21, 48 rooms, 22 with bath; old-fashioned and somewhat oppressive. *Bryghia,* Oosterlingenplaats 4, all rooms with bath, is recent (no restaurant).

First class reasonable: *Princess,* excellent, looks old, but is quite recent; good restaurant. *Speelmanshuys,* Zand 3, recent.

Moderate: *Barge* boatel, Komvest, all rooms with bath or shower, has the *Westhinder* boat as restaurant. *Fevery,* Collaert Mansionstr. (no restaurant). *Tybaertshof,* Vogelzangdreef, two miles out, off road to Roesclare.

If you are hard pressed for accommodation, the restaurant *Panier d'Or,* on Grote Markt, has a few guestrooms. Try *Rembrandt-Rubens,* Walplaats 38 or *Atlantic,* St. Jorisstr., moderate to inexpensive.

Restaurants: In full view of the magnificent belfry, you can eat at these terrace restaurants: *Civière d'Or, Panier d'Or.* A good place is the *Central,* Markt 30. *Westhinder* is a floating restaurant at Komvest.

The dining rooms of the *Duc de Bourgogne,* and *Weinebrugge* (at Loppem, two miles out) are excellent: both (E).

DAMME. Historic small town near Bruges. Restaurants: *Bij Lamme Goedzak* (E-M); *Drie Zilveren Kannen* (M), try the duckling pâté.

Two miles out, on canal, *Bruegel,* lobster "Mère Jenny" in rural spot (M); *De Siphon* (M-I) is renowned.

DENDERMONDE. Hotel: *Het Guldenhoofd.*

FURNES (VEURNE). Hotel: *'t Belfort,* reasonable.

Restaurants: *De Beurs, Oud Veurne, Retorika, De Spillon, De Kleoffe* and *'t Paviljoen.*

GHENT (GENT, GAND). Hotels: First class reasonable: *Europahotel,* finely located on Gordunakaai, 40 rooms with bath, and *Carlton,* Koningin Astridlaan 40, 25 rooms with bath, well sited for exhibition visitors, are both good, but neither has restaurant. *Sint Jorishof,* Botermarkt 1, claims to be the oldest hotel in Europe, 71 rooms, 32 with bath. *Parkhotel,* Pr. Wilson Plein, 38 rooms, 22 with bath, is expensive. The new *Holiday Inn,* 120 rooms, at crossing of Amsterdam-Paris and Ostend-Brussels motorways, is 5 kms from city centre.

Moderate: *Grand Vatel,* Maria Hendrikaplein 9, an excellent small residential hotel; next door, the *Terminus.*

Restaurants: *Vieux Strasbourg,* Vogelmarkt 27 and *Cordial,* Kalendenberg 9, are generally considered best and can be expensive if you don't choose carefully. You can have a meal at *Cordial* as late as 2 a.m.; specialty: waterzooi. The excellent *Patinje* (M-E), Gordunakaai 94 is closed from 15 Jly. to mid-Aug. *Venise* (I), is on Koornmarkt. Try the *Raadskelder* (Town Hall) for excellent beer in a medieval atmosphere.

In Ghent's vicinity you can dine superbly in medieval surroundings at *l'Hostellerie du Château,* Laarne Castle. Fairly expensive.

Resorts for sailing, angling, and swimming along the Leie, between Ghent and Deinze, include **Deurle,** 8 miles southwest and **Astene,** a bit farther on: here you can stop at *Wallebeke* (M), for a meal. In Deurle, stay at the *Ralley St. Christophe,* 18 rooms, first class superior. At **Laethem St. Martin** (6 miles out), eat at the *Klokkeput* or its smarter counterpart, *L'Equipe,* both (M).

KORTRIJK (COURTRAI). Hotels: First class reasonable are the new *Porsel,* near the Porsel Towers; *Damier,* Grote Markt, half of rooms with bath; *Boerenhof,* Walle 168, a transformed farmhouse, expensive.

Near the station, *Nord* is moderate, *Continental,* inexpensive.

At Rodenburg, pleasantly situated in a garden, is the *Marquette* hotel and restaurant.

OUDENAARDE. Hotel: *Pomme*

d'Or, small, inexpensive, with restaurant (M).

ST. NIKLAAS. Hotels: *Serwir,* Koningin Astridlaan, is on the expensive side, but has good food, modern amenities and two thirds of rooms with bath. *Spiegel,* Hoek Markt, has 20 rooms, 7 with bath. Reasonable.

Restaurant: *Begijnhofken* (M-E), has rustic décor.

WEVELGEM. About halfway between Kortrijk and French frontier. Restaurant: *Cortina* (M), an excellent halt. 20th-cent. Flemish opulence.

YPRES (IEPER). Restaurants: On Grote Markt, all offering good food, are the *Britannique, Sultan, 't Klein Stadhuis, Miroir* and *Old Tom* (last two less expensive). *Hostellerie St. Nicolas* on Steurstraat, has delicious food.

One of Belgium's gastronomic high-spots, *Hostellerie Mont Kemmel,* is only 8 miles away. It's also an excellent hotel, reasonable.

In the vicinity of Ypres, on the shores of Dikkebus Lake, *Dikkebus,* is a pleasant little hotel, and so is *Hostellerie de l'Etang,* near the lake of the same name.

ZEDELGEM. 7 miles from Bruges, on road to Torhout, a marvelous but expensive hotel-restaurant is *Bonne Auberge.*

CHURCH SERVICES. *Catholic,* in all parish churches. *Protestant:* Bruges, Witte Leertouwerstraat, Sunday service 10 a.m.; Church of England, Ezelstraat, morning service 10:30 a.m. Ghent: Brabantsdam, Sunday service 10 a.m. Ypres: St. George's Memorial Church, a moving reminder of the first world war; evening service on Sundays.

SPORTS. *Canoeing* and *sailing* are popular activities on the Leie and Schelde rivers. These two rivers, along with others in the Schelde basin, offer the *fishing* enthusiasts a varied catch of shad, eel, bream, pike, and perch. There is also *tennis* and, at Waregem, *horseracing.* At Laethem St. Martin, about 6 miles from Ghent, is the 18-hole *golf* course of the Royal Golf Club des Buttes Blanches (Ghent autobus, St. Pierre Station golf stop).

Well-equipped *camping* sites are located at St. Kruis (near Bruges), at Aalter, Drongen, and Heusden in the Ghent area, at Ruien and Wachtbeke; in the St. Niklaas area, at Belsele, Kemzeke, Lokeren, Temse, and Waasmunster.

USEFUL ADDRESSES. *City Tourist Offices:* (Bruges) Markt; (Kortrijk) Town Hall; (Ghent) Borluutstraat 9; (Ypres) Town Hall. *Certified guides*: in Bruges, at the City Tourist Office; in Ghent, at Guides' League, Baliestr. 36.

Car hire: *Van Renterghen Travel Agency,* Grote Markt 13, Bruges; *Autolux,* Ghent.

Excursion boats: Bruges-Damme (bus 4 takes you to landing stage); Ghent-Deurle, information, Benelux Co., Voormuide 77, Ghent.

Exploring Flanders

The Flemish have a great sense of spiritual unity and, even though they were once supporters both of Jansenism and of Calvinism, their unity today revolves more than ever around the Catholic Church. Flanders is a country of large families, and the Flemish-speaking people of Belgium now outnumber the French-speaking. Luckily for the visitor, the Flemish are good linguists. Moreover, the connection with England dates back over many centuries, not only in the commercial field but also in tourist visits and more especially in the migrations of political and wartime refugees.

Ypres, Victim of History

While Ghent is queen of the rivers and islands, and Bruges for some centuries was queen of the sea, Ypres—with the spire of Saint Martin's Cathedral and the sturdier but less aspiring tower of the Cloth Hall—is queen of the Flemish plain. Senior partner in the great triumvirate of Flanders, Ypres was probably in the thick of the textile industry when Menapian cloth was the prized possession of the matrons of ancient Rome. Centuries before Edward III of England gave Bruges the handling of the English wool trade, Ypres was the active centre of a mighty industry that, in the 14th century, gave her the right to annex the Poperinghe countryside and break up the competing looms of the *buiten-poorters* or country citizens.

When you see the Cloth Hall you will realise that only an industry on a large scale—an immense scale by medieval standards—could have justified this provision and this lavish architecture. It dates from the year 1214, and the cathedral is from the same period. Unfortunately, however, little of the original structure is left in either. What you see today has been reconstructed from the ruins of World War I, when the name of "Wipers" stood for the destruction, suffering, and dogged resistance of that last salient of Belgian soil, which never fell.

It is right and fitting that the Cloth Hall should be restored, and so gigantic an enterprise is not for overnight accomplishment. The building has, or had, scarcely its like in the world. Its rebuilding is an act of piety scarcely influenced by the spirit of social usefulness which was never wanting from the original. In the cathedral you can still see the tomb of Bishop Jansen, the Bishop of Ypres whose studies of Saint Augustine produced a "heresy" that divided the Christian world through the second half of the 17th century. When you look at them, in comparison with the size of the town itself, remember the men who built the originals would be surprised to think that a day would come when Ypres would be smaller than London (in the 13th century it was a city of 100,000 inhabitants, today it has less than 20,000).

It may well be that you will take little interest in the reconstructed 17th-century house-frontages that are to be found in a number of streets. Ypres, as she has risen out of the rubble of 1914-18, is essentially a modern town. She is lucky in having a great past round which to build, to have lost whatever she may have possessed of the works of 17th-century architects, and to be at work on her rebuilding at a time when social architecture is awakening from its long sleep.

Some consciousness of this is shown in the Menin Gate, a masterpiece of classic simplicity, built as a lasting memorial to the 250,000 officers and men of the British Commonwealth who lost their lives on the Western Front in World War I. Of these, some 55,000 have no known graves, and their names are engraved on panels on the gate itself. Every evening, traffic through the Menin Gate is stopped for a few minutes while buglers, recruited from the local fire brigade, blow the "Last Post" on silver bugles endowed by the British Legion. Only during World War II has this nightly rite been interrupted and, on the night of Ypres' liberation, the "Last Post" was blown before the last enemy had marched out of the town.

The ancient moated fortifications of Ypres were strengthened by Vauban in the 17th century, and even the bombardments of the 20th century did not destroy them. If you walk up the stairway in the Menin Gate, you will find yourself on the ramparts. You can follow them round as far as the Lille Gate where, nestling below a large cypress and with turf greener than is elsewhere to be found in Belgium, is one of the most picturesque of the many British war cemeteries. These cemeteries are maintained by the Imperial War Graves Commission on soil freely given in perpetuity by the Belgian government, in acknowledgment of the fact that the liberty of their country was brought at a price that included blood other than its own.

The upkeep of the cemeteries has created in Ypres a thriving British community. Among all the reconstruction and modern building, it seems unlikely Ypres will forget that of all her eventful history, the years 1914-18 are the most memorable. If you return to the Grote Markt, pass through the archway of the Cloth Hall and follow round past the cathedral, you will come to the little British Church of Saint George, with its abundance of war memories and, behind it the Pilgrims' Hall, built for those who visit Ypres in quest of family graves.

The tremendous events of the 20th century have all but eclipsed the memories of earlier centuries. There is, however, a link with a remote past: on the second Sunday in May, *Kattenwoensdag,* cats (nowadays only stuffed woolen cats) are flung by the town jester from the belfry-top to the crowd below, after a "Cat" procession with more than 1,700 participants. This is a survival from some ancient, supposedly sun-worshipping, pagan celebration; far more cruel was this observance in the Middle Ages, for then real cats were the victims.

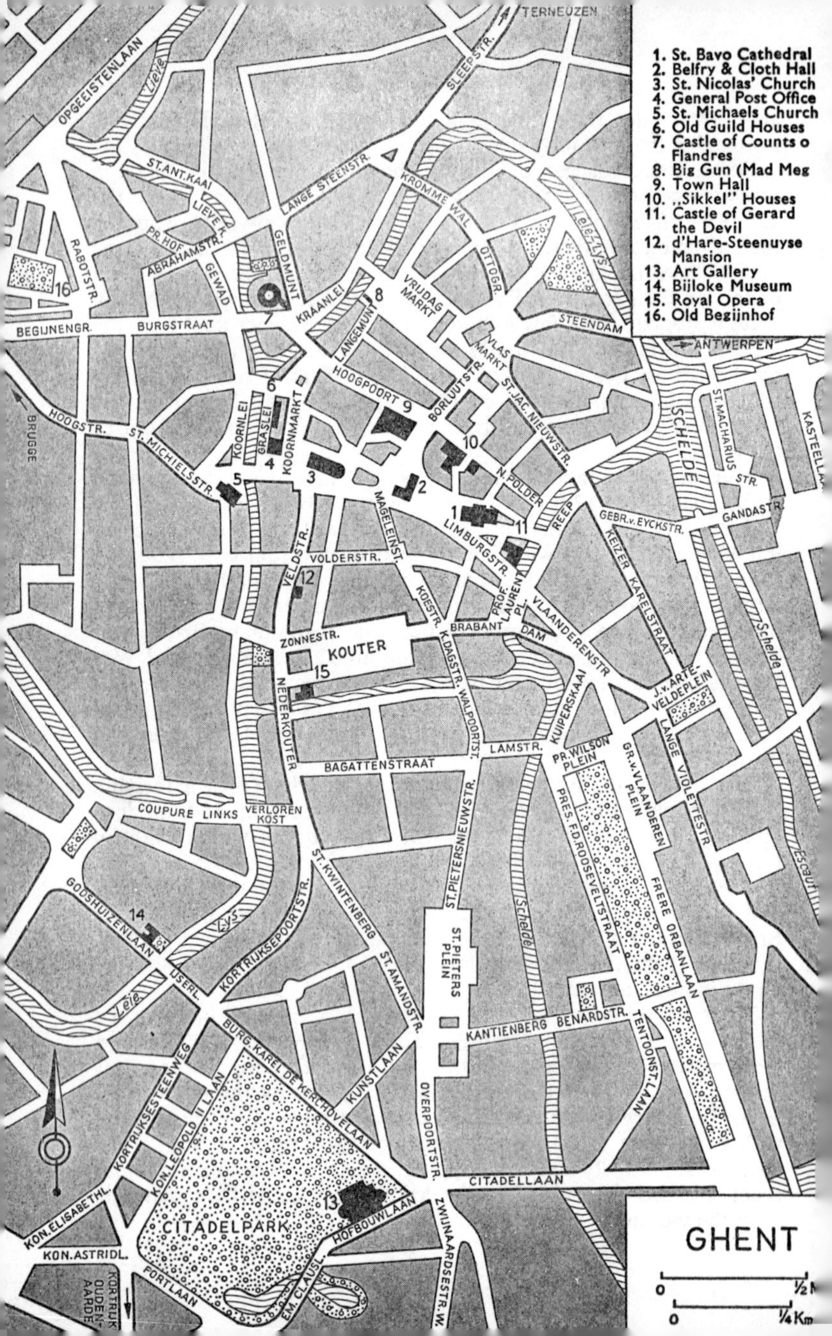

1. St. Bavo Cathedral
2. Belfry & Cloth Hall
3. St. Nicolas' Church
4. General Post Office
5. St. Michaels Church
6. Old Guild Houses
7. Castle of Counts o Flandres
8. Big Gun (Mad Meg
9. Town Hall
10. „Sikkel'' Houses
11. Castle of Gerard the Devil
12. d'Hare-Steenuyse Mansion
13. Art Gallery
14. Bijloke Museum
15. Royal Opera
16. Old Begijnhof
GHENT
0
½ M
0
¼ Km
TERNEUZEN
ANTWERPEN
BRUGGE
KOUTER
CITADELPARK
SCHELDE

The names around Ypres sound like a repertoire of battlefields—Poperinge, Passendale, Kemmel Hill, Ploegsteert. British cemeteries, of course, are almost everywhere, but the country is attractive for walking. Westouter, near Loker, is a typical Flanders village, worth a short halt.

Ghent, "Florence of the North"

If Ypres has lost touch with her remoter past, Ghent has absorbed hers. No city, except perhaps Florence, has had a history so full of dark incident and valiant strife; and in none do the buildings of many centuries jostle one another in so lively an existence of present social usefulness. Ghent does not live in the past; her past lives in her. She has more to show you, if you care to look for it, than any city in Belgium or any city of comparable size in the world. Yet she does not worry unduly about bringing her treasures to your attention.

But the town (pop. 230,000) is not an inanimate museum, as is often said of Bruges. Like Florence, it is full of flowers, for it is the centre of a great and learned horticultural industry. Due to the flowers there is always color in the streets of this grey city, where there is much that dates from the Middle Ages and earlier, but where nothing is self-consciously medieval and where every stone is part of 20th-century life. Incidentally, at Lochristi, six miles out, a Begonia Festival is held on the last weekend of August (the begonia is the national flower of Belgium).

True it is that you can no longer see the palace where Charles Quint was born, with its "six gateways flanked with towers, its gardens where there wandered bears and lions, its 300 halls each with its lock and key, and above them all its tower of glass." All that is left of this splendor is the name of Prinsenhof for a dingy industrial street; and, indeed, Charles Quint, though perhaps the most illustrious of the city's sons, has been the one she has seemed most anxious to forget. Not till 1966 did they erect a statue of him, to replace the one they angrily removed to substitute another of the tribune Jacob (or Jacques) van Artevelde. Ghent has always been proud of her civic liberties, which cost her much blood in defending them against the counts of Flanders and the dukes of Burgundy. She does not seem to have forgotten it was against Charles that her citizens revolted in 1535, or that it was he who disbanded the Abbey of Saint Bavo, even then nine centuries old, for the sake of erecting a military citadel. It is there that Edward III of England resided during his negotiations with Van Artevelde in 1341, and that his queen gave birth to John of Gaunt, Duke of Lancaster.

If you are to understand Ghent, you must not regard it as an antique. It is no more old than a man is old for having a long line of ancestors. True enough, its pedigree traces unbroken through the history of the two abbeys, those of Saint Bavo and Saint Peter, founded by Saint Amand in the 7th century. Ever since the centre of gravity of the wool trade shifted eastward from Ypres, it has been Ghent which has taken the natural leadership in all the troubled days through which Flanders has passed. It was from here that Jan Borluut led his troop of citizens to victory on the field of the Golden Spurs (1302) against the flower of French nobility. From here Philip van Artevelde led his levies against the last of the counts of Flanders to the victory of Beverhout. It was here that the commune executed the councillors of Charles the Rash, and the revolt against princely privilege rebuffed the besieging armies of the Emperor Frederick III. In the religious troubles of the 16th and early 17th century, the Pacification of Ghent (1576) freeing the city from its Spanish garrison, is one of the high points. But the intransigeance of the Ghent Calvinists lost them the support of the rest of Flanders and left them an easy target for Alessandro Farnese, Duke of Parma, in the service of Philip II. Returned to the Catholic faith, Ghent had to face a time of economic difficulty; but it was her Bishop, Maurice de Broglie, who in 1814 launched the religious assault that was the basis of Belgium's separation from the predominantly Protestant Netherlands 16 years later and of her establishment as an independent state.

Ghent is as proud of the Vooruit (Socialist) building as it is of the ancient buildings; and as proud to count among its sons such men as Edward Anseele, the pioneer of socialism, and Maurice Maeterlinck as it is of the Van Artevelde or the overprolific painter, De Crayer. It is a town of great civic pride, and it is a saying that everything done in Ghent is done well. This is certainly true of all the major manifestations of the city's consciousness, such as the stupendous flower show, *Floralies*, held every 5 years (ending in a 5 or 0), the international trade fair held in a park setting every September and the European Music Festival, Aug. 20 to Sept. 20, each year.

Hub of Trade

You must know the city well to realise that it is built on a hundred islands. It stands at the confluence of two rivers: the Leie, which brings its waters from the flax country around Kortrijk, and the Schelde. These waterways have played a big part in Ghent's prosperity. They were one of the causes for the shifting of predominance in the wool trade from Ypres, and Ghent's nearness to the flourishing port of Bruges was a valuable asset. When the wool weavers of Flanders were ruined by English competition, and Antwerp was handling the hated English cloth that Bruges had refused to touch, Ghent turned her attention to the grain shipments coming downriver from France. Her shipping trade grew important, and you will still see the storehouses around the Graslei and Koornlei where the commune stored the tolls, taken in kind, which were put by against times of scarcity. On top of this trade, Ghent began to develop a trade in linen, but it was not till the early 19th century that her textile prosperity again waxed strong.

In 1800 Lievin Bauwens, a leading citizen and later burgomaster, whose statue you will find before the castle of Gerard the Devil, returned from England with the secrets of mechanical spinning and weaving of cotton. (The "Jenny", a power loom smuggled out of Britain piece by piece, is exhibited in the Castle of the Counts.) Within a decade, the Ghent cotton industry had sprung from nothing to employ 10,000 workers, housed in emergency camps.

Since then Ghent has not looked back. The textile industry has had its ups and downs, but the closing of the Liverpool cotton market has given Ghent the opportunity to establish her own, though still on a smaller scale. The seabound traffic, of course, suffered by the closing of the Schelde during the troubles with the Dutch, but this difficulty is now in the far past. A canal has been built through Dutch territory to Terneuzen in the Schelde estuary, making the Ghent maritime traffic independent of Antwerp. In point of fact, the canal needed deepening, and the lock at Terneuzen broadening, in line with present-day traffic, especially tanker traffic. These requirements have lately been settled between Belgium and Holland in the Benelux framework, along with the Antwerp-Rhine canal and the Lanaye bottleneck. Behind the canal, at the northern end of the city, Ghent possesses a first-class seaport, which did outstanding service to the Allied cause in 1944, and has lately been streamlined and enlarged to give access to merchantmen up to 60,000 tons.

Ghent thus combines, with its activity as a flower centre, the roles of Liverpool and Manchester, as a seaport, cotton market and a textile centre. There is much other industry around the canal, and more to come through the modernizing of this most crucial waterway. Oddly enough, it is in the Stadhuis (Town Hall) that the city has its most forceful reminder of its troubled history.

The façade on the Hoog Poort, begun in 1518, differs completely from that on the Botermarkt, which was finished almost a century later. The original plans, by Keldermans and De Waghemaker, would have made it a rival to the town halls in Brussels and Leuven; but, in the meantime, with civic revolt and the religious troubles, Ghent virtually lost her status as an independent commune. By the time work could be resumed, taste had changed and the old plans were regrettably abandoned. This is one of the Ghent grievances against Charles V (Quint); and, in revenge, she exhibits in the Hall of Civil Marriages a monster canvas showing Charles' grandmother, Mary of Burgundy, vainly interceding with the town authorities against the execution of her two ministers, Hugonet and d'Humbercourt.

Peerless Art Treasures

On a summer evening, viewed from St.-Michielsbrug (St. Michael's Bridge), Ghent's noble medieval buildings acquire a fairytale quality under the floodlights: in the background to the left, the truculent lines of the castle; in front, the gabled guildhouses of the Graslei; and farther on, the menacing silhouette of the Belfry, surrounded by the spires of St. Nicolas' Church and St. Bavo's Cathedral. Here you have a magnificent sight.

The city's greatest treasure is undoubtedly the *Adoration of the Lamb*, the big polyptych by Hubert and Jan van Eyck in a side chapel of Saint Bavo's Cathedral. This astonishing 15th-century masterpiece, one of the earliest known paintings in oil, has had many adventures. The nude figures of Adam and Eve were objected to by Joseph II, and even replaced for a time by clothed figures. The central panel was taken to the Louvre in 1799 and only recovered after the fall of Napoleon. It has since been twice stolen by German invaders and its last recovery was from an Austrian salt mine. Meantime the panel of the Just Judges was the object of one of the most daring thefts ever known, and the alleged thief died without disclosing its hiding place. Apart from these adventures, the polyptych alone is worth the visit to Ghent. The cathedral, in which the rather flashy marble of the choir screen and the richness of the Baroque monuments are more striking than pleasing, also contains another precious 15th-century painting, *Christ On the Cross* by Justus of Ghent (who later went to Urbino to teach the Italians to paint in oils), and an interesting Rubens, painted in 1623, of the conversion of Saint Bavo.

Most authorities now deny the legend that the gilded dragon adorning the pinnacle of the Belfry was a crusaders' trophy from

Istanbul. The Belfry, indeed, is another building that never achieved its original design, which would have taken it a full 100 feet higher. It houses a carillon of 52 bells, but the famous tocsin bell Roeland—another of Charles Quint's offences was that he confiscated it—was smashed in the 17th century. On the ground floor of the Belfry is a built-in recess, which housed the iron coffer conserving the charters of privilege granted to the city. The ancient prison gate, close to the Belfry, has a fine portal depicting a strange incident: an old prisoner condemned to die from hunger fed by his daughter's breast.

Adjoining the Belfry is the 15th-century Cloth Hall, whose construction, interrupted when the city's Protestant weavers left for England, was only completed in the last century.

Guardians of a Stormy Past

To get an idea of what Ghent stood for in its earlier days, you must turn up through the delightful Groentenmarkt to the Gravenkasteel. Here, washed by the dirty protective water of the Leie, and superbly buttressed and elegant even in its massive solidity, the castle of the Counts of Flanders dominates the town. One look at it is enough to make you appreciate the reality which must have underlain the strife for civic freedom, and the courage that went into it. Your visit to the castle follows a course determined by imperative arrows, and departure from them is often injudicious. The count's apartment contains an interesting collection of instruments of torture. A fine panoramic view of the city can be obtained from the top of the imposing tower.

The castle, founded in the 9th century, was built up in the 12th on the model of the crusaders' fortified mansions in Syria. Before it is St. Veerleplein, where the pillar surmounted by the Flemish lion marks the site of the scaffold used for the religious executions of the 16th century.

It is natural to proceed from here, away from the Leie, to the Vrijdagmarkt, the traditional forum of the city, used as a place of execution, and also for the disputes among the trade guilds. It was here the riots broke out on the Bad Monday of 1345 between the weavers and the fullers, resulting in 500 deaths. Here, too, the Counts of Flanders were installed on their entry into their capital; and here they held their armed tourneys, took the oath to maintain the privileges of the city, and made their declarations to the people from the Tooghuis, the door of which still exists. The Vooruit building takes its place worthily among a number of interesting buildings of several periods, the most noteworthy of them being the guildhouse of the tanners dating from the late 15th century.

In the Middle Ages the city was dotted with fortified manors. The best known of these "private fortresses" is the Castle of Gerard the Devil, a particularly tough gentleman. Its Romanesque crypt is of exceptional grandeur. The Rabot is a reminder of the 1488 siege by the Austrian Emperor Frederick III and of his defeat by Ghent's burghers under Philip van Cleef. When Charles Quint destroyed the entire defence system of the city in 1540, this fine specimen of medieval military architecture, quite unaccountably, escaped his wrath.

Mad Meg (Dulle Griet), the 15th-century secret weapon, was manufactured around 1430. This 16-ton gun, made entirely of wrought iron, fired heavy stone-balls with a noise that earned it a fitting nickname. Replaced since by ballistic missiles, she stands today opposite the Kraanlei and its charming Renaissance gabled houses.

Array of Religious Relics

The Church of Saint James (Sint Jacob) nearby has a central tower dating from about 1200, but the interior is uninteresting. Jostling the church on one side is a 17th-century Cistercian abbey now used as the town and university library and housing also a secondary school. Equally jostling on the other side is the Church of Saint John. This crowding together of churches is not untypical of Ghent, which has 50 or more churches and was, during the 18th century, famous for its great number of monasteries. Of the latter, the chief trace is the Byloke, lying beside the Leie a short distance south of the Gravenkasteel. This was founded by the Cistercian sisterhood in 1228 to look after the big civil hospital endowed by Ermentrude van Uttenhove. The abbey buildings are given over to an archeological museum, which contains some extremely interesting pre-Van Eyck mural paintings. The refectory and the Chamber of the Poor are worth seeing for their own sake. In addition, the museum contains a miscellaneous collection of articles connected with the history of Ghent, including reproductions of 17th- and 18th-century Ghent homes and a most entertaining assembly of 18th- and 19th-century means of transport from the sedan chair to the early motorcar.

Ghent has two relics of medieval religious life typical of the Belgian Lowlands, the Begijnhofen (Béguinages). The *béguines*, lay sisters of humble origin, lived in communities less secluded than those of the convents. The Ancient Begijnhof, founded in 1234, was abandoned during the 19th century, but is still worth a visit. Close to the Rabot fortress, its houses have been preserved and one can still capture their medieval atmosphere. The Klein Begijnhof (Small Béguinage) is a picturesque town within the city, where forty *béguines* still wearing the ancient Flemish headdress occupy quaint cottages.

Of the two abbeys founded by Saint Amand, that dedicated to Saint Peter survives only in some unclassified remains and in a church built 1,000 years after Saint Amand's day. It is the work of the monk, Pieter Huyssens of Bruges, though in fact it was not finished till long after his day. As the work of a leading master in Baroque, it is worth study though it contains little that is remarkable.

The abbey buildings of Saint Bavo, on the other hand, are a beautiful survival, if not of the original 7th-century edifice or even of the 10th-century reconstruction, at least of 12th- and 13th-century work befitting a religious house of this importance. It was, in fact, the biggest landowner in Flanders during the 14th century, and it was here that Edward III made his sojourn and that John of Gaunt was born. The abbey rose to its apogee near the end of the 15th century, when the abbot was Raphael de Mercatel, one of the bastards of Philip the Good. Most of the buildings survived the austere resolve of Charles Quint to create here a fortress to survey the ebullient burghers of Ghent; and quite a lot survived the property greed that characterized the early 19th century. The museum of stonework is interesting to students, but to the normal visitor the charm of the place is in the buildings themselves, the cloistered gardens, and the magnificent 12th-century *Lavatorium* with its canopied vault, one of the earliest examples of crossed ogive construction.

Other churches deserving a special mention are Saint Nicolas' and the Church of the Augustinians. The former has the third of the great towers of Ghent (the others being the Belfry and Saint Bavo's Cathedral). The tower itself dates from about 1230. In the Augustinian Church, the main point of interest is the series of carved confessionals. Right behind St.-Michielsbrug is the last church to be built in the centre of the city, named after the same saint. Started in 1440 and completed two centuries later—the period of Gothic decadence—it shows many an architectural impurity. Besides some fine stained-glass windows, its main treasure is a splendid *Christ On the Cross* by Van Dyck.

If you see the scheduled sights of Ghent in double-quick time, you will perhaps have gained knowledge and interest, but you will not have felt Ghent's charm nor gained a real knowledge of her spirit. For this, you must wander in the old town, most of all along the Graslei and the Koornlei, noting the gable-fronted houses with their rich ornamentation, which somehow avoids—as the Grand' Place in Brussels does not—the stigma of being over-ornate. See the Butchers' Guildhall from the Kraanlei, and above all see the lordly dwellings of the 13th and 15th century called the *Groote Sikkel, Kleine Sikkel*, and *Achter Sikkel*, after the Van der Sikkel family.

Superb Patrician Mansions

Though the Ghent of which you will see most relics is the Ghent of the 13th to 16th centuries, you must not forget the Ghent of the *équipages* and the powdered footmen. The patrician heritage was never dead, and the nobility maintained mansions as magnificent as in any other capital in the world. Nowadays, most of these sumptuous buildings are given over to other uses, and many of the furnishings are dispersed or destroyed. Nevertheless, in Nederpolderstraat you will find, housing the Ophthalmic Institute, the old home of the Van der Meersch-Maes, where the magnificent staircase is eloquent of a great period.

You could get a closer view of the same period in the Hôtel Hane-Steenhuyse in Veldstraat, but this is no longer a museum. This was the refuge of Louis XVIII during Napoleon's memorable comeback, the "Hundred Days". You will notice here the characteristically unostentatious front on the street and the superb grandeur of the garden frontage (1768). The house, with its splendid ballroom and its furnishings, which still remain, has had a number of illustrious guests, including Alexander I of Russia and William I of Orange. Chateaubriand, who later met Talleyrand here, was in the house during the period immediately before Waterloo, while the Duke of Wellington was a guest in the Hôtel Clemmen on the opposite side of the same street. On the corner of this street and Volderstraat is Hôtel Schamp; in 1814 this was the lodging of John Quincy Adams and the other United States delegates, who, during one of the first of Ghent's giant flower shows, signed the Treaty of Ghent ending the Anglo-American war.

Other buildings from the period of elegance which deserve a mention include the Hôtel d'Oombergen, occupied by the Royal Flemish Academy, in the Koningstraat.

A later building with a very exquisite interior is the theater in Kouter, built in 1848 by the architect Roeland. In the same square is the Hôtel Faligan, built in 1755, the home of the Cercle Noble.

The Waas Country

If you are driving to Ghent from Antwerp, you might fancy a

detour via Sint Niklaas, Dendermonde, and Aalst (Alost). The landscapes are big and broad. Two rivers, the Schelde and the Dender, water these lands and flow on to Antwerp. Onetime capital of the Waas country, Sint Niklaas can look back on 500 years of independence, granted by the Counts of Flanders in 1241. Its vast square is the largest in Belgium. There, among ancient houses, rises Sint Niklaas' Church, which has undergone many alterations since its construction in the 15th century. The city museum has two rooms devoted to Mercator, the geographer and inventor of the grid system, born in nearby Rupelmonde in 1512. His famed navigational planisphere is visible there, and so are some rare maps created by him.

Dendermonde, where the two rivers meet, was often a victim of its strategic position. Normans, burghers of Ghent, Spaniards, Marlborough and, in 1914, the Germans, sacked this city; each destruction was followed by a rebirth. On one occasion Dendermonde suffered devastation at the hands of its own citizens. Rather than see their town fall to Louis XIV, they inundated the whole region. It is little wonder that only a few monuments survive. One, the church of Onze Lieve Vrouw, right behind the Butchers' Hall, has the air of a fortress. It houses two Van Dycks, an altar by the great sculptors, Fayd'Herbe and Duquesnoy, as well as some early Romanesque baptismal fonts. The façade of the Stadhuis is decorated with statues of local potentates and of the city's patron saints. The well-proportioned Belfry contains one of the country's finest carillons.

Driving southward, you enter fertile hop country, hence Aalst's centuries-old fame for beer. Saint Martin's Church is yet another Flamboyant Gothic masterpiece of that father-and-son team, the Waghemakers. Rubens and his teacher, Otto Venius, are both represented, but the highlight of this church is the tabernacle by Duquesnoy. The old Town Hall dates back to the 13th century. Beneath the slogan *Nec spe, nec met u* (Neither by hope nor by fear), two statuettes in the Belfry's recess explain what was meant by these proud watchwords: they represent a down-to-earth merchant and a warrior. Loiter along the few remaining old streets, and visit the town museum, where the display of medieval furniture will delight you.

Bruges (Brugge), Northern Kin of Venice

If it were not for people in modern clothes, it would be difficult in Bruges to realise that you are living in the 20th century. There is scarcely an edifice in the city that does not date from a prior period, and you can even go to the cinema in a 15th-century building. Scarcely a façade on street or canal fails to conjure up visions of a teeming past.

While the canals have led to Bruges being called the Venice of the North, there is much in the character of the town to deserve her alternative name—Bruges la Morte. She has, in fact, been the victim of circumstances, in that her early splendor was eclipsed through events far outside her control. To understand this, you should begin, not with Bruges itself, but with the nearby townlet, the ancient fore-port of Damme, birthplace (in 1235) of the father of Flemish literature, Jacob van Maerlant, and of legendary Thyl Uylenspiegel. This peasant lad, through the sanguinary farces that he adroitly played on the occupying Spanish soldiery, contributed greatly to the rural population's resistance to the Duke of Alba's reign of terror in the 16th century.

Here the waters of the Reie, which flows through Bruges, broadened into the Zwin, which, flowing down past Sluis, gave access to the North Sea. The Maritime Law of Damme was the Bible of the Hansa merchants. Today, Damme is a quiet commune of barely a thousand inhabitants. Both the Church of Our Lady, begun about 1230, and the Stadhuis, dating from about two centuries later, bear witness to a more prosperous past. Indeed, were it not that the nave was destroyed in the religious troubles, the church would look oddly large for a town of this size; and it is still difficult for many to realise that the town was important enough to have been the scene of the weddings of two dukes of Burgundy—of Philip the Good to the Portuguese Isabella and, in 1468, of Charles the Rash to Margaret of York, sister of Edward IV of England, who had sailed upriver with her noble escort.

Even at this time, the seeds of Bruges' decline were being sown. The Zwin was blocking up with the sands of the Schelde. Eighty years later Lancelot Blondeel—painter, architect, and engineer—was drawing plans for replacing the Zwin by a canal to link Bruges with the sea at Heist. This, however, came to no fruition, for in the meantime English cloth was ruining the Flemish weavers and Bruges, having haughtily refused to handle it, saw its trade and its privileges transferred to Antwerp.

It was not until the very end of the 19th century that the idea revived of giving Bruges new access to the sea. The canal to Zeebrugge (which means merely Bruges-on-Sea) and the Mole, which stretches out for over a mile to protect the outer harbour from the west and north, are essentially 20th-century achievements. Its port is being steadily improved. Bruges is making great progress as an industrial port, and the fact that the port is actually on the coast is proving important for quick-moving traffic. Bruges now has a population of 110,000.

History Shaped by Maritime Commerce

The story of Bruges is so tied to the sea and ships that it is hard to give it an existence without them. You will, indeed, see in the Grote Markt a statue of Pieter de Coninck and Jan Breydel, whose great exploit was to organise the Bruges Matines of 1302, when the Flemish workers (Klauwaerts, or Men of the Claw) mercilessly slaughtered the French. This insurrection led to the great Battle of the Golden Spurs, where Flemish weavers won the day against the French. The golden spurs, gathered by the thousand from the slain French noblemen, were hanging from the vault of the choir in the Church of Our Lady in Kortrijk until 1382, when the French, victorious at Westrozebeke, brought them home again. Even a sea town had to fight for its liberties in those stern days, though Bruges had by that time possessed a charter, granted by the Count of Flanders, Philippe d'Alsace, for a century and a half. It was the same count who built the sea wall between Bruges and Damme; and the standing of Bruges in Europe is indicated by the fact that there is reference to this in the *Inferno* of Dante.

It is now nearly 200 years since the demolition of the Waterhalle, the covered barge-port that spanned the canal and fronted on the Grote Markt on the side where the Provincial Palace (and main post office) now stands. But it was long before this that the old glory died. At its height Bruges had all the wealth of a great merchant city, and you will find to this day traces of peoples and influences that do not belong to the various sovereigns who have reigned in Flanders nor to the wars which have been fought across her territory. Such a trace is the Saaihalle though only a wall-plaque remains to mark the site of the House of the Smyrna Merchants.

Bruges retained its glory for about three centuries, and was at its peak under the dukes of Burgundy. It was, in fact, a favored resort of the dukes, and two of the Treasurers of the Golden Fleece had their abodes in the city. It was not only to the dukes, however, that it owed its prosperity. Here came merchandise from the seven seas, and around its point of discharge were congregated the merchants and the rest of the trading community, including the agents of the princely banking houses. If Hugo van der Goes' *Nativity* found its way to the Uffizi in Florence, it was because the Portinari were established in Bruges as agents of the Medici.

Bruges possesses two major treasures, one religious, the other artistic. The first is the Relic of the Holy Blood, which is kept in the Chapel of the Holy Blood. The façade, dating from 1530, is a fine piece of early work under Italian Renaissance influence. The crypt chapel, dedicated to Saint Basil, goes back to the end of the 11th century and contains a bas-relief of this period. The Relic itself is in the upper chapel, in a fine *châsse* made about 1617 by the Bruges goldsmith Jan Crabe. The Relic was, according to tradition, given to Count Thierry d'Alsace during the Second Crusade (1149). The count presented it to the city of Bruges. It is exhibited every Friday morning, and once a year—on Ascension Day—all Bruges is *en fête* and the devout and curious come from all over the world for the procession of the Relic through the city. This pageant, which follows a long and tiring route, includes impersonations of many characters from the Scriptures, from Adam and Eve to the Apostles, and the re-enactment of many Biblical scenes. In the passion play that is enacted every five years in the Grote Markt, several hundred amateur actors, chosen amongst the citizens of Bruges, make up the cast.

The Memling Collection

The city's second treasure is the collection of the work of Hans Memling, housed in the Hospital of Saint John. The hospital itself has been in continuous operation since 1188, and is one of the best unspoilt examples of the architecture of the period. The Memling collection includes the *Mystic Marriage of Saint Catherine,* a big and rather obscure work, and a delightful portrait presumed to be Maria Moreel, the daughter of the burgomaster who was one of the painter's patrons. The pearl of the collection, however, is the *châsse* of Saint Ursula, showing the Ursuline legend in six small paintings—more akin to miniature work than to the normal work of the master—and in which the characters are robed in the clothes of Memling's own day, thus presenting a fine picture of Burgundian Bruges.

Before leaving the hospital grounds, don't miss a visit to the pharmacy, probably the oldest in the world and still dispensing prescriptions. It's medieval charm and dignity are enchanting.

Almost opposite the hospital is the Church of Our Lady, the most important of the many Bruges churches, with its nave dating from 1230 and the Paradise Porch (1465). Its treasures include a lovely, though rather disdainful, white marble *Madonna and Child* by Michelangelo, another of the masterpieces returned since the war from a Nazi-protected sojourn in a Salzkammergut salt mine. This statue was commissioned by the Mouscron merchants in

Bruges, and brought here in 1506. The fondness of the Burgundians for Bruges is brought out here by the tombs of Mary of Burgundy and her father, Charles the Rash. The forest of Wijnendaal, where Mary had the fatal fall from her horse, is a few miles south of Bruges; and it was in the château surrounded by those same woods that King Léopold III made his equally historic decision to surrender with his army in 1940.

The tombs of Mary and her father are in the Lanchals chapel. You will notice the swan among the Lanchals armour, and recall that the name (Lange Hals) means Long Neck. You will have noticed, too, the swans on the decorative Bruges canals; according to legend, they are maintained in memory of the magistrate Pieter Lanchals, done to death by the commune in 1488. His offense was that he took the part of Maximilian of Austria, the famous husband of the lamented Mary of Burgundy, when the men of Bruges revolted against him and imprisoned him as a hostage within their walls. The swans are the tardy reparation the city made to its murdered magistrate's widow.

You will find another reference to the Lanchals episode when you visit the Groeninge Museum, depicted in the two rather terrifying panels by Gerard David illustrating the judgment of Cambyses —a Herodotean legend that involves the skinning of the corrupt judge to make a chair-cover on which his son sits as his successor. These works were ordered by the Bench of Magistrates shortly after the death of Lanchals. The painter took some years in their execution, and maybe his heart was not fully in them, for they are not in the same class as his *Baptism of Christ,* in the same museum. This is a later work, dated 1508, and is generally regarded as the finest work of this Dutch pupil of Hugo van der Goes, who was the last important master of the Bruges school. The school can be studied well in the museum. It contains, indeed, none of the rare works of Hubert van Eyck, but it has Jan van Eyck's portrait of his wife, his *Virgin with Saint Donat,* and one of Canon van der Paele, who has obligingly removed his spectacles for the occasion. Memling's *Saint Christopher* is another tribute to the family of Burgomaster Moreel, showing him and his wife with their five sons and eleven daughters. There is also a dramatic *Death of the Virgin* by Hugo van der Goes, and a beautiful *Virgin of the Sorrows* attributed to Roger van der Weyden, the Tournai painter who learned the mysteries of the Bruges school and appropriated them to enrich the life of Brussels.

Beside the Church of Our Lady is the home of the Gruuthuse family, built in the 15th century. The head of this family was the companion and sage adviser of Charles the Rash. As a museum the house is intensely interesting, especially the 16th-century Flemish kitchen and the collection of old Flemish lace. The striking courtyard forms the setting for the summertime "Sound and Light" spectacles, held every night except Tuesdays.

Imposing Public Buildings and Intimate Markets

The work of the College of Europe needs no introduction to those who follow the affairs of the present day, and its presence here is a reminder that Bruges is nothing if not international. Besides its specific post-graduate programme, the college pursues many cultural and scientific activities, and has an 8,000-volume library dealing with problems of contemporary Europe, particularly in the field of European integration. Though postwar events, especially in the currency field, have robbed Bruges of much of its English colony, it is proud to have counted Sir Frank Brangwyn as one of its citizens. His most striking work, however, is outside the city in the strange, very international monastery of Saint Andrew, where some of the windows are from his design and a number of his most powerful drawings are kept in the chapter house.

It is a short walk along the enchanted canal by the Rozenhoedkaai to turn through the rather surprising fish market and, up the narrow street of the Blind Ass (Blinde Ezelstraat), to find yourself in the Burg (Borough Square). Here, besides the Chapel of the Holy Blood, you will find the Stadhuis, the Palace of Justice, and the Old Registry of Civil Liberties (Oude Greffie van het Vrije). The Palace of Justice is on the site of the former Palace of the Frank, and contains the famous Fireplace of the Frank (De Schouw van het Vrije), from designs by Lancelot Blondeel, in which the elders of Bruges are reminded in marble of the story of Susanna and the Elders.The Burg frontage of the Palace of Justice is 18th-century work, but behind, across the canal, you will see the well preserved façade of the 16th-century Palace of the Frank with its gables and mullioned windows.

From the Burg, another minute's walk will bring you back to the Grote Markt, under the shadow of the Belfry—"thrice destroyed and thrice rebuilded" (Longfellow)—rising to its famous octagonal tower above the 13th-century market buildings. This is not the mother of all the Belgian carillons—a distinction that belongs to Mechelen—but it is certainly one of the most famous in what Thomas Hardy called the "Land of Chimes". The climb of the 400 steps to the top is well worth the effort.

Proceeding along Steenstraat, you will pass the colourful fruit and flower market in the Simon Stevin Plein to reach the Cathedral of The Holy Saviour (Sint Salvator). The first chapel on this site was founded by Saint Eloi in the 7th century. Though nothing of this remains, the base of the tower dates from about 1120 and its rather uninspired top is unmistakably 19th-century. The spatial arrangement of the church is most pleasing, and the side walls are hung with a number of interesting canvases by Van Orley and Claeissens. There is a heavy marble screen with some good ironwork, and the stalls beside the choir are fine examples of 15th-century wood carving. Here, too, are the armorials of the knights present at the 13th Chapter of the Order of the Golden Fleece (1478). It was, in fact, at Bruges that Philip the Good had founded the order almost half a century earlier.

At the end of Steenstraat you will come to the broad square, formerly the railway station, which is still busy finding its place in the scheme of the Bruges of today. You will do well to continue your walk along the broad concrete road to the rail station, now outside the town. It is a low, functional and unfussy building in a setting of trees, lawns and canal-water, whose garden display in front makes it one of the more attractive stations in Europe. The building is by Van Kriekinge (1939), and the mural paintings in the booking (reservation) hall are by René de Pauw.

Most Picturesque Spots in Town

Returning from the station, a right turn from the main road will take you past the modern hospital of Saint John to the Minnewater, the most picturesque spot in this picturesque town, separated from the canal by an equally picturesque lockhouse. You can sit under the trees by the almshouses (Godshuizen) and the lace shops before crossing the bridge into the Begijnhof. The green, tree-shaded quadrangle with the little old houses and the robed and coiffed beguines is a subject dear to many painters, as it was to Sir Winston Churchill. There is a small folklore museum to be seen, and the house of the Grande Dame. The public may attend services in the Church of Saint Elizabeth, reconstructed in the 16th century after the burning of the 13th-century chapel.

The gateway to the Begijnhof dates from the foundation of the institution in 1245, by the then Countess of Flanders, Margaret of Constantinople—the same Black Margot (Zwarte Margriet) who was captured by the King of France, incontinently married her tutor at the age of ten, and as impetuously repudiated him and her children at the age of 21 to marry again and raise another family. All Europe was involved in the legitimacy squabble that ensued, and it was over thirty years before a political compromise was forced on the rivals by Louis IX of France (Saint Louis): the second family took the county of Flanders and the first took Margot's other domain of Hainaut. Thus, the cunning politics of France, having acutely ensured a discordant atmosphere between the menacing Hainaut and the quarrelsome Flanders with its English backing, legitimised for the latter the countship of Margot's son, Guy de Dampierre.

A walk along the ramparts from the Minnewater will bring you to Saint Catherine's Bridge across the encircling canal whence, turning left and following the girdle of the city, you will pass the Gentpoort and re-enter the town by the Kruispoort which leads into Peperstraat and to the astonishing Church of Jerusalem, a pseudo-Oriental edifice. Three journeys to Jerusalem were made to ensure the church being an exact replica of the Church of the Holy Sepulcher. It was consecrated in 1428. There is a raised choir, and a sinister sculptured altarpiece surmounted by three crosses. The founders were more successful in the stained glass, in which they are themselves commemorated.

Hard by the church is a lace-making school working under the instructions of nuns, and the local Folklore Museum. Striking northward (Balstraat) to Carmerstraat, you will come to the 18th-century chapel of the English Ladies (Engels Klooster), one of the several aristocratic British religious settlements that took root in Belgium in this period. At the end of the same street is the house of the Guild of the Archers of Saint Sebastian, another link with England through the patronage of the exiled Charles II and, in less contentious conditions, by the recent honorary membership of Queen Elizabeth II of England, and her husband, the Duke of Edinburgh. Farther north, beside the Reie before it crosses the canal-girdle on its way to Damme, is the Hospice de la Poterie, a 13th-century almshouse for old ladies, with its 14th-century church (notice the brass candelabra) and a museum containing pen-sketches rather doubtfully attributed to the Van Eyck brothers and their sister Margaret. Also beside the Reie, just south of the hospice, is the old Abbey of the Dunes, which houses a truly remarkable collection of illuminated manuscripts. On your way back into Bruges you pass the Church of Saint Walburga, by Brother Pieter Huyssens, whose work in Ghent we have already noticed.

Returning to the Grote Markt, and leaving it by the northwest corner and the Sint Jacobstraat, you will come to Sint Jacob's Church, which is especially worth visiting for the lovely Luca Della Robbia Madonna in pottery and the tomb—flanked by his two wives—of Gerry de Gros, a Treasurer of the Golden Fleece. Another treasure of the church is the *Coronation of the Virgin* by

Albert Cornelis, a 16th-century master of whose work little has yet been identified. There is also some work by Blondeel, and a *Madonna of the Sorrows* by Pieter Pourbus. In the same street, Number 19 is the house occupied by another Treasurer of the Golden Fleece, Pierre Bladelin, who eventually relinquished it to the Medici agent, Tomaso Portinari. Bearing round from here to the right, you will come to the town theater, and the Poorters Loge, a 15th-century building which was the house of the "inside" burghers—those who lived in Bruges itself, as opposed to those who were centred on the Palace of the Frank, the "outside" burghers. In the façade of this building is the little, and unexplained statue of a bear, known as *Beertje van de Loge*. He was installed there in 1477, and is now revered as the oldest inhabitant, and in the same way as the Manneken Pis in Brussels, he has several costumes which are worn on different occasions.

Walking down beside the Poorters Loge, you will come into the van Eyck Plein, with a good 19th-century statue of Jan. Beyond this is the Spiegelrei (Quay of Mirrors), now the deadend of the canal that once linked the Reie with the Grote Markt. The truncated canal leads you in one block to the Reie; follow the river round to the right (upstream) when you reach it at the end of the cutting. Rather than follow the Predikheerenrei through another cutting to the girdle-canal, you will probably follow the river round to your right again—this is the boundary of 12th-century Bruges—past Dyver to the Steenhouwerskaai and on again to the Quai of the Rosary. The canal and river quays are Bruges itself. The tabloid way of enjoying them is to take a 40-minute trip in a motorboat. The canals have recently been dredged and cleaned at a cost of some five million dollars, and a quiet stroll round the quays can be relaxing and interesting. Do not neglect the northern cutting; you can reach it, at the Augustijnenrei, by walking north with the theater on your left and the Poorters Loge on your right. Farther round, beyond this enchanted quay, you will find the Convent of the Black Sisters, and the 19th-century statue of Hans Memling.

Furnes (Veurne), Locale of a Colorful Procession

A 30-mile drive from Bruges southwestwards and almost parallel with the coast will bring you to Furnes (Veurne). It is a good plan to see the one while the other is fresh in your mind, for the Procession of the Penitents, which takes place on the last Sunday in July at 3:30 p.m. and to which Furnes owes its fame, has the same Gothic spirit as the Bruges Pageant of the Holy Blood. This observance always attracts a great crowd. There is some doubt as to whether the procession dates back, as is claimed, to the 12th century—to the time when Count Robert II of Flanders, after his miraculous escape from shipwreck, fulfilled his vow of presenting to the first Flemish church he saw (the Church of Saint Walburga) the fragment of the True Cross which he had brought from the Holy Land. This precious relic would of course account for the Holy Cross entering very deeply into the consciousness of the townsfolk, and it may well be that it would serve as basis for the alternative theory that the procession started in 1644, as an intercession against the plague and against an outbreak of war between the Spaniards and the French.

Be this as it may, the procession differs from that of Bruges in that it does not concern the Holy Relic itself, but exhibits the passage of hooded and black-robed penitents carrying their own heavy crosses through the town. It is interspersed, in the same way as the Bruges event, with costumed set-pieces. It is organised by a local devout society, which is also responsible for the less spectacular but very sincere procession making Stations of the Cross every Friday in Lent.

Furnes was a key-point during the Spanish occupation, and the visitor is apt to see a very real Spanish influence in the buildings, which have been comparatively untouched by time and suffered little in the two world wars. The flamboyant Flemish Renaissance is tempered here by Spanish dignity and severity. You can still see the Spanish Guard House and the Spanish Officers' Mess, and both the Stadhuis and the Palace of Justice date from the Spanish period. The Stadhuis (town hall), which dominates the vast square, has a graceful loggia and its interior is panelled with magnificent skins brought by the Spaniards from Cordoba. The two churches are older, but the oldest parts in Saint Walburga date from a century or more after Robert II who died in the year 1111. Saint Nicholas' has a fine brick tower, erected in the 13th century. Its greatest treasure is the *Crucifixion,* a painting attributed to Van Orley.

Dixmude's World War I Memorial

A 10-mile drive in a southeasterly direction brings you to Dixmude, chiefly remarkable for the IJzer (Yser) Tower, which stands by the river as a memorial to the resistance of King Albert's troops during World War I. This impressive monument has, in the course of years, become the symbol of Flemish, rather than Belgian national aspirations. It is the centre of a pilgrimage, the IJzerbedevaart, on the third Sunday in August, when many thousands of Flemish patriots crowd into Dixmude. The proceedings begin with an open-air Mass, after which there are speeches and Flemish patriotic songs and a vastly impressive laying of flowers on the memorial. So great are the partisan passions involved around this memorial that it has, since the war, been severely damaged by a bomb. The Flemish patriots (they are not, for the most part, separatists) have so far identified the tower with their own cause that the slogan is that Flanders will build its tower again. The fact that it is a national memorial seems to have been passed over.

This charming old town was completely razed by four years' continuous shelling, and whatever you see in the way of period architecture is a reconstruction of old Dixmude (Diksmuide), including Saint Martin's Church. You can still visit the network of trenches outside town that gives you an impression of living and fighting conditions in World War I.

Kortrijk (Courtrai) and Oudenaarde

The tides of war have swept so fiercely over Dixmude that little is left to remind you of an earlier history. The same could be said of Roeselare, a town which you will pass in the 25-mile drive to Menen (Menin). You are here at the French frontier, and the town was one of those held against the French in the 18th century, largely because the fortifications had been perfected a century earlier by the French expert, Vauban. From here, taking the Brussels road, you quickly come to Kortrijk, the capital of the flax and linen industry, and a town that has never grown poor. It is a busy town and does not seem to lay itself out for the idler or the sightseer. The main Cloth Hall was almost wholly destroyed in World War II, but Kortrijk's connection with flax will be obvious to you from the fields round about, even though it is no longer in the chalkless Leie itself that the flax is now retted. The Church of Our Lady, also damaged in the war, once contained the golden spurs of the French knights picked up by the victorious men of the loom on the battlefield (just outside the town) in 1302. It does in fact contain the *Elevation of the Cross* by Sir Anthony van Dyck, painted in 1631 during his Antwerp period. The chapel of the counts of Flanders is also worth seeing, both for its own sake and for that of the delicate late 14th-century statue of Saint Catherine, the authorship of which has never been satisfactorily settled. The Stadhuis, a 15th-century Flamboyant Gothic building, contains two fine fireplaces.

Situated between the churches of Saint Martin—with its Baroque tower—and Our Lady, the fine Begijnhof takes us back into the Middle Ages. This little township of whitewashed, gabled houses, and the silence that surrounds it, excludes a rarely equalled old-world charm. Medieval but of a different character are the powerful Broel towers that once guarded the bridge over the Leie.

Keeping on the Brussels road you pass through Oudenaarde, which certainly deserves a stop, for it was the mother of the art and industry of tapestry-making before its workers emigrated—not, like the weavers to England, but to France—and you will see some magnificent early tapestries in the Town Hall. The building itself is one of the showplaces of Belgium, ranking with the town halls of Brussels and Leuven in architectural splendour. It stands by itself at one end of the Grote Markt, with its detailed ornamentation and its queer crown-topped tower above which stands the gilded Hanske 't Krifgerke (Battling Jack). It was built in the third decade of the 16th century by the Brussels architect, Van Pede. The interior is well worth seeing, both for the tapestries and for the fireplaces. In the second floor museum are the 12 *simarts*, metal pots in which the municipality would send round the wine required by a visiting nobleman for the banquet he would undoubtedly be giving. This early gesture of encouragement for the tourist industry fixed 12 as the number of filled *simarts* to be presented to an emperor, though a king's ration was limited to six and a prince would get only two.

Saint Walburga's lofty tower was made top-heavy by the bulb crowning it. The church of Onze Lieve Vrouw van Pamele (13th century), is of a much purer style and one of the finest examples of Romano-Gothic in northern Europe. The Cloth Hall is of the same period, while Margaret of Parma's House is in late-vintage Gothic. Tired of affairs of state, Charles Quint used to come and visit the lovely Jeanne van der Geenst in this house, where Margaret, child of this love affair who later became regent of the Lowlands, was born.

In front of the Town Hall is the fountain presented by Louis XIV, a reminder that here you are not far from the French frontier, and that the importance of Flanders in Franco-British, Franco-Spanish, and Franco-Austrian rivalries led to Oudenaarde's being four times occupied by the French and eventually to the Duc de Vendôme's defeat by Marlborough under its walls (1708). In Saint Walburga's Church you will find the tombs of four priests drowned in the Schelde by the Protestants, and a picture of the incident. There is another picture, too, of the buying back of Christian slaves from Turkey, a work that was organised from Oudenaarde.

Two war memorials connect Oudenaarde with the New World. It was here that the Belgian corps of volunteers was formed in 1864 to help maintain Maximilian's shaky empire in Mexico. One monument commemorates those who fell at the Battle of Tacambaro. The other memorial honors American soldiers who gave their lives helping to defeat Imperial Germany in World War I.

At the French-Flemish Language Border

Continuing on the Brussels road, at Nederbrakel you are in green, hilly country with a fine view over the Flemish plain. A right-hand road leads you quickly to Geraadsbergen, a curious survival, fast becoming industrialised. You are here at the extreme frontier between the French and Flemish languages and within a mile or two of the formal frontier between Flanders and Hainaut provinces. You will be surprised to see, in a niche in the Town Hall, a replica of the Brussels Manneken Pis, a memorial presented by the city of Brussels in tribute to the courage of the people in recovering the original statue from the Duke of Cumberland's soldiery after the Battle of Fontenoy. Geraardsbergen is built on the sides of two hillocks on one of which, grandiosely called La Vieille Montagne, stands a little chapel containing the little black miracle-working Vierge de la Vieille Montagne, to whom a processional pilgrimage is organised on the first Sunday in Lent. This is the prelude to the Cracknel Festival, which begins with the filling of a cup of wine containing a number of small live fish. The burgomaster, aldermen, and certain other notables pass the cup from hand to hand, each drinking till he has swallowed one or more of the fish. After this the cracknel cakes are flung among the crowd, and the festival has begun.

Crossing the main Brussels-Ostend road you arrive at Deinze, one of the oldest towns in Flanders, though little remains of the past glory which was its own from its purchase by Robert de Béthune (1316) through the creation of its Marquisate (1625). There is a good deal of 13th- and 14th-century work in the church, but the blowing up of the tower in 1918 did a great deal of damage necessitating elaborate restorations.

A little farther on is Tielt, which was a fortified town as long ago as 1172 and a prosperous textile centre when the Burgundian troops set fire to it in 1579. The 13th-century carillon tower rises above the market building.The carillon itself, which is Tielt's main claim to modern fame, was installed in the 17th century. The old hospital of the Alexian sisters is another foundation of Black Margot, or Margaret of Constantinople, Countess of Flanders and foundress of the Begijnhof of Brughes. A Bee Museum was opened recently in the restored outbuildings of the Château of Tielt.

A wandering barber and native of Tielt, Oliver Necker was one of the greatest self-made men of the Middle Ages. Better known as Olivier le Daim, he became the friend and confidant of ruthless Louis XI, one of France's greatest kings. After Louis' death in 1484, Parliament's first action was to have him hanged.

The route has covered the main centres in Flanders, politically divided into two provinces—East (with Ghent as its county town) and West (centred on Bruges).The route has also covered the chief parts of the Flemish countryside, except for the uninteresting section between the Ghent-Bruges road and the Dutch border.

THE BELGIAN COAST

Endless string of Beach Hotels

For some 40 miles, from the French frontier to the Dutch, the Belgian coast stretches in its unbroken belt of sand. The country behind is mostly polder country, lying below sea level, relying much for its protection on the line of reeded sand-dunes that hide the sea from large parts of the broad coast road, and on the great seawall *(Zeedijk* or *Digue)*, which adds to the protection of the chief built-up areas. It is a paradise for summer holidays, though at the peak of the season you will find more people there than you would ordinarily expect in Heaven.

There is good reason for the popularity of the coast. The sea stretches northward with no landfall for many hundreds of miles, and the freshness of the air strikes many miles inland. The water is shallow and the tides are long, but there can be strong currents, so watch out for the warning flags. There is a big area of sand kept clean by the forces of nature and firm to the feet and the horse's hoof. Moreover, Belgian children have but short school holidays except for the two months of high summer, when *Le Littoral* or *De Kust* is their summer playland. Landladies expect children with the summer months, and lay themselves out to make things easy for parents. This is a great industry—tourism ranks as the third greatest industry in Belgium—and you will find none of the "no dogs or children" notices that leave such a bad taste in the mouth.

Practical Information for the Belgian Coast

WHEN TO COME? The holiday season on the coast runs from mid-May to mid-Sept. reaching its peak in July and August, when prices are up by nearly 30 percent. In this country of uncertain weather it is just as safe to spend a few days early in June or sometimes in September as during the principal summer months.

Only a few miles inland are such art cities as Bruges, Furnes, Damme, and slightly farther on, Ghent and Ypres. A cloudy or inclement day can thus be turned into an unforgettable voyage into the past.

Unless you book accommodations well ahead, you should avoid the area on July 21 (Belgium's National Day), August 15 (Feast of Assumption), and weekends nearest these dates. At these times, Belgium as a nation swarms to the coast.

Events: Regional events are plentiful. They start as early as *February* with carnival processions at Blankenberge and Heist. In early *March* Ostend stages its masked Ball of the Dead Rat, a stupendous affair embracing the whole town. Later in the month its traditional carnival cortege takes place. The arrival of spring is celebrated in *April* with a vast Flower Market at Koksijde (Coxyde); fishermen make a pilgrimage to the statue of Our Lady "Star of the Sea," washed ashore in the 16th century. The 8th of *May* is a double V-Day in Ostend, commemorating the *Vindictive's* exploit in World War I and Germany's capitulation in World War II. In *June,* Koksijde is in the fore again with a 2-day celebration, comprising a historic procession and Giant's sortie. Yet another traditional procession, the Ommegang, takes place at Ostend, ending with a religious ceremony, the Blessing of the Sea. Nieuwpoort repeats its yearly procession of St. John on the last Sunday of that month.

There is a popular shrimp-catching contest on horseback at Oostduinkerke early in *July* and a folklore cortege at Koksijde. Only a few miles inland, Furnes (Veurne) stages its famed Penitents Procession, while Ostend has its yearly Seafarers Day. King Albert Commemoration Day is held in *August* just outside Nieuwpoort and there is a naval cortege and blessing of the sea at Knokke-Heist on 15 Aug. each year. Toward the end of the month the festivities wind up with a Flower Corso at Knokke.

The Summer Festivals at Ostend and Knokke are an uninterrupted succession of musical, artistic, and theatrical events that last throughout July and August. During the same period both resorts stage topical art exhibitions of the first order in their casino's gallery.

"Gastronomic Weekends" are a feature at Ostend. Inclusive price of 950 frs. per person for accommodation, meals in the Casino, etc. Evening dress recommended. Knokke-Heist offers "Evasion Weekends" at about 1200 frs. per person.

WHAT TO SEE? Though you came primarily to laze about and enjoy the golden sand and the sea, you will probably want to vary this pleasant monotony by a short outing. Nature lovers will visit the splendid dunes between De Panne and the French border or, at the other end of the coast, the Zwin marshes covered with sea lavender that blooms in July and August. This is a site of 370 acres, where bird watchers have the opportunity of seeing and hearing more than 100 species of birds. Birds abound at the Zwin Aviary outside Zoute for the benefit of amateur ornithologists. Crossing the Zwin, one can climb up the high dunes and be rewarded with a magnificent view of the North Sea, the mouth of the Schelde, the "Isle" of Walcheren, and the hinterland with its Belgian and Dutch steeples. You can visit the tiny Dutch township of Sluis, near Knokke. A fast car-ferry crosses the Schelde to Walcheren.

At Zeebrugge you can board the M.S. *Groot-Brugge* and visit the port. Or see the Naval Museum, partly devoted to the famous battle of 1918. Three miles inland, the ancient village of Lissewege merits a visit.

The house of the painter James Ensor at 27 Vlaanderenstraat, Ostend, has re-opened.

HOW TO GET ABOUT? Visitors from Britain may choose one of the drive-on/off car ferries, from Dover to Ostend or Zeebrugge or Tilbury to Antwerp; or one of the several air services that connect London, Lydd, Southend, Birmingham and several towns in the north of England with the much improved international airport at Middelkerke (for Ostend).

There is a fast electric train from principal Brussels stations to Ostend every hour and almost as often to Blankenberge and Knokke. One of the finest highways on the Continent connects Ostend with Brussels, and an excellent parallel trunk road via Ghent and Maldegem connects with Knokke-Zoute and with Blankenberge via Bruges. There's a fine coastal road (Route Royale) from Knokke to De Panne, and fast, comfortable trams run every half hour from one end of the coast to the other.

For inland excursions you may use the numerous bus lines connecting the large coastal localities with Bruges, Furnes, etc. Special excursion buses.

SPORTS. Sailing enthusiasts will find ample opportunity to spend their holiday on the water. A permanent breeze along the coast offers splendid facilities for *yachting.* Regattas are frequently held in Ostend; best known is the Ostend-Blankenburg race. In addition to these two places, Zeebrugge and Nieuwpoort have also good yacht harbors. There are many navigable canals throughout the area for *canoeing.* You can play *golf* on the 9-hole courses at Zoute. The coast is dotted with *camping* sites, the biggest concentration found between Bredene and Klemskerke. *Horseracing* meets take place almost daily during July and August at Ostend's Wellington Racetrack; international *jumping* tournaments are organized by Ostend and Zoute. At De Panne and Oostduinkerke there is 3-or 4-wheeled *land-yachting. Tennis* tournaments take place during the season at Ostend and Zoute. There are hundreds of tennis courts along the coast; all resorts and some hotels have their own facilities. Safe *swimming* at the splendid Olympic pool (with restaurant and café) at Knokke. Indoor pools at Palais des Thermes and near beach, Ostend.

Warning for swimmers (and especially non-swimmers): bathe only at official beaches patrolled by lifeguards. Red flag means bathing prohibited; green, bathing open, lifeguards on duty; yellow, bathing risky, but lifeguards on duty.

Children's sports and playground at the *Pinguin Club,* Zeedijk, Knokke.

SPAS AND CASINOS. The Palais des Thermes at Ostend offers mineral baths for the treatment of rheumatism with water from a well sunk to over 1,000 feet, along with electro-therapy and other cures.

You may invest your savings in chips of 10 to 1,000 francs at the casinos of Ostend, Knokke-Zoute, Blankenberge, and Middelkerke, and see what happens.

HOTELS AND RESTAURANTS. There are over a thousand hotels and pensions, from the simplest to the most luxurious, along the coast. You should experience no difficulty in finding accommodation at short notice, except during the peak periods, around July 21 and August 15. Value added tax is included, but 16% service charge is added to the bill and there is no need for extra tipping either in hotel or restaurants.

Though older hotels have restaurants, often very excellent ones, and are willing to quote *en pension* terms, many new ones quote only for bed and breakfast and serve no other meals. The latest construction phase incorporates kitchenettes in hotel rooms, or pairs of rooms, even when there is a restaurant on the premises.

Recently, for administrative purposes, five closely connected resorts have been regrouped as Knokke-Heist. They comprise Albertstrand, Duinbergen, Heist, Knokke and Zoute. But since visitors are not concerned with administration, we treat them here separately.

ALBERT-STRAND. Hotels: *La Réserve*, very luxurious with sports amenities; 42 rooms and 3 suites, all with bath. Tea dances and music. Due to be enlarged to 120 rooms plus a therapeutic center with hot seawater bath. The *Résidence Albert*, 27 rooms with bath, is also deluxe.

First class reasonable: *Nelson, Astoria* and *Du Soleil.*

Moderate: *Lido*, 36 rooms, 20 with bath; *Simoëns,* 40 rooms, 18 with bath; *Trianon,* 43 rooms, half with bath.

Restaurants: Good are *Less Flots Bleus, Rubens, Esmeralda* and *Don Pepe.*

BLANKENBERGE. Small fishing port grown into noisiest and gayest of the beach resorts. Caters to all tastes. Has about 148 hotels.

Hotels: Leading and first class superior: *Petit Rouge,* Zeedijk.

First class reasonable: *Idéal,* on Zeedijk, followed by nearby *Laforce; Azaert,* Molenstraat.

Moderate: *Du Louvre* and *Imperial,* both on Kerkstraat.

Restaurants: Best are *l'Huitrière* (M-E), de Smet de Naeyerlaan 1; *des Colonies,* Kerkstr. 95; *La Grande Marée,* Bakkerstr. 6; *St. Hubert,* Manitobaplein 15.

There are restaurants galore on the Zeedijk, all very reasonable. One of the best is at the casino.

BREDENE. Center of largest camping sites. Hotels: *Europa,* moderate; *Meiboom,* inexpensive.

COXYDE (see Koksijde).

DE HAAN (LE COQ). Has some very good hotels and a splendid beach.

Hotels: *Hôtel des Dunes,* Léopoldplein (breakfast only), and *Belle Vue,* Koninklijk Plein, one third of their rooms with bath, are moderate. *Familles,* Koninklijke Baan, is inexpensive.

Restaurant: *Hostellerie au Coeur Volant* (E), Normandiëlaan (book ahead), is outstanding. Specialties are hot lobster à l'armoricaine and chicken flambé au whisky.

DE PANNE (LA PANNE). Westernmost beach resort of the coast. Has about 60 hotels and pensions.

Hotels: *Parc,* Dumontlaan, 48 rooms, 22 with bath. *Terlinck,* Zeedijk, 55 rooms, 32 with bath, slightly more expensive, but both first class reasonable, as is *Royal,* Zeelaan, 40 rooms, 22 with bath.

Carlton and *Des Princes* are inexpensive, while *Astrid,* Duinkerkslaan, is even more modest.

Two good pensions in Nieuwpoortlaan: *À l'Avenue* and *Ville de Roubaix,* both moderate, as is the *Strandmotel* in the same street.

Restaurants: Among many, best is *Le Catinou,* Bortierplaats.

DUINBERGEN. Pleasant family resort, conveniently situated near Knokke. Two excellent hotels in Patriottenstraat: *Bel Air* and *Soleil,* both first class reasonable. *La Dunette,* almost in same category, well situated, with excellent restaurant, the *Wielingen.* Several small hotels and pensions.

HEIST. Next door to Duinbergen. Hotels: The *Royal,* on seafront, and 80-room *Grand* next to it, are first class reasonable.

At nearby Westkapelle, the elegant *Ter Zacle* is first class superior with apartments, modern rooms and heated outdoor pool.

Ter Dycken (M) is a good restaurant with rustic décor.

KNOKKE. Has about 100 hotels and pensions. Prices lower than at Albert-Strand or Zoute.

Hotels: Leader is *Nouvel Hôtel,* first class reasonable, followed by *Aquilon, Mayfair, Select* and *Princes,* all good, reasonable.

Moderate: *Westland, Zwinneblomme,* and *Le Chapon Fin.*

Restaurants: *Toison d'Or* and *Panier d'Or,* are excellent. *Grand Chef,* Lippenslaan, is (M). Good value are *Firenze, La Petanque, Marmite, Eric* and *La Patate.*

KOKSIJDE (COXYDE). *Terlinck* and the rather bigger *Royal Plage,* both on the seafront, are moderate. Also on the seafront is *Louise,* inexpensive. (See also nearby St. Idesbald.)

Restaurant: *Gentilhommière* (M).

LISSEWEGE. Hardly south of Zeebrugge, this old-world village has some outstanding restaurants: *Goedendag* (15th-cent.), and further south, near the vestiges of an abbey, *Hof Ter Doest.* Both (M-E).

MIDDELKERKE, family beach near Ostend. Has about 25 hotels and pensions, most of them small, with good cuisine.

Hotels: *Zeebries,* 42 rooms with bath, newest and largest; *Excelsior* (breakfast only); *Floralies,* on seafront, expensive; *Orchidées,* not on seafront, reasonable, has fewer bathrooms; *Rotonde* and *Regent* (M).

At the Casino, the *Sirène* (M), is recommended for a meal.

NIEUWPOORT. Small fishing port and yacht harbor slightly inland. Known for its good cuisine. The actual beach is two miles out.

Hotels: *Peter Pan* is best but very small. *Sandeshoved* is largest (125 rooms, 68 with bath), but does not accept overnight guests in principle, reasonable. *Tourisme,* quite inexpensive. The *Park Hotel,* 175 Albertlaan, has 21 rooms, all facilities, and some furnished flatlets.

Restaurants: *Thalassa,* on seafront, offers the famous local fish soup (bisque). You can choose your live lobster at *L'Huitrière,* between town and beach, with their own oyster park. The *Rôtisserie de l'Espinette* is the place for grills.

OOSTDUINKERKE. Famed for its shrimp-fishers on horseback, has wide sands. Hotels: *Westland* on the western zeedijk is an "all rooms with bath" hotel, with fitted kitchenettes. A good pension, the *Britannia.*

OSTEND (OOSTENDE). This "Queen of Belgian beaches" has about 200 hotels and pensions. In winter gastronomic weekends at the casino are popular.

Hotels: The *Royal Club Hotel* is a former royal residence. On seafront with private park; 14 rooms with bath, TV. Dining room and bar on ground floor. *Palais des Thermes,* 157 rooms, most with bath, is deluxe. Thermal springs and cure; covered pool.

First-class, fully equipped and comfortable but without restaurants, are *Ter Streep* (indoor pool), *Die Prince* and *Melinda,* all near the casino, *Riff* and *Prado;* the smaller *Ambassadeur* has good restaurant.

The *Westminster, Ostend Palace* and *Admiral* all have bath or shower to every room, and good restaurants.

Somewhat better are *Bellevue-Britannia, Wellington* and *Imperial.*

The *Royal Ascot,* Hertstr. *Viking,* Boekarestr., *Europe,* Kapucijnenstr., are all moderate.

The numerous inexpensive hotels include the *Bécasse* and *Flandria,* facing the yacht harbor, with excellent, moderately expensive restaurants. *Kingston,* 59 Koningstr., inexpensive and comfortable.

If in transit stay at comfortable, moderate *Terminus-Maritime,* Ostend Station, 29 rooms. For longer stay, try *Mon Rêve,* 77 Aartshertogstraat.

Restaurants: The *Hôtel Bel Air,* Van Iseghemlaan, has a remarkable restaurant; just as good is *Le Beau Site,* Albert I Promenade. *Le Périgord,* at the casino, is fashionable. All (E).

Prince Albert and *Mercator* (M-E) on the port, are excellent. The latter prepares sole in a dozen different fashions. *La Bonne Auberge* (M) Brabantstraat, is small, pleasant. Excellent food at *Freddy's Grill* and at *Rôtisserie Tournebroche,* both (E). Italian cooking at *Villa d'Este* (E), Albert I Promenade.

ST. IDESBALD. Up-and-coming end of Koksijde, but hotels have still to rise to their opportunity. Best is *Vlierhof,* tiny, with typical Flemish interior, first class reasonable, followed by *Albertum,* moderate. But the inexpensive *Touring* and *Soll-Cress* are quite good, as also, among the pensions, is *Lydia.*

Restaurant: *Aquillon* (M-E), has good reputation.

WENDUINE, has 2½ miles of wide, sandy beach, dunes, restful woods.

Hotels: *Mouettes,* Zeedijk, facing sea, and *Wellington,* de Smet de Naeyerlaan, vary between inexpensive and first class reasonable. *Prince Albert,* Manitobahelling, moderate.

WESTENDE, family resort known as "Pearl of the Coast", has splendid promenade.

Hotels: Best is *Melrose,* tiny, first class reasonable, followed by the *Splendid,* 14 rooms, comfortable, with very good restaurant. *Noble Rose,* 15 rooms, is less expensive, with Flemish interior and good cuisine. Pension *Michel,* moderate, cozy restaurant.

Restaurant: The *Bristol* (M-E), is outstanding.

ZEEBRUGGE. Beach on the left of harbor. Hotel: The *Asdic,* 23 rooms with bath, is first class superior.

Three outstanding restaurants: *Le Chalut* and *Mon Manège a Toi,* both facing the port, both (M-E); *Willy* (M), excellent.

ZOUTE, smartest beach resort on the coast, mainly residential, but there are some 35 hotels and pensions.

Hotels: *Memlinc Palace,* 90 rooms, deluxe; closely followed by *Claridge's,* facing sea, then *Carlton, Shakespeare, Ascot* and *Ducs de Bourgogne,* all first class superior.

The *Links* is first class reasonable.

Moderate: *Norfolk, Eldorado,* both on Elisabethlaan. *Victoria,* Golvenhelling, 50 rooms, half with bath, *Dormy House,* in same road, both near the golf links can be expensive if you choose the best rooms, as can *Balmoral,* almost next door.

Restaurants: *Breughel,* Wielingenstr., in an ancient setting, features grills. *Auberge St. Paul* (has a few rooms). Both (E). *Marcassin* (E), Strandhelling, is not of the same standard. *Relais du Comte Jean,* Osthoekstr., top cuisine, rustic décor. In the lower drawer, but still tops in many respects: *Manderlé,* Kustlaan and nearby, *Le Perchoir,* Place du Triangle, open day and night.

The former summer residence of Léopold III, in the Zwin nature reserve, now has the well-known *Chalet du Zwin* (E).

NIGHTCLUBS, DANCING. As you can well imagine, the mortality rate among these seasonal establishments is very high and you had better check to see whether the place of your choice is still running. What usually happens is that a year later they open under a different name, so while their names may be different from season to season, addresses may be right. This general rule is not valid for nightclubs run by local casinos; whatever their losses, they keep right on—roulette will always fill financial gaps. Economic considerations being thus set aside, you usually get more than your money's worth: two dance bands and headline cabaret entertainers from Paris, London, and New York and no fleecing.

BLANKENBERGE. *Sunset,* leading nightclub at the casino. Next to it *Canzonetta del Mare,* Hoogstraat. *Eden,* Zeedijk, has a family type floorshow. Ditto for *White Horse Inn,* Langestraat. The *Casino Theater* offers variety shows. At the giant *Lamme Goedzak* dancehall in the casino boy meets girl easily, while the *Hit-Club* is a teenagers' rendezvous. Good band at *Résidence l' Amitié.* At the *Continental Palace* you can go dancing or listen to a show band at the brasserie, at rock bottom prices. Another popular place is *The Beatles,* Weststraat and *King's,* same location. Good bands at *Taverne Bristol* and *Thalia,* latter on Weststraat.

DE PANNE. Dancing at *La Chandelle, Djinn* and *Rialto.*

KNOKKE-HEIST, a nightclubber's paradise; several places open year round. The casino offers dinner-dancing to two orchestras, gala nights with international stars, theater, films, ballet and exhibitions.

In the casino building are *Patrick's Club* and the *27 Club.* The smart set is found in the *Gallery Club;* the *Ranch, De Hoeve, Dixieland* and *El Gringo* are reasonable.

MIDDELKERKE. Nightclub at the casino; dancing at *V.I.Ps., Bunny, Ugly, Le Noeud* and *Mia-Cara,* all moderately priced.

OSTEND. Best, *La Champagne,* run by casino. Two bands, short cabaret. Prices very reasonable. Girlie shows at *Maxim's,* Van Iseghemlaan, and *Elysée* in Langestraat. *White Horse Inn* in Iseghemlaan is music-hall type; first floor, same management. *Wiener Weinstube* dispenses sweet music and inexpensive wines to the lovelorn. You can take a large choice along Van Iseghemlaan and Langestraat by moving from the *Groove* to the *Mecca,* via *Versailles,* the *King's Club* and *Elysée,* unless you get bogged down at *Van's* or *Number One.*

USEFUL ADDRESSES. *British Vice-Consulate,* 21 IJzerstr., Ostend. *Police Emergency:* Blankenberge, tel. 410-09; Knokke, tel. 649-42, ambulance is tel. 610-10; Nieuwpoort, tel. 233-44; Ostend, tel. 717-11; De Panne, tel. 412-57.

Tourist information: For the whole coastland: *Westtourism,* 55 Vlamingstr., Bruges, tel. (050) 373-44. *Blankenberge,* Town Hall; *Knokke-Le Zoute-Albert Plage,* Stadhuis (Town Hall) and in July-Aug., Heldenplein; *Nieuwpoort,* Town Hall; *Ostend,* Wapenplein; *De Panne,* Town Hall.

To rent furnished villas or flats (apartments) on coast, apply to estate agents (*agence immobilière*). A full list is available from the Tourist Office, with indications of the cost. The usual letting period is a month or half month. Enquire whether bed linen, table linen and cutlery are available.

Exploring the Belgian Coast

Geographically, the coast falls into sections, divided by Nieuwpoort—so called when the Yser changed its course and formed its estuary there eight centuries ago. Ostend, the fishing port, which was enlarged in the 15th century, became the chief port of access to the southern part of the Low Countries; it was fortified, besieged, and fought over in the 17th and 18th centuries, and eventually became one of the smarter watering places of the early 19th century. Zeebrugge was the final solution to the problems set up by the decadence of the port of Bruges; the old access to the latter, the Zwin, is now a stretch of botanically interesting dry land between the limit of Zoute and the frontier of Dutch Zeeland.

Zoute, Smartest Resort

Nearest resort to the Dutch border, Zoute (Het Zoute, Le Zoute) is a high class residential area, with comparatively few hotels. It is sometimes called the Garden of the North Sea, with its 300-acre nature reserve (part of which is in Holland) in the Zwin area, which also contains the former residence of Léopold III—where there is a fine restaurant. This silted-up former estuary of the Zwin river, where the salt water gets into the soil at certain seasons, has resulted in some beautiful and rare flowers growing there, and the bird life is unique in Belgium. There is a big tennis club, 50 courts, and an excellent golf club that draws custom from most of the players in the country. There is a shopping street, Kustlaan, which is quite the most fashionable word in luxury shopping for anything from chocolates to clothes.

Among the staple amusements at Zoute is the hiring by the hour of small motorscooters. Though this is a rather costly way of moving round among the seaside resorts, it adds to the feeling that here there is more space than at most of the other resorts. On the eastward side, towards Holland, you can ride or walk in the woods. It is a short ride over the Dutch frontier to Sluis, full of "sex-shops" forbidden in Belgium.

Knokke, Albert-Strand

Albert-Strand, where the 1976 meeting of the European Federation of Conference Towns is to be held, used to be thought more democratic than rich Zoute or middle-class Knokke. But now, with a casino and a fabulous hotel, *La Réserve,* the balance has been swinging towards Albert-Strand. One of the advertised attractions of Albert-Strand was, and still is, boating and canoeing on the Lac de la Victoire. These diversions were never very exciting, but they have acquired a new interest since participants may now see into the part of the lake separated off as the *piscine* and playground of the Réserve, and for those who can identify film stars in swimsuits this is a real attraction. The casino over the way is the center of the many things that go on in Knokke. It contains two nightclubs and a spacious *salle de fêtes,* which attracts some of the best singers and entertainers from all over the world. At the casino, too, are organized the conferences and congresses that occur almost every week. The gambling rooms are most easily reached from the back, facing the *Réserve.*

Duinbergen, Heist and Zeebrugge

Until recently an unpretentious little place, Duinbergen has now numerous smart villas, and counts as one of the more fashionable family resorts. It merges into Albert-Strand at one end and into its larger brother, Heist, on the other. There are tennis courts close to the seafront and others in the pleasant little garden city between the dunes and the road.

Heist has a small fishing port, the fishing village lying beyond the railway line away from the sea. Like Blankenberge, it caters to a clientele of a more popular sort—trades-people, office and factory workers, and their families.

Both these resorts make much of the contrast with the costlier fare at Knokke and Zoute. In point of fact, so far as hotel charges go, there is not a lot to choose between one resort and another for equivalent accommodation. It is true, however, that in the smaller places your hand is far less often in your pocket.

At Zeebrugge the tourist quarters appear to have inserted themselves almost apologetically beyond the foot of the Mole. Though restaurants and nightclubs are now finding their way here, they are not yet obtrusive and you can still pass an idle vacation without being constantly on the spend. You might, if you can find a willing owner, take a motorboat trip up the canal to Bruges, which is always in sight from the Mole on a clear day.

During the last war, the Germans removed as scrap the beautiful little statue (by Dupont and Smolderen) of Saint George. A replica—oddly enough, not the original—was found on a Hamburg scrap-heap, and the port authorities were haggling with the Allies for years to let them have it as a replacement for the stolen original.

In addition, Zeebrugge is also a center of pilgrimage for all Britons, and indeed for all whose blood stirs at great feats of heroism, because of the exploit of the Royal Navy in blocking the sea channel to the U-boat base in the moonless midnight of Saint George's Day in 1918. This achievement, incidentally, was something of an echo of the act of the Royal Navy's ancestors six centuries earlier, when they sailed into Sluis—the outer port of Bruges at that time (1340)—and tackled the French fleet at their moorings.

Coming westwards, Zeebrugge is the first of the main fishing ports. The coaling station on the Mole brings big ships in for brief visits, and the Harwich train-ferry carries the quick-moving consignments of vegetables and other produce coming from Italy and the south, while car ferries bring tourists from Dover, but there are very few hotels. There is an interesting little museum covering the history of the port in the two world wars.

If experts can solve the problem of shifting sands, Zeebrugge may yet become one of Europe's most important ports for passenger traffic. In fact, plans are under consideration for the improvement of its facilities to receive giant, low-cost, transatlantic tourist liners, and to make more extensive use of its advantages as an oil port.

Blankenberge and Fashionable Le Coq

Next beyond Zeebrugge is the great metropolis of Blankenberge, giant of the Belgian seaside, with its 148 hotels (50 more even than Knokke) and its specialized establishment designed to deal with workers' holidays-with-pay. This, too, is a fishing port, and the catch arrives at the very door of the fish market that stands cheek-by-jowl with the shelter designed near the miniature golf links to keep holiday-makers away from the wind. Here, too, is a pier, with its concert hall at the end, and a casino where, as at Knokke, you can play roulette subject to a 5 percent tax if you win.

A reminder of Blankenberge's long existence as a fishing port is the Church of Saint Anthony, a Gothic building with 17th-century additions; but Blankenberge is essentially the town of the striped awning. The town has its own yacht basin.

A detour of seven miles to the southeast brings you to Lissewege, a sleepy little village, once a powerful medieval city. Its massive church tower, worthy of a cathedral and visible from many miles away, is the only witness to a rich past.

When you get to Wenduine, you are beginning to realize the terror of the sea in this polder country. The seawall here is called the Graaf Jandijk, after Jean de Namur who began its construction nearly seven centuries ago. The choir and sacristy of the church are of about the same period, and the church appears on very early maps. The town is now a small one, and its chief industry is entertaining the tourist.

Three miles farther on is De Haan (Le Coq), the enchanting little place that is becoming the fashionable resort of the coast. It almost rivals Zoute in fashion and expensiveness, luckily not in the crowds that flow in on the public holidays. Here, too, you can add golf to your holiday amusements. De Haan is largely a villa resort and, as at all the Belgian bathing places, most of the villas are to let during the "fat months" of summer.

Towards Bredene the dune wall against the sea is naturally broad and there is room on its back for the Royal Golf Club. At Bredene itself there is no promenade but the beach is large and perfect for families; at the rear is an 800-meter stretch of beautiful sand dunes. This is a great center for camping.

Ostend

So we come to that paradox of watering places, Ostend, which has managed to expunge from its fair face so much that has disfigured it in the past. The Europacentrum skyscraper and the twin spires of the Church of Saints Peter and Paul are the first warning to the mariner that he is nearing the port, but the appalling old Kursaal mercifully disappeared, together with most of the ugly buildings that marred this queen of seaside resorts at the end of the last century. All that was gay and colorful in the period was caught by James Ensor, the English painter, who took Belgian citizenship and lived and died in Ostend.

Ostend is the oldest settlement on the Belgian coast, and its history goes back to the 10th century. From here the Crusaders sailed for the reconquest of the Holy Land. For centuries a pirate hideout, the House of Orange made Ostend a fortified outpost of their realm in 1583. One of the first railroad lines on the Continent (Ostend-Mechelen) was inaugurated there in 1838, and a regular mailboat service to Dover started as early as 1846. In 1918 the Royal Navy's *Vindictive*, loaded with cement, was sunk at the port's entrance, immobilizing the German submarine base there. As part of Hitler's Atlantic Wall, the city was raided several times during World War II.

The town has kept what was worth saving, and lost the rest as completely as she has lost the fortifications of the Dutch, and the speculative fever that made the Compagnie d'Ostende the pale but modish equivalent of the English South Sea Company. It is a good-looking Ostend that emerged from the postwar bout of reconstruction, and now you can play roulette and baccara in the modern Kursaal. There is also a racetrack, where meetings are transferred from the Brussels courses in the summer. Ostend is full of the usual sporting facilities and many festivities. It is prettily laid out, and the fishing port keeps you picturesquely in touch with as much as you need of the realities of life. There is always a vital flow of traffic through the town because of its position, as the railhead for Europe reached from Dover, and the fact that the London-Istanbul road starts here.

Proceeding westwards from Ostend, you come into the country where horses are used in catching shrimp. At Middelkerke the staple sport is land-yacht sailing on the sands, and the tennis courts are good. The overloaded little airport has been greatly enlarged and modernised and handles a big (mostly cross-channel) summer traffic. Middelkerke is becoming fashionable, and has a pocket-size casino where the play is seldom high. Westende, two miles farther on, has a number of reasonably priced hotels and some excelent holiday facilities. Almost next door to it, Lombardsijde is the ideal spot for camping or caravaning. Its church houses a statue of the Virgin, washed ashore in the 16th century, and ever since considered by the local fisherfolk as their patron saint.

At Jabbeke 8 kms from Ostend a holiday farm *Noordhof*, run by the Ostend tour operator Transeurope, is open at weekends and can accommodate 16 guests. The inclusive cost is about 800 francs per person per day with a 20% discount for children under 12. The price includes a daily 90-minute horse ride and use of the swimming pool and cycles or horse-drawn carts.

From Nieuwpoort to La Panne

At Nieuwpoort, three miles farther on, you are again on historic ground. Here you are at the mouth of the Yser (IJzer) River with its 1914-18 associations, and here it was that the sluice gates were opened, flooding the polder country to the discomfiture of the advancing Germans, and playing a decisive role in the defense of the Ypres salient and the Channel ports. Two cemeteries, one Belgian and the other British, will remind you of the part Nieuwpoort played in World War I. Besides the bust of Geeraert, the water-control expert who directed the flooding, you will find British, French, and other memorials. Impressively situated, too, despite its Meccano-like pillars, is the memorial to King Baudouin's grandfather, Albert the Soldier King.

You will soon discover, of course, that Nieuwpoort town is quite separate from Nieuwpoort Bad. The former has sustained the scars of war, and was all but knocked out of existence. The Church of Our Lady was destroyed in 1914, restored, burned again in 1940, and again refurbished. The attraction of Nieuwpoort for the tourist lies largely in the presence of the estuary, which makes it a good yachting center and the scene of regattas.

Two Modest Resorts

The next resort is Oostduinkerke, which includes Groenendijk. The seaside resort has the same name as the inland town because the territory of the commune goes down to the sea.

Koksijde (Coxyde) and its sub-commune, Saint Idesbald, are both ideal for a simple holiday. The dunes here are very high and the remains of the 13th-century Dunes Abbey seem like an exciting desert discovery. Saint Idesbald has a few modest hotels and is rapidly growing in popularity.

De Panne

So we come to De Panne (La Panne), three miles from the

French frontier, the last spot on Belgian soil where King Albert stubbornly stuck out the war in 1914. The place has another connection with the royal family: it was here that Belgium's first king, Léopold I, set foot on the soil of his realm in 1831. De Panne has attained a certain popularity as a family-holiday base.

HAINAUT AND SAMBRE-MEUSE REGION

Cradle of Walloon History

The two main roads out of Brussels into the Hainaut region are the Chaussée de Mons, which forks at Halle, giving you the choice between the road through Enghien and Ath to Tournai, and the road through Braine-le-Comte and Soignies to Mons. The Chaussée de Charleroi forks just behind the Waterloo battlefield, where you take either the road through Nivelles and Thuin to Beaumont, or the highway to Charleroi and into the country between the Sambre and Meuse (Maas). All of these roads lead into France, which will serve to remind you that you are in a proud old country that was the nursery of French kings, the bait of dynastic marriages, and for many centuries the buffer between expansive France and quarrelsome Flanders.

If Hainaut is heavy with the history of strife between France and her neighbors, it is full, too, of the contrast between industry and a smiling countryside. It is a country where farming is run on different lines from that of Flanders, and here you will find less of the strip-farming of the Flemish and many more well-run farm units worked on modern—even model—lines. Yet Charleroi is the center of the engineering industry and the central coal basin; and at Mons you soon forget Saint Waudru in favor of the great black country of the Borinage. Here the slagheaps dot the countryside. At Wasmes, on the Tuesday of Whitsun, a little girl is carried in procession to commemorate the "Pucellette" whom the villagers were constrained to sacrifice annually to a nearby monster until delivered by Gilles de Chin more than 800 years ago. Here you are, in contrast, only a couple of miles from Quaregnon, where the old mine tips and pithead gear still remind the villagers that, as lately as under a decade ago, their men-folk were working a mile underground.

The people of the Borinage are fast growing accustomed to the dramatic transformation which, in less than a decade, has delivered almost all of them from the servitude of the mines and taken their wives (part-time) and daughters into ultramodern factories at Frameries and Ghlin. Their traditions remain, and they work out their day with simple faith, a good deal of alcohol, and a large number of Italian colleagues, originally brought here for mine work, often with their wives and families, who have made this their permanent home. They find in pigeon-racing one of their chief recreations, though around Charleroi the Sunday morning cock-crowing contests are also popular and characteristic of the café life. It all marks a strong contrast with the Allied Supreme Headquarters (SHAPE), with its ultra-modern buildings, its satellite communications, the new military number plates and all the appurtenances of modernity centered at Casteau, only five miles from Mons.

Practical Information for Hainaut and Sambre-Meuse Region

WHEN TO COME? The "season" in southwest Belgium is from May to Sept. Off-season travel, despite its many advantages, can be pretty dull in these parts, even if the weather is good—which it isn't likely to be. Some of the outstanding carnival events, or the prospect of good hunting or fishing in the Viroin valley, might prompt you to come earlier. If so, here's good luck to you.

Events: The world-famous Binche Carnival, held on Shrove Tuesday (usually in *February*), goes back to the 16th century. There is a fine cortege at Tournai almost at the same time. La Louvière has its two-day carnival in *March*. Again in Binche, there is a remarkable procession in honor of St. Ursmer in *April*. In Mons you can see hundreds of participants in sumptuous costumes of the Renaissance on Trinity Sunday in *May*, assisting at the mock slaughter of Lumçon, the giant dragon. Walcourt and Thuin hold their traditional Military Marches. The Grand Prix of Chimay for racing cars and motorcycles now enters its fourth decade. The "International Musical Encounters" at Château de Chimay's little rococo theater during end of *June*/early *July* are a prominent feature of Belgium's musical life. Military Marches can be seen in June at Florennes and Morialmé, and in *August* at Couillet, Ham-sur Heure, and Jumet. On the fourth Sunday of that month, Ath stages a great cortege during which David slays Goliath, and celebrations last two days. A Plague Procession, nearly a thousand years old, is held at Tournai on first Sunday in *September*.

WHAT TO SEE? There are two historic and art cities—Mons and Tournai—to visit. Tournai is delightful and merits leisurely exploration on foot. Beloeil, which the Belgians fondly call their Versailles, and Chimay, farther to the south, are late French Renaissance châteaux housing innumerable treasures. Additional castles: Ecaussines, Attre, Ham-sur-Heure, Antoing, Chièvres, Moulbaix, and many others.

HOW TO GET ABOUT? Charleroi is on the direct Paris-Dortmund (TEE *Parsifal)* line, about 2½ hrs. from Paris, while Mons is about 2 hrs. from Paris on the Paris-Amsterdam run. Almost hourly fast trains also run from Brussels to these points and to Tournai. By car, most of the localities in this area may be easily reached from Brussels over first class paved roads: Charleroi, 33 miles; Mons, 34 miles; Tournai, 49 miles. From Paris to Tournai, take the motorway via Lille

MUSEUMS AND CHÂTEAUX. Mons has about ten museums. Most important is the *Centenary Museum,* in Mayeur Garden. Its collection includes a Two World Wars section, numismatics, porcelain. The *Musée des Beaux Arts* (Fine Arts Museum) in Rue Neuve shows works by painters of the recent Mons School; often stages art exhibitions. *Maison Jean Lescarts* is an interesting museum of furniture and Mons folklore. *Chanoine Puissant's Museum,* Rue Notre-Dame: archeology, manuscripts, incunabula, unique collection of old lace. *Treasury of St. Waudru Collegiate Church.*

Tournai: The collection of ancient and resistance weapons is housed in Henry VIII's tower, *Grosse Tour.* The picture gallery *Musée des Beaux Arts,* Enclos St. Martin, has some Impressionist masterpieces by Manet, Seurat, etc., and the Flemish School is represented by Breughel, Rubens, Jordaens, Gossart, and others. The *History and Archeology Museum* is in the medieval Pawnhouse in Rue des Carmes. A stimulating *Folklore Museum,* Réduits des Sions, was restored in a very lively manner after heavy war damage, through donations of rare pieces by Tournai citizens.

Châteaux: The following are living museums and can be visited daily: *Attre,* near Ath, intact 18th-century interiors. *Beloeil,* finest in Belgium. *Chimay,* with charming theater. *Ecaussines,* same region, early medieval feudal castle. *Ham-sur-Heure,* near Thuin. *Mariemont,* north of Morlanwelz, 16th century (closed Fri.).

HOTELS AND RESTAURANTS. This region has an abundance of hotels. None are in the luxury class, except for the *Amigo* at Casteau, near the SHAPE headquarters, where new hotels and hostelries are mushrooming. In any given price range you are assured a high standard of service. This is definitely a gastronomic province: trout is a specialty of the Sambre-Meuse region, and while there, we suggest that you try it *aux amandes* (with almonds), *à l'escavèche* (in jelly), *en papillotte* (wrapped in parchment and fried).

ATH. Hotels: *Central,* Grand' Place, and *Guide,* Marché-aux-Toiles, both inexpensive.

Restaurant: *Régence,* on Grand' Place, good.

ATTRE. Four miles south of Ath, near Brugelette, with impressive 18th-cent. château.

Restaurant: *Auberge du Vieux Chaudron* (M-E), excellent.

BEAUMONT. Vestiges of fortified city. Hotels: *Commerce* and *Les Rocailles,* very modest.

Restaurants: *Hostellerie Charles Quint.* Specialty is brochet à l'escavèche (pike). Also has 10 rooms, inexpensive.

At nearby Soire-St.-Géry (2½ miles south), *Le Prieuré,* expensive, is an excellent restaurant; ancient décor, also has a few rooms.

BELOEIL. Louis XIV-style château. Hostelry *La Couronne,* close to entrance has 12 rooms, 6 with bath. Rustic décor, good value, inexpensive. There's a moderate restaurant at back of the castle's park (you have to drive round).

BINCHE. Has no decent hotel, but you can eat extremely well at *Bernard* (M), Rue de Bruxelles and at *Philippe II* (M-I), Ave. Albert I.

You can stay at nearby Morlanwelz, where there is a fine château. *Chez Mairesse,* 10 rooms, 4 with bath, is moderate; its restaurant, however, is one of the best and most expensive in the country.

BONSECOURS. A frontier halt on
BOUSSU-EN-FAGNE. After a mile or so north of Couvin, turn left. Anthe Peruwelz-Valenciennes road.

Hotel: *La Cornette* on Grand' Place, inexpensive.

other mile and you are at *Manoir de la Motte.* Authentic medieval setting, small, moderate.

CASTEAU (see Mons).

CHARLEROI. Traditional good cuisine in this town.

Hotels: Two first class reasonable hotels, *Parking,* Blvd. Tirou, part of a business center; *Siebertz,* Quai de Brabant, slightly cheaper; has best restaurant in town. Only moderately priced is *Aux Caves d'Artois,* Place Buisset, 30 rooms, 20 with bath. Next door *Hôtel des Alliés,* and at No 19, *Derby,* both inexpensive. Also good, *Bernard,* near Place Buisset, close to station.

Restaurants: Tops, *Ducs de Bourgogne* (E), Quai de Brabant. *Solms,* 16 Rue du Collège is less expensive. *Prince de Chimay,* Rue Léopold, and *Mouton de Panurge,* Rue Neuve, are also good.

At Loverval, 3 miles south on the road to Philippeville, in pleasant surroundings, is an excellent hostelry, the *Chardon* (M).

CHIMAY. Famous château. Hotels: *Commerce; Emmaus,* good. At Virelles Lake: *Moderna, De la Place.* All inexpensive.

Best restaurant *Edgar et Madeleine. Armes de Chimay* (I) excellent.

COUVIN. On the Brussels-Rheims road, near French frontier. Hotels: *St. Roch,* converted fortified farm in splendid park; 16 rooms, 11 with bath. Moderate. Its restaurant is (E).

Two miles south (N5), *Forges de Pernelle,* moderate, as is its restaurant.

HAM-SUR-HEURE. Famous château.

Hotel: *Au château,* inexpensive. *Auberge St. Roch,* restaurant.

HAVAY-BOIS-BOURDON. Halfway between Mons and Maubeuge (France), before reaching frontier.

Restaurant: *Savoy* (I-M), good.

LENS. Eight miles from Ath on route to Mons. Restaurant: *Auberge de Lens* (E), a good halt, has rustic interior.

MARIEMBOURG. *Hôtel des Fagnes,* inexpensive. The restaurant is (M).

MAZEE. Ten miles to the northeast of Couvin in the Viroin valley.

Hotel: *Le Vieux Moulin de Chaupny,* an ancient watermill converted into hostelry, moderately expensive, has 4 rooms. Telephone (060) 391-44 before undertaking trip. Fishing.

MONS. Capital of province and art city.

Hotels: Leader is the *Raymond,* 27 Blvd. Charles-Quint, 76 up-to-date rooms, first class reasonable. Next in the hierarchy: *Europ-Hôtel,* 9 Rue Léopold, followed by the very small *St. Georges,* 15 Rue des Clercs and the *Résidence,* 4 Rue Masquelier, all moderate. Inexpensive are *du Parc,* 9 Rue Fétis and *de la Cloche,* Place Léopold.

At nearby Ghlin, *Château de Milfort* and *La Marmite,* both moderate.

Close to Casteau (SHAPE), at Masnuy St. Jean in the Chaussée de Brunhault, the *Amigo* of Brussels has a 58-room hotel in the same deluxe category.

The *Esso Motor Hotel,* on Hwy. E10, outside Casteau, has 70 rooms, restaurant, coffee shop. Expensive.

Restaurants: Many restaurants and road houses are mushrooming within striking distance of SHAPE: it's still uncertain which will last. Right opposite the entrance to SHAPE is the *Maisières,* where you can dine well.

In Mons, *Devos* (M), Rue de la Coupe, near Grand' Place prepares a delicious caneton aux griottes (duckling with black cherries) for the asking. *Restivo* (I), Rue d'Enghien, is Italian. The *London Tavern* is a restaurant-pub (don't expect English dishes). *Pâtisserie Saey* has two buffets for those in a hurry, in Rue des Capucins and Grand' Place. You'll find Greek, Chinese, Italian, even Vietnamese restaurants around town, as well.

MONTIGNIES ST. CHRISTOPHE. Four miles from Beaumont on the "short-cut" road to Mons. Roman Bridge. *La Villa Romaine,* excellent halt, moderate. *Pont Romain,* inexpensive.

OLLOY-SUR-VIROIN. Six miles north of Couvin. Two hostelries, *La Champagne,* inexpensive—but not its restaurant—and *Viroin.* Fishing may be arranged.

PHILIPPEVILLE. Charles Quint's once-fortified city. Renowned for cuisine. *Croisée,* Rte. de France, moderate hotel-restaurant. *Princes de Liège,* Rte. de Givet, inexpensive, but not its restaurant. In same category is *Armes de Philippeville,* Grand' Place, with Spanish cuisine. Another address for good inexpensive accommodation and food is the *Grand Bonnet,* Grand' Place.

SOIGNIES. Fortresslike St. Vincent's Church, housing many treasures of religious art.

Hotel: *Moderne,* inexpensive, has good restaurant.

THUIN. *Regina,* tiny, inexpensive.

TOURNAI. One of Belgium's important art towns.

Hotels: deluxe *Holiday Inn,* 88 double rooms, pool, restaurant, etc.

Of those in station square, best is *Neuf Provinces,* moderate. *Armes de Tournay,* Place de Lille, moderate. *Ecu de France,* on Grand' Place is a former stage-coach halt, a delightful example of Flemish Renaissance; inexpensive.

At Mont St. Aubert, 4 miles north, on a by-road: *Hôtel du Lion,* 12 rooms, inexpensive.

At Blandain, 3 miles west, *Le Prieuré,* once an abbey, is now a deluxe hotel. Each bedroom suite has a different décor. Meals can be prepared according to taste, mine host supervising all the cooking. The wine cellar is extensive.

At Froyennes, 2 miles west, the *France* restaurant is (E-M).

TREIGNES. Ten miles northwest of Couvin, in the Viroin valley. Castle.

Hotel: *Buchet,* inexpensive, provides shooting and fishing.

VILLE-POMMEREUL. For 8 miles follow Mons-Valenciennes road, turn right toward Thulin, another 6 miles and you are at the *Relais,* an excellent, almost luxurious, but very small hotel. All rooms with bath. Hunting-lodge-style manor. Perfect food; don't count the cost here. Best book ahead.

VIRELLES. See *Chimay*.

WALCOURT. Picturesque locality on a by-road between Philippeville and Beaumont. *Clef d'Or,* inexpensive, has good cuisine. *Aigle,* inexpensive. At nearby Berzée, *Notre Dame de Grâce* is an inn.

NIGHTCLUBS. Captains (and lower ranks) of industry in Charleroi patronize *Parisiana* (floorshow), in one of Rue Léopold's sidestreets, and *Manhattan,* 6 Rue du Comptoir (with bowling); *La Réserve* at the Palais des Beaux Arts, Ave. de l'Europe, *Champi,* Place Charles II, and *Mistral,* Rue Neuve, are also popular. For the younger set there is *Le Carré Blanc,* 18 Rue Léopold.

Framed in traditional wrought-iron grillework, is St. Niklaas' Hôtel de Ville (Town Hall), situated on a vast square, the largest in Belgium.

Rich in art and history, the Meuse Valley region offers such gems as the Château of Jehay (above) and the city of Dinant, ranged along the river with its blue-tinted roofs, citadel, and bulbous-spired church.

In Mons, the favorite haunt is *The Drug's* discothèque, on Grand'Place.

USEFUL ADDRESSES. *City Tourist Offices* (Syndicats d'Initiative): Almost every locality has its tourist office, usually in the town hall. Here are the more important ones: Charleroi, Hôtel de Ville; Mons, 20 Grand' Place; Thuin, Hôtel de Ville, Grand' Rue; Tournai, Halle aux Draps, Grand' Place. *Car hire:* Avis, Blvd. Gendebien, in Mons.

Golf: Royal Golf Club of Hainaut, Erlisoeul, near Mons.

Camping sites are located at Leugnies, Mons, Nimy, Rance, Tournai, Virelles, and Walcourt.

Exploring Hainaut

The Brussels-Tournai road enters Hainaut at Enghien (Edingen), on the linguistic frontier, where there is the remnant of a fine park laid out in the 17th century by the dukes of Arenberg, who bought the town from Henri IV, King of France. The convent church contains a splendid mausoleum by the well-known Renaissance sculptor, Jean Mone, in honor of Guillaume de Croy, a Belgian priest, later primate of Spain.

It is worth taking the turning to Lessines (from Ghislenghien) to see the hospital of Notre-Dame-à-la-Rose, a 13th-century foundation by one of the dames of honor to Blanche of Castile, though most of the buildings date from the 16th and 17th centuries and the chapel from the 18th. This may be visited each day except Saturday and contains some fine old furniture.

Lessines, itself a town of porphyry quarries (some of which you can visit) is on the Dendre, which you will meet again when you have returned to the main road and gone on to Ath. Lessines is the birthplace of Hennepin (La Salle's companion), who was the first explorer to sail up the Mississippi River to 46° North latitude, in 1680. The Vauban fortifications at Ath, put up by order of Louis XIV after he had personally supervised the siege and capture of the town, have disappeared; but there remains a vestige, the Tower Burbant, of a much older fortification, erected around 1150, with a massive wall some ten feet thick. The main attraction in Ath, however, is the festival of the last Sunday of August. The town is famous above all for its giants, colorful reed-built citizens, eight in number and including Goliath (Gouyasse), Samson, the four sons of Aymon and others, who spend most of the year in Wenceslas Cobergher's little 17th-century Hôtel de Ville. By traditional arrangement, Goliath and his wife are married on the eve of the festival.

Chièvres is a very attractive little village with a charming square and a 16th-century château of the powerful de Croy family. Passing Chièvres and Neufmaison, you take a sharp right turn to Beloeil. Here, by courtesy of the Prince de Ligne and on payment of some 50 francs, you can visit the "Versailles of Belgium", with its great garden-park laid out in the manner of Le Nôtre, its ornamental lake, its swans and its fountains. The château itself, rebuilt from the original plans after the fire of 1900, is not quite the same place as was described by Marshal Charles-Joseph de Ligne, but its treasures give you an absorbing journey through the great events of Europe in which the princely family and the château have played their part for nearly a thousand years. Lovers of antiques and old books will want to spend days on end here; paintings abound, from Holbein to Caravaggio, and curiosities like Marlborough's pistols or Marie Antoinette's lock of hair are not lacking either: all outlined against a background of Flemish and French tapestries.

The tomb of the de Ligne princes is in Beloeil village church, which stands in a shaded square and there is still a feudal atmosphere about the place. Beyond Beloeil you join the main road again at Leuze, where it is worth while visiting Saint Peter's to see the consistent 18th-century furnishings.

Tournai, Cathedral and Art Town

After Leuze comes Tournai, pop. 35,000 (the Flemish call it Doornijk), within a few miles of the Flemish language frontier on the road to Courtrai and of the French frontier on the road to Lille. Strategic pivot whenever France and Flanders were at loggerheads, Tournai has origins which go into a very distant past. Birthplace of Clovis (465 A.D.) and burial place of Childeric (481 A.D.), there is that within it which is more French than France itself. Early French drama can be traced back to Tournai: it was here that the play *Farce du garçon et de l'aveugle* was performed in 1295. It was the Tournaisian mantle of Clovis that Napoleon assumed when he wore on his coronation robe the emblem of the bees. Childeric's tomb was discovered with a fabulous treasure during excavations for building in 1653.

The town has lived through many vicissitudes and, with its air of spiritual detachment, it resisted the English in 1340, repudiated the Burgundian suzerainty a century later, and was besieged by Henry VIII of England who erected defences of which part, the Round Tower, still stands. Wolsey was enriched by appointment to the Bishopric of Tournai a few years before he became a Cardinal. Within a few decades the town was again besieged, this time by the Spaniards who were met by the epic defence of Christine de Lalaing, the governor's wife. In her husband's absence she successfully held out for over two months, leading many sorties, until relief came. Later it was seized by Louis XIV, fortified by Vauban, recaptured by the Allies and handed over to the Austrian regime from whom Louis XV seized it after the Battle of Fontenoy.

Tournai was war-scarred indeed when it emerged from the holocaust of 1940-44. The Grand' Place had simply disappeared and the Cloth Hall and the Hôtel de Ville were in ruins. Over a thousand of the city's ancient houses were totally destroyed and several hundred badly damaged. Today's Grand' Place is a product of postwar town planning, respectful of the past and quite sucessful in recapturing it. One good thing came out of the bombardment, for the damage of the Church of Saint Brice revealed fragments of very ancient frescos and made possible the planning of a positive restoration.

The Cathedral

Most important of all was that, for all the bombardment, the great Cathedral of Notre Dame stood intact. Indeed, the damage to surrounding buildings revealed the line and majesty of the cathedral so that they could be better appreciated. For all that, the cathedral is a strange building. As at Antwerp, the exterior does not prepare you for the large scale of the interior and, unless you are well acquainted with Germanic architectural forms, you are bound to fancy there is something unfinished or temporary in the hat-like cones that crown the five towers. However, you will see between the west doors the 14th-century statue of *Our Lady of the Sick Folk* (or *Our Lady of the Grape*) which will prepare you for great treasures on more accustomed lines. Started in 1110, it took only 60 years to build.

Inside the cathedral you will at first be amazed, perhaps even appalled, by the heavy and over-ornate screen. The nave, however, will in its structure have prepared you for the masterly Ile-de-France grace of the 13th-century Gothic choir. The cathedral contains a great number of treasures. The Rubens *Souls in Purgatory* is so heavily restored as to be worth little to the student, but the remains of the 12th-century mural paintings in the transept are most interesting, as also are the well restored transept windows by the 14th-century master, Arnold of Nijmegen. There are a number of other important paintings by Metsys, Pourbus, De Vos, and Blondeel, and the high altar is by an 18th-century artist, Gaspard Lefèbvre. The great treasure of the cathedral, however, consists in the three reliquaries known as the *Châsse de Notre-Dame*, the *Châsse de Saint Eleuthère* and the *Châsse des Damoiseaux*. The first, in vermeil, is the work of the greatest of the Meuse-side silversmiths, Nicholas of Verdun, and is dated 1205.

The second is attributed to an illustrious pupil of the same master, Hugo d'Oignies, a work in silver as also is the third, a much later work of Bruges origin (1571). There is also a Byzantine cross of the 7th century, containing a relic of the True Cross.

An ecclesiastical treasure to Belgian and Briton alike is Saint Thomas à Becket's chasuble. He spent some time at Saint Medard's Abbey in Tournai in 1170 before returning to England to meet a violent death.

Tournai has at various times in its history been a school of the arts. Tournai sculpture was famous at least 800 years ago and you can see evidence of this in the *Porte Mantile* of the cathedral. In the 15th century Robert Campin was a leading Tournai painter, though little is now known of his work unless it is right to identify him with the Maître de Flémalle. One of his pupils was Roger van der Weyden, who afterwards worked in Bruges and Brussels, and another was Jacques Daret. At about the same period tapestry became one of the city's fine arts. It was at Tournai that Simon Marmion of Valenciennes started his school of illumination work. At the same time, Tournai brass- and copperwork was a rival to that of Dinant, and wrought-iron work was also flourishing. In the 17th century, a new school of painting grew up among the followers of Michel Bouillon, and in the next century Tournai porcelain began to be at its best. Around the turn of the 18th century, carpet-making became another artistic outlet.

Unfortunately, the iconoclasts left little of the Tournai statuary, but the Musée des Beaux Arts houses, in a modern but extremely satisfactory building by Victor Horta, an exceedingly fine collection of all that is best in all the Tournaisian arts, including a number of fine sculptures by Charlier.

The belfry dates back to the 13th century and its carillon is one of the finest in the country. If you can muster enough courage to climb its 256 steps you will get a splendid panorama of this ancient cathedral city. In the Rue Barre Saint Brice you will come across two dwelling houses of the 12th-century Romanesque period. In the same street and elsewhere you will find rows of Gothic houses, some Renaissance buildings, and a number of Louis XIV dwellings.

The bombings have brought up vestiges of a Roman *castrum* visible near Place Reine Astrid. You will get the finest view of Tournai from the fortified water-gate, the Pont des Trous, part of the city's medieval defence system.

No Irishman will want to leave Tournai without a visit to the field of Fontenoy, where the Celtic cross in Irish sandstone commemorates the Irish contingent that fought against the English. It brings back memories of the Treaty of Limerick. Fontenoy is best reached by following the road to Peruwelz.

SHAPE and its Impact

Only five miles from Mons on the road from Brussels, you will see a big complex of new buildings and read the sign: "Supreme Headquarters Allied Powers Europe". Here, since the NATO crisis of 1966, and the move from Paris into Belgium, SHAPE has now dug itself well into its new home. You will see the odd-shaped radio mast which was the instrument, in June 1967, by which General Lemnitzer made the first of the NATO phone calls transmitted by way of a man-made satellite hovering 18,000 miles above the earth.

The lightning installation of the headquarters and the personnel is still referred to as the SHAPE miracle. By the fall of 1967, permanent housing had been provided for all the 2,400 families.

Three-quarters of the personnel are English-speaking (56% American) and the official languages are English and French. Even in the little village of Casteau itself, there are crowded attendances at the classes in English which, in Mons, have become one of the main events in everybody's life. There is the SHAPE school, with sections to prepare each nationality for their prescribed examinations, so little language barrier exists already. It is also a standing instruction that the personnel should integrate to the maximum with the local population; and indeed the inhabitants have not been backward in their welcome. A family arriving to take up a SHAPE posting is at once caught up in the whirl of corporate life. The SHAPE worker hears of all the 1,500 sporting, cultural and social clubs, from chess to athletics—the marathon race is already an annual event—from baseball to horseback riding. His wife is at once a member of the Women's Club, the guest of the energetic Belgian Welcome Committee (known as ASPREAS), run from Mons by Vicomtesse de Walckiers.

Apart from SHAPE village itself, inside the H.Q. area, with its own shopping center, nearly 1,800 families are housed around the countryside. Most of the SHAPE wives use the H.Q. supermarket, mainly for items to which they are accustomed and which are not yet in the local shops, but the influx has brought much trade to shopkeepers, as well as to cafés and restaurants, in this pleasant district.

Barges and Wedding Feasts

The road from Brussels to Mons will take you through Braine-le-Comte and Soignies. From the former you will surely turn left, on the Nivelles road, to see the quite astonishing barge-lift at Ronquières. It has been rumored that there is something on similar lines, though admittedly smaller, somewhere where nobody has been in Soviet Russia; but, to all western knowledge, Ronquières ranks as one of the seven wonders of the world. The Belgians are very proud of it, and often forget it was only saved from perdition through a Swedish firm's energetic investigation to correct their mis-estimates of the rock formation. It has, however, been successfully operating since late in 1968; and you will be able to buy a bag of *frites* while you watch a 1,350-ton barge sail into a mammoth tank, and the tank, water, and barge hauled uphill for three-quarters of a mile, passing through a lock and continuing its trip on a viaduct. The whole thing is worked by closed-circuit TV control, and is surmounted by an elegant 300 ft.-tower which, apart from the control room in the lower part, is largely there to give you a first class view of the countryside. This is the Brussels-Charleroi canal; and Ronquières, by cutting out bends and small locks, has curtailed this short waterborne journey by days rather than hours. There are not many of the big Ruhr-type barges using it yet; but their number is growing.

Returning to the main road and passing through Braine-le-Comte, you may perhaps want to turn again into the valley of the Sennette, where the Castle of Ecaussines-Lalaing grimly bars the old trade route into Brussels from the French country beyond Mons. It was restored in the 15th century, and is the scene of the annual Marriage Feast held every Whit Monday for marriage-minded spinsters and bachelors. Its vast halls, old kitchen and museum are worth a visit. Escaussines d'Enghien also possesses its château, a pleasant 18th-century affair with a 16th-century chapel.

Mons, City of Coal and Carillon

If you turn off to the right to pass through Le Roeulx and see the château of the Princes de Croy, with its fine 18th-century façade, you will go on to Mons through the edge of the mining district which gave the Borinage its essential character. Mons is the administrative capital of Hainaut, a town traditionally founded by Saint Waudru, daughter of a count of Hainaut, in the 7th century. In the 12th century it was given up-to-date fortifications by Baudouin of Mons, and in the Rue du Prince you can still see some vestiges of these. Despite its industrial character, Mons (pop. 35,000) does not sprawl; it keeps pretty well within the limits laid down by Jean d'Avesnes in the 13th century, though the fortifications of the Dutch, built in 1818, were gleefully demolished and the town was somewhat enlarged without losing its character. Its red-bricked, elegant but grimy 17th-century houses remind us of the reign of Louis XIV.

The first thing to strike you will be the absurd belfry, and you may agree with Victor Hugo that only its size saves it. He likened it to "an enormous coffeepot, flanked below the belly-level by four medium-sized teapots". It is, in fact, a 17th-century effort. It dominates the hillside, and you will be surprised to hear it spoken of locally as the *tour du château*, or simply *le château*. This is a reference to the castle of the counts of Hainaut, which stood nearby, and of which you can still see the subterranean passages and the Chapel of Saint Calixte. The belfry houses a carillon of 47 bells, for the Montois were famed as bell forgers. At the top you have a fine view over the country.

The church of Saint Waudru is a fine specimen of 15th-century Gothic, though parts date from much later. It was started in 1450 by the ladies of Saint Waudru's noble chapter of secular canonesses, and Matthew de Layens is said to have made the original plans. Jacques du Broeucq built the screen which was unfortunately taken down in the late 18th century, though some of the statues and basreliefs are still preserved in the church. The artistic traditions of Mons itself are represented in the windows in the choir and transept, by the Eve family, and also in the church's exceptionally fine treasure of plate and reliquaries. One of the latter is probably by Hugo d'Oignies. (There is also a good collection of this craftsman's work in the Convent of the Sisters of Notre-Dame at Namur.) For examples of Hainaut pottery and glass in Mons you must go to the Musée du Centenaire, housed in the building of the old Mont de Piété (municipal pawnshop) just by a pretty little garden which abuts on the Hôtel de Ville.

There are also two interesting museums of local interest, that in the Maison Jean Lescarts behind the Beaux Arts and the one in Rue Notre-Dame where the Canon Puissant collection is found. In the latter street, too, the restored 13th-century Chapel of Saint Margaret houses a collection of religious art.

It's on Trinity Sunday, the day of Saint George's fight (for the gallant Cappadocian saint, a dragon specialist, is now identified in local tradition with the montois hero, Gilles de Chin) with Lumeçon the dragon, that this otherwise sleepy town goes mad with joy. A cavalcade of costumed citizens accompany the monster, who descends from the castle to the Grand 'Place. There, to the tune of a 13th-century ballad the combat takes place.

The Binche Carnival

While you are at Mons, it is worth taking a ride down the Charleroi road, past Saint Symphorien, with its feudal castle and its memories of the Order of Saint John of Jerusalem, to discover the tailoring town of Binche. This amusing little town, once the delight of the daughters of the counts of Hainaut, is the scene every Shrove Tuesday of the most remarkable manifestation in Europe, which has even led to the suggestion that the town gave its name to the English word "binge". The key to the show is the procession and dance of the Gilles, who wear for the occasion an ornate and heavily padded costume, and headdresses of thick ostrich plumes mounted in white top-hat-like headgear. They carry baskets of oranges, which they fling pellmell among the crowd, and oranges are brought to Binche by the truckload for the great day. On this day, the good burghers of Binche keep their doors open and champagne flows with fine abandon. The young men who are not among the Gilles arm themselves with inflated sheep-bladders, and woe betide the tourist who has ventured into the town without wearing a fancy hat. He is certain to learn that a blow from a sheep-bladder can sting.

The festival may have Teutonic origins, but a more probable explanation of the whole thing may be found in the 15th century. When Mary of Hungary, sister of Charles Quint, was in residence, the town around her lived in a state of uninterrupted carnival. This was just after Peru was conquered by the Spanish, and it is likely that the oranges of Binche symbolize the gold of the Incas, just as the Gilles are supposed to represent the defeated Indians. The Château of Binche is now in ruins. That of Mariemont, restored by Albert and Isabella, burned out and replaced, was left with its park to the nation. It contains excellent collections, including Tournai porcelain.

Thuin, and Nearby Abbeys

Thuin is a little town of pretty hanging gardens, in which there still remains the tower of the fortifications erected in the year 972 by Notger, Prince Bishop of Liège. On the third Sunday in May, there takes place in Thuin a religious *marche militaire*, one of many such which you will find in the country between the Sambre and the Meuse. At this time the relics of Saint Roch are guarded from brigands and robbers by a big escort in many and various uniforms, all colorful and imposing.

The Abbey of Aulne, one of the most important ecclesiastic remains of the country, is only a few minutes' drive from Thuin and worth a visit. Of vast proportions, it comprises a hostelry, a farm, and a fine church, dating from the 16th century. More modest but more ancient (7th-century), the Abbey of Lobbes has a remarkable Romanesque church. So, by a pleasant road, you come to Charleroi. A very short, worthwhile detour at Gozée brings you to Ham-sur-Heure and its remarkable château, reconstructed by command of Louis XV of France. No less remarkable is the 15th-century Gothic altar-screen in Saint Martin's church.

The city of Charleroi is now one of the more important in Belgium. Its history goes back into no remoter past than 1665, when the Marquis de Castel-Rodrigo renamed the village of Charnoy in homage to his monarch, Charles II of Spain. He had seen strategic importance in this crossing of the Sambre with the great road due south from Brussels, and here he erected a fortress which seems to have had little success since it was occupied without much difficulty by Louis XIV a few years later, and, 136 years later, by Napoleon, advancing to Waterloo. And it was through here the Emperor fled a few days later. The former village of a thousand souls had become a commune of 20,000 inhabitants by the middle of the 19th century, when industry—Charleroi is mainly a metal-working and engineering town—began to cluster round the coal-fields of the center. Today Charleroi is an urban agglomeration with over a quarter-million inhabitants. It is no use looking here for signs of a prosperous past, for to Charleroi the present is what matters. The city is justly proud of its two outstanding modern civic buildings: the Industrial Exhibition Halls and the Palace of Fine Arts (Palais des Beaux Arts).

Between Sambre and Meuse

The Sambre at Charleroi, with its surrounding canals, is an industrial river, a complex of wharves, warehouses, and cranes. The main highway from Charleroi to Namur takes you through Presles, the reputed site of the battle between Caesar and the Nervii—with its Roman ruins, more numerous, though perhaps less in their context, than those at Gerpinnes—and so on to Fosse, with the charming houses of the Canons surrounding the church. Here the best known of the *marches militaires* of the Sambre-et-Meuse country is held once in seven years. It is dedicated to Saint Feuillen, the 8th-century Scottish missionary, and lasts from 9 a.m. to 4 p.m. Three thousand performers assemble, wearing all the uniforms in which foreign troops have kept order in southern Belgium for many centuries. (Next in 1977.) *Marches* of a similar character are held in other parts of this region.

The axis of Entre-Sambre-et-Meuse is the road running due south from Charleroi. It takes you through Somzée, where you will want to turn off to the right to see Walcourt, on the Eau d'Heure. In the interesting 12th- and 13th-century Church of Saint Materne you will find more of the exceptional work by the great Hugo d'Oignies, and a miracle-working silver Madonna which is the pretext for the local *marche militaire* on Trinity Sunday each year. Its *jubé,* a Gothic gallery, is a remarkable piece of filigree stonework. A little to the north is Berzée, where there is a castle-farm, early predecessor of the walled-in farmyards with their defensive implications. Returning to the main road, you will find a 17th-century version of the same thing at Daussois.

An interesting example of Renaissance town planning can be seen in this region. Mariembourg, constructed in 1542 and named after Charles Quint's sister, Queen of Hungary, fell to the French in 1554 and was destroyed, so that little trace of the quadrangular plan remains. In 1555 he had another fortified city built farther north, named Philippeville in honor of his son, the king of Spain. Its ramparts have disappeared but the town has retained its original aspect until this day.

Chimay, Home of Madame Tallien

Westward from Couvin is the road to Chimay, which will lead you through Gomrieux and past the Pierre-qui-tourne, a conical druidic survival standing on a plateau. From here you come quickly to Chimay, on the westward edge of the Fagne moorlands where the château, were it not for its ugly bulbous spire, would be strangely reminiscent of the Cotswolds. The statue of Jehan Froissart, historian of the Hundred Years' War and Canon-Treasurer of Chimay, is in the main square; but the memory which keeps Chimay alive is that of Madame Tallien, known to revolutionary France as Notre Dame du Thermidor. Her great beauty and strong personality saved her from the guillotine. She married her protector, Tallien who, upon her instigation, managed to have Robespierre outlawed and "liquidated" in July 1794, thus putting an end to a reign of terror that decimated the country's population. She later married the Prince Caraman de Chimay, and so ruled in this château which had known the lordships of the De Croy, the Chatillon and the Henin, and had been taken by assault by Don Juan of Austria and Turenne. The warrant for her arrest, signed by Robespierre, is still preserved here. One of the features of the château is the little rococo theater, the scene of an annual music festival, end June-early July.

Here the road strikes north, parallel with the French frontier, to Brussels. To your right, the Lake of Virelles invites you to halt. Here you can swim, go boating or fishing, and have your catch prepared by one of the many inns along its shores.

Rance has been famous for centuries for its quarries. Its pink marble decorates Saint Peter's in Rome and the palace of Versailles. Another few miles on is the ancient town of Beaumont, dominated by the ruins of its once formidable fortress.

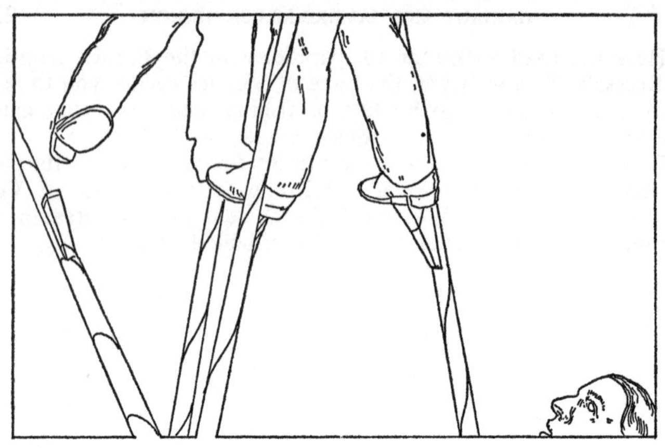

THE MEUSE VALLEY

Historic Cities and Idyllic Countryside

by

SUZANNE CHANTAL

(Mme. Chantal, an outstanding French novelist, also has several travel books on various European countries to her credit. Her particular affection for the Meuse region, which is reflected in the chapter below, is easily understandable, for she was born there.)

Certain corners of the earth retain a quality pure and untouched by man; others present unbounded depths and haunting echoes of the centuries of struggle and hardship which man has invested in their making. It is these regions that are curiously attractive to the traveler.

You feel this mark of centuries of history in the Meuse valley, where, resting side by side, are graves of primitive hunters and tombs of soldiers killed by the gunfire of World War II. The Meuse banks have felt man's keenest suffering from ancient times until today.

The Meuse has always marked the pulse-beat of all Western Europe. The Romans understood its importance as one of their principal causeways from Cologne to the sea. Later, the valley was the seat of the Liège Diocese, and the cradle of Charlemagne's empire. The matchless school of Mosan metalwork developed along the river's banks as it winds through France, Belgium, and Holland. It is this art that has perpetuated the name of the Meuse in such masterpieces as the baptismal font of Renier de Huy, the silver ornaments of Hugo d'Oignies, and the reliquaries of Nicholas of Verdun.

The Carolingian civilization, outwardly Germanic, was essentially Christian. When the empire of Charlemagne disintegrated, leaving the valley a vulnerable wedge between two strong powers, the Meuse frontiers were reinforced not only with fortified castles, but with the spiritual aids of monasteries and abbeys. The country developed Christian virtues and magnanimous qualities which were felt throughout the world of that time. Saint Lambert of Liège became known as the "fountain of wisdom", drawing students and clergymen from all northern Europe.

As finely tempered and enduring as the bronze and silver of their art, the people of the Meuse early acquired the characteristics they possess today—daring, courage, industry, lustiness, and independence. Julius Caesar called them the bravest of all the Gauls.

For more than a thousand years these people have battled valiantly for liberty, warring against tyrants and invaders. They have even fought among themselves, neighbor against neighbor, cousin against cousin, without mercy. The region is filled with soldier graves of every epoch, from ancient Roman mausoleums to the flowery plots of Bastogne.

But all this tragic drama has not been able to dim the beauty of the valley, nor to quench the lust for life which burns in its people. Because they know so well how to die, the Mosans know equally well how to live.

The Four Ages of the Meuse

Although the Meuse has its source in France and its end in Holland, and less than one-third of its long course is through Belgium, it is, nevertheless, only in the latter country that the river is its unique self. From Agimont on the southern border, to Maaseik on the northern frontier, it flows in gentle, modulated curves rather suggesting the four stages of human life.

Beginning in the Ardennes, a young and impetuous stream foaming along narrow ravines, it batters down all obstacles, gathering other impetuous torrents, and thus, noisy and violent, it arrives at Dinant.

From Dinant to Namur it becomes quite beautiful, its banks bedecked with wild roses and marked by castles and chapels. An elegant, worldly set live along its borders, and the lawns of millionaires' villas extend to the water's edge near Wépion and Profondeville.

But at Namur it meets the Sambre, whose waters are tainted by the slag-heaps of Borinage. The Sambre is a beggarly river, coming from a rustic background, but abruptly exposed to the fire and tumult of coal mines, the flames of blast furnaces, the acid scum of rolling-mills. After this confluence with the Sambre, the Meuse becomes deeper and more powerful, fit for useful work. At Liège it is very much a part of the city's life, carrying to and fro an endless procession of tugboats, freighters, and barges.

Through Liège the Meuse is grey and sluggish, and occasionally reinforced by canals. After Liège, the river loiters through the Limburg countryside, where fishermen idle on either bank. The Meuse, called the Maas in Flemish-speaking Belgium and in Holland, is official guardian of the frontier between Belgium and the Low Countries, but it is a peaceful sinecure, since there is never a quarrel from one bank to the other. The two borders have the same red-roofed farm buildings, the same big villages shaded by cherry trees.

You can go up or down the Meuse by boat, breaking the sameness of the voyage by excursions into such picturesque river-regions as Marlagne, Condroz, Famenne, or Herve. Each tributary valley is full of personality and fantasy.

With the coming of spring, from the walnut trees of the Ardennes to the orchards of Limburg, the country is one vast splendor of verdure, and resounding with church bells and the music of holiday processions which fill the streets. Distances are so short in Belgium that you can go everywhere and see everything without fatigue. It is never more than a mile or two from one village to another, and the Meuse landscape is subtle and ever changing.

Practical Information for the Meuse Valley

WHEN TO COME? The chief tourist season in this region runs from May to October. During these months there is a wide range of historical, folklore, and sporting events: festivals, nautical pageants, regattas, outboard motorboat and dinghy races, and fishing. Through the summer, on a Saturday afternoon each month, you can hear chamber music in its natural setting—in one or other of the private châteaux of the Namur country. It is more a music party than a concert and the price includes your buffet tea.

Events: The Grand Féerie de Namur is a succession of activities early in *July*. This is also the month of the International Folk Dance Festival at Yvoir. Each peak-season weekend boasts a special event, while in *August* the city stages the Grand Prix de Belgique motorcycle races on the Citadel circuit as well as an international swimming contest. Historic buildings and some of the finest natural sites along the Meuse are floodlit throughout the season. In *September,* Dinant presents a folklore procession in which the amusing Knights of Flamiche appear.

WHAT TO SEE? No matter what mode of transportation you choose to reach the valley of the Meuse, Namur will most likely be your first port of call. Capital of the province, Namur offers easy access to the whole region and, as a city, has a wide range of attractions. The Meuse valley and parts of the Ardennes can be visited in a day. Namur Tourist Office's "Ardennes-Service" gives information on local accommodation, congresses and sports clubs.

If you are interested in medieval religious art, you will find rewarding collections at Namur, Dinant, and Hastière. This is Belgium's château country, with remarkable edifices (see under "Museums and Castles") in a fairytale setting. Citadels of more recent construction overlook the cities of Huy, Namur, and Dinant. You will find remarkable grottos at Dinant, Hastière-Lavaux, Rochefort, and, farther inland on a much vaster scale, at Han-sur-Lesse.

HOW TO GET ABOUT? *By train:* Namur is a principal stopping place for all trains (including the fast TEE expresses) on the Ostend-Brussels-Luxembourg-Basel route, and the Liège-Charleroi--Paris line, as well as for local services from Brussels to both Namur and Dinant. *By road:* Namur may be reached from Brussels in under an hour, Dinant is only about 17 miles from Namur. The roads in general are in excellent condition and, even in the most remote spots, are asphalted. At weekends, however, you will find driving is easier (and usually more interesting) on the secondary roads.

By boat: A trip worth making is by excursion boat upriver from Namur to Dinant; from there you may continue, by changing boats, to Heer-Agimont near the French frontier. The return journey for this second lap requires an overnight stop at Dinant. You can also take a short excursion by boat from Dinant to Anseremme or vice-versa.

SPORTS. All Meuse valley localities have bathing beaches and some have up-to-date *swimming* pools. *Rowing* facilities are available under the auspices of the Clubs Nautiques at Namur and Dinant, while for *canoeing*—particularly by the not-too-skillful—the Meuse is ideal. You may travel downstream on the Lesse by boat or kayak, with a pilot, from Houyet to Anseremme—a tricky proposition if you do it in your own craft. Kayaks may be hired at Dinant. You can *water-ski* at Waulsort, Wépion, Profondeville, Yvoir, and Dinant. *Yachting* is also a favorite sport and there are yacht harbors at Namur, Profondeville, Dinant, and Waulsort. *Tennis* courts abound everywhere. For *gliding* and amateur aviation there is an attractive little airfield at Temploux.

If the Meuse is not an angler's dream, *fishing* can still be a satisfying pastime. A state license is needed where fishing areas do not belong to someone (mostly hotel proprietors). In local post offices, tourists can purchase licenses for a day's or several day's fishing.

Mountaineers, expert or novice, will find plenty of opportunity to test their *climbing* skill. The abrupt, rocky cliffs provide an excellent training ground for up-and-coming Alpinist, but are not without danger. The best known are those of Marches-les-Dames, Dave, Anseremme, and Waulsort.

The Namur country is ideal for *horseback riding*. There are 20 livery stables in the Province (list from the Tourist Office), where you can hire horses for

150-200 frs. per hour, whether for lessons, organized outings or for a private ride. Many of the stables organize treks of several days, with pre-arranged overnight accommodation for horse and rider. An enjoyable outing is the ride along the Lesse river. At Ciergnon, near Dinant, you can have riding holidays on a residential basis at the *Cercle Equestre d'Herock*.

The young folk, if they are keen and over 13, enjoy the Monday-to-Saturday camps at the Henriet farm at Dailly-les-Couvin, near the French frontier, which costs about 2,000 frs. including insurance, and gives them a specially exciting week, in which they learn practically everything there is to know about the care of the horse and its handling.

CASINOS. The casinos at Dinant and Namur are open all year round. While the former is on a more modest scale, Namur casino is the last word in luxury. Its gastronomic feasts, usually at weekends, are well worth attending.

MUSEUMS AND CASTLES. Certain ancient sites, such as Andenne and Huy, have their own museums, but most of the region's treasures are concentrated in **Namur:** The *Archeological Museum,* Rue du Pont, houses prehistoric, Roman, and Merovingian collections. Near St. Aubain's Cathedral, the *Diocesan Museum* displays the work of Mosan silversmiths, a Merovingian *châsse,* and outstanding pieces of Dinant copperwork. Those interested in antique weapons will find 6,000 of them at the *Citadel Museum.* In the Rue Saintraint, you may visit the *De Croix Museum,* charming 18th-cent. home of the Marquis de Croix, today housing regional art and history. Specially worthwhile is the *Musée des Arts Anciens* which has a splendid collection of Mosan art in many fields. In the courtyard, too, is a separate museum of the work of the Namur 19th-century painter Felicien Rops.

Among the outstanding castles and châteaux of the region are the following:

Annevoie, Louis XIV castle in French-style park; guided visit of gardens, about one hour; periodic displays of antiques. Open Easter-Nov. 1.

Crupet, near Spontin, worth a short detour. Dates from 14th century; still inhabited. Unique example of fortified farm.

Franc-Waret, may be visited Sundays; fine paintings and tapestries.

Freyr, near Waulsort; one of the most impressive edifices of its kind in Belgium; beautiful interiors, including Louis XV woodwork and furniture. Recently repaired.

Jehay-Bodegnée, 10 miles from Huy on road to Tongres; one of finest architecturally; still inhabited, contains fine archeological collection; open weekdays, May-Oct.

Lavaux Ste. Anne, 17th-cent. moated castle, contains hunting museum, and there is a wild animal park (including boar) in the grounds.

Spontin, feudal castle, good example of medieval military architecture; still inhabited but open to public from Mar.1-Oct. 31.

Vèves, near Celles; this 15th-cent. castle is perhaps the most romantic of all. It has recently reopened after extensive repairs.

Walzin, perched like an eagle's nest on a high rock; dates from 16th cent.; open Thurs. only.

HOTELS AND RESTAURANTS. The Meuse valley is far from suffering shortages of hotel accommodation. Nevertheless, you should book ahead during July and August, especially if you want a room with bath. The smaller hotels are equipped like most of their counterparts everywhere and are extremely clean. Service is good. Special features of this region—more so than anywhere else in Belgium—are the culinary *auberges* and *hostelleries.* Behind the often modest façade of an inn lurks not so much the cost of accommodation as the astronomic price of the meals which you are expected to take there. First consult the menu-card exhibited outside the establishment, and you'll know where you are.

AGIMONT. Southernmost point in the Meuse valley.

Hotels: *Manoir d'Agimont,* off the main road. Former château of the Count of Paris, pretender to the French throne. Moderate, 20 rooms, excellent restaurant. *Deux Tilleuls,* small, inexpensive. On the right bank of Meuse, at Heer: *Hôtel de France,* 8 rooms, 2 baths, inexpensive.

ANDENNE. Halfway between Huy and Namur.

Hotel: *Hôtel du Commerce,* 12 rooms, inexpensive, good cuisine.

Restaurant: at Ohey, four miles out on the Chiny road, is the *Monjoie* (M), pleasant décor. Has a few rooms.

ANHEE. Three miles north of Dinant. Ruins of Montaigle and Poilvache.

Hotel: *Terrasse,* 6 rooms, expensive for what it is; food excellent.

ANNEVOIE. Hotels: *Bellevue,* overlooking river, 8 rooms; *Bon Accueil,* 6 rooms. Both inexpensive.

Restaurants: *St. Christophe,* good and reasonably priced.

ANSEREMME. All hotels overlook Meuse or Lesse, open April-Sept. *Windsor,* 79 Rue Caussin; *Hôtel de la Lesse,* Pont Saint-Jean, large terrace. Both moderate.

Restaurant: *Freyr* (M), with panoramic view.

BAUCHE-EVREHAILLES. Four miles from Yvoir, in the Bocq valley.

Hotel: *La Bonne Auberge,* 9 rooms, first class reasonable. Excellent cuisine prepared by owner; the blow to your wallet won't be too heavy.

BEEZ-SUR-MEUSE. Château and Romanesque church.

Hotel: *Le Grand Roi,* 10 rooms, half with bath. Excellent value, inexpensive. Restaurant specialty: escavèche de Meuse.

BOUVIGNES. Hotel: *Auberge de Bouvignes,* 6 rooms, moderate. Its restaurant is excellent but fairly expensive.

CRUPET. Hotel: *Hôtel du Centre,* 9 rooms, simple.

Restaurant: *Les Ramiers* (M-E), gastronomically recommended.

DAVE. Five miles south of Namur, on right bank of the Meuse, ancient château.

Hotels: *Auberge d'Amée,* small and cozy, 6 rooms, moderate. Restaurant open until late, Italian specialties; terrace, tennis. *Beau Rivage,* also moderate.

DENEE-MAREDSOUS. In the Molignée valley, near the famous abbey.

Hotel: *Auberge de Maredsous,* only a few rooms. Try their trout and the cheese made by the monks.

DINANT. The center of Meuse tourism, has many hotels and pensions. Avoid on Sundays in peak-season.

Hotels: Best is *Hôtel des Postes,* Ave. Cadoux; 25 of its 60 rooms with bath. First class reasonable. Also good: *Henrotaux,* Ave. W. Churchill, has only a few rooms with bath. *Hostellerie Thermidor,* 3 Rue de la Gare, moderate, 8 rooms, 5 with bath. *Couronne,* Rue Sax, moderate; *Commerce,* Place St. Nicolas, inexpensive.

Restaurants: Best is *Hostellerie Thermidor* (E), with M. de Wynter himself presiding in the kitchen; pâtés and crayfish à la Dinantaise are his specialties. Or try the *Central,* Place Reine Astrid, or *Auberge d'Alsace,* Ave. General Garcia. *A la Ville de Bruxelles,* Place Reine Astrid, caters abundantly at many levels. For oriental food, the Chinese restaurant on Ave. W. Churchill, near the bridge.

An excellent restaurant outside town at 365 Rue Rémy Himmer, *Moulin de Leffe,* is in the Fonds de Leffe valley; fishing.

EVREHAILLES. See *Bauche.*

FALMIGNOUL. Near Waulsort. Has four hotels, all very simple.

GODINNE. Halfway between Namur and Dinant, on the right bank of river.

Hotels: *Grand Hôtel,* 15 rooms, 4 baths, moderate. *Etrangers,* moderate; *Chambéry,* inexpensive.

HASTIERE. On both sides of Meuse, abbey-castle.

Hotels: *Tilleuls,* small, moderate. *Abbaye,* 14 rooms, *Ardennes,* and *Du Centre,* smaller, all inexpensive.

HUY. Hotels: *Aigle Noir,* Quai Dautrebande, several of its 20 rooms have baths, first class reasonable. Slightly less comfortable, the 350-year-old stagecoach halt, *Hôtel de la Cloche,* Quai de la Batte, has only 6 rooms, moderate. In the same category, *Du Fort,* Chaussée Napoléon. *Nord,* Pl. Zénobe-Gramme, inexpensive.

Restaurant: At Villers-le-Temple, 10 miles from Huy, there is first class fare at the *Commanderie* (E-M), a 13th-cent. manor and 15-room hotel.

LUSTIN. Vacation center opposite Profondeville. Hotels: *Chalet de Frênes,* fine view from terrace, moderate, 10 rooms, 4 baths; excellent with good restaurant (M). *La Cigogne,* nice terrace, small, moderate; outstanding restaurant.

Restaurant: *Floraire,* moderate to expensive, has a few rooms.

NAMUR. Hotels: The *Amigo,* recreated from a château at the summit of the Citadel, is best, first class superior. Rooms and suites for 60 guests have bath, TV, radio. Located in a park overlooking the Meuse valley. Indoor pool.

First class reasonable: *Flandre,* 14 Pl. de la Gare; 35 rooms, 15 with bath; food excellent.

Queens, Ave. de la Gare, is best among the moderate hotels, 25 rooms, a few with bath. The *Couronne,* Pl. de la Gare, and the small *Porte de Fer,* Ave. de la Gare, are very satisfactory, inexpensive. The latter has no restaurant.

Restaurants: In addition to the hotel restaurants, there are several other eating places. *Aux Armes de Namur,* 82 Rue de Fer, and *Berote,* 8 Ave. de la Gare, both excellent and most reasonable. Good French cuisine at *Le Bayard,* Place Wiertz (M). *Le Champeau* (I-M), Ave Golenvaux, at the Maison de Culture. On the Citadel plateau there are a few inexpensive restaurants.

The younger set, from Namur and far afield, spend their evenings dancing at *La Ferme Blanche* on the Charleroi road at Malonne, which also runs a lively stable.

PROFONDEVILLE. Vacation center in pleasant surroundings.

Hotels: *Frisia,* on the Dinant road, moderate. *Parc,* similar, has excellent but fairly expensive restaurant. *Chanteraine* and *Auberge d'Alsace,* are small and inexpensive.

Restaurant: *Le Périgord,* renowned for its cuisine, as is *Rhétorique,* both (M-I).

SPONTIN. Hotels: *Auberge des Nutons,* first class hostelry, reasonable. *Hotel du Bocq,* small and unpretentious, as is *Cheval Blanc.*

Restaurant: *Auberge des Nutons,* above.

TEMPLOUX. At an easy distance of Namur, is the *St. Martin,* modern, first class reasonable.

WAULSORT. Southwest of Dinant, ancient abbey transformed into castle. From here you can visit nearby Château of Freyr. Hotels: *Grand Hôtel Regnier,* with terrace overlooking Meuse, 53 rooms, 7 baths, moderate; try their anguilles de Meuse en *matelotte* (eel stew) or chicken in tarragon sauce. *Mondego,* is inexpensive, 21 rooms, 3 baths.

WEPION. Vacation center 3 miles south of Namur.

Hotels: In town, *Le Lido,* first class reasonable, is the leader; only 10 rooms, but nearly all with bath. Terrace restaurant. *Le Wépion* and *Chalet,* 6 rooms, both inexpensive.

The *GB Motel,* on outskirts, is recent, has lovely river view; 130 large rooms with bath, TV, air-conditioning. Restaurant, coffee shop.

Restaurants: *Chez le Père Courtin* (M), famed gourmet rendezvous. *Moulin de Provence,* in same bracket.

YVOIR. Hotels: *Hostellerie Vachter,* has only 8 rooms, all with bath, first class. Its restaurant (E) is justly famous. *Les Mésanges,* is almost first class. *Ermitage,* a few of its 14 rooms with bath, moderate. *Auberge de Bruxelles,* is small but satisfactory, terrace, inexpensive.

USEFUL ADDRESSES. City tourist offices (Syndicat d'Initiative): *Dinant,* 37 Rue Grande (near casino);*Huy,* 4 Quai de Namur; *Namur,* Place Léopold.

Excursion boat information: (Namur to Dinant and French frontier) *Pittance,* 16 Ave. Churchill, Dinant.

Yachting: *Namur,* Royal Yacht Club of Sambre and Meuse, 117 Chaussée de Dinant, at Wépion.

Exploring the Meuse Valley

Embarking at Hastière-par-delà, quite near the French border, and known for its 11th-century Romanesque church, you reach Dinant in about two hours, after a trip between rock cliffs, pierced with caves full of shells and fossils. The bare rocks overhanging the river have been worn by time and weather into curious shapes, and they are named accordingly—*The Camel, The Dog* etc. The ancient Abbey of Waulsort, founded by Scottish monks in the 10th century, has been transformed into a château and rivals in landscaping its neighbor, the Château of Freyr, designed by Le Nôtre. The orange trees in the French-style garden are over 300 years old. Louis XIV of France and the King of Spain, Charles II, met here in 1675 to put an end to the prolonged strife between the two countries, an occasion when coffee was consumed for the first time in Belgium.

Anseremme is quite a busy, flourishing community, with riverside restaurants that serve excellent fried fish; and an attractive aquarium with a full and well-presented collection of the aquatic life of the Meuse and Lesse which, in a whirl of water, joins it here. Long before you reach Dinant, the city's sentinel—the rock of Bayard—comes into view. It is a tall, needle-like stone, detached from the sharp cliff. According to legend, it was Bayard, the dauntless steed of the four sons of Aymon, who split the mammoth boulder when jumping across the Meuse. These four sons color all the early lore of the Meuse valley with their eternal strife and patriotic valor. They fought a long war against Charlemagne, and almost every château of the region has sheltered them.

Dinant

When Louis XIV laid siege to Namur he installed Madame de Maintenon, his morganatic wife, at Dinant, where she was near enough to comfort him in his trials and tribulations. The city rests in an enchanting background, but it has never been able to keep a single one of its historic monuments through an endless history of war, fire, and siege. Dinant was involved in every war that affected the Mosan valley—against the people of Liège, the Burgundians, the French, and, more recently, the Germans. The sack of Dinant by the Duke of Burgundy in 1466 saw the city razed and 800 of its citizens, tied back-to-back, drowned in the Meuse. Not less frightful was the struggle of 1914, and the ghastly reprisals that ensued. Incredibly enough, Dinant not only survives and rebuilds its shattered ruins but maintains its traditions and its gaiety.

The ancient art of hammered copper made Dinant an illustrious center of metalwork; even England sent to Dinant for beaten and engraved copper. This art thrived and prospered through the 13th and 14th centuries, but it received a mortal blow under the pillaging of Charles the Rash. The craft lost its originality, becoming, at last, a banal feature of the shops. For some time, conscientious artisans have devoted themselves to resurrecting and applying the secrets of the old masters of metal-work. Another local craft is the manufacture of *couques:* hard gingerbead baked in molds which often are masterpieces of woodcarving. The local artists' fancy knows no limits and you can buy these edible souvenirs in all *patisseries* and candy shops in town.

Dinant is a perfect port-of-call, for it has fine hotels and restaurants, as well as easy access to the neighboring valleys of Lesse and Molignée. A lift, by the way, carries visitors up the Rocher (high rock) to the citadel, and another one, departing from the town center, brings you to Montfort Tower. On your way down you can visit the prehistoric caverns of Mont-Fat.

Adolphe Sax, inventor of the saxophone, was born here in 1814. His home has been converted into a small museum.

Castles Everywhere

Take a boat trip through six river locks and you will have plenty of time to enjoy the purple foxgloves and bluebells along the banks, and to consider the history of the old castles and fortresses that line the way. It was at Crèvecoeur that three lovely noblewomen threw themselves from a high window to escape Henry II, the infamous French king. Bouvignes, squatting below, shows some traces of its important past: the only remaining gate of the city ramparts; *la maison du baillage,* a perfect example of the Spanish occupation period; and an early Gothic church. Nearby, on the right bank of the river, the ruins of Poilvache Castle appear. The countryside around is dotted with ancient fortified farms.

At Anhée you can make a detour to visit Maredsous Abbey, a successful turn-of-the-century imitation of early Gothic on a site of wild beauty. Romantically set in the Molignée valley, the ruins of Montaigle Castle have a sad tale to tell, for it was in the courtyard that the medieval knight De Bioulx accidentally pierced his daughter's heart while duelling with her lover.

From Yvoir, a picturesque locality on the right bank, you should make a circular trip to Spontin's feudal castle, still inhabited but accessible. It will give you a good idea of the evolution of a baronial hall from the 12th to the 17th century. Continuing towards the Meuse, you will pass Crupet—a fortified moated manor of the same epoch and of a most curious shape—and Mont, a typical village of the region. Opposite Godinne, at Annevoie, there is a small Versailles, all parks, fountains, and little pools. A million tulips can be seen here during April and May, and the lovely Château Montpelier is open to the public in season.

The riverbanks rise higher and higher, becoming more crowded with a chaos of boulders. Some of these conceal hidden wonders, such as the formation at Frappecul, behind which is the Chauveau Cave. The Rock of Tailfer guards the entrance to the delightful valley of Fond-de-Lustin. At each lock the riverbanks offer enticements to come ashore for tea and sightseeing. More houses appear among the wild undergrowth, lawns extend to the water's edge, and the river is alive with swimmers, canoeists, and sailboats. The Meuse is busy all summer with this pleasant holiday traffic, but since the war some of its elegance has been spoiled by ever-multiplying cottages and inns.

Namur

Past Profondeville, Wépion, and the ancient Château of Dave, the stern silhouette of Namur comes into view. The citadel broods on a promontory above the confluence of the Meuse and the Sambre. Happily, Namur's greatest treasures have remained intact in the Sisters of Our Lady Convent. They are the works of Hugo d'Oignies, the monk-jeweler who dedicated to Christ his art as silversmith. His crosses and reliquaries are ornamented with squirrels and stags, and jewel-studded interlacing leaves. On one Mosan reliquary you will see represented a joust between men on stilts. This once was a popular sport in the Walloon country. Why did the men of Namur cling so to their stilts? No doubt because the Meuse often flooded its banks, leaving a treacherous film of mud and slime, but there is a much more amusing explanation furnished by an ancient chronicler. Following a rebellion of his subjects, the noble lord, Jehan, ruler of Namur, laid siege to the city, and reduced it to a state of famine. Emissaries were sent to plead for mercy, but Jehan outraged, replied that he would see no one who came "on foot, horse, carriage, or boat". It was then that the city fathers conceived the idea of sending their ambassadors on stilts. It worked. The duke laughed when he saw the long-legged committee, and that was the end of the strife.

Namur (pop. 35,000) is a city of immaculately curtained 17th-century pink-brick houses, rich Baroque churches, gardens, an outdoor theater, and a casino. A comfortable cabin lift takes you right up to the citadel. The fortress owes its present shape to the Dutch who, after the Napoleonic Wars, reinforced the strategic château of the counts of Namur.

The early 18th-century cathedral is one of the finest examples of Baroque in Belgium and owes its authenticity to an Italian architect, Pizzini. It shelters an authentic Jordaens, a debatable Van Dyck, and several Rubens copies executed under the master's watchful eye by one of his pupils.

The heart of the victor of the memorable Lepanto naval battle, which saved Christendom from the Turks' onslaught, rests here. Don Juan of Austria, camping outside Namur in 1578, was sent a pair of gloves by a lady admirer. They were the gift of intrigue, and a promising prince died from their poison at the age of 31. Some historians like to think this was a Belgian patriot's act of resistance. But the shocking way in which Don Juan's body was cut up and smuggled in saddlebags across hostile France into Spain tends to show a somber picture of the most powerful monarch of the age. Philip II of Spain, envious of his illegitimate half-brother's military and amorous successes, gave him the most thankless job in the realm—the governorship of the Low Countries. The Pope wanted to help Don Juan to a kingdom within the Spanish dominion and that was probably too much for the master of half the world. The curious Baroque Saint-Loup Church nearby was described by Baudelaire as a "sinister and courtly marvel" with "the interior of a hearse, terrible and delightful, embroidered in black, pink, and silver."

Some of the finest works of the silversmith Hugo d'Oignies can be seen at the Convent of the Sisters of Notre Dame, and there is a notable 8th-century Carolingian *châsse* at the Diocesan Museum.

Those addicted to gambling will find the Namur Casino a pleasant place in which to lose their money: sumptuous premises, a first class restaurant, and a dance band at weekends will help to soften the blow.

You should certainly go to visit the Cistercian Abbey of Marche les Dames. It is a peaceful sight, with silent cloisters and terraces smelling pungently of boxwood. Not far from the abbey, King Albert I of Belgium met his death while climbing a sheer cliff.

Inland, past the fortified farm of Wartet and the medieval Castle of Fernelmont, lies the Château of Franc-Waret, still owned by descendants of the Marquis de Croix, Spain's governor of California. Admirable paintings of the Flemish School and Brussels tapestries designed by Van Orley decorate the walls, and among the many exhibits you can see the gold and platinum keys presented by the city of Lima to Théodore de Croix when promoted to Viceroy of Peru and Chile.

Andenne owes its origin to a convent, the nuns of which—under protection from the counts of Namur—had the strange privilege of governing this township for over a thousand years until 1785, when Joseph II put an end to their reign. It was one of the early manufacturing centers of potters, and its Ceramic Museum is well worth a visit.

Romantic Huy

The birthplace of Renier de Huy and Godefroid de Clair, Huy is the epitome of romantic towns. It may, or may not have been the birthplace of the naughty Arlette; but it certainly obtained its civic charter, one of the first in Europe, in the same year (1066) in which William, the fruit of her indiscretion, conquered England. Here, too, Peter the Hermit brewed up the first crusade, and his tomb is here to this day. Lying at the confluence of the Hoyoux with the Meuse, Huy is a winding tangle of narrow streets dominated by a towering cliff on whose top broods a fortress. Don't miss the copper fountain in the Grand' Place, the town hall carillon ringing out *Brave Liègeois* every hour, the view from the fort, the Collegiate Church—a fine example of 14th-century flamboyant Gothic—with its rose window, or the tortuous byways around the Convent of the Black Friars. On the riverbank you can see a fine example of medieval Meuse valley architecture, the Hôtel de la Cloche, dating back to 1406. A cable-car connects for over two miles, the hill beyond the citadel with the left bank and offers a splendid panorama of town and country.

The Meuse lingers another instant along the mall shaded by lime trees, past the University of Peace, foundation of the late Father Pire, Nobel Peace Prize winner (soon to have a monster nuclear power station for neighbor), traces a lazy curve about the Château of Neuville, and then forsakes its borders of ivy and honeysuckle for banks lined with railroads and brick factories.

Liège, the Spirited City

Rows of drab houses ranged along stone quays serve as introduction to Liège, and there is the city itself, bustling and clattering among protecting hills. Now dignified and industrious, the river is equally divided between coal barges and gay little sailboats. Reflected in its slate-grey waters are the steeples and coal shafts.

Here the river spreads out and loiters among many islands, lagoons, and shop-lined bridges. Until the beginning of the 19th century, Liège remained a perfect Walloon Venice. But the Meuse, which once covered this entire area, has through the centuries become narrower and deeper. The shallow lagoon has been filled in and surmounted with great boulevards; while the old quarter of the city retains nothing of its watery past but a few street names: "Island Bridge", "Sovereign Bridge", "Under Water". If you would capture the true, poignant beauty of Liège, approach it from the riverbanks.

Do not look for grandiose monuments, vast perspectives, or triumphal avenues (except for the new motorway accesses). Liège, pop. 450,000, is a chaos, a confusion resulting from years of strife. Crouching at the bottom of a hilly pocket, it has no space for a big square, and the only order imposed on its tangle of streets is that of the Meuse, which obliges certain thoroughfares to follow its quays. Liège is a symbol of contradiction, and rebellion against rule and order. And even more than he is hotheaded, the Liège citizen is stubborn. Still, he is a good fellow, openhearted, generous, and always ready to laugh and drink with the next one. Paradoxically, Liège, a city that works hard day and night in a glare of strip mills, is also a city of quiet home life, where families dine bountifully, and spend hours sitting about the table. Yet, it must be said, the people of Liège also spend hours *not* sitting about the table, for all the pleasures of café life can be found in this, one of the gayest cities of Belgium (except summer, which is a bit more dull, as the university's 15,000 students are not here).

In the midst of this uproar of factories, a school of notably sensitive musicians sprang up. César Franck and Grétry were born in Liège and the famous violin school exemplified by Bériot, Vieuxtemps, Ysaye, and Thompson developed here.

The city has clung steadfastly to old Walloon traditions. You will find evidences of them in the picturesque and touching Museum of Folklore. But for a more lively study, perhaps the most typical entertainment of Liège is to be found in the theater in Rue Féronstrée, contained in two marionette shows where all the heroes of Mosan legends can be seen: the four sons of Aymon,

Geneviève de Brabant, Charlemagne, and even Napoleon, along with assorted Biblical or contemporary figures. The puppets are large or small according to their historical significance. The great Emperor Charles weighs about 78 pounds, while his archers are small enough to be manipulated six at a time in the puppeteer's hand. A commentary, by the witty Liègeois Punch, Tschantches, is part of each performance, whether it represents the Nativity Scene or the latest tid-bit of contemporary scandal.

The history of Liège is one long struggle by its bishop-princes against powerful neighbors, and by citizens against its rulers. Individual liberty—*pauvre homme en sa maison est roi*—was granted by charter as early as the 12th century, coinciding with the discovery of large coalfields. The city's increasing prosperity was broken by 70 years of Burgundian rule and recurrent insurrections, culminating in the destruction of Liège by Charles the Rash in 1468. After his death the De La Marck family played an eminent role in her resurrection.

A fundamentally boisterous population willingly joined the French Revolution and chased out the last ruling prince-bishop. After Napoleon's fall, the proud city suffered Dutch rule. Liège volunteers, dispatched in haste to Brussels, played an important part in the 1830 Revolution that finally sealed Belgian independence. The story of the heroic defence of that independence in 1914 is one of the fairest laurels in Belgium's flag.

Practical Information for Liège

WHEN TO COME? City of nearly half a million inhabitants, Liège offers a great variety of pastimes, and may be visited all year round. Special attractions that might influence your choice of date include: End of *May*, the Liège International Fair, showing the latest achievements in mining, metallurgy and electricity. Ten days after Whitsun, the Corpus Christi procession dating from 1246. *Sculpture and Light,* a pioneer lumino-dynamic show, using latest electronic techniques, is held in Boverie Park each Sunday from mid-*June* through August. On the island between the Meuse and the Ourthe—the "Republic of Outremeuse"—there is a boisterous popular fair, called the *fête des potales,* on 15 *August. September* is the month of the Liège Fortnight, a festival that includes an important musical event, the international competition for string quartets. In *December*, on Christmas Day, the Republic of Outremeuse stages the annual Feast of the Nativity, with innumerable "live cribs" all over the crowded island.

WHAT TO SEE? In the city, a large number of museums reflect all aspects of the region's arts and crafts, history and folklore. Historic buildings and fine churches abound. You can take excursions on the river as far as the Dutch frontier. Interesting side trips will bring you into the Ardennes valleys; to the grotto of Remouchamps; to Spa, the famed watering place where you may gamble at the casino; to the gigantic dam near Eupen; and along the Ourthe River, dotted with charming old villages. At Henri-Chapelle, halfway between Liège and Aachen, is the vast American military cemetery.

HOW TO GET ABOUT? The Trans-Europe-Express (TEE) offers direct service to Liège on its Paris-Dortmund (*Parsifal*) and Ostend-Frankfurt (*Saphir*) runs; there are also frequent express trains from Brussels. By road Liège may be reached from Brussels via the Brussels-Liège motorway (E5). Good rail and bus networks help to explore the surrounding countryside. In the city itself there are trolleybuses and buses. Self-drive cars are also available.

SPORTS. A spirited sports city, Liège offers a variety of distractions throughout the year. *Football* (soccer) is the most popular sport and you may view, from Sept.-end May, some exciting Belgian championship and international games at the grounds of the city's first league clubs: F.C. Liègeois, Rocourt Stadium; Standard Club at Sclessin Stadium which is also Tilleur Football Club's home. During the summer season the various motoring organizations offer *automobile and motorcycle racing* at Francorchamps, near Spa. *Boxing* is also very popular and during winter several important events are staged at the Palais des Sports.

The Meuse is ideal for *rowing,* and there are two clubs fostering this stimulating sport: Royal Sport Nautique and Union Nautique, both at Parc de la Boverie. *Golf* can be played in Angleur, at the Golf Club du Sart-Tilman. To *swim* in the Meuse, you must go north to Visé; but in Liège you have the excellent Piscine Couverte, 33 Blvd. de la Sauvenière. The leading *tennis* club is R.T.C. Liège, Sart-Tilman, at the site called "Belle Jardinière".

HOTELS. There are several good hotels, usually with excellent restaurants. The older ones are small and service, therefore, is more personalized than you will find on the average in cities of this size.

Two American-sponsored hotels in near deluxe category are: *Ramada Inn,* Blvd. de la Sauvenière, central, and *Holiday Inn,* Rue du Parc, across the Meuse river.

Just out of town, on the Liège-Aachen motorway, is the 100-room *Post House* with grill restaurant.

First class superior: *Moderne,* 29 Pont d'Avroy, 68 rooms with bath and reasonable for short term stays. *Couronne,* Pl. des Guillemins, 79 rooms with bath, is near the station and noisy.

First class reasonable: *Cygne d' Argent,* 49 Rue Beeckman, 21 rooms, about half with bath.

Moderate: *Univers,* 116 Rue des Guillemins, 56 rooms, 10 baths; *Angleterre,* 2 Rue des Dominicains, 50 rooms, 20 baths, good.

Among the inexpensive spots: *Le Vénitien,* 2 Rue Hamal, is comfortable.

ENVIRONS OF LIEGE. At **Chaudfontaine,** small thermal spa 7 miles southeast, with a casino: *Des Bains et Périgord,* and *Palace,* both same size (40 rooms) and ranging between first class reasonable and moderate. *La Source,* inexpensive.

At **Herstal,** a suburb of Liège, is the first class superior *Euromotel,* a recent venture by Wagon Lits/Cook.

At **Visé,** historical art town on bank of the Meuse, 10 miles east: 20-room *Pont,* is leading establishment, inexpensive; others include *Touristes, Métropole, Liège, Tourne Bride,* all very simple. Try the local specialty, goose à l'instar de Visé. On Robinson Island, water sports, dancing, fishing. Pleasure boats leave from Liège Passerelle at 10 a.m., and 1:30 p.m. (Check with the Tourist Office).

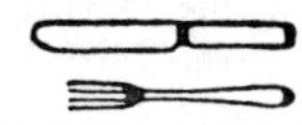

RESTAURANTS. Liège cuisine is refined and noted for specialties of goose, thrushes (*grives*) and a white sausage that is the pride of local butchers (*boudin blanc de Liège*). In addition to all the classic creations of French and Belgian cuisine, Liège offers such local specialties as *écrevisses à la Liègeoise* (crayfish cooked in white wine sauce and butter) or *rognon de veau à la Liègeoise* (veal kidney cooked with juniper berries, with a dash of gin added before serving). Perhaps your tastes are more modest, and you'll be quite happy with the illustrious Ardennes ham, cured over smoldering oak. Another simple, and inexpensive, course is *salade Liègeoise*, a stew prepared with French beans, potatoes, onions, and lard. If your culinary ambitions go higher, try *oie à l'instar de Visé,* goose cooked in wine, then fried and served with a *sauce mousseline* made of eggs, melted butter and garlic. For dessert there are fruit tarts of all kinds and pancakes (*crêpes flambées*). Your afternoon coffee session should consist of *gaufres Liégeoises*—prepared in front of you in most places—and coffee with whipped cream, still a bone of contention between Liège and Vienna.

Clou Doré (E), 33 Rue Mont St. Martin, is highly atmospheric, full of antiques; it also has a few deluxe rooms. Recalling bygone days is *Vieux Liège,* in a 16th-cent. Mosan Renaissance house at 41 Quai de la Goffe. You can eat well, too, in the riverside *Palais des Congrès*. Less expensive but still in the top gastronomic class, *Rôtisserie l'Empereur,* 15 Pl. du 20 Août, and *Rôtisserie Dinantaise,* 75 Rue Grétry.

Atmosphere in an ancient residence, *La Batte,* Quai de la Batte. Equally good, *Chez Septime,* 12 Rue St. Paul. Both (M).

For seafood, *La Coquille,* 14 Rue des Clarisses. Closed mid-July to mid-Aug.

Good cuisine at straightforward prices can be enjoyed at the bistro, *Chez Marcel,* 39 Rue Basse-Wez (small, so reserve).

Italian food, cheery folklore, at *La Strada,* 15 Rue Vinâve d'Ile. Other Italian spots: *San Remo,* Pl. Général Leman, and *Chianti,* 4 Pl. Delcour.

Pont d'Avroy (I), 32 Rue Pont d' Avroy, where you may taste in season one of their 13 preparations of mussels. Excellent.

All department stores have good restaurants and snack bars.

ENVIRONS OF LIEGE. At **Chaudfontaine** you can eat extremely well in attractive rustic décor at *Cense Blanche* (E). At **Herstal,** a suburb, the *Sans Secret* (M), is recommended. In the suburb of **Seraing,** restaurant on 24th floor of *Europa Tower,* prices not so high as the building. Three miles out, on road to **Marche,** *Sart-Tilman* (M-E), excellent. At **Angleur,** suburb, *l'Orchidée Blanche* (E), 457 Rte. du Condroz, open till 1 a.m.

NIGHTCLUBS. Liège people enjoy music and dancing, but don't favor night spots. They are quite content to visit cafés in the evening, or the *British Pub* (a Watneys house) at 14 Rue Tête Boeuf. Nightlife dies down after 1 a.m. The only nightclubs: *New Inn,* 4 Pl. St. Paul, offers sweet music and soft lights; no floorshow. *Le Tabarin,* 14 Rue Bergerue, starts its somewhat daring floorshow at 10:30 p.m.; quality debatable, prices reasonable. For lonely males: try the dancing and drinking clubs in Rue du Port d'Or and Rue St. Adalbert.

MUSEUMS. The most important art gallery is the *Musée des Beaux-Arts,* 34 Rue de l'Académie. Collection of French paintings since Ingres; Corot and Impressionists (Boudin, Monet, Pissaro) well represented; works by Vlaminck, Utrillo, Picasso, Léger, and German Expressionists. A room devoted to modern Belgian painting shows Permeke, Ensor, Evenepoel, and Laermans. Open from 11-12:30 and 2-5, except Tues. *Armorer's Museum,* 8 Quai de Maestricht, holds more than 8,000 pieces and shows development of gunsmith techniques over six centuries. One of its unique showpieces is the 14-barrel flintlock ancestor of the machine-gun, invented by English Col. Thornton in 1793. Same opening times.

A few houses farther on, the *Curtius Museum,* in pure Mosan Renaissance style, holds an important archeological collection. The section on glass retraces the history of this material since its origins. Open 11-12:30 and 2-5, closed Tues, open Wed. 7-10.

The *Ansembourg Mansion,* 114 Rue Féronstrée, houses remarkable pieces of Liège-style 18th-cent. furniture. The *Walloon Folklore and Art Crafts Museum* is at No. 136 in the same street. Rooms have commentaries in different languages. Both open 10-12 and 2-5, but closed Wed. and Thurs. respectively.

The Diocesan Museum, installed in the cloister of St. Paul's Cathedral, holds rich collections of religious and Meuse valley art. For admittance apply to guardian, 6 Rue Bonne Fortune.

Guided visits are conducted Tues. evening at 7:30, at Curtius Museum and at Ansembourg Mansion at the same hour on Wed. except July-Aug., admittance free on Sat.

In the heart of the city, underneath Pl. St. Lambert, you can visit Sun. morning between 10-12 the *Hypocaust,* an interesting heating system introduced by the Romans and visible amid the vestiges of a Belgo-Roman villa. Remains of a neolithic cave and of St. Lambert's Cathedral (destroyed by fire in the 12th cent.) may also be seen here. (From June to Sept.)

THEATERS AND MUSIC. The *Théâtre Royal* has an opera, operetta, and ballet company. If you understand French you will enjoy a visit to *Théâtre du Gymnase,* or the *Rideau de Liège,* (puppet shows); still more of the puppets at the *Théâtre de la Jeunesse,* Rue de Surlet. At the *Trianon,* plays are in the Walloon dialect. At the Conservatoire, 27 Blvd. Piercot, you can hear the Liège Municipal Symphony Orchestra and the best international soloists. Lunchtime concerts are held Oct.-Apr. every Thursday at the Salle de l'Emulation. The well-known Quatuor de Liège string quartet holds a recital every Sunday at 11 a.m., at the Vertbois chapel, from Oct.-Apr.

SHOPPING. Liège is the hometown of the world famous Belgian shotgun. This is your opportunity to pick and choose, and here are a few reliable addresses: *Bury-Donckier,* 11-13 Passage Lemonnier; *Defourny,* 7 Rue Gérardrie; *Dumoulin,* 55 Rue St. Gilles; *Masquelier,* 88 Rue Cathédrale. Herstal, a suburb, houses several outstanding gunsmiths.

The best Belgian crystal-ware, Val St. Lambert, coms from Liège and the folowing shops specialize in it: *Art et Lumière,* 29 Rue de l'Université; *Boland,* 30 Rue Vinâve d'Ile and 6 Rue St. Paul; *Moreau Frères,* 16 Pl. Maréchal Foch.

You will find the best shops in the Rue Pont d'Avroy, Rue Cathédrale, Passage Lemonnier, Rue du Pont d'Ile, Rue Vinâve d'Ile, and the Galeries Charles Magnette and Moderne.

CHURCH SERVICES. Catholic services in all parish churches. Protestant, 22 Quai Marcellis; Adventist, 29 Blvd. Frère Orban; Redemptionist, 1 Quai G. Kurth; Jewish, 19 Rue Léon Frédéricq; Mormon, 118 Rue Campine.

USEFUL ADDRESSES. *British Consulate,* 45 Rue Beeckman. *City Tourist Office,* 5 Rue Gen. Jacques, and Guillemins Station. Police, tel. 23-28-28.

Exploring Liège

Do not hope to follow any set route in your rambles through the town; Liège streets are laid out like jig-saw puzzles. If you are surprised by the number of churches, remember that Liège is an ancient Episcopal city. The martyr, Saint Lambert, was its founder, and until 1789, it was governed by bishops.

So, in spite of bitter anticlerical demonstrations, like that in which old Saint Lambert Cathedral was destroyed in 1794, Liège remains a city devoted to its saints. Each has his particular cult of healing: Saint Apolline cures toothaches, Saint Donat protects against lightning, and Saint Ghislain saves children from nervous disturbances. There must be at least 100 steeples surmounting old churches which may be modest but are never uninteresting. Saint Jacques is the most beautiful, in Flamboyant Gothic, but with a Romanesque narthex and a Renaissance porch. Saint Paul's Cathedral also mingles three architectural styles. Among its ornaments is the gold reliquary offered by Charles the Rash, Duke of Burgundy, to expiate his sins. It seems small enough atonement, considering the fact that he had razed the entire city—except for the churches—and massacred all the able-bodied men. But the Church of Saint Barthelemy is the real gem of Liège. Its baptismal font, dating from 1108, is the finest work of Renier de Huy, and is decorated with reliefs representing four famous baptisms. It is one of Belgium's greatest treasures.

The old bishop's palace, now the Palace of Justice, hides beautiful courts surrounded by porticos with sculptured capitals behind a banal façade. The council chamber has rich Brussels tapestries. Without any doubt, this early 16th-century edifice is one of the most impressive secular buildings left in northern Europe. One of Liège's finest houses is the Curtius Mansion, built about 1600 by Jean de la Corte, who supplied munitions to the King of Spain. Even in those days manufacturers of arms made a good living, and this red brick Renaissance building cost about one million gold francs. It is now the Archeological Museum. The fine houses of wealthy middle-class Mosans are grouped on Mont Saint Martin, in a maze of winding streets, stairways and secret gardens. In early days, a bishop of Liège who became Pope, instituted Corpus Christi Day, and it is still celebrated with great ceremony.

But the most popular Liège procession is that of Outremeuse, that little island locked between the river and the Ourthe. On Saint Nicholas' Day, each window is transformed into a street-altar and the entire parish follows the parade of the Black Virgin. In August, amidst the happy tumult of a traveling fair, they bring out the *bouquet,* a prodigious structure of artificial flowers.

Outremeuse, nicknamed the "Free Republic", is a little world apart. People used to live there all their lives without crossing the bridge that leads to the city. The community was enough for them, with its narrow, noisy streets and its sidewalks and savory-smelling shops. Strolling along, you see many niches sheltering doll-faced Virgins bedecked with wreaths. Every house has its potted plants and shining copper decoration, its good smell of hot pies and coffee. Families often have eight or ten children all of whom are loyal to the family kitchen. There is probably a Mosan expression for "the pies that mother used to make", for every son comes home to mama on Sunday for another round of her incomparable soup and pies. The citizens of Outremeuse are honest and hard working, impulsive and notably choleric.

Coal and Industry

Liège citizens are small shopkeepers, artisans, miners, or steel workers. They are proud of their fearsome reputation and even of their nickname, "coal heads". Since 1198, when a blacksmith named Hullos discovered coal deposits near Publement, Liège has been a prosperous, industrial city. These natural resources, plus hard work and perseverance, have made the people great ironworkers and stubbornly independent citizens. However, it must be said that the Mosan miners have a very high standard of living, and it is among these families that Belgium finds her most skilled technicians and engineers. The first Continental locomotive was built here and Liège men taught the Swedes over a century ago how to make their peerless steel.

For a really good view of this city, created by water, coal, and years of labor, you should go in the evening to the top of one of the three hills which overlook the city. Robermont is a hill where 50 patriots were executed in 1914. On another hill is the citadel sentinel of the valley. There, in October 1468, 600 heroic Mosans from Franchimont Castle scaled Sainte Walburge Hill in an attempted surprise attack on the Burgundians camped there; the effort failed, and all were massacred. Sainte Walburge was also the scene of a great battle in 1830, when Belgium gained its independence from Holland. The citadel resisted the German attack in August 1914 long enough to allow the French command to regroup their forces for the decisive Battle of the Marne. It was again one of the first objectives of the invasion in May 1940. From this hill there is a fine view of the city below.

But the most pleasant place from which to contemplate the city is the wooded hill of Cointe: the Park of Birds is a hospitable point from which you can see the great curve of the Meuse gleaming in the midst of the city.

Liège does not forget its indebtedness to coal and its by-products. One of the principal squares is named Cockerill, after the Englishman who played an important part in the region's industrial progress. The ugly black mine shafts are called locally, "pretty flowers", and the flaming mill chimneys have earned the city the title of the "burning city". The place exudes a warm cordiality, and if you are looking for elegance, you can find that, too. There are fashionable shops and fine hotels, usually adjoining excellent restaurants. At the Trois-Ponts, at an altitude of 300 meters, 30 country cottages are being built to form the new holiday village of Les Gotalles, which will have facilities for winter sports.

You might consider a river trip in one of the little passenger boats. Embarking from Flémalle, at the city limits, you will pass the industrial complexes of Val Saint Lambert, Ougrée, and Jemeppe. Then rounding the green spur of Cointe you will cross the mouth of the Ourthe River and come to the flowery Botanical Gardens. Next comes the rose and gray bishop's palace, then the university. You will come to the old quays of La Goffe and La Batte with their bird markets and apothecaries, their street singers and ironmongers. Finally, a mighty statue of King Albert dominates the entrance to the canal, a gigantic enterprise he inspired.

Cutting across rich Limburg pasturelands, the Albert Canal goes obliquely towards the North Sea. But the Meuse follows a less ordered route, passing Visé, an old town which possesses the oldest Mosan reliquary, the *châsse* of Saint Hadelin. It is attributed to Godefroid de Huy. The town hall's onion-shaped belfry reminds us of Dinant and that we are still in the Meuse valley. At Maaseik the Meuse finally leaves Belgium, to pursue its course through Holland to the North Sea.

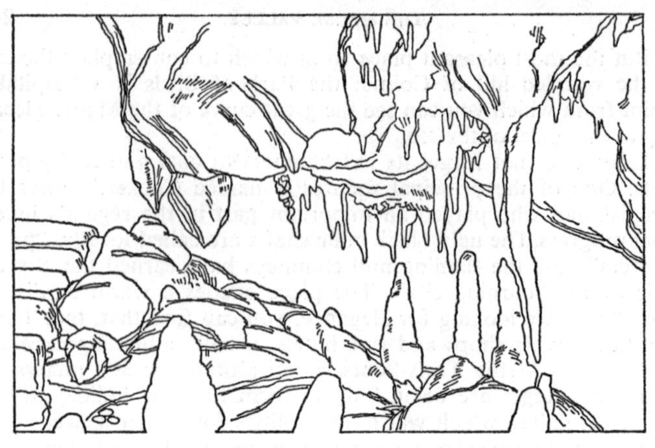

THE ARDENNES

Fast-Flowing Rivers and Wooded Glens

More a geographical area than a province, the Ardennes east of the Meuse River take in part of Belgian Luxembourg, as well as portions of the provinces of Namur and Liège, and to the north the two cantons of Eupen and Malmédy, German from 1815 until returned to Belgium by the Treaty of Versailles in 1919.

This perfect vacationland lacks nothing, and is loved by poet and picnicker, geologist and hunter alike. Spa, La Roche, and many other places offer comfortable hotel accommodation. But for those traveling on a modest budget, every road has hospitable inns. Certain manor houses are now youth hostels, and camp sites are easily found. In the midst of pine woods, on rocky crests, and near wild caverns, one finds young people from France, Holland, Germany, and England sharing the warmth of campfires.

But while life in the cities is expensive, camping is paradise, at half the cost. It is always easy to find good Ardennes ham, smoked over oak chippings. There is fresh white bread, cold beer, and coffee with hot milk kept warm on the cast-iron stoves that electricity seems powerless to make obsolete. The most out-of-the-way inn will serve you wonderful fried potatoes in a twinkling and afterwards, a pie or a sugar tart. So take your walking shoes and a heavy sweater, a bathing suit, and a camera and follow the trail of students, scouts, and young couples who are trying, like you, to ex-

The belfry of the church at Mons dominates the city, whose citizens still call it "the tower of the château".

The Grand Duchy of Luxembourg, one of the smallest states of Europe, has its full share of castles. The ruins of the Château of Beaufort preserve an authentic 15th-century atmosphere, even including a grim torture chamber.

plore all the paths, climb all the peaks, and photograph all the castles.

You will need to be careful to keep to the beaten track when you get into the highland country in the east. These are the High Fenns, or *Hautes Fagnes* around 2,000 ft. above sea level and close to the German Eifel country (and in fact, German is the easiest language here). A large part of the country, however, is marshy and if you are walking, particularly after dark, you must be careful to stick to roads and footpaths which are well laid out; and avoid, most of all, following unidentified lights, for in such country the will-o'-the-wisp is no fairytale.

Practical Information for the Ardennes

WHEN TO COME? The Ardennes, ideal vacationland, offers a wide choice for your holiday planning. The most suitable period for visits to this richly wooded region runs from May to September. You might, however, want to join in the infectious merrymaking during carnival time. *February* sees the opening of the season of fun at Malmédy where harlequins, jesters, and *haguettes* (long-arms) run about the streets during four days teasing the onlookers.

Nearby Eupen pays homage to Prince Carnival on Rose Monday with a sumptuous procession of multi-colored groups. On mid-Lent Sunday Stavelot revives the carnival season. White-clad Blancs Moussis with long red noses, hit about with pigs' bladders and are full of other clownish capers.

In mid-*April,* La Roche stages the Courses du Côte, an international and exciting road circuit event in sub-mountain country for cars, motorcycles and sidecars. *May* resounds to a hunting-horn fanfare at St. Hubert on Whit Monday. Each month of the season there is an important car or motorcycle race on the Francorchamps circuit.

On the third Sunday in *June,* Verviers stages a costumed cortege and *July* sees the annual St. Hubert Music Festival in the town of the same name. From early July to end *August,* Sound and Light performances at La Roche Castle ruins. If you know French, the Spa Theater Festival in August will interest you. Spa holds its corso fleuri on the 15th of August, a few days before the international tennis tournament. Stavelot's chamber music festival, held in the abbey refectory, has become a tradition. Also in August, the legend of St. Hubert, patron of hunters, is enacted.

In *September* (2nd Sun.), Bouillon has a parade of ancient costumes. The sound of hunting horns fils the air on 3 *November.* The giant matchmaker comes out in *December* at Arlon's famed Lovers' Fair. The Nut Fair of Bastogne, where marriage is also the prevailing topic, is a friendly rival.

WHAT TO SEE? The charm of the Ardennes lies in subtly shaded differences and every tourist has his own personal preference. There is a whole cluster of grottos, notably Han in the Lesse valley; also the historic castle of Bouillon and the ancient town of Durbuy. This is not an area that offers much to the art lover, but those interested in archeology and folk customs will find the museums of Arlon, Eupen and Virton worth a visit. The archaic charm of Spa will remind you that it was for three centuries the playground of Europe's nobility. Cheerful little towns, rustic villages, and elegant manors add their attraction to the landscape of rivers and wooded hills.

HOW TO GET ABOUT? Aside from the Brussels-Arlon-Luxembourg, and the Liège-Arlon-Luxembourg trains, which stop only once or twice en route, train services are slow and complicated. There is a widespread network of buslines and you can probably reach even the remotest village by public transport. For the adventurous, one good way of seeing the many lovely hidden little châteaux and farm houses is to hire a small motor scooter for a few days; no license needed.

MOTORING. To get the maximum of enjoyment out of your trip, you should tour the region by car. Asphalted roads will take you to all parts of the Ardennes highlands. From Brussels, direct roads lead westward (N.2 and N.3) to Liège and thence to Spa, 80 miles; southwestward (N.4) to Bastogne, 95 miles. From Holland, the region is directly reached from Maastricht or Hasselt. From Germany, the road enters from Aachen. Bastogne is easily reached from Luxembourg. From France, follow N.77 after Sedan.

SPORTS. The rivers Ourthe, Vesdre, Amblève, and Semois are ideal for *canoeing* and so is the Lesse, although it is not without danger between Houyet and Dinant. The most attractive *boating* excursions will take you from Houyet to Anseremme on the Lesse and from Chiny to Lacuisine on the meandering Semois. You can devote your vacation to *fishing* for eel, trout, pike, and crawfish in all the above-named rivers as well as the Salm and Warche. Most riverside hotels have their own fishing stretches. The whole region is dotted with *camping* sites. Well-marked and well-chosen footpaths increase the pleasure of *hiking*. You may play *tennis* in all sizeable localities, and *golf* may be practised on the beautiful links at Spa. Barely two miles from the center of this city is an airfield for *sport flying*. There are six good *ski-runs* when the weather is right, which is rather chancy and rare. Best is at Ovifat, reached from Robertville; good centers are reached from Spa and Malmédy. You can hire skis, but the stock of boots is apt to run out.

MUSEUMS. At **Arlon:** Province of Luxembourg Museum, 13 Rue des Martyrs, with archeology of the gallo-roman period, folklore, chimney backs, cast-iron works. **Bastogne:** The "Nuts" Museum, named for General McAuliffe, Place McAuliffe, contains history of the siege of Bastogne. **Bouillon:** Ducal Museum, 1 Rue du Petit, a 17th-cent. house with archeology and folklore collection. At **Han** there is a museum containing objects found in the grottos. **Spa:** Municipal Museum. **Stavelot:** Tannery Museum and Treasury of the Church of St. Sebastian. **Virton:** Gaumais Museum.

SPAS AND CASINOS. The original **Spa,** whose name became a genetic term for health resorts, has several mineral springs of high iron content. Baths with carbonized water, as well as mud and turf baths are natural therapeutic agents for all forms of arthritis, and particularly for gout. **Chaudfontaine,** close the Liège, has warm springs which are slightly radioactive. Both these resorts have their casino where roulette and baccara are played all the year round. Spa's casino opens at 4 p.m.

REGIONAL GASTRONOMIC SPECIALTIES. Sausage products in general, and Ardennes ham in particular, are deliciously cured over smoldering oak for a long time. During the hunting season, ask for some of the dishes prepared with wine-soaked hare (*civet de lièvre*), roebuck (*chevreuil*), or young wild boar soaked in Orval Abbey's beer (*estouffat de marcassin à bière*).

HOTELS AND RESTAURANTS. Ardennes hotels are noted for comfort and good food. While the old-fashioned hotels of Spa have become institutions, the accent today is on more countrified sites, and modern standards are slowly gaining ground. The hotels listed below represent only a few of the many establishments available. You will have no difficulty in finding accommodation, provided you avoid the weeks of July 21 and Aug. 15.

Rates are reasonable, probably the lowest in Belgium. Most of the hotels offer special weekend (1 night) or extended weekend (2 nights) terms.

ALLE. Hotels: The first class reasonable *Auberge d'Alle,* 12 rooms, has restaurant (E). *La Charmille,* 16 rooms, 3 with bath, moderate, meals can be expensive. The same goes for *Fief de Liboichant.*

A modern recreation center, *Recrealle,* on the banks of the Semois, includes many sports and amusement facilities, a closed park for children, caravan site and fishing facilities.

ARLON. Largest city in Luxembourg province.

Hotels: *Arly,* 81 Ave. Luxembourg, first class superior, recent. *Ecu de Bourgogne,* 10 Pl. Léopold, antique furnishings; *Druides,* 106 Rue Neufchâteau, both moderate. *Courtois,* 45 Ave. de la Gare, inexpensive.

Two good addresses outside town: *Peiffeschof,* 10 rooms and *Beau Séjour* (at Châtillon). Both inexpensive. You can fish there in the three neighboring lakes.

Restaurants: *Relais du Nord* (M), 2 Rue des Faubourgs, is best, and less expensive than *Métropole,* Marché-aux-Légumes.

ASTENET, in the region of Eupen. Hotel: *Château Thor,* a fortified manor of the Middle Ages. Moderate, fishing privileges.

AVE-ET-AUFFE. Just over 3 miles from Han Grottos.

Hotel: *Hostellerie du Ry d'Ave,* Ardennes interior, moderate. Owner presides in the kitchen.

AYWAILLE. Hotels: *Villa des Roses,* good halt, moderate. *La Brassiene,* modest. Several others.

BARVAUX. Hotels: *Buron* and *Grillon,* inexpensive, as is *Cor de Chasse,* half a mile north.

BASTOGNE. Hotels: Leader is *Lebrun,* moderate, 24 rooms, 11 with bath. In season their young wild boar (marcassin) in cream sauce is delicious.

BOHAN. Near French frontier.

Hotels: *Table des Fées* and *Dauby.*

Restaurant: *Auberge du Printemps,* worth a detour.

BOMAL. Restaurants: At Juzaine, a mile away, two good halts, *St. Denis* and *Vieux Moulin,* both (M), the latter with a few rooms.

BOUILLON. Historic city and castle.

Hotels: *Poste,* 60 rooms, 14 with bath, first class reasonable. Napoleon III stayed here. Has the best restaurant in town, overlooking river. Somewhat cheaper is the splendidly situated *Panorama,* 65 rooms, 14 with bath. *Le Tyrol,* beautiful view, nice furnishings, 16 rooms, moderate. *Semois* and *Aux Armes de Bouillon,* are in the moderate to expensive class and have excellent restaurants. Good camping at Halliru.

CELLES. Near the interesting Church of Foy Notre Dame.

Restaurant: *Val Joli* (E), excellent. You might try duckling "à la normande". Also has a few rooms.

CHAMPLON (BARRIERE DE). An important crossroad 15 miles north of Bastogne. Excellent overnight halt.

Hotels: *Hostellerie de la Barrière,* old Ardennes atmosphere; 24 rooms with bath, moderate. Delicious food on the expensive side; specialty: wild fowl. *Les Bruyères,* 20 rooms, nearly all with bath, slightly cheaper; and *Bon Coin.*

CHINY. Starting point of boat trip to Lacuisine.

Hotel: *Comtes de Chiny,* first class reasonable.

CIERGNON. Summer residence of royal family.

Hotels: *Auberge de la Collyre,* small, inexpensive; garden restaurant. At Herock, 2½ miles northeast, *Hostellerie d'Herock,* inexpensive; restaurant (E).

COMBLAIN-LA-TOUR. Hotel: One of the best in the valley, *St. Roch,* has a nice garden-terrace overlooking river; 20 rooms, 7 with bath, moderate.

COO. Cascade and chairlift.

Hotels: *Cascade, Baron* and *Liège,* all inexpensive.

DOHAN. Hotels: *Auberge du Moulin,* nearly all rooms with bath, first class superior; restaurant very expensive. *Hôtel de la Vallée,* modest but comfortable.

DOLEMBREUX. Halfway between Liège and Aywaille, turn right toward Esneux.

Hotel: *Normandie,* moderate.

DURBUY. Restaurants: Two gastronomic high spots: *Sanglier des Ardennes and Vieux Durbuy,* both (M); the game dishes in season are excellent. You can stay at either.

EMBOURG, a few miles out of Liège, on the road to Spa, *La Vieille Auberge,* regional specialties, rustic interior.

EUPEN, with the giant dam just outside the city.

Hotels: *Schmitz-Roth,* Pl. de l' Hôtel de Ville, and *Bosten,* 2 Rue Verviers, are best, both moderate.

Rotterwäldchen, two miles out of town on the road to Monchau, is inexpensive.

Restaurant: *Chapeau Rouge,* 38 Aachenerstr., gastronomic food, but prices not astronomic. Has a few rooms.

FLORENVILLE. Good overnight halt.

Hotels: *Hôtel de France,* 40 rooms, some with bath, inexpensive. At Martué, 2 mile north, *Gais Lurons,* 32 rooms.

FRANCORCHAMPS. Hotels: Right at the motor racetrack, and named after its most dangerous curve, *Eau Rouge* is patronized by some of the star drivers. Small, moderate, and open only during the race meetings. *Bruyères,* 25 rooms, 9 with shower. Rather higher up are *Roannay,* exquisite food, expensive, rooms moderate. *Moderne,* inexpensive.

GLEIZE (LA). Mountain village.

Hotels: *Les Princes,* park, angling, inexpensive. *La Fermette,* small, very modest.

Restaurant: Delicious meals at *Ecuries de la Reine* (M), highly atmospheric.

GRUPONT. Château of Buslin.

Hotel: *Ry de Belle-Rose,* inexpensive, not so its dining room; offers free angling.

HABAY-LA-NEUVE. *Hostellerie du Pont d'Oye,* small, moderate. Restaurant can be expensive.

HAN-SUR-LESSE. Hotels: *Voyageurs,* 41 rooms, 17 with shower; *Ardennes,* inexpensive. *Lesse* is rock bottom but has good restaurant.

HERBEUMONT. Hotel: *Hostellerie du Prieuré de Conques,* former abbey, 15 rooms, 10 with bath; fine cuisine, well worth its price: Superb location on river Semois. Hunting parties, best book ahead.

HEYD. One of the few top-comfort hotels in the Ardennes is *Le Lignely,* first class position, amenities and food. Try the sole soufflé.

HOCKAY. Hiking center near Francorchamps.

Hotels: *Beau Séjour* and *Belle Vue,* both inexpensive.

HOTTON. Restaurant: *La Commanderie,* moderate.

HOUFFALIZE. Hotels: *Grand Hôtel du Commerce,* 22 rooms with shower; *Ermitage,* moderate, good restaurant; try the pâté maison. Inexpensive, *Les Nutons,* also has an excellent restaurant.

Two miles southwest: *La Clef des Champs,* inexpensive. Their jambon d'Ardennes is home cured.

HOUYET. Starting point of canoe or boat trip down to the Meuse.

Hotels: *de la Lesse*, 9 rooms, inexpensive. At nearby Payenne: *Auberge du Grand Virage*, small, modest.

Restaurant: On road to Dinant (2½ m.), *Marquisette* (I), has a few rooms.

LIGNEUVILLE. Hotels: *du Moulin*, 23 rooms, 7 with bath; angling; *Georges*, 15 rooms, 6 with bath. Both are socially top-drawer and rank as moderate plus; but the *Amblève*, essentially a family hotel, is moderate and comfortable, with good food.

LORCÉ-CHEVRON. Hotel: *de la Vallée*, charmingly situated, halfway between Nonceveux and Stoumont off the main road (cross river and railroad), 6 rooms; moderate. Temple of good eating (E).

MAISSIN. A Breton calvary in honor of 10,000 French soldiers of World War I buried here.

Hotel: *Mathot* is the largest and best-equipped, first class but moderate.

MALMÉDY. Hotels: *Maison Geron*, first class superior, with adjoining restaurant *de la Chapelle*. *Globe*, 10 rooms, 2 with bath. *International*, both moderate.

On hilltop, overlooking town, *Ferme Libert*, a converted farmhouse with much to commend it.

Less than 4 miles from Malmédy, on the Eupen road: *Tros Marets* (E), is a gourmet's shrine; a few moderate rooms.

MARCHE-EN-FAMENNE. Important road junction, teeming with hotels and restaurants. *Cloche*, near station, 10 rooms, nearly all with bath, moderate.

There is a motel, *Las Vegas*, off the main road two miles farther south.

Best restaurants: *Manoir*, closed Tues. You can eat cheaply, or expensively if you choose duckling with pineapple (canard aux ananas) or grouse in wine sauce (coq au vin).

MARTELANGE. On Luxembourg border. See Grand Duchy section.

MONT RIGI. Highest point in Belgium, some 10 miles east of Spa. *Hôtel du Mont Rigi*, 8 rooms, inexpensive, good restaurant.

NADRIN. Near the Hérou gorge.

Hotel: Leader is *des Ondes*, 16 rooms, 4 with bath, first class reasonable. Best food in town.

At nearby Nisramont-Ortho: *Rochers du Hérou* commands a fine view, inexpensive.

NASSOGNE. Halfway between Marche and St. Hubert.

Hotels: *La Forêt* and *Beau Séjour* (provides riding horses) are both inexpensive.

NEUFCHATEAU. Restaurant: *La Potinière* (I-M), also has 12 rooms.

NEU-MORESNET. Hotel: *Eural's Country Club Benelux*, on the Liège-Aachen road. Small apartments, covered pool, riding; meals (I-M).

NEUPONT. *Le Baligan*, an excellent hostelry moderate, restaurant (E).

NOIREFONTAINE. About two miles from Bouillon. The *Auberge Moulin Hideux* has a few expensive rooms and a restaurant which is out of this world. Better book by phone: 462-15.

NONCEVEUX. Near the Fonds de Quareux.

Hotel: *Chaudière*, 29 rooms, inexpensive.

Restaurant: *Ma Bicoque*, (M).

OCQUIER. Three miles northeast of Durbuy.

Hotels: Château d'Amas. *Castel du Val d'Or*, is a converted farmhouse, inexpensive, but not its restaurant.

REMOUCHAMPS. Interesting grottos.

Hotel: *Cheval Blanc*, first class reasonable.

ROBERTVILLE. Large lake, camping.

Hotels: *des Bains*, is best, most rooms with bath, moderate to first class. *Du Lac*, inexpensive, very pleasant.

LA ROCHE. No less than 37 hotels and pensions. Biggest is *Hôtel des Bruyères*, 35 rooms, 6 with bath, moderate. Best is *Air Pur*, Rte. de Houffalize, small, but rather expensive. Panoramic location on the hillside outside town; restaurant (E), unique in the region. The *Ardennes*, Rue

Beausaint, is also a good bet. Very good, moderate, is the *Belle-Vue,* Ave. du Hadja, nice terrace. *Les Merlettes,* Rte de Houffalize, is charmingly situated; pool, miniature golf, moderate.

Les Sorbiers, on Rte. de Houffalize, and *Les Genêts,* Rue St. Quoilin, are excellent pensions.

Restaurants: *Chalet* or *Prevot,* both outstanding for trout and other regional specialties.

ROCHEFORT. Grottos; ancient city, a vacation center.

Hotels: Best is *Hostellerie des Falizes,* on the road to Han, moderate; good restaurant (E). Closely followed by *La Fayette,* Rue Jacquet, 14 rooms, moderate, good food. Inexpensive but good, *Central,* Pl. Albert, has nice terrace. *Trou Maulin,* Rue de Marche, inexpensive, offers riding and angling facilities.

ROCHEHAUT. Hotels: *Chalet Ardennais,* small, moderate, fine view. *Au Naturel des Ardennes,* inexpensive. So is *Passage d'Eau.*

ST. HUBERT. In legendary St. Hubertus Forest.

Hotels: *Abbaye,* inexpensive. *Luxembourg* and *Cor de Chasse,* modest but satisfactory.

At Poix St. Hubert, 4 miles west: *Val de Poix,* 25 rooms, 10 with bath, first class reasonable, good food. Try pâté de canard en croûte or duckling with fresh cherries. Less expensive, *Hôtel St. Hubert* is also first class.

SPA. Hotels: Right in the heart of the town, *Cardinal,* has 36 rooms, most with bath, first class reasonable, nice restaurant. *Rosette,* 34 rooms, 12 with bath, has a well-known restaurant. Try their chicken (poularde au whisky). *Hostellerie Ardennaise* is centrally situated, next to the post-office.

Near the road to Francorchamps is the *Château Sous-Bois,* 20 rooms with bath, large park and gardens. Formerly a mansion, it is quietly located and is first class superior.

Among moderately priced hotels is the historic *Park Hotel,* Ave. Reine Astrid, 23 rooms. Try the *Portugal,* 8 Pl. Royale, if slight motor traffic does not bother you. Halfway between moderate and inexpensive is the *Auberge du Grillon,* which looks ancient but isn't.

Restaurant-inns: *Vieille France* (E), on the way to Lake Warfaz, where good food meets rare wines. Do not go if you are in a hurry; try one of their lobster preparations or chicken in tarragon sauce (poularde à l'estragon); has 6 rooms, 4 with bath. *Grand Cerf* (E), Rte. de la Sauvenière, excellent. We suggest champignons farcis au beurre d'escargot (mushrooms stuffed with herbs and garlic butter) or lobster McKinlay. Its 10 rooms (6 baths) are moderately priced.

At Balmoral: You may live at the very modern *Eurotel,* first class superior, with heated pool, beautiful view, or at the moderate *Les Clématites,* on the road to Tiège.

At Nivezé, halfway to Spa, the moderate *Orleans* has a pleasant garden, excellent cuisine.

At Tiège, three miles northeast of Spa on the road to Verviers: *Charmille* is a hotel of old reputation, first class reasonable. They prepare an excellent Russian-type goulash (boeuf Stroganoff).

At Warfaz Lake: *La Crémaillère* has a few rooms and good restaurant. *Hôtel du Lac* is moderate, and *Chalet du Lac* inexpensive.

At La Reid, attractive village 5 miles before Spa, on road from Remouchamps, are two outstanding restaurants: *Auberge Menobu,* which also has 6 rooms, and *Retraite de L'Empereur,* both (M).

STAVELOT. Hotels: *Val d'Amblève,* on the Malmédy road; cozy, 10 rooms, outstanding food, beautifully served. *Orange,* Rue de Spa. Both moderate.

THEUX. Historic ruins of Franchimont, fortified church and fine town hall.

Hotels: On the Spa-Liège road, *Les Erables* is a pleasant overnight halt and inexpensive, 8 rooms: *Ile de Franchimont,* 15 rooms, on a small island, offers free angling. *Ambassa-*

deurs, inexpensive, has the better restaurant.

TILLF. Liège patrons' favorite weekend spot. *Casino,* between moderate and first class reasonable, over half the 15 rooms have bath; early 17th-cent. building; in the restaurant (E), brochet de l'Ourthe au coulis d'écrevisses (pike in crayfish gravy) is one of the numerous specialties offered.
Restaurant: *Romeo et Michette* (M), excellent, terrace dining.

TROIS-PONTS. Starting point of a panoramic circuit.
Hotel: *Beau Site,* 18 rooms, inexpensive; restaurant (I-M).

VERVIERS. Hotels: Recent is the *Amigo,* deluxe, a younger brother of the Brussels Amigo, 60 rooms with bath. First class reasonable, *Europe,* 21 rooms, half with bath. *Park,* and *Charlemagne* are moderate.
Restaurants: *L'Ecuyer* is best in town. But even better is the atmospheric *La Chefnée* at 530 Rte. de Jalhay. Slightly cheaper, *Le Vénitien,* Place Verte.

VIELSALM. On the Salm, tributary of Amblève, angling.
Hotels: Best are *Bellevue* and *Myrtilles,* 7 rooms with bath. *Central,* inexpensive.

VILLERS, near Orval. *Val d'Or,* excellent, first class reasonable.

VILLERS-SUR-LESSE. Hotels: *Beau Séjour,* inexpensive, excellent; park, angling, swimming. At Jamblinne: *L'Oasis* has outstanding cuisine. Try pâté maison as a start and, in season, grouse in wine sauce (coq au vin).

VIRTON. "Capital of Belgian Lorraine."
Hotels: *À la Porte des Ardennes* is inexpensive. *Siméon,* modest.

VRESSE-SUR-SEMOIS. Restaurant: *Pont St. Lambert* (M), good, has a few rooms.

XHOFFRAIS. *Tchession,* a good hotel-restaurant (M).

USEFUL ADDRESSES. *City Tourist Offices* (Syndicats d'Initiative): Arlon, Place Léopold; Bouillon, Porte de France; Florenville, Grand'Place; La Roche, Hôtel de Ville; Malmédy, Pl. Albert; St. Hubert, Pl. Verte; Spa, Casino Building.

Sport flying: airfields at St. Hubert, Spa-La Sauvenière and Temploux. Canoeing information: C.C.C.W., 123 Rue Hocheporte, Liège. Golf course: Golf Club des Fagnes, Spa.

Exploring the Ardennes

Which road will you take? They strike out from Liège like the strands of a spider's web, each running through the most diverse landscapes, from quiet, outdated watering places to the lonely forest of Malmédy and the high valley of the Ourthe. Motorists have their choice of a score or more delightful drives.

You can also explore the Rivers Ourthe, Semois, Lesse, Sure, Ambleve, Our and the Lake of Nisramont by canoe and kayak. (Information: Gilbert Haesendonck, 6663 Engreux-Houffalize).

The Ourthe Valley

The banks of the Ourthe are favorite haunts of the Liège population, rich and poor alike. They are lined with a curious mixture of taverns, summer houses, and castles. The cliffs of Sy mark a stopping place. This is where you leave the placid farm country of the Lower Ourthe to enter the Ardennes, a silent, brooding region. The slate-roofed villages are farther apart and hidden among walnut groves. The cliffs are higher and difficult to climb.

Durbuy is like a stage-set for an operetta. In the main street, the Grain Market and a ducal palace seem much too big for the village. Durbuy has only 350 inhabitants, but its title is "the biggest little town in Belgium". This nickname has a historical background: Durbuy, in the 14th century, was granted city rights, but after a brilliant period while the dukes of Ursel were rich and powerful, the community reverted to its present somnolent life, in which everybody knows everybody else.

La Roche-en-Ardennes, however, is something right out of a fairytale. Its romantic ruined castle (with wild game park and *Son et Lumière*) belonged to the counts De la Roche, who were famous for dispensing justice and home-made money. Although it was sorely tried during World War II, La Roche remains a vacation center; its hotels are good and its promenades numerous. Blue earthenware is the outstanding local craft, and visitors are admitted to the workshop in the Rue Rompré. La Roche is teeming with butcher's shops and no tourist leaves without taking home some *saucisson* or *jambon d'Ardennes*.

A round trip to the top of Le Hérou is a matter of five or six hours. The going is rough, but from the summit there is a breathtaking view. The cliff falls in a straight line to the turbulent river, and the panorama that spreads for miles before your eyes is vast and profoundly silent. The center of this scenic area is the small village of Nadrin. From here you can undertake the descent of the Ourthe by canoe, a 10-mile course of unique beauty.

Houffalize lies in a deep valley which the Ourthe has hollowed out over the ages. Its early Gothic church holds some remarkable treasures, like the chorister's desk, the altar, and the ancient local squires' sculptured tombstones. Miraculously, the church escaped destruction during the 1944 Ardennes battle, when almost the whole town was wiped out.

This is the magic forest of the Ardennes, where Saint Hubert, while hunting on Good Friday in 683, saw a stag bearing a lighted cross between its antlers. A Benedictine abbey was erected on the site, and there the saint's bones were kept. But when Belgium was invaded, the monks hid the coffin, and hid it so well that it has never been found. The sanctuary is still visited by pilgrims, and each year, to a fanfare of hunting horns, an open-air Mass is said.

The Battle of the Bulge: Bastogne

The villagers near Bastogne take upon themselves the care of the graves of American soldiers who fell in the Von Rundstedt offensive in December 1944. It was the last German attempt to block the Allied armies that were approaching Germany.

Von Rundstedt's scheme, bold and cunning, was to launch three movements, a northern one towards Liège, through Saint Vith, a southern one towards Sedan, and a central one towards Bastogne. Saint Vith resisted, the southern attack miscarried, but the Bastogne offensive was sucessful. The area was poorly defended: it had been considered too wooded to permit engagements between motorized troops. German tanks drove furiously through the forest in the direction of Bastogne, an important road center. The American 106th Division was deployed throughout the region but it was an unseasoned unit. Frightful weather added to the chaos; fog and snow paralyzed every movement. Soldiers were continually cut off from their base, and supplies and ammunition were wearing thin. It was soon evident that Bastogne was surrounded, but the American 101st Airborne Division, which had been rushed to the area, held firm. When Brigadier General McAuliffe was asked to surrender, he calmly replied, "Nuts."

The resistance continued, rendered more difficult by a violent snowstorm, more poignant by the approach of Christmas and it was a grim holiday for GI's buried in icy mud. Burning houses blazed through the thick fog, lighting up every target. The townspeople helped the troops as much as they could, using their linen sheets to camouflage scouts who were clearly marked against the snow. The desperate struggle lasted for days. Finally at dawn, the miracle happened. Suddenly the thick moist veil lifted, revealing the German tanks, and the Americans were able to use their last stocks of ammunition effectively. Bastogne was encircled, but it held out. Soon after, Allied planes dropped arms and supplies to the stranded division and 2,000 planes pounded the Germans.

Those who come to kneel before graves in Bastogne cemeteries will never know the brutal cold and flame of that winter battle, but they will find, instead, among the brave citizens, a warm memory of those who died as heroes. Bastogne, also proudly called "La Nuts City" by the inhabitants, is the guardian of the impressive Mardasson Memorial outside the town's precincts, dedicated to the American troops who lost their lives in the Battle of the Bulge.

The Vesdre and Amblève Valleys

The Vesdre has all the charming potentialities of its neighboring rivers, but it is captured almost at its source, and made to serve industry. Its tributary, the Gileppe, is dammed just above the textile-manufacturing cities of Pepinster and Verviers. This dam, built in 1867, was considered gigantic at the time, and the lion that dominates it has been photographed as often as that of Waterloo. The artificial lake set amongst green hills possesses an idyllic beauty. A mighty dam has been built since World War II, just outside Eupen, largest locality of the German minority in Belgium.

The river has its spots of rustic simplicity, when it flows placidly through orchards or busily turns old mill wheels. And famous writers have been entranced with the Vesdre: Sir Walter Scott loved the area near the Château de Theux, and Victor Hugo said the Vesdre "is sometimes a ravine, often a garden, always a paraise." Chaudfontaine's thermal sources, in the outskirts of Liège, have been a convenient pretext for the setting up of a well-run casino. A few more miles in an unlovely, industrialized setting and the Vesdre disappears into the Meuse.

The Amblève rises in a region as devout as Oberammergau. In Montenau 135 village players present the Passion of Our Lord every Sunday of Lent. Later the river passes the noble abbeys of Malmédy and Stavelot which were ruled for eleven centuries by abbot-princes subservient only to the emperor. They were cultivated and worldly, generous and well informed. The houses are curious, with their visible beams, and the old abbey is remarkable. Since the Napoleonic Wars most of this region was German until the Versailles Treaty (1919), but the Walloon language never died. Malmédy, rebuilt since World War II, is justly renowned both for its cuisine and carnival, one of the merriest in Belgium. During the hunting season, the vast silence of the pine forest is broken by the galloping of horses and the flourish of hunting horns. The local nobility takes great pride in their horses and packs.

It was at nearby Stavelot that St. Remacle discovered in 648 that his mule had been devoured by a wolf, and it is said that he founded the town by the simple expedient of saying "To the stable, wolf"—"Stave, leu" in local dialect. It is not recorded whether or not the wolf obeyed, but Stavelot certainly does exist and conserves a beautiful 13th-century reliquary of its founder in the parish church where you may also see a fine 17th-century gilded and silvered reliquary bust of a saint with the improbable name of Popon. Stavelot, though hardly a city, is a particularly active cultural center holding art exhibitions throughout the year, and a summer chamber-music festival.

A couple of miles to the south, the Amblève drops from a height of 45 feet with a great splashing and rebounding of spray. These are the Coo Falls with an old stone bridge and water mill. You get an excellent view of the countryside, hemmed in by a meandering river, by taking the somewhat frightening chair lift to the

Belvedère Jean. The Amblève narrows, and is squeezed between slopes so hot and thickly wooded that the valley is called "The Congo". Soon it reaches the strange Fonds de Quareux and, at Nonceveux, it is joined by the Ninglinspo, which descends in great leaps, carving out pools called "Diane's Bath" or "The Naïades".

Through the countryside the Amblève leaves a network of subterranean streams; it has hollowed out the mysterious caverns of Remouchamps, whose great Cathedral Chamber is more than 109 yards long. After you have left the caves' galleries to admire the Calypso Passage and Titan's Bridge, you can take a boat trip on the underground Rubicon River. The feudal castle, still inhabited, is not accessible to the public, but you can get a good view of it from the banks of the Amblève. The River Salm, its largest confluent, offers some good trout fishing. The principal centers are Trois Ponts and Vielsalm.

The High Fenns

East of the Salm and of Spa is the High Fenn country, which, at an altitude of 1,000 ft, ranks as low-lying country. The high point is Baraque Michel, windswept but magnificent; and from there you strike southward to Robertville, where you are just below the Ovifat ski slope and just above the great manmade lakes which are the retention reservoirs for the power supply. From here you strike westward for Malmédy, a pleasant little town, or, if you continue southward, you pass Amel among the headwaters of the Amblève river, and so come down to romantic St. Vith and, close to the German border, Burg Reuland, beside the river Our, which flows southward to divide Luxembourg from Germany.

Spa Stands for Thermal Resort

The town of Spa used to be an international society spot, for it was for centuries one of the favorite resorts of czars and queens, statesmen and philosophers. Pliny the Elder, that Roman forefather of travel writers, even mentions the healing powers of Spa's springs. It was a blacksmith from Breda who, in the Middle Ages, rediscovered its waters, and who purchased from the Liège bishop-princes some woodland near Pouhon fountain. This spring is now called Pouhon Peter the Great, since that sovereign visited it many times. Before him had come Montaigne and Queen Margot, Christina of Sweden and the fugitive Charles II of England. But it was Henry VIII's court physician, a Venetian named Augustino, who first used the waters in the treatment of rheumatism. The list of illustrious visitors who followed his example fills the town's Golden Book. You can see some of the celebrities depicted in the Pouhon frescos.

In the 17th century two English doctors, Andrews and Paddy, came to Spa to study the virtue of its waters. They gave the term *spa* to several ferruginous sources in their own country, and it eventually became the generic term for health resorts throughout the English-speaking world. Spa reached its zenith as a watering place and rendezvous of high society during the 18th and 19th centuries. Many fine houses of that period, today classified as historic monuments, give a glimpse of that gracious past.

The cure was not painful and the neighborhood was delightful. But visitors might have been bored without the high-stake gambling at the casino. They played *pharaon, biribi* for rubles, ducats, piastres, francs, or what-have-you. Finally, in 1751, Bishop-Prince Jean Théodor gave the gambling monopoly to a Scotsman, who made a fortune. Other gaming houses were opened: the *Vauxhall,* the *Redoute* and the *Levoz.*

Spa has changed considerably. It is now Belgium's health center of socialized medicine. The Vauxhall shelters an orphanage, a casino has replaced the Redoute. Amusements are a little more varied and include beauty and other contests. The golf course is one of the loveliest in Europe. There is even a small airfield tucked into a forest clearing and, a little farther, on the way to Stavelot, Francorchamps circuit lies in a most attractive mountain setting. European and Belgian autoraces and motorcycle contests are fought out here several times a year.

In 1918, the Kaiser installed his general headquarters at Spa and had a concrete underground shelter built at the Neubois Château. After the armistice was signed, Hoover, Pershing, and Foch lodged in Spa.

With the introduction of new healing methods, the draw of the seaside, and the strides made in foreign travel, Spa has lost its allure as an international social health center. It has become a pivot of tourism in the Ardennes, holding the motorist for a day or two but not longer.

Spa abounds in excellent hotels, some of which are in Balmoral, a wooded ridge overlooking the city and Warfaz Lake. Its admirable situation has caused many well-to-do townspeople and outsiders to build their elegant villas there. An interesting contemporary sight in this city of memories is the ultra-modern bottling plant of *Spa-Monopole;* guided tours take place daily during the season. From June till the end of September, there is a display of thousands of begonias on Avenue Reine Astrid, in the town center.

A 10-minute drive north will take you to Theux, dominated by the ruins of the Castle of Franchimont. They relate the sacrifice of the castle's 600 defenders, who in the 15th century dashed to their capital, Liège, and died to the last man against the overwhelming forces of the French king and Charles the Rash, Duke of Burgundy. Sacked by the French, the castle remains a silent witness to this heroic exploit.

The Lesse Valley of Grottos

If you plan to explore the course of the mysterious Lesse River, you must start at Dinant. After tracing a number of meanders, through defiles and gorges, the stream completely disappears in a most disconcerting way, only to reappear a few steps farther on. The Meuse is only 32 miles from the source of the Lesse, but that river is so sinuous and curving that its course measures at least 105 miles before it empties into the large river.

It begins deep in the Ardennes, between two forests and almost immediately encounters obstacles in the form of rocks and bolders. Coming up against the Belvaux promontory, the Lesse disappears underground. In the subterranean caverns, the river has carved the crystal palace of the Han Grottos. These were first discovered in 1814 by four young men who ventured into the prodigious labyrinth. They carried torches and left a trail of flour in order to retrace their steps. You can imagine their astonishment when they came upon an enchanted scene of sparkling stalactites in vaulted rooms of cathedral-like proportions. A further room, the Cave of Cataclysms, was discovered in 1962, and one or two more caves opened in 1971.

The nearby Rochefort Grottos, subterranean work of the Lhomme have their marvels too, including a natural throne made of varicolored stone in the Sabbath Room. But the Han Grottos are the real treasures of natural beauty.

The Lesse becomes more and more amazing. Going by boat from Houyet to Dinant you will pass through landscapes more varied and surprising than the scenes of any stage show. The region is called the Chaleux Circle; where you can see plainly the rock strata showing the stages of the formation of the world's crust. In Furfooz Ridge, the Lesse hides under a rocky shell. When it finally emerges, the Lesse flows towards and empties into the Meuse and for some distance colors that river with a cold, deep green current.

The Lesse region boasts many other castles. Villers has three of them: Vignée, Jamblinne, and that of the counts of Cunchy.Vèves, near Celles, is a beautifully preserved example of medieval military architecture. Lavaux-Saint-Anne, now government property, is farther to the south. It houses an exciting Hunters' Museum, with some wild boar in the paddock across the moat. These castles form a circle around the royal estate of Ciergnon, favorite weekend haunt of King Baudouin and members of the royal family.

At St. Hubert itself, there is a fine 17th and 18th-century church where victims of rabies formerly came to seek a cure and were chained to the wall opposite the reliquary enshrining the remains of the patron saint of hunters. North of the town, at Fourneau St. Michel, is a small museum of ancient crafts, where there is a fascinating reconstruction of a foundry which operated for a short time in the late 18th century. Its first cannons were sold to the young American republic during the War of Independence, but no more were ordered when the first batch exploded on being used, and the foundry went bankrupt. In the foundry is what may well be the world's largest collection of ancient waffle-irons.

The Semois Valley

The Semois is an unpredictable, disconcerting river, flowing through the chalky Gaumais country, the calm Belgian Lorraine, and jostling its way through rocky Ardennes hills. It follows the highway very often, hiding behind rows of trees and tobacco sheds. Tobacco is the valley's source of wealth, and in September you can smell the drying tobacco throughout the entire countryside.

If you are prepared to walk a few hundred yards, away from the road, you will be rewarded by some splendid views. Leave your car and go picnicking to Roche la Dame near Bohan, to Raven's Rock (Rocher du Corbeau), on a side road between Alle and Rochehaut, or to the Pulpit (Chaire à prêcher) near Corbion. Before reaching Bouillon, you can see the Tombeau du Géant (Giant's Tomb), hemmed in by the meandering river. Another fine view is offered by walking across the main road to the Rocher du Pendu (Rock of the Hanged Man).

The highway climbs ceaselessly, crosses the Frahan crest and slides down the shady slope past the Giant's Tomb, at Botassart, to arrive at Bouillon and its château perched above the Semois. This was the castle of Godefroy de Bouillon, Defender of the Holy Sepulcher, a heroic crusader who died in the Holy Land after having refused the title of King of Jerusalem. This fortified castle has been defended and conquered countless times, for it occupies one of the most strategic spots in the Ardennes. Its ruins are a grandiose sight and within their walls you may still see the Hall of Justice, various prisons, the gallows, and a 250-foot well, hewn into the rock. During the tourist season the castle is floodlit every night. Perhaps the best view of Bouillon's 140 ft. of unscaleable walls is from the top of the "Austrian Tower" (Tour d'austriche). From this vantage point the memories of a thousand years of strife are tempered by the sight of the Semois as it flows past houses and fields. The town was, from 963 until 1794, the capital of a small free state.

After Bouillon, the Semois is again turbulent and twisting, making its way through great oak forests. You can hire canoes in Dohan or Cugnon for short excursions on the river. Herbeumont, a spotless mountain village, is over a thousand years old. The ruins of its castle and the small church, dating back to the 12th century, are worth visiting. At Muno, there is a choice between penetrating into the Shakespearian Forest of Arden whose fringes begin here, or heading towards the more pastoral landscapes of Gaume.

The Gaumais Country, and Orval Abbey

Belgian Lorraine, called La Gaume, begins at Florenville, a neat little town from where you can reach Orval Abbey in a few minutes by car. Near Chiny, the river is covered with flowers. Here you can take a most interesting boat trip to Lacuisine or you can go still farther on to the Forges Roussel, which once employed 200 workers, until one fine morning it sank under the lake waters. Now only a little turreted castle remains to mark the spot.

Deep in the forest, you come upon Orval Abbey, once so powerful that its yearly revenue surpassed 1,200,000 pounds, and 300 towns and villages were subservient to it. Any traveler was welcome to three days' lodging. But when Napoleon's General Loyson pillaged the countryside, he set fire to the abbey and its ruins were almost forgotten until 1926, when Cistercian monks set about rebuilding it. By means of special stamp series, charity balls, and donations, a new abbey was built of warm brownstone. Great artists collaborated in the reconstruction, and so Orval is once more a fascinating sight for tourists. If the monks no longer offer free board and room, at least they offer you excellent bread, and their justly famous beer. They observe the spirituality and discipline of their medieval predecessors, and their monastery has once again become a religious focal point of considerable influence.

The legend of Orval's buried treasure is almost as generally accepted as the yarn of Captain Kidd. Quite a store of gold could conceivably be hidden in the maze of underground passages which connect the old abbey with seven surrounding lakes. After all, Orval means Valley of Gold. But the real treasure of Orval is the abbey itself, standing once more amidst its church and cloisters.

Virton, farther south, is a typical Lorraine city with its red-tiled roofs and narrow streets. Its regional museum shows old utensils, over a hundred *taques* (artistically-worked fireplace plates made of iron) and many other objects of popular art. One of the excursions will take you to Montauban. On this hill some astonishing 2,000-years-old Roman vestiges were discovered recently and a museum has been erected on the spot to house the finds.

But it is in ancient Orolaunum, the Arlon of today, that we can measure the extent of Roman civilization in this province. Its museum contains Belgo-Roman archeological remains of the first importance. The carvings on the 2nd-century tombstones provide an interesting picture of daily life in those times: Christianity had not yet affected this region, and the opulence and hedonism of the still-pagan Romans is revealed.

Endless wars have stripped Arlon of its ancient monuments. This lively city, with its broad avenues and neat houses built of heavy stone, will not impress lovers of the past. Yet Arlon is the oldest known settlement in Belgium.

Belgium's southernmost village is Torgny, where the Belgian State runs an experimental climate station. Mediterranean-type flowers grow in the open and this is the country's only wine growing area.

THE LUXEMBOURG SCENE

LUXEMBOURG AND ITS PEOPLE

Key Industrial Country in a Fairyland Setting

by

D. NED BLACKMER

(David Ned Blackmer, an educator and former journalist, is an American who has resided in Luxembourg at different periods since 1947.)

When you try to locate Luxembourg on a map, look for "Lux." at the heart of Western Europe. Even abbreviated, the name runs over: west into Belgium, east into Germany, south into France, as the country's influence has done for centuries.

The shape of the land is roughly that of a wooden shoe resting on its heel with the toe pointed toward Holland. This is appropriate enough, as there are certain tenuous affinities between the Luxembourg and Dutch languages, and the royal houses of both countries have an attachment to Vianden, a majestic castle in the Luxembourg Ardennes, ancient cradle of the Orange-Nassau dynasty.

This land of 999 square miles (51 long by 36 wide) offers variety and contrasts out of all proportion to its size. On the northern borders of Luxembourg and down along the Our and Sûre rivers is a rugged, wildly beautiful highland country studded with castles from four hundred to more than a thousand years old, rich in history, where industrious present-day Luxembourgers have created a lovely lake and one of the most ingenious hydro-electric installations in the world. Castles still abound as you travel south through rich farmlands lying in the broad, central valleys of the Attert, Eisch, Mamer, and Alzette rivers, or follow the eastern frontier down the Wine Route through the lush Moselle Valley. In the southern plains, above green farms, rise turrets, not of the past, but of great industrial installations that make Luxembourg the world's highest per capita producer of steel. Turning back north from the French border, a twenty-minute drive brings the capital into view, its spires towering above the south-central plain. Seen through early morning mists it revives the magic of Camelot. It is the nerve center of a thousand-year old seat of government, a functional working element of the European Communities, a spot where the past still speaks, the present interprets, and the future listens.

The Historic Background

There is no scientific evidence that people lived in Luxembourg earlier than the Pleistocene period, although it is not impossible. From that time, however, the evidence is definite and may be seen; much of it in the excellently-organized National Museum, more throughout the land itself. At Oetrange were found traces of Magdalenian man, at Reuland a nearly complete Mesolithic skeleton. Megalithic remains near Diekirch and Manternach show that Neolithic man lived here and, later, the Celts, perhaps the best known of our prehistoric forebears.

Despite their different tribes, of whom the Treviri (Trier) and Mediomatrici (Metz) were most important in Luxembourg, the Celts were united in Druidic faith. On the Titelberg, at Helperknapp, Widenberg, and through the Mullerthal were refuges where Celtic priests, the Druids, confirmed the people in loyalty among themselves and resistance to all invaders, deep-rooted characteristics which Luxembourgers show today.

In historic times Caius Julius Caesar, having repulsed the Helvetii and subdued the Belgae, turned his legions toward the Treviri. Although the leader, Indutiomar, perished in battle in 53 B.C., the people fought on until defeated at a river, probably the Alzette below Luxembourg. Roman dominion over the area lasted nearly five centuries, and Ardennes smoked ham and Moselle wines found their way to the Lucullan feasts, to be praised by Roman poets like Ausonius and Fortunatus. Yet Augustus, Tiberius, Vespasian and other of the eagle emperors faced attempts by the people to regain independence. Roman paganism did not succeed in stamping out the officially forbidden Druidism, but Christianity was established early in Luxembourg, probably before the fourth century.

As archeology and written records span the flow of time, tying today to the remotest past, so the history of Luxembourg is marked by actual bridges, or their remains. During the development of the Moselle waterway, which provides a fine navigational link between the French canal system and the Rhine complex, there were discovered at Stadtbredimus the iron-sheathed piles which supported the old Roman bridge. At Ettelbruck, the very name of the town (Attila's Bridge) recalls the Hun's passage as he hacked his way to Chalons. Nearby is the Hunnebour, a choice picnic spot, where legend has it the hordes watered their steeds. In Luxembourg City and throughout the land are bridges which recall some chapter of history. To find and identify them, and through their tangible evidence to touch some bygone episode of our story, is an engaging pastime.

After the ebb and flow of the Suevi, Alani, Vandalii, Huns, and Visigoths, by the middle of the fifth century the area was firmly Frankish. The urban civilization spread by Rome, which left fine mosaic floors, stonework, and many artifacts for us to see, receded and a new rural culture arose.

With the conversion of Clovis to Christianity in 496, missionaries brought their message through the forests and fastnesses of Luxembourg, where local pagan religions and Druidism persisted (traces still linger in spots). In their tracks arose the monasteries which united the people and exercised so vital an educative and civilizing influence from then throughout the Middle Ages. Not the least of these is that of Echternach, founded in 698 by St. Willibrord, an Anglo-Saxon from Northumberland.

Under Charlemagne, Luxembourg was a part of the great Frankish realm, and the emperor caused some thousands of Saxon families to be established in the Ardennes region, then thinly populated, an ethnic transplant which left signs in the people and on the land. Out of the dismemberment of Charlemagne's domains rise the beginnings of Luxembourg, as Luxembourg, with a history uninterrupted to our times.

On April 12, 963, the Abbey of Saint Maximin in Trier, by a deed which can still be examined in the Municipal Library, granted Sigefroi, youngest Count of Ardennes, certain lands that included the ruins of a Roman fort known as Castellum Lucilinburhuc. This citadel stood on a land bridge at the crossing of the great consular road, Paris-Reims-Arlon to Trier with the road from Metz toward Aix-la-Chapelle. The remains of the fortress Sigefroi erected were presented to public view on the thousandth anniversary of his purchase, after having been hidden for centuries beneath and within the fortifications which grew from his original castle. From this stronghold, Sigefroi's sword reached out and a town and country grew up that were called Lützelburg.

The House of Luxembourg

It is well to remember that from these times and for several centuries, countries were defined not so much by boundaries as by the families who lived in such castles and the influence they exerted through prowess at arms, interlocking oaths of fealty, and intermarriage, both upon the country round about their citadels and often upon distant lands.

The influence of the House of Luxembourg waxed and waned through the centuries. William (1096-1128) was the first to be officially designated Count of Luxembourg. From the fortress town of Luxembourg and from castles among the Ardennes crags, succeeding counts of Luxembourg extended their domains and sway by the sword. From Esch-sur-Sûre, Hollenfels, Bourscheid, and their other strongholds they sallied forth to the Crusades. Luxembourg knights stood with Godfrey of Bouillon in the Holy City and Luxembourg barons in subsequent Crusades fell in Asia minor and Mesopotamia. The country suffered from the absence of its lords protector—and from their return. Debt-ridden, they sold, gambled, and generally mismanaged their estates into bankruptcy.

A Medieval modern Woman

Countess Ermesinde (1196-1247), upon the death of her father, Henry IV the Blind, was in a sorry fix. A minor, her County of Luxembourg attached by the House of Hohenstaufen, the County of Namur which her father had united to Luxembourg seemingly lost to her, she needed protection. Marriage with Théobald of Bar (Bar-le-Duc), a descendant of Wigerik, Sigefroi's father, restored her lost patrimony and added the Counties of Durbuy and Laroche. After Théobald's death, Ermesinde, now 18, married Waleran of Limburg who brought her the Marquisate of Arlon as dower. When Waleran died in 1225, Ermesinde took the government into her own hands.

Her administration re-established Luxembourg's prestige, and her reforms prefigured later developments. Power was drawn from the separate and feuding lords to a central sovereign by the creation of officers of the court, a kind of council of state; by appointing competent provosts rather than allowing functional offices to be handed down in a family; by establishing a court of feudal justice (which lasted with modifications until 1795); by bringing villages and free towns under her own authority. Charters of freedom were given Echternach, Thionville and Luxembourg, but Ermesinde furthered the cause of freedom on more essential levels in extending the rights of justice to the burghers in all but criminal cases, giving them freedom to move about and dispose of their own goods and chattals, limiting the *droit du seigneur*, establishing a primitive form of social security, and by other acts assuring individual liberties we today take for granted. Aware that freedom depended upon intellectual and moral development, she established schools, convents, monasteries, and other institutions of education and culture. At her death, she who had begun as a weak and defenseless girl in a man's cut-throat world, left a sovereign and united nation, competently administered, full of social institutions whose effects remained for centuries.

The Power Game

In the 14th century the House of Luxembourg made its bid to dominate all Europe. In 1308, Henry VII, known as an enlightened prince, a just man, and gifted administrator, was elected to the throne of the Holy Roman Empire through the influence of his brother Baldwin, Archbishop of Trier, and Pierre d'Aspelt, Archbishop-Prince-Elector of Mainz, one of the most astute politicians of the day and himself a Luxembourger. Henry VII's reign fulfilled its promise. He lies in the Cathedral of Pisa, prematurely dead of malaria during an expedition which he hoped would bring the continent under united rule.

John, Henry's son, was the full embodiment of the knightly ideal. War was the temper of the time and John battled his way up and down Europe from the Carpathians to Crécy. For the first thirty years of his reign, until he lost his sight and became known as John the Blind, only four springs passed when he did not set out upon a major military adventure, which carried him triumphantly from the Schelde to the Vistula and from the Baltic to the Po. Count of Luxembourg, King of Bohemia, John the Blind is Luxembourg's national hero still. A man of his word, he responded to the appeal of Philip VI when Edward III of England invaded France and, sightless on the battlefield of Crécy, ordered his followers to lead him into the heart of the fight where he was slain. The victorious Black Prince is reported to have said, "The battle was not worth the death of this man." He took the three ostrich feathers of John's helmet and adopted his maxim, *Ich dien,* "I serve". The feathers and motto still figure on the coat of arms of the Prince of Wales.

Charles IV, son of John the Blind, achieved by marriage and treaty the dominion his father had sought by the sword, and *his* son, the Emperor Wenceslas, brought the rule of the House of Luxembourg its greatest extension. From the North Sea to the borders of Muscovy, and from the Baltic to the Alpine cantons and beyond, the red lion of Luxembourg held his paw on a domain roughly 500 times the size of today's Grand Duchy. The Grand Duchy proper was, at its largest, four times its present size. With Sigismund (1368-1437), emperor after Wenceslas, the great epoch of Luxembourg's imperial glory passed The people themselves cannot have greatly mourned, for imperial power had meant that Luxembourg's rulers resided abroad and increasingly looked upon the home country as a source of troops for their armies and revenues for their support. Six years after the death of Sigismund the country had lost its independence, its autonomy, and its dynasty, to become a province under Philip the Good, Duke of Burgundy. It was to remain subject for just over 400 years—variously under Burgundy, Spain, France or Austria. Throughout this foreign rule the procession of conquerors filed through the capital of the little country that accepted them and tried elaborately to pretend they weren't there. Although always a special province with specific rights, the rulers never let Luxembourgers forget that they were now a subject people; and the Luxembourgers never forgot that they had been free. Their birthright of freedom was a passion that centuries of occupation could not dim.

Division and Independence

Yet, given the politics of the times, the men who controlled the destinies of nations dared not free Luxembourg. The capital, through successive fortifications and because of its strategic position, had become too significant to bypass and too strong for any powerful nation to leave exposed to others. The Congress of Vienna, attempting to solve this problem among others, gave the eastern portion of the Duchy to Prussia, ceded the remainder to William of Orange-Nassau, raised the title of the dismembered country to Grand Duchy, and guaranteed its independence. Strange independence! It brought to the capital a temporary Prussian occupation army that stayed for 52 years. In 1839 another dismemberment gave more than half of William's territory to

Belgium. Independence, neutrality, and autonomy were guaranteed anew to the tiny remnant—but the Prussian garrison stayed. The trouble was that too many nations turned uneasy eyes to this fortress-capital at the pivot point of Europe. Accordingly, in 1867, the European Powers met in London to certify Luxembourg's freedom and to insist that the fortress be dismantled.

The usually undemonstrative Luxembourgers danced in the streets as the Prussians departed and hastened to underline their regained freedom by affirming anew their constitution. On October 19, 1868, this charter proclaimed to the world: "The Grand Duchy of Luxembourg forms a free state, independent, and indivisible."

Progress and Stress

The history of Luxembourg since 1868 is that of a country stepping from the position of a feudal province to that of an autonomous modern nation in less than 100 years. Progress has been interrupted twice: in 1914-1918 by Wilhelm II's Germany and in 1940-1945 by Hitler's dream of a thousand-year Reich.

Luxembourg emerged from the turmoil characterizing the close of the 18th century and the opening of the 19th, exhausted and impoverished; a primarily agricultural country which could hardly feed itself. Thousands of people emigrated, so that there are few Luxembourg families without relatives in some other part of the world. With the discovery that fine steel could be made from the iron ore deposits in the south of the country, using the innovations of the English engineers Thomas and Gilchrist with phosphorus for smelting, a great industry arose. The development paid off two ways, for it was found that the wastes from the smelting provided exactly the fertilizers needed to make the soil of the northern and central farm lands commercially productive. Prosperity followed upon intelligent exploitation and hard work, and emigration dwindled.

The war of 1914-1918 put an end to this period and the Grand Duchy was again an occupied country. More than 3,000 Luxembourgers died fighting with the Allies, a huge per capita sacrifice for so small a nation. Peace brought unsettled conditions until a plebescite was held to determine whether the Grand Duchy should become a republic and elect a president, or that Charlotte, sister of the Grand Duchess Marie-Adelaide who abdicated at the close of World War I, should accede to the throne. The people voted overwhelmingly for Charlotte and, as Grand Duchess, she enjoyed undiminished popularity throughout her reign.

In 1921, a customs and economic treaty was signed with Belgium: public welfare and social security administrations were inaugurated and women gained the right to vote. The Grand Duchy became a member of the League of Nations, and Luxembourg pavilions in expositions like the Paris and New York Fairs demonstrated to the world what a small country could achieve. Emile Mayrisch, Luxembourg steel magnate, was elected head of the International Steel Cartel, and by the eve of World War II the Grand Duchy ranked seventh among the world's producers of steel. Until 1940, despite the depression, productivity and prosperity grew.

On May 10, 1940, a full-scale Nazi invasion overran the country within hours. The royal family and members of the government escaped to found a government-in-exile. But it was within the country that the people stubbornly, systematically, heroically resisted. After all, Luxembourgers had centuries of training for this. Young Luxembourgers escaped *Festung Europa* to enlist with the British, Canadian, Free French, Free Belgian and United States armies. When military service in the Wehrmacht was imposed, Luxembourgers nailed the country's flag to the masts of their factories and went out on strike. Such acts, of course, entailed reprisals, deportations and privations, but no suffering could modify the peoples' determination to maintain their identity. The suffering was monstrous. At war's end, largely owing to the Battle of the Bulge, 45 percent of the farm land could not be tilled, the homes of 60,000 people were rubble, 160 bridges and tunnels had been destroyed, miles of railway track had been removed and the rolling stock hauled away, over half the roads were destroyed, and the steel plants practically burnt out from forced overproduction.

Despite all, Luxembourg was soon on its feet after the war, thanks in large part to the peoples' sense of purpose, their solidarity and hard work. The farms, increasingly mechanized, returned to prosperous bearing, homes were rebuilt, the railway system was restored and expanded, as was the highway system, and the steel plants, until other countries overtook their rebuilding program, briefly carried Luxembourg to sixth place in production. A conscious attempt to attract other industries, to reduce dependence on steel, led to the establishment of factories making rubber tires, plastics, machinery, chemicals, among other things, a policy of diversification still followed. By the fifties Luxembourg, in terms of gross national product per capita, was excelled only by the U.S.A., Australia, Sweden, Canada, and Switzerland. Having attained one of the highest living standards, it is unlikely the people will relinquish it.

European Involvement

Against this background, Luxembourg rediscovered its European importance. A participant since 1943 in building the Benelux Economic Union, since 1950 in the Coal and Steel Community, in the European Defense Community until its demise, since 1957 in the European Economic Community, in the Council of Europe, EURATOM, OCDE, GATT, and a host of other acronymic entities, Luxembourg has demonstrated in practical ways its faith in a common destiny for Europe, and its expertise in international negotiation. More than once the suggestions of Luxembourg diplomats have been a catalytic factor leading to syntheses of policy or organization which opened the way for wider collaboration, deeper ties among nations. It is a rôle only a small country can fulfill without arousing suspicions, and one in which Luxembourg has earned respect by its clear, honest, and highly effective statesmanship.

The newest bridge in Luxembourg, named for the Grand Duchess Charlotte, unites the city proper with the plateau of the Kirchberg, from which the tall European Center building dominates the townscape, a symbol and a nucleus of the European vocation of the capital. It is the home of the Secretariat of the European Parliament, for three months of the year the meeting place of the Council of Ministers of the European Communities. The Grand Duchy is the seat of the Court of Justice of the European Communities and will be the home of any other juridical bodies to be formed by the Communities. The European Investment Bank has been transferred to Luxembourg, augmenting the importance of the country as an international financial center, a development dating back to 1929, as many holding companies know to their satisfaction; and the Luxembourg Stock Exchange both quotes and issues international stocks in all foreign currencies.

In this period of transition when individuals and nations are preoccupied with the search for identity, may it not be that this small country, which has preserved its character over centuries of contention to rise from economic disaster to a respected place in the councils of the world, offers an example worth looking at thoughtfully? From experience, Luxembourg knows how dangerous it is to live on past glories, but it draws from its heritage the lessons to seek new initiatives, make new efforts and, in collaborative endeavors, to maintain its progress.

Yet, on the surface, the city and the country seem to go a placid way, with the customary rhythms of life hardly ruffled by international figures, the comings and goings of diplomats, modern pressures, or the jet flights which tie this country in the heart of Europe to the ends of the earth in hours. A Luxembourger is a Luxembourger, and this attitude of his, fined in the crucible of history, is cast of steel and gold.

The People's Character

Mir woelle bliewe wat mir sin, "We want to remain what we are", is the national motto of Luxembourg, not only carved above the porticoes of town halls or painted in houses, as you will find, but also written in the hearts of the populace as a whole, as their story demonstrates. But what *is* it they want to remain? What caprice makes them so ardently insist upon an identity apart from their more powerful neighbors? A former Foreign Minister of Luxembourg, Joseph Bech, noted some years ago, "It has often been said . . . that the Grand Duchy is only an artificial creation of European diplomacy. This is not true. From the 15th century onwards Luxembourg was a distinct principality, enjoying its privileges as such whether under the domination of Burgundy, of Spain, or of Austria." An English historian wrote, "Surrounded by France, Germany and Belgium, this little country is neither French, Belgian nor German, nor a mixture of the three, but has an entirely distinctive physical, social and ethnical character of its own."

The saying that Luxembourg is less a country than a state of mind is nearly true, for it is in the minds and hearts of its people that the Grand Duchy finds its character. Their strength lies in their will to "remain what they are"—a simple farming and industrial people whose lines have, nevertheless, gone out to all the earth. Consciously close to their land, it is only natural that the primary concern of the majority should be with simpler, more eternal matters like births, deaths, marriages, crops, or whether the price of steel warrants asking for higher wages. The concerns of the young people are the concerns of young people everywhere; their period of rebellion takes the forms of their era but then, with marriage, a job and children, the impulse is integrated into the longer line of traditional progress. Those who rebel violently usually leave the country.

Along with simplicity, Luxembourgers are quite cosmopolitan. The necessarily international character of Luxembourg's business, its place as co-capital with Brussels of the European Communities, a growing population that impels young men to seek employment abroad, and a deep love for travel have led Luxembourgers to every continent. There are more people of Luxembourg origin in the United States than in the Grand Duchy, and more in the city of Chicago and its environs than in Luxembourg's capital. Wherever they go, whatever their adopted country, Luxembourgers settle in as good citizens, but they always retain strong ties with the Grand Duchy. Whoever speaks the mother tongue, Letzeburgesch, has a passport into a sort of club with members in Africa, the Orient, Australia, the Americas, and the islands of the Seven Seas.

Luxembourgish is a spoken tongue as far removed from modern German as the Dutch language. It is learned from the cradle. Schooling begins in German, and French is added in the early years. Secondary school offers a choice of English, Italian, or Spanish. The official language, and the language of cultural exchange is French, but the country is truly bilingual—not to say trilingual or perhaps more.

Homes in Luxembourg differ greatly. There are farm cottages, thick-walled, with beams black with age, and there are residences which can only be described as regal. Housewives pride themselves on the order, cleanliness, and comfort of their homes, and on their cooking. Despite the use of many modern kitchen aids, including frozen foods, market days see ladies of all levels shopping with gourmet care. Pastries are a national institution, and an afternoon *klatsch* in tea-room or at home is a regular affair. Cafés, even more numerous and active than pastry shops, function as club, office, and home-away-from-home. There's always time for a glass of Moselle wine or *en gudden Humpen* of Luxembourg's famous beers. Nor is it necessarily "time out" for as fashions and social engagements are discussed over tea, so in the café business, political affairs, and the all-important sports debates go forward.

Life here has its pace, both through the days and through the years. If it seems cut-and-dried, it is a framework only within which Luxembourgers find ample interest, and within which cultural development is limited more by the individual than by society.

The Royal Family and the Constitution

His Royal Highness, the Grand Duke Jean of Luxembourg, Duke of Nassau, Prince of Bourbon-Parma, is the executive of a constitutional monarchy. Sovereign power resides in the Nation, while the Grand Duke exercises it in conformity with the Constitution and the laws of the country.

In 1890, when union with the crown of Holland ended, the present Luxembourg National Dynasty was founded. Since that time, the members of the royal family have shown a devotion to the interests of the people which has earned them a merited respect and popularity. While the Grand Duchess Charlotte was confirmed by the people of the Grand Duchy in her hereditary rights, these rights began to devolve upon the present Grand Duke not just at birth but with his coming of age on 5 January 1939, when he was invested as heir apparent to the crown and the grand ducal property trusts and assumed, with his other hereditary titles, that of Hereditary Grand Duke of Luxembourg. When, on 9 April 1953, he married Princess Josephine-Charlotte of Belgium, the bride became the Hereditary Grand Duchess of Luxembourg. On 12 November 1964 the Grand Duchess Charlotte, after a 45-year reign, abdicated in favor of her son. In the instant of the signature, the full grand ducal powers were transmitted to the present royal couple.

For the exercise of these powers Grand Duke Jean was unusually well prepared, not only by years of study with tutors and in schools and universities, in one of which he read law and political science, but also by ten years service on the Luxembourg State Council. This ruler, then, is not simply symbolic but, within the Constitution, a functional monarch.

The Constitution of the Grand Duchy, which the Grand Duke in acceding to his powers swore to observe, guarantees equality before the law, the natural rights of person and family, the right to work, the organization of social security and health protection, freedom of trade unions, the inviolability of the home, freedom of religion, freedom of speech and of assembly, with guarantees in detail of liberty and justice to individuals and communes. Also, "Every foreigner on the territory of the Grand Duchy shall enjoy the protection afforded to persons and property, except as otherwise provided by law."

The members of the Chamber of Deputies are elected by universal free suffrage for terms of six years. Half the country votes every three years for candidates from the Social Christian, Worker Socialist, Democratic, and Communist parties. The communes are administered by communal councils and by the college of burgomasters and aldermen.

Luxembourg's Social Structure

To understand the social structure of Luxembourg, its politics, or its spirit, it is necessary to understand the role religion plays in the life of its people. About 95 percent of the population is Roman Catholic. Rome may be the home of the church, but Luxembourg is one of its strongholds. Still, the people differentiate between practicing and non-practicing Catholics, and the *non-pratiquant* is frequently quite explicit in defining his position. Practicing or not, all of the family customs are scrupulously kept—baptism, confirmation, first communion. While there is religious instruction in the schools, in the higher grades there is the choice between Catholic doctrine and a lay course in ethics and morality. Traditions count. The Octave celebrations in early May and the Whit Tuesday *Springprozession* at Echternach draw pilgrims from neighboring countries to keep these ancient feasts. In the capital or walking the country lanes, one can still hear the sound of church bells. Wayside shrines are found everywhere, usually decorated with flowers. The greatest shrine is probably the sanctuary of Our Lady of Luxembourg in the cathedral. To many Luxembourgers she is the first citizen of the country, and is credited with numerous miracles (among others, saving the city from siege and from the Plague).

Freedom of worship is also an old tradition, however, and both the rabbi of the Jewish consistory and the official Protestant pastor (Reform and Augsburg confessions) are paid by the state, as are the priests. Many other Christian and non-Christian faiths are to be found. Hospitals, old-age homes, and some other official institutions, are usually staffed with nuns but state-owned, as is customary in many predominantly Roman Catholic countries.

The Arts

All of the arts, except perhaps lumia, and all tendencies and schools of the arts, are to be found in Luxembourg. If there is only one practitioner of some extreme trend, far from being lost or ignored, he is known and gets a hearing, whether sympathetic or otherwise. The names of Joseph Kutter, an expressionist painter whose work has been compared to Vlaminck's and Roualt's, and the photographer, Edward Steichen, are well known abroad, but there are other pleasant discoveries to be made in many fields if the visitor can give a little time to the search. Appreciation of the arts is widespread and clues can easily be picked up from galleries, the announcements of shows, the *Agenda Touristique*, or from official agencies. Little Theater groups, book clubs, lecture series, concerts and opera circuits, and the cultural activities of the legations provide many points of contact. Despite connoisseurs in every art, no single field has a sufficient following to permit artists, and particularly young artists, to live exclusively from the sales of their works. This leads some to go abroad to seek success, but many more take a regular job to support their muse. If the professional level is scant, the amateur level is highly professional and must stem from a real love.

The artistic activity in which most Luxembourgers are at home is unquestionably music. Every village, suburb, and section of town has at least a band, an orchestra, and a choral group. Town and village bandstands get much use beginning about mid-May, and there are concerts of one kind or another regularly in the Place d'Armes in Luxembourg City.

Toward the end of summer a music competition is held with prizes offered in many categories. If you stay in Luxembourg a week you are bound to see a parade, and no parade is complete without half a dozen bands.

Perhaps the best souvenir that you will carry away with you from Luxembourg will be a vivid recollection of a visit that was too short, to a country rich in history, past and present; with an easy, friendly people who welcome the stranger without envy since they consider themselves particularly blessed and want to remain what they are—solid, forward-looking citizens of one of the smallest of the United Nations.

THE FACE OF LUXEMBOURG

PRELUDE TO LUXEMBOURG

Practical Information

WHAT WILL IT COST? See the *Facts at Your Fingertips* section at the beginning of this volume for general information and specific hotel rates.

Planning ahead saves time and money. The National Tourism Office, P.O. Box 1001, Luxembourg, will send you booklets on hotels, campsites, holiday apartments, and the Grand Duchy itself. Upon arrival, the NTO information center at the airport or near the rail station, or one of the Syndicat d'Initiative offices in all main towns, can prove useful.

If you are traveling on a budget, economize by avoiding travel in the high season, or staying in the capital, or major towns like Echternach, Diekirch, or Ettelbruck. Within walking distance of these centers are smaller towns and villages where you can establish yourself more economically and enjoy the same scenery. There are good reductions in full board hotel rates between Easter and Whitsun, after Whitsun to 1 July, and after 15 Sept.

Prices were held well during 1975 and will probably not rise more than the 9% predicted for 1976. The National Tourist Office has long assured the touring public of its assistance in cases of over-charging by hotels and restaurants. Any complaint may be addressed to the NTO, documented if possible.

Some local costs: Wine (0.7 liter), about 200 frcs.; measure of gin, 45 frcs., of whisky 55; man's haircut 100 frcs., but razor-styled haircut 150; woman's shampoo and set 165 frcs.

Movie 70 frcs., opera 280 for good average seat; American or British cigarettes 25 frcs., local 21 frcs.

Cost of living: The legal hourly wage for an adult skilled laborer is 105 frcs., for unskilled 87 frcs., while the minimum monthly employee's wage is 15,040 frcs. A strong system of social security, medical benefits and pensions reinforces the structure.

A kilo loaf of bread costs 18 frcs., milk is 18 a liter, and a pound (about 500 gr.) of beefsteak is about 140 frcs.

A 2-bedroomed unfurnished apartment, in a good residential section of Luxembourg City runs about 8,000 to 10,000 frcs. a month.

WHEN TO GO? As in Belgium, July-August is the peak season; in winter there is very little to do and many hotels are closed. April, May and June are excellent months for seeing the Luxembourg countryside at its best and freshest, though it is also attractive in the fall. For seasonal events, see the *Facts at your Fingertips* section at the front of this book.

WHAT TO SEE? The Highlights of Luxembourg. These are difficult to segregate, since Luxembourg is all highlight in miniature. Wherever you go, wooded hills crowned by old castles meet your gaze. The chief places to visit are: the capital, Luxembourg City; the medieval town of Echternach; Luxembourg's own picture-book town, Esch-sur-Sûre; Wiltz with its museum of the Battle of the Ardennes; Clervaux, whose abbey recreates the monastic life, and its castle with displays of scale models of other strongholds; and the fairy-tale fortress of Vianden, 9th century; Rumelange, with its Musée des Mines *in* a mine; and for a spa, Mondorf-les-Bains.

HOW TO GET ABOUT? By Rail: The Luxembourg National Railways offer several interesting reductions. Weekend roundtrip tickets valid from 6 p.m. Friday to Monday are sold for the price of a half-fare return ticket to whatever points you choose, except the frontier. These tickets are also sold whenever there is a holiday.

Low-priced season tickets are sold all year and are valid for 5 days. They can be used on any of the lines of the Luxembourg Railways for an unlimited number of journeys. Half-price group tickets may be had upon application in writing 10 days before the trip. Children under 12 travel at half rate.

By Bus: The bus service to all parts of the country is good. There are also attractive bus tours: contact the Renseignements office in the central station, or the Tourist office in Luxembourg City. Or take the excursion coaches of *Voyages Henri Sales* in Luxembourg City, of *Touring-Cars* at Echternach, or of *Autocars Simon* at Diekirch, Ettelbruck, and Larochette.

Motor excursions leave the Place de la Gare and the Place d'Armes, Luxembourg City, daily during the season.

By Boat: The M/S. *Princesse Marie-Astrid* plies on the Luxembourg Moselle from Wasserbillig to Schengen with intermediate stops, and has a restaurant on board. Season, April-Oct.

MOTORING. Roads are excellent but occasionally narrow, and the hilly nature of the country means, of course, more curves and slower average speeds than usual. The Automobile Club of Luxembourg assures permanent road service and other assistance or advice motorists may need. We list here a two-day motor tour which will take you through the most attractive parts of the country:

Depart Luxembourg City-Mondorf-les-Bains-Moselle Valley (Remich-Grevenmacher-Wasserbillig)-Echternach-Little Switzerland (Berdorf-Beaufort-Müllerthal-Larochette)-Diekirch. Approximately 75 miles

Diekirch-Vianden Castle-Stolzembourg-Clervaux Castle-Wiltz-Bavigne-Esch sur Sûre-the Upper Sûre dam and lake (approximately 50 miles).

Upper Sûre Valley-Bourscheid Castle-Erpeldange-Ettelbruck-Berg-Mersch-Castles Hollenfels and Ansembourg-Septfontaines-Koerich-Steinfort-return to Luxembourg City.

FISHING. Most rewarding, with fast streams and well stocked rivers—notably trout (almost everywhere) grayling, perch and dace. You need a Government permit and a permit from the owner of the fishing rights which, in many cases, is your hotel. The official permit comes from the District Commissioner in Luxembourg, Diekirch or Grevenmacher, and costs 150 francs a year for internal rivers. In frontier rivers (Moselle and Sûre) it is required only for livebait or spoonbait fishing (200 frcs.) or boat-fishing (400 frcs. or 50 frcs.) a day). Trout season on internal rivers is April-Sept, white fish June 25 till end-Feb. Special rules for lake-fishing (Our and Sûre), apt to be rather more expensive.

OTHER SPORTS. The District Commissioners also issue 5-day *hunting* (shooting) permits on request, but the application must be franked by the owner of the hunting rights for the area. The Luxembourg *golf course,* 4 miles from the city, has become extremely popular with visitors these last few years. The 18-hole course, more challenging than most found on the Continent, has a length of 7,400 yards. The well-run clubhouse has become a social center. Those who like *horseback riding* can apply to the Fédération Luxembourgeoise des Sports Equestres, 90 Rte. de Thionville, Luxembourg City. Riding tours through the country can be arranged.

The Grand Duchy has many rivers suitable for small craft or canoes. The broadest and the safest for *canoeing* is the Moselle. The Wiltz is of a more capricious type and requires continuous attention as does the Clerve. The Our, with its wooded gorges, is the wildest, but most rewarding is the Sûre, for its length and for the thrills it offers.

Addresses to write to for further information on the above, all in Luxembourg City:

Fédération Luxembourgeoise de Canoë et de Kayak, 25a Blvd. Grand-Duchesse Charlotte.

Club St. Hubert (for hunting), 71 Ave. Guillaume.

Fédération des Pêcheurs Sportifs (for fishing), 14 Rue du Fort Wallis.

Walking Tours: Enthusiasts will find the wooded and hilly regions a real paradise. Excellent, well-marked footpaths take you along attractive countryside without causing undue fatigue. The *Guides Auto-Pédestre* show how best to combine motoring and hiking. *Circuits Trains-Pédestres* gives you comparable advice for the railways.

Best walking tours: Seven Castles track—from Gaichel (Eischen to Mersch; Victor Hugo track—Ettelbruck to Vianden, via Brandenbourg; Mathieu track —Wiltz to Vianden; Moselle track—Wasserbillig to Stromberg. Circuit of the Lake of the upper Sûre.

SPAS AND CASINOS. Mondorf-les-Bains has modern installations fed by springs of hot thermal waters, discovered over a century ago and heavily mineralized. They are well known for the treatment of liver and other intestinal complaints and for all forms of rheumatism. The casino, daily concerts, tennis, boating, swimming, and lovely walks complete the holidaymaker's activities. The season lasts from Feb. to Christmas.

THE CAPITAL AND COUNTRYSIDE

Varied Beauty in Miniature

Luxembourg is organized to be seen at the pace which best suits the traveler. The railroads, highways, navigable streams and cleared footpaths reach all parts of the land so that whether afoot, by cycle, canoe or automobile, whatever the means of transportation, one can race or ramble at will both through the centers of interest and the intriguing, unexpected byways. Even a bird's-eye view can be arranged: inquire at the airport. A glimpse of the entire country may be had in three or four days. The leisurely pace pays, for the Grand Duchy opens its heart most freely to those who muse over ruins, who see more in the grape harvest than labor in the fields, who sense drama in an open-hearth furnace.

The National Tourist Office is a mine of helpful information on what to do and see in Luxembourg if you write them in advance, particularly if you wish to keep within a budget.

Practical Information for Luxembourg City

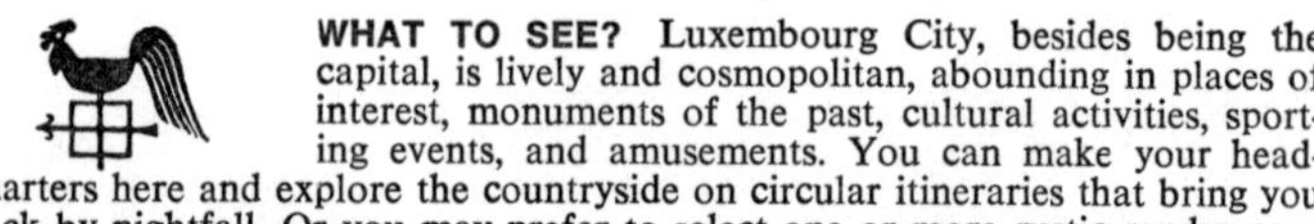

WHAT TO SEE? Luxembourg City, besides being the capital, is lively and cosmopolitan, abounding in places of interest, monuments of the past, cultural activities, sporting events, and amusements. You can make your headquarters here and explore the countryside on circular itineraries that bring you back by nightfall. Or you may prefer to select one or more rustic rendez-vous and gain a more intimate understanding of this charming region.

SHOPPING. The choice of souvenirs is difficult. Unless one wants a steel girder there are few typically Luxembourg products. Many shops offer souvenirs, but Luxembourg suffers with the rest of Europe from mass-produced mementos and the decline of the native crafts. Leather goods are well-made and there are craftsmen who can do miracles in wrought iron. Cast iron fireplace backs, a traditional feature of Luxembourg hearthsides and now collectors' items, have reappeared in minature. If you are worried about weight, arrangements can be made to mail this decorative souvenir to destination. The Luxembourg crest, a red lion rampant on a blue and white field surmounted by the Grand Ducal crown, is applied to articles in all price ranges, is distinguished and has a long history. Record shops sell discs of choral and orchestral groups presenting Luxembourg national and folk songs.

It is sometimes possible to find a good piece of peasant woodwork. You may also care for a bottle of *Quetsch* or *Mirabelle,* often best if it is a local brew bought from a country inn. Arrangements to send wines home, or to friends, can be made.

HOTELS. Luxembourg has more hotels per square mile than almost any other country. Everywhere you go you will find a clean if simple establishment with excellent and plentiful food at prices that are among the cheapest in West Europe. Most hotels have rooms with private bath, but all have bathrooms available, although some charge extra for a bath.

Many hotels (list on request from National Tourist Office) offer greatly reduced prices off-season and some of them encourage tourism by granting special terms for a 3-days stay.

LUXEMBOURG CITY. All first class superior: Best are the *Aerogolf,* 150 rooms, the *Holiday Inn,* 260 rooms, indoor pool, sauna, all rooms air conditioned. *Um Bock,* 6 rooms, in the old town. *Kons,* 167 rooms, opposite railroad station. *Cravat,* more intimate, 63 rooms. *Des Ducs,* 11 rooms, for VIPs. *Rix,* 22 rooms, whose restaurant (closed Sun.) claims fish in fresh seawater. *Eldorado* is modern with 48 sound-insulated rooms, TV provided, and free beer and bottled water in refrigerator. *Sonesta,* 29 rooms, all new. Opposite rail station, *Alfa,* 200 rooms. *Central-Molitor,* 36 rooms, and *International,* 60 rooms, excellent restaurant.

First class reasonable to moderate: *Italia,* 15-17 Rue d'Anvers, 22 rooms; *Continental,* 86 Grand Rue, 34 rooms; *Dauphin,* 42 Ave. de la Gare, 37 rooms; *Ancre d'Or,* 21 Rue du Fossé, 14 rooms; *Terminus,* Pl. de la Gare, 50 rooms; *Empire,* Pl. de la Gare, 45 rooms; *Carlton,* 9 Rue de Strasbourg, 46 rooms; and *Schintgen,* Rue Notre Dame, 34 rooms.

Moderate: Best are: *du Théâtre,* Rue des Capucins, 21 rooms; *Français,* Pl. d'Armes, 21 rooms; *Air-Field,* at Findel Airport, 11 rooms; *Graas,* 78 Ave. de la Liberté, 32 rooms.

At Dommeldange, two miles out on the Echternach road, is the *Euro Parc,* modern country setting; 32 rooms with bath. Fairly expensive.

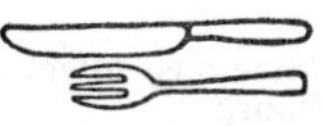

REGIONAL GASTRONOMIC SPECIALTIES. Luxembourg cooking combines German heartiness with Franco-Belgian finesse. Smoked pork and broad beans or sauerkraut *(carré de porc fumé)* is of Teutonic origin, as are *quenelles de foie de veau,* a tasty dish of minced liver balls. *Cochon de lait en* gelée (jellied sucking pig) is a more authentic local dish. The preparation of trout, pike, and crawfish is excellent, as befits a country rich in mountain streams. Trout is best cooked in wine sauce, or simply boiled and accompanied by a white *sauce mousseline.* You can get the excellent smoked Ardennes ham (*jambon d'Ardennes*) all year round, while you should not miss sampling during the shooting season the hare in thick wine sauce (*civet de lièvre*), or young wild boar (*marcassin*). If you don't mind eating song birds, try roast thrush (*grives*).

Pastry shops are numerous and the rich assortment of cakes is excellent. No wonder you have difficulty in finding a seat in the smarter tearooms of the capital during "gossip hour." Ask for *tarte au quetsch*. Outstanding desserts are prepared with the aid of local liqueurs, and the better restaurants will make to order the delicious *omelette soufflée au kirsch*. During the carnival season a special dry cake is much in favor, bearing the appropriate name *les pensées brouilées* (mudded thoughts).

Luxembourg's white Moselle wine is a dry hock resembling the wines of the Rhine perhaps more than the fruitier wines of the French Moselle. The main types are *Riesling, Rivaner* and *Auxerrois*. There are sparkling wines (*vin mousseux*) prepared by the champagne method. They also taste like champagne and are less than half the price. The *goût américain* has a sweeter tang than *brut*, so watch what the label says. By another system of fermentation they get the *vin perlé*, less effervescent but very pleasant to the palate.

Brewing beer is an old, established, traditional industry. Belgium, herself an eminent beer producer, imports large quantities of different makes of Luxembourg beer. Among the best known are *Diekirch, Mousel, Clausen, Funck* and *Bofferding*.

Quetsch, made from small blue plums, is a traditional Luxembourg "fire-water" drink. Other varieties are *Mirabelle* and *Prunelle*, both made from plums, and *Kirsch*, made from cherries. All are served ice-cold, often as a chaser to a long drink and while excellent, they should be treated with caution. When at Beaufort, try the delicious local blackcurrant wine (*cassis*).

RESTAURANTS. Most hotels have restaurants, so finding an eating place is no problem. For food that is out of the ordinary, here is a list of the best restaurants. In the listing below, (E) indicates expensive, (M) moderate, and (I) inexpensive charges.

LUXEMBOURG CITY. *L'Empéreur*, Ave. de la Porte Neuve, is for prestige dining, as is *Au Gourmet*, where coq au vin is a specialty. The *Pavillon Royal*, 20 Blvd. Royal, and *Astoria*, 14 Ave. du 10 Septembre, are one price step down, but still excellent. All (E).

Du Commerce (M), 13 Pl. d'Armes, and *Pole Nord* (I), 2 Pl. de Bruxelles, have years of dependable quality. There are two of the well-known *Wimpy* establishments, one on the Ave. de la Liberté not far from the station and the other in Pl. d'Armes. Both (M). Upstairs in the latter is the *Kofferpaan* (M), a very good steakhouse. *Rôtisserie Ardennaise* (E), Ave. du 10 Septembre is good, better on some dishes. The *Italia*, 15 Rue d'Anvers, and *Roma*, 6 Rue Louvigny, serve good Italian fare but also other specialties, both (M); on the east side of Place Guillaume, at 21 Rue de Fossé, is a genuine trattoria. The restaurants of the hotels *Ancre d'Or* and *Paris* are good value, both (M).

On the Place d'Armes are three related eating spots: at *La Marmite* you can have a full, regular meal; *Le Rendezvous* is a snack bar, while *Le Cellier* offers wine-tasting with cheese, crackers and conversation in a wine-cellar atmosphere. All (M).

Um Bock (M-E), 6-8 Rue de la Loge, near the State Museums, offers a range of dining in an atmosphere characteristic of Luxembourg.

Just outside town, the *Euro-Parc*, at Dommeldange (E), serves good food in woodland surroundings. A runner-up is the *Grunewald*, 10 Rte. d'Echternach, and many golfers (who have paid their green fee) enjoy the pleasant atmosphere of the *Golf Club* restaurant. Both (E).

LUXEMBOURG
0
300 m
0
1/8 Mile
1. City Hall
2. Central P.O.
3. Cathedral
4. Gr. Ducal Pal.
5. National Mus.
6. Theatre
7. Central Station
8. Station P.O.
DIEKIRCH
AV. DE LA FAIENCERIE
PASTEUR
PONT GR. D. CHARLOTTE
COTE D'EICH
AV. D. L. PORTE NEUVE
BOUL. DE LA FOIRE
BOUL. DU PRINCE HENRI
ROYAL
R. DES BAINS
AV. D'ARLON
ARLON
AV. DE L'ARSENAL
BOULEVARD JOSEPH II
GRAND RUE
R. PHILIPPE
BOULEVARD
PL. GUILLAUME
R. NOTRE DAME
BOUL. F. D. ROOSEVELT
AVENUE MONTEREY
BOUL.
AV. DU 10 SEPT.
VITRON
LONGWY
AV. MARIE THERESE
PT. ADOLPHE
PL. DU St ESPRIT
Alzette
BOCK
R. DE LA PORTE DE TREVES
TRIER
B. GEN. PATTON
HAMM
B. D'AVRANCHES
BOULEVARD GR. DUCH. CHARLOTTE
AVENUE DE LA LIBERTE
BOUL. DE LA PETRUSSE
RUE GOETHE
RUE ZITHE
RUE D'ANVERS
AV. DE LA GARE
BOUL. PETRUSSE
RUE ADOLPHE FISCHER
RUE DE STRASBOURG
Petrusse
ROUTE D'ESCH
RUE DE HOLLERICH
RUE D'ALSACE
RUE DE L'ACIÉRIE
RUE DES JARDINS
R. DE THIONVILLE
METZ
THIONVILLE

EVENING ENTERTAINMENT. Pick your leading nightclub (they all close at 3 a.m.) from the *Splendide*, 18 Rue Dicks, *Charley's* or *La Réserve*, both on Place des Martyrs. The floorshows are fair and the prices not excessive. Nightlife rolls along quietly in Luxembourg, except for the discothèques, which are numerous and vibrant.

CAR HIRE. *Avis*, 13 Rue Duchscher, tel. 48-95-95; *Hertz*, 25 Ave. de la Liberté, tel. 48-54-85; *Intenent*, 88 Route de Thionville, tel. 48-81-21.

Sightseeing coaches: *Voyages Henri Sales*, 17 Bd. Royal.

The *Automobile Club du Grand Duché de Luxembourg*, 13 Rte. de Longwy, Luxembourg-Helfenterbruck, can be helpful in untangling any red tape.

USEFUL ADDRESSES. Embassies: *United States,* 22 Blvd. E. Servais; *British,* 28 Blvd. Royal.

National Tourist Office: Air Terminal, Pl. de la Gare. *City Tourist Office*: Pl. d'Armes.

Exploring Luxembourg City

Luxembourg City is like no other city on earth. All ages exist together in a kind of helter-skelter harmony and yet the place seems ageless. One can live in almost any era. Charming anachronisms, which still reflect the vitality of other days, are in every street. One good introduction is to enter the city from the east. The road winding down from the plateau, into the gorge cut through the centuries by the Alzette and Petrusse rivers, goes up into the city across the tongue of cliff known as "the Bock". From pre-Roman times until the later bridges to town were built, this was the principal approach to the settlement on the heights.

The ruined tower, called the "Broken Tooth", is a remnant of the ramparts elaborated from Sigefroi's original fortifications, just beyond it at your left. This once haughty fortress is the cradle of the House of Luxembourg, which gave emperors to Germany, kings to Bohemia, and queens to France.

Legendary accounts of Luxembourg's founding differ. Some claim Sigefroi sold his soul to the devil, who built the fortress in a single night. Another story says Sigefroi, riding through the Alzette valley, was captivated by a maiden who sat on the rocks, singing as she combed her hair. Love flamed and marriage followed. As a wedding present, the lady Melusine, in one night of magic, built her husband a castle crowning the heights. The bride would tell nothing of her origins and made the condition that Saturday was to be hers alone. Sigefroi agreed. If Melusine had unearthly beauty and fairy powers, Sigefroi was very human. An exceptional husband, he kept his promise for years, but in the end, doubt, jealousy, and friends' solicitude had their way. He peeked. Melusine was bathing and, in her Saturday seclusion, had turned back into a mermaid, her right as naiad of the Alzette. Sigefroi gasped in dismay. Melusine turned her stricken face to him and vanished into the rock, where she remains. Every seven years she comes back for a moment, sometimes as a beautiful woman, sometimes as a serpent holding a golden key in her mouth. The brave man who dares kiss the beauty, or take the key from the snake, will release Melusine from her enchantment and gain all Luxembourg's wealth. On the other hand, Melusine knits: one stitch a year. Should she finish before she is released, Luxembourg and all its inhabitants will vanish into the rock to share her fate.

Markets and Monuments

From the Bock, walk up Rue Sigefroi to the first open square, the Marché-aux-Poissons (Fish Market), site of the oldest buildings. To the right is the National Museum (open daily, free, except Mon., 10-12 a.m. and 2-6 p.m.) that houses priceless works of art and, among other interesting exhibits, a model of the citadel in its heyday. (A walk outside along the ramparts, and a very little imagination, recreate the past. Time is worn thin here and the squeak of armor can often be heard above the traffic.) Leaving the museum, return to Fish Market Square. To the left, beyond the round bay window, lettered in Gothic script with the national motto: *Mir woelle bleiwe wat mir sin,* the building by the gaslight has been the Masonic Hall since the 19th century. If you stand on the large manhole lid, facing the café with the tawny stone colonade, you are on the spot where John the Blind, Count of Luxembourg, King of Bohemia, received the burghers in the 14th century. Petrarch wrote of his reign. Although quite blind, on the battlefield of Crécy in 1346, he ordered his followers to lead him to the heart of the fight. Two survived and told the story of John's end, his famed sword singing murder to the last and a hill of dead beneath its bloody edge.

The Rue de la Loge, not two yards wide in spots, brings one to the back of the palace. The upper windows once marked the apartments of the royal family. Left and around in front, the double stone stair leads to the Chamber of Deputies. The Spanish section, built in the 16th century, is the oldest part of the Grand Ducal Palace. One of the consoles supporting the balcony shows the cross of Burgundy. The ornamentation bears the stamp of Italian Renaissance influence.

Down the Rue de la Reine, Place Guillaume opens out, filled with stalls, noise, and color if it's market day, until it is hard to see the City Hall at the left or the statue to the poet Michel Rodange. The arcade at the right connects with the Place d'Armes, which features a bandstand, where the band of the *Garde Grand-Ducale* plays regularly.

Down Rue de la Poste is the Post Office. A right turn there brings one to the Grand' Rue—Main Street. Turn right the length of the shopping center until you see a turreted building on a corner. There, where the main street goes right, turn left through the alley and you come out on a fine terrace with a magnificent view: down below the near-precipice, the old quarter of Pfaffenthal with its medieval buildings; across, the plateau that contains the Fort of the Three Acorns and the Malakoff Tower; beyond, the tall European Center building on the Kirchberg; down the valley, the Grand Duchesse Charlotte bridge, soaring 280 feet above the Alzette; and, immediately below, the Three Towers, which in 1050 marked the outer ramparts of the town. It's an easy descent to the Spanish Tower that hangs over the valley; you can stroll back up Rue Wiltheim, passing under the portcullis of the towers, to the Fish Market. A left turn there, and right at the Church of Saint Michael (1320), brings you onto the Chemin de la Corniche. Below is the quarter called the Grund, with prisons across the Alzette and, on the plateau, the Hospice of Rham and ruins of the second ring of fortifications from the days when Luxembourg was "the Gibraltar of the North". Following the Corniche, mount through the yard of the Vauban barracks, cross the Place du Saint Esprit, and follow Boulevard Franklin D. Roosevelt right, to the back of the cathedral.

The Cathedral and Casemates

From this side, one enters through the section added in 1935-1938. The sacristan (office to the right) takes pride in showing the treasures of the cathedral to those truly interested: the monumental sarcophagus of John the Blind; the royal family vault, done in blue and gold mosaic to designs created especially by Vatican artists. Leave through the cathedral proper (1613-1623), a splendid example of latter day Gothic in the former Low Countries. This is the shrine of Our Lady of Luxembourg and the object of the chief religious event of the year, the Octave. From the third to the fifth Sunday after Easter, thousands of pilgrims come on foot in procession and pray for the continued protection of the miraculous statue of the Holy Virgin. In the closing ceremony the Madonna is carried in procession from the cathedral to flower-decked altars erected in the streets throughout the city.

Turning left from the porch of the cathedral, and left again in Rue Chimay, brings one to the Place de la Constitution and an entrance to the casemates. In her glory, Luxembourg was protected by three rings of defenses comprising 53 forts and strongpoints, all tied together by some 16 miles of tunnels and casemates hewn from the solid rock of the citadel. Ten gates controlled admittance through the walls, and Luxembourg was, in effect, 440 acres of solid fort. A guided trip through the casemates is a unique experience, a veritable voyage into past ages. (Open only in summer.) From the Place de la Constitution there is a good view of the majestic arches of the Pont Adolphe, which span 255 feet and rise to a height of 126 feet.

The municipal park, which begins just beyond the head of the bridge, is the site of a demolished ring of forts.

Across the bridge rises the lofty tower of the Savings Bank, and two blocks farther down the Avenue de la Liberté is the imposing office of A.R.B.E.D., the steel company that plays so important a role in the economic life of this pocket-sized Grand Duchy.

From the head of the Old Bridge, the Passerelle, the Montée de la Petrusse drops down into the valley. At the foot of the hill is the Chapel of Saint Quirinus, built in the 4th century, one of the oldest shrines in Christendom.

One could walk for days through the medieval suburbs of the Grund and Pfaffenthal or among the ruins on the plateau.

Of special interest to Americans is the United States Military Cemetery three miles east from Luxembourg City center. Some 10,000 American soldiers fell in Luxembourg during World War II, most of them in the Rundstedt offensive. A few more than half that number lie buried in a spacious field, surrounded on three sides by pine woods. Among the thousands are the graves of General George S. Patton, Jr., 3rd U.S. Army commander, and Brigadier General Betts, Judge Advocate General of the U.S. Army of Occupation.

A little under a mile down the road is the German Military Cemetery.

Practical Information for the Regions

HOTELS

BEAUFORT. Public skating rink, swimming pool. The top hotel here is the *Meyer*, which has 44 rooms. There are close to a dozen others from which to choose, the *St. Jean*, 15 rooms, and *Cigrand*, 10 rooms, being the best known.

BERDORF. About a dozen hotels, although most open for the tourist season only. Among the best: *Bisdorff*, 17 rooms; *l'Ermitage*, 16 rooms; *Parc*, 38 rooms; *Herber*, 35 rooms. (*Parc* and *Bisdorff* have pools.)

BETTEMBOURG. *Au Relais*, 10 rooms. The town has a large amusement park for children (*Parc Merveilleux*).

BIGONVILLE. A good fishing center. The *Molitor*, 12 rooms, inexpensive, has fishing rights in the Sûre.

BOULAIDE. Also near the Sûre

River. You can fish here if you stay at the *Hames*, 15 rooms.

BOURSCHEID. The best hotels are at the river beach: *Week-End*, 14 rooms, *Bel-Air*, 10 rooms, and *du Moulin*, 23 rooms. All offer fishing facilities.

CLERVAUX. 12-cent. castle, bowls, minigolf. Has an embarrassingly wide choice for such a small place.

Du Commerce, 45 rooms, has pool; *Claravallis*, 28 rooms; *Central*, 34 rooms; *de l'Abbaye*, 45 rooms; *Koener*, 24 rooms; and *des Nations*, 46 rooms. All moderate.

CONSDORF. Good base for walking tours. *Beau-Sité*, 10 rooms, *Mullerthal*, 14 rooms and *Mersch*, 18 rooms, are best. Two others.

DIEKIRCH. Rooms and cuisine are best at the *Hiertz*, 7 rooms, followed by *Kremer*, 29 rooms, *Beau Séjour*, 38 rooms, or *de la Paix*, 10 rooms. There are several others, largest being the 50-room *Parc*.

ECHTERNACH. Over 30 hotels. The *Bel-Air*, 60 rooms, is the best, followed by *du Parc*, 34 rooms, with indoor pool, *Grand*, 40 rooms, *Universel*, 33 rooms, *de la Sûre*, 35 rooms.

Also good: *du Commerce*, 45 rooms, *St. Hubert*, 35 rooms, and the more modest *de Luxembourg*, 12 rooms.

EHNEN. Small *de la Moselle*, and *Simmer*, primarily a restaurant, are both quite good.

ESCH-SUR-ALZETTE. Biggest industrial city (steel). The best hotels are small but comfortable: the *Astro*, 27 rooms, *Mercure*, 12 rooms, *Auberge Royale*, 8 rooms, fine cuisine, and the *Le Carrefour*, 20 rooms, are all moderate, as is *de la Poste*, 17 rooms.

ESCH-SUR-SURE. Has numerous hotels, among them: *Astrid*, *Hôtel des Ardennes*, and *Beau-Site* and *du Moulin*, on the river bank, are all good. All moderate.

ETTELBRUCK. Busy market center for farmers and good tourist spot. At the *Central*, 22 rooms, some with bath, you'll get excellent meals and comfort; local atmosphere. *Cames*, 10 rooms, *Herckmans* and *Solis* are also good.

GAICHEL (EISCHEN). Good excursion center. *La Bonne Auberge*, 15 rooms; *de la Gaichel*, 18 rooms; fishing. Cuisine in both is out of this world: choose their specialties.

GOEBELSMUHLE. By courtesy of the *Schroeder*, 12 rooms, you can enjoy some excellent fishing.

GREVENMACHER. Great wine center. *Govers* with 24 rooms, and *de la Poste* with 11 rooms, are the leaders. *Le Roi Dagobert* is also attractive.

GRUNDHOF. On the Moselle, not far from the Hallerbach gorge and grottos. *Brimer*, comfortable, 21 rooms, miniature golf, badminton. *Ferring* has a good, inexpensive restaurant.

HALLER. The *Hallerbach*, 24 rooms, has a superb table in this ideal spot for walking.

KAUTENBACH. Another tucked-away hamlet from which to ramble through the hills. *Hatz* and *Huberty* are recommended.

LAROCHETTE. Dominated by romantic old castle. *De la Poste*, moderately expensive. In same category, *Hôtel du Château*, 40 rooms, *Résidence*, somewhat cheaper.

MARTELANGE. Luxembourg half of a village on the Belgian Arlon-Bastogne road. *Maison Rouge*, 10 rooms, small but excellent.

MERSCH. *Marisca*, 21 rooms, and the smaller *du Hunnebour*, are good.

MONDORF-LES-BAINS. More than 20 hotels and pensions, most of them open from Apr.-Oct. only.

The first class superior *du Grand Chef*, 46 rooms, has an excellent restaurant where you can sample Luxembourg crawfish (écrevisses) at its best. *Terminus-Golf*, 45 rooms, first class reasonable, is closely followed by the less well-fitted and moderate *Beau-Séjour* and *Welcome*. More modest are the *de France* and *Astoria*, while *Astrid* is rock bottom. Excellent swimming pools here.

MÜLLERTHAL. In lovely valley of the Ernz Noire. The *Central* (open Mar.-Oct.) is modest but satisfactory.

RODANGE. Best is *Arens,* with many creature comforts for the price. Possibilities for fishing or horseback riding.

REMICH. Pleasantly situated on the banks of the Moselle. The leaders are: *des Ardennes, Belle-Vue, Esplanade,* and *Chalet Beau-Lieu.*

SEPTFONTAINES. In the Eisch valley. *Des Roches* offers riding.

STEINHEIM, near Echternach. Excellent cuisine at *Gruber*, 22 rooms.

STOLZEMBOURG. North of Vianden, with its once proud castle overlooking the Our valley. *Theisen,* a small inn. Good fishing.

TROISVIERGES. *Lamy* has a restaurant. If full, try *des Ardennes* or *Orion.*

VIANDEN. Best is the *Heintz,* 30 rooms and a villa for overflow; *Victor Hugo* and the *Hof van Holland* are very good. Really inexpensive are the *Réunion,* and l'*Espérance.*

WASSERBILLIG, Tarry at *Relais International* on the banks of the Moselle.

WILTZ. *Du Vieux Château,* comfortable and well known for its cuisine, has 13 rooms; *du Commerce,* 12 rooms, *Belle-Vue,* 10 rooms, and *Beau-Séjour*, 42 rooms.

RESTAURANTS

BERDORF. *Bisdorff* is excellent and *Kinnen* can be recommended. Both (E).

DIEKIRCH. *Hiertz* (E), Rue Clairefontaine, will prepare a quite unusual kidney "tossed in the pan" (rognon de veau sur canapé).

BOUR. The restaurant *Janin (Beau-Site)* is well worth the trip. (M).

ECHTERNACH. Good restaurants at most of the bigger hotels with *Bel-Air* (M) top.

EHNEN. A picturesque village, worth a lunch halt. *Simmer* (E) is famed for fish specialties such as brochet (pike) à la mode de chez nous; fine view over the Moselle.

ESCH-SUR-ALZETTE. *Auberge Royal,* and *Au Bec Fin,* both (M), are good.

GAICHEL (EISCHEN). If you arrive from Belgium at Arlon, take route 8 to Gaichel. You'll find two excellent country inns: *La Bonne Auberge* (E), which specializes in young wild boar in wine sauce (in season), and *de la Gaichel* (E), expert in preparing lobster and crayfish.

GREVENMACHER. The restaurant *de la Piscine* (I) is worth a stop for lunch overlooking the Moselle.

GRUNDHOF. *Brimer* (M), where M. Charles Brimer sets a splendid table.

LEESBACH. *Du Vieux Moulin* (I), in the Valley of the Seven Castles well merits a visit.

MANTERNACH. The *Restaurant aux Rochers* (E) is first-rate.

MONDORF-LES BAINS. You'll eat well at the *Grand Chef* hotel. Specialty: grills; *Astoria* and *International* are also good. All (M).

VIANDEN. The *Hostellerie Trinitaires* (M), in Hotel Heintz, is atmospheric, first class. At the *Oranienburg* (M), two generations of Hoffmanns, who have cooked for royalty, present a sound menu.

WASSERBILLIG. Pleasantly situated near the Moselle, *La Frégate* (M); good halt for an excellent meal.

WELSCHEID. Northwest of Ettelbruck; it's worth the trip to eat at Emile Reuter's (M).

WILTZ. The cordial atmosphere of the restaurant in the hotel *du Vieux Château* (E) makes for pleasant dining. The terrace is a refreshing spot in summer.

YOUTH HOSTELS. Plentiful and rewarding, for they are often parts of ancient fortresses and castles. You'll find them at Clervaux, Echternach, Hollenfels, Luxembourg City, Vianden, among other places. *Luxembourg Y.H.A.*, 18 Pl. d'Armes; *Gîtes d'Etapes Luxembourgeois* (Catholic Y.H. network), 23 Blvd. Prince Henri, are two addresses for further information.

USEFUL ADDRESSES. Local Tourist Offices: *Echternach,* Porte St. Willibrord; *Diekirch,* Place Guillaume; *Ettelbruck,* Town Hall; *Esch-sur-Alzette,* Town Hall; *Beaufort,* Rue Gang; *Clervaux,* 93 Grand'rue; *Larochette,* Place de la Gare; *Vianden,* Victor Hugo House; *Mondorf-les-Bains,* Casino; *Wiltz,* Castle.

Exploring the Grand Duchy

The northern part of the country, called the Luxembourg Ardennes, has a good many similarities with its Belgian namesake. Romantic winding valleys of fast rivers cut into the plateau of high hills.

The Ardennes Region

To see the Ardennes, take Route 7 from Luxembourg to Diekirch. The church is ancient, with parts that are from the 7th and 9th centuries. Some well preserved 4th-century Roman mosaics give an idea of the villas the Roman masters of this land built during their occupation. From before even these times the "Devil's Altar", a Celtic dolmen, has survived. In the people, too, a strong strain remains. Nineteenth-century Luxembourg folklore has a Druidic flavor and one may even still find an old farm woman who talks just a little too familiarly to her cat.

Route 17 leads from Diekirch to Vianden. Roman stonework can be traced in the ruins, but the castle on the hill dates from the 9th century, even though the important and more beautiful additions were made during the 11th, 12th, and 15th centuries.

In 1350 Adelaide of Vianden married Othon of Nassau, by which event the fortress is the ancestral castle of both Queen Juliana of the Netherlands and Luxembourg's Grand Duke. A national monument, it belongs to the Grand Ducal family.

Vianden is a picturesque little town, with its old houses and narrow streets stretching from the hill to the two banks of the Our. The church, quaint in itself, holds interesting old tombs. Nearby is a most rewarding folkloric museum. The Victor Hugo Museum, a reconstruction of the house where he lived, commemorates this genius' sojourn here.

You get a fine view from the bridge, but if you take the chair lift, a much vaster panorama embraces the town, castle, and the winding valley. If you walk a short way up-river from the bridge, you will find yourself abruptly in the twentieth century, where a mighty pumping-station takes the river water to the high summit and releases it for sale as peak-hour electric power to Germany (across the river).

Vestiges of the castles of Stoltzembourg, Falkenstein, and Roth are within walking distance. Continuing from Stoltzembourg through the excursion center of Hosingen, one turns left from Route 16 toward Clervaux, in the heart of the Ardennes. Walking along almost any of the wood paths above town, one can believe oneself to be in Shakespeare's Forest of Arden. Up the hill beyond the new church rises a monument to Luxembourgers' honesty. In 1798 the young men of the country were called to the French army. Ardennes farmers, armed only with ancient weapons, axes, pitchforks, scythes or big clubs (*Kloeppel*), led anti-conscription rioting. When experienced French soldiers arrested the leaders of the Kloeppelkrich, the President of the Military Tribunal was moved to clemency. He tried to persuade the farmers to say that their guns had not been loaded and their aims misunderstood. *"Mir koenne net lé'ien!"* "We cannot lie," they replied and the guillotine or the firing squad killed thirty-four men who wouldn't lie to save their lives.

Farther on is the Benedictine Abbey of Saints Maurice and Maur (1910), built on the lines of the famed Abbey of Cluny. The exhibit at the abbey recreating the monastic life is a window on the past which merits meditation. In the park of Clervaux, near the Chapel of Notre Dame de Lorette (1786), stands the rocky pulpit of Saint Hubert, a 7th-century missionary, who became the patron saint of hunters. The unique lines of Clervaux Castle were destroyed in December 1944 but have recently been fully restored. In 1621, Philip de Lannoi, reputed to be an ancestor of the late President Franklin Delano Roosevelt, left this castle to seek his fortune in America. On display in the castle are scale models of other medieval citadels and displays of arms and uniforms from World War II.

To return, Route 16 through Hoscheid to Diekirch, Route 14 through Medernach and Larochette, Rte. 9 to Mersch, and 7 to Luxembourg lead through beautiful countryside. For the country between Wiltz and Ettelbruck, Route 12 through Bridel and Kopstal leads to the Hunnebour (Hun's Springs), an ideal picnic ground. Legend has it that Attila's army camped here. Continue on Route 12 through Saeul to Redange. There, change to Route 23 through Folschette, Koetschette and Arsdorf. The views of the Upper Sûre at Hochfels and the countryside around Boulaide are worth seeing. From Bavigne, Route 29 leads to Wiltz.

An industrious little city, Wiltz has a real "uptown" and "downtown", the difference in level being something like 500 feet. The lords of Wiltz, powerful vassals of the counts of Luxembourg, used to dispense justice under the cross, which dates from 1502. A pleasant drive along the Wiltz River brings you in a few minutes to Kautenbach, a good center for fishing expeditions. The castle was built in the 12th century and remodeled in 1631. In the parish church are the tombs of the counts of Wiltz. But here in these rugged hills more recent history jostles the past. The tank mounted at the bend of the road winding up into Wiltz is a reminder of other and heavier armor than that of the old knights; armor that clanked along these roads to break the back of the Rundstedt offensive.

From Wiltz, about 2 miles south on Route 15, a right turn takes you to Esch-sur-Sûre, another ideal angling place, well provided with hotels. Completely circled by hills, this stronghold was well situated for defense. Legend says that an Eschois Crusader brought back a Turk's head, hung it outside the castle gate. The head disappeared, but it is said that the Turk reappears to warn the inhabitants of Esch of impending disaster. Some will tell you that the head was seen just before the country was invaded in 1940. Just over a mile upstream is one of the dams of the Sûre with its artificial lake.

Leaving Esch-sur-Sûre by the same road, follow the Sûre valley to Bourscheid, or turn left from Route 15 at Heiderscheid. Continue through the village to the castle. The seigneurs of Bourscheid must have had an eye for beauty as well as warfare. Commanding three valleys, the situation of the castle, 500 feet above the Sûre, needs no story of the past to evoke response.

From Michelau the road will lead you back to Ettelbruck, a tourist crossroad where information and supplies are available. Route 7 leads past the Grand Ducal Castle of Colmar-Berg to Luxembourg.

Echternach to Müllerthal

Route E42 northeast from Luxembourg towards Echternach goes through Junglinster, where certain spires of Radio Luxembourg's transmitter masts tower over 750 feet in air. Visits to one of the most powerful stations in Western Europe can be arranged. Route E42 continues into Echternach, where the longstanding bond between Britain and Luxembourg is visible. Echternach still centers around Saint Willibrord, the Northumberland missionary to the Ardennes. In the 7th century, he founded a Benedictine abbey which, throughout the Middle Ages, exercised a gentling, educative, civilizing influence. Today the buildings house a boys' school. In the basilica the remains of Saint Willibrord are enshrined in a Carrara marble sarcophagus. Frescos dating from the 1100's decorate the crypt, where traces of the original chapel erected by the saint are visible.

Annually on Whit Tuesday some 15,000 pilgrims gather from Western Germany, from Lorraine, from the Grand Duchy, from all the territory that once was Luxembourg for the *Springprozession*. The origin of this festival is lost in time, but it has become a feast of Saint Willibrord.

About 9 a.m. the solemn tolling of a seven-ton bell gives the signal for the departure of the procession of devout pilgrims, which winds slowly through the streets to the music of bands, of violins, accordions, or singers. To an ancient, subtle tune the faithful dance, forward three steps and back two, through the streets of the town. "Holy Willibrord, founder of churches, light of the blind, destroyer of idols, pray for us." This phrase is chanted over and over again. Miraculous cures are attributed to this act of devotion and to the properties of Willibrord's fountain in the church. Towards two o'clock, the last wave of dancers has surged into the basilica and been blessed. The streets are still jammed especially in the square in front of the 12th-century Town Hall. Moselle wines speed recuperation shortly, and to godliness is added a gaiety that lasts into the small hours.

In Echternach you have reached a region Luxembourgers love to call their Switzerland. If the hills are not alps they exercise, nevertheless, a gentler attraction, and you should not shy away from a healthy walk of just under an hour to the Gorge du Loup (Wolf's Crag), a fearful looking crevasse. But Echternach is not all history and hiking. Its recreational facilities include tennis, swimming (pool of river), horseback riding, canoeing and fishing in ideal surroundings.

Route 19 up the Lower Sûre through Bollendorf-Pont, Grundhof, and Wallendorf leads to Reisdorf where a left turn winds through Bigelbach to Beaufort's 15th-century castle, which has kept much of the old atmosphere and a torture chamber with an authentic rack. Beaufort kirsch and cassis liquors are renowned and available on the terrace.

Returning through Vogelsmuhl the road enters Berdorf, where there is a pagan altar with bas-reliefs of the ancient gods. This is the middle of the Müllerthal (Miller's Dale) which, from the variety of the rock formations, gets the name of "Little Switzerland". Though miniature, there is enough difficult climbing to provide a good workout. Grottos and caves to explore are numerous in this region and will appeal to enthusiasts. The best known are those of Hallerbach.

Turning right at the town of Müllerthal, through Waldbillig and Christnach, you reach Larochette, where two ruined castles overlook the Ernz Blanche River. Continuing Route 14 to Heffingen, a right turn leads to Fischbach, the summer residence of the Grand Ducal family. Farther on there is a splendid view just before arriving at Rollingen where a left turn into Route 7 returns to Luxembourg.

The Moselle Valley and the Steel Country

The Moselle valley is best reached by taking Route 1 out of Luxembourg City. After passing Roodt-sur-Sûre, at the junction with Route 14, the road through Manternach leads to Wasserbillig where the Sûre joins the Moselle at this frontier town.

Route 1 south from Wasserbillig leads to Grevenmacher whose wine festival on the Thursday after Easter draws many connoisseurs. Here you may visit the Cooperative of Vinegrowers' mammoth cellars or the caves of Bernard-Massard. There the method of making champagne will be explained to you and also illustrated by several glasses of the sparkling wine that enjoys a somewhat overrated prestige in Britain and America.

Route 10 continuing south leads through Wormeldange, another wine center, to Remich, of Roman origin. Remich has a delightful, wide and tree-shaded riverside promenade and facilities for boating and fishing. The wine cellars of Saint Martin are open and worth visiting. A bit south of Remich at Bech-Kleinacher, is a museum in a typical Moselle 18th-century house with artifacts and explanations which make clear the traditional development of the vintner's art.

The road leaves the Moselle to wind through Ellange to Mondorf-les-Bains. This is Luxembourg's great thermal spa. There are orchestral concerts during the season and the Luxembourg, French, Belgian, British, and American national holidays are celebrated, usually with fireworks. The village church has some interesting frescos.

At Bettembourg, the *Parc Merveilleux,* with its miniature farm and zoo in a fairy wood setting, offers plenty of entertainment to young and not so young.

Route 6 to Dudelange leads to the steel country. Farther on, in Kayl, is the Madonna called Our Lady of the Miners. South from there, Rumelange has installed what may be the world's most authentic mining museum—in a mine. Famous for roses as well as great steel production, Esch-sur-Alzette is proud of both; it puts a great rose garden within stone's-throw of the steel plants, which can be visited on certain days. From the nearby Galgenberg, France, Germany, Luxembourg, and Belgium may be seen from a single point.

Our last stop before reaching the French frontier is Rodange. For railroading buffs, a steam engine hauls a tourist train from Rodange to Fonds de Gras on Sunday afternoons. If you are lucky, you'll still find an archeological souvenir at Lamadeleine, at the foot of Mount Titus (Titelberg). If you are unlucky, you will get some consolation from looking at the rare pieces exhibited at the Roman Museum. Titelberg was an old Celtic settlement, later a Roman camp. There is a monument to the first American soldier killed on Luxembourg soil in World War II, September 9, 1944. Route 4 leads directly back to Luxembourg.

Valley of the Seven Castles

The valley of the Eisch, known as the Valley of the Seven Castles, is one of the most picturesque of the circuits near Luxembourg. Route E9 west leads to Steinfort, the entrance to the valley. The road continues through Koerich to Septfontaines, situated below the cliff where perches a ruined castle once used by Knights Templar. The old section of the church was built in 1316. The road continues to Ansembourg, where the old castle dominates the height and the valley is graced by the new castle.

Marienthal, once the home monastery of the order of White Fathers, lies in the valley below Hollenfels. At the Castle of Hollenfels is a youth hostel. The castle tower is 9th-century and the carving in the Knights' hall merits inspection. All roads north lead to Mersch, in the geographical center of Luxembourg. The town is a center, too, for excursions. There are wall paintings, mosaics, a villa, sculpture, looking much as they did when the Caesars reigned. A step later in history, the castle reflects early feudal times. Over the town brood the three towers that identify it at a distance. Route 7 returns to Luxembourg City.

TOURIST VOCABULARY

USEFUL EXPRESSIONS

English	French	Dutch - Flemish
Please	S'il vous plaît	Alstublieft
Thank you very much	Merci beaucoup	Dank U zeer
Good morning, sir	Bonjour, Monsieur	Dag, Mijnheer
Good evening, madame	Bonsoir, Madame	Goeden avond, Mevrouw
Good night	Bonne nuit	Goede nacht
Goodby	Au revoir	Tot ziens
Excuse me	Excusez-moi	Pardon
I understand, I don't understand	Je comprends, je ne comprends pas	Dat begrijp ik, dat begrijp ik niet
Hunger, thirst	Faim, soif	Honger, dorst
Yes, no	Oui, non	Ja, neen
Yesterday, today tomorrow	Hier, aujourd'hui, demain	Gisteren, vandaag morgen
This evening, this morning	Ce soir, ce matin	Vanavond, vanmorgen
How much?	Combien?	Hoeveel
Expensive, cheap	Cher, bon marché	Duur, goedkoop
Where? Where is? Where are?	Où? Où est? Où sont?	Waar? Waar is? Waar zijn?
Is this the right way to...?	Est-ce bien la route de...?	Is dit de goede weg naar...
Can you direct me to the nearest...	Pouvez-vous m'indiquer le plus proche...	Kunt U mij... dichtst bijzijnde... wijzen?
doctor	médecin	de... dokter
hotel	hôtel	het... hotel
garage	garage	de... garage
post office	bureau de poste	het... politiebureau
police station	poste de police	het... postkantoor
telephone	téléphone	de... telefoon
To the left	A gauche	Links
To the right	A droite	Rechts
Bus or trolley stop	Arrêt	Bus/tramhalte
Entrance	Entrée	Ingang
Exit	Sortie	Uitgang
Admission free	Entrée libre	Vrije toegang
Open from... to...	Ouvert de... à...	Geopend van... tot...
No smoking	Défense de fumer	Verboden te roken
Gentlemen	Messieurs	Heren
Ladies	Dames	Dames
Town Hall	Hôtel de Ville	Raadhuis (Stadhuis)
Art Gallery	Musée d'Art	Schilderijenmuseum
Cathedral	Cathédrale	Kathedraal (domkerk)

RESTAURANTS AND DINING

Please give us the menu	Donnez-nous la carte s'il vous plaît	Mag ik het menu zien?
What do you recommend?	Qu'est-ce que vous recommandez?	Wat kunt U aanbevelen?
We will have the table d'hôte	Nous prendrons le prix-fixe	Wij nemen het menu
Please serve us as quickly as possible	Servez-nous aussi vite que possible	Bedien ons zo vlug mogelijk, alstublieft
Please give me the check (bill)	L'addition, s'il vous plaît	Ober, mag ik afrekenen
Have you included the tip?	Est-ce que le service est compris?	Service inclusief?
Waiter! Waitress!	Garçon! Mam'selle!	Garçon! Juffrouw!
Please give us some . . .	Servez-nous, s'il vous plaît . . .	Geeft U ons wat . . .
Bread and butter	Du pain et du beurre	Brood en boter
Toast	Du pain blanc grillé	Geroosterd brood
buttered	beurré	warm gesmeerd
dry	sans beurre	zonder boter
Jam	Confiture	Confituur
Marmalade	Marmelade	Marmelade
Bacon and eggs	Oeufs au bacon	Eieren met spek
Fried eggs	Oeufs sur le plat	Spiegeleieren
Boiled egg	Oeufs à la coque	Gekookt ei
soft-boiled	peu cuit	zachtgekookt
medium	mollet	halfzacht
hard-boiled	dur	hardgekookt
Pork chops	Côtelette de porc	Varkenskotelet
Roast lamb	Rôti d'agneau	Gebraden lamsvlees
Roast mutton	Rôti de mouton	Gebraden schapenvlees
Roast veal	Rôti de veau	Gebraden kalfsvlees
Roast beef	Rosbif	Rosbief
Cod	Morue (Cabillaud)	Kabeljauw
Eel	Anguille	Paling
Flounder	Limande	Bot
Halibut	Flétan (Elbot)	Heilbot
Herring	Hareng	Haring
Mackerel	Maquereau	Makreel
Plaice	Plie	Schol
Salmon	Saumon	Zalm
Trout	Truite	Forel
Crab	Crabe	Krab
Crayfish	Ecrevisse	Rivierkreeft
Lobster	Homard	Kreeft
Oysters	Huitres	Oesters
Shrimp	Crevettes	Garnalen
Snails	Escargots	Slakken
Spring chicken	Poulet de grain	Piepkuiken
Chicken	Poulet	Kip
Duck	Canard	Eend
Wild duck	Canard sauvage	Wilde Eend
Goose	Oie	Gans
Partridge	Perdreau	Patrijs

Rabbit	Lapin	Konijn
Hare	Lièvre	Haas
Fried	Frit	Gebakken
Roasted	Rôti	Gebraden
Smoked	Fumé	Gerookt
Stewed	En ragoû, étuvé	Gestoofd
Rare	Saignant	Bleu
Medium	A point	Half gaar
Well done	Bien cuit	Goed gaar
Asparagus	Asperges	Asperges
Beans	Fèves	Bonen
String beans	Haricots verts	Snijbonen
Brussels sprouts	Choux de Bruxelles	Brusselse spruitjes
Cabbage	Chou	Kool
Carrots	Carottes	Wortelen (Pekens)
Cauliflower	Choux-fleur	Bloemkool
Cucumber	Concombre	Komkommer
Mushrooms	Champignons	Champignons
Onions	Oignons	Uien (Ajuin)
Peas	Petit pois	Erwten
Potatoes	Pommes de terre	Aardappelen
boiled	à l'eau	gekookte
fried	sautées	gebakken
French-fried	frites	frites
mashed	Purée de pommes de terre	Aardappelpuree
Sauerkraut	Choucroute	Zuurkool
Spinach	Epinards	Spinazie
Tomatoes	Tomates	Tomaten
Turnips	Navets	Koolraap
Apple	Pomme	Appel
Cherries	Cerises	Kersen
Grapes	Raisins	Druiven
Lemon	Citron	Citroen
Orange	Orange	Sinaasappel (Appelcien)
Pears	Poires	Peren
Fruit salad	Macédoine de fruits	Vruchtensla
A bottle of ...	Une bouteille de ...	Een fles ...
A pot of ...	Une théière, cafetière ...	Een potje ...
A glass of ...	Un verre de ...	Een glas ...
A cup of ...	Une tasse de ...	Een kop ...
Water	Eau	Water
Iced water	Eau glacée	IJswater
Mineral water	Eau minérale	Mineraalwater
Milk	Lait	Melk
Coffee	Café	Koffie
Coffee with hot milk	Café au lait	Koffie met warme melk
Tea, iced tea	Thé, thé glacé	Thee, thé glacé
Hot chocolate	Chocolat chaud	Warme chocolade
Beer	Bière	Bier
Wine (red, white)	Vin (rouge, blanc)	Wijn (rode, witte)
Sugar	Sucre	Suiker
Salt	Sel	Zout
Pepper	Poivre	Peper
Mustard	Moutarde	Mosterd

AT THE HOTEL

Can you recommend a good hotel	Pouvez-vous me recommander un bon hôtel?	Kunt U me een goed hotel aanbevelen
Which is the best hotel?	Quel est le meilleur hôtel?	Wat is het beste hotel?
Have you anything cheaper?	Avez-vous quelque chose de meilleur marché?	Hebt U iets goedkoper?
What is the price, including breakfast?	Quel est le prix avec le petit déjeuner?	Wat is de prijs met ontbijt?
Does the price include service?	Le prix s'entend-il service compris?	Geldt de prijs inclusief bediening?
At what time is . . .	A quelle heure . . .	Hoe laat is hier . . .
breakfast	le petit déjeuner	het ontbijt
lunch	le déjeuner	het middageten
dinner	le dîner	het avondeten
Please wake met at . . . o'clock	Je voudrais être réveillé à . . . heures	Ik wil graag om . . . uur gewekt worden
I want this dry-cleaned	Envoyez cela au nettoyage	Kunt U dit laten stomen? (. . . droogkuisen?)
I want these clothes washed	Envoyez ces vêtements à la lessive	Wilt U alstublieft deze kleren in de was doen.
I would like to have a . . .	Je voudrais avoir	Ik zou . . . willen hebben
single room	Une chambre à un lit	Een eenpersoonskamer
double room with twin beds	Une chambre à deux lits	Een kamer met twee bedden
double bed	avec un lit à deux personnes	een tweepersoonsbed
with bath	avec salle de bain	met bad
Another pillow	Encore un oreiller	Nog een kussen
Another blanket	Encore une couverture	Nog een deken
Soap, towel	Savon, serviette	Zeep, handdoek
Coathangers	Cintres	Klerenhangers

TRAVELING BY TRAIN

Timetable	Horaire	Dienstregeling
Through train	Train direct	Doorgaande trein
Slow train	Train omnibus	Stoptrein (Omnibustrein)
Fast train	Train rapide	Sneltrein
Express train	Train exprès	Exprestrein
Weekdays only	En semaine seulement	Alleen op werkdagen
Sundays and holidays only	Seulement les dimanches et jours fériés	Alleen op Zon- en feestdagen
Return ticket	Billet aller-retour	Retour
One-way ticket	Billet aller	Enkele reis
Fare	Prix du billet	Prijs van het reiskaartje
Compartment	Compartiment	Coupé
Dining car	Wagon-restaurant	Restauratiewagen
Sleeping compartment	Compartiment de wagon-lit	Slaapcoupé
First class	Première classe	Eerste klas

Second class	Seconde classe	Tweede klas
Connection	Correspondance	Aansluiting
Delay	Retard	Vertraging
All aboard	En voiture	Instappen

AT THE POSTOFFICE

Air mail	Par avion	Luchtpost
Ordinary mail	Comme lettre ordinaire	Gewone post
Special delivery	Comme exprès	Express
Cable	Télégramme	Telegram
Stamp	Timbre	Postzegel
Registered	Recommandée	Aangetekend
Insured	Valeur déclarée	Verzekerd

MOTORING

How many kilometers is it to . . .?	Combien de kilomètres jusqu' à . . ?	Hoeveel kilometers is het naar . . ?
I want . . . liters of gasoline	Je voudrais . . . litres d'essense	Ik wens . . . liter benzine
Fill it up, please	Faites le plein, s'il vous plaît	Bijvullen, alstublieft
Will you . . .	Voulez-vous . . .	Wilt U . . .
grease the car	graisser la voiture	de wagen smeren
change the oil	changer l'huile	de olie vernieuwen
check the oil	vérifier l'huile	de olie controleren
wash the car	laver la voiture	de wagen wassen
clean the windscreen (windshield)	essuyer le parebrise	de voorruit schoonmaken
top up the battery with distilled water	remettre de l'eau distillée dans les accumulateurs	de batterij met gedistilleerd water bijvullen
change this wheel	changer cette roue	dit wiel verwisselen
test the tyre (tire) pressures	vérifier le gonflage	de spanning van de banden controleren
fill the radiator	remplir le radiateur	de radiateur bijvullen
There is something wrong with . . .	Il y a quelque chose qui ne va pas lans . . .	Er mankeert iets aan
I will come for the car at . . . o'clock	Je passerai prendre la voiture à . . . heures	Ik zal de wagen om . . . uur komen halen
What will it cost?	Combien cela coûtera-t-il?	Hoeveel kost dat?
May I park here?	Puis-je stationner ici?	Mag ik hier parkeren?
Axle (back)	L'essieu arrière	Achteras
Axle (front)	L'essieu avant	Vooras
Bearing	Un coussinet	Lager
Body	La carrosserie	Carrosserie
Bonnet (hood)	Le capot	Kap
Brake	Le frein	Rem
Carburet(t)or	Le carburateur	Carburator
Clutch	L'embrayage	Koppeling
Crankshaft	Le vilebrequin	Krukas
Cylinder	Le cylindre	Cylinder
Dashboard	Le tableau de bord	Instrumentenbord
Exhaust	L'échappement	Uitlaat
Bumper	Le pare-choc	Bumper

Gear box	La boîte de vitesse	Versnellingsbak
Headlights	Les phares	Koplampen
Ignition	L'allumage	Ontsteking
Jet or carburetor	Le gicleur	Sproeier
Number plate	La plaque d'identité	Nummerplaat
Oil can	Le bidon à huile	Oliekan
Petrol tin (gas can)	Le bidon à essence	Benzineblik
Spark(ing) plug	La bougie	Bougie
Speedometer	L'indicateur de vitesse	Snelheidsmeter
Steering wheel	Le volant	Stuurwiel
Tail light	La lampe arrière	Achterlicht
Tyres (tires)	Pneu	Banden
Valve	La soupape	Klep (van de motor)
Wheel (spare)	La roue de rechange	Wiel (reserve)
Windscreen wiper	L'essuie-glace	Ruitenwisser
The toolbox	La boîte à outils	Gereedschapskist
Bolt	Le boulon	Bout
File	La lime	Vijl
Hammer	Le marteau	Hamer
Jack	Le cric	Crick
Nail	Le clou	Spijker
Nut	L'écrou	Moer
Pliers	La pince	Buigtang
Screw	La vis	Schroef

Sound your horn	Avertissez!	Signaal geven
Slow	Allure modérée!	Langzaam
Proceed at walking pace	Avancer au pas	Stapvoets rijden
To the right	A droite	Naar rechts
To the left	A gauche	Naar links
Crossroads	Croisement	Kruispunt
No admission	Défense d'entrer	Verboden toegang/inrit
Keep to your right	Gardez votre droite	Rechts houden
Level crossing	Passage à niveau	Spoorwegkruising
Road up for repair	Route en réparation	Opgebroken rijweg
Road blocked	Rue barrée	Versperde weg
No traffic allowed	Sens interdit	Verboden voor alle verkeer
One-way street	Sens unique	Eénrichtingverkeer
Traffic lights	Signaux lumineux	Verkeerslichten
Turn	Tournez	Keren
Straight ahead	Tout droit	Rechtuit or Rechtdoor
Maximum speed	Vitesse maximum	Maximum snelheid
Deviation	Détournement (Déviation)	Omleiding (Wegomlegging)

DAYS OF THE WEEK

Monday	Lundi	Maandag
Tuesday	Mardi	Dinsdag
Wednesday	Mercredi	Woensdag
Thursday	Jeudi	Donderdag
Friday	Vendredi	Vrijdag
Saturday	Samedi	Zaterdag
Sunday	Dimanche	Zondag

NUMERALS

The answers to many of the questions you ask will be given in numbers, hence you need to know what they sound like. Here they are, with approximate pronounciations following in parentheses:

one	un, une (ung, een)	een (ayn)
two	deux (duhh)	twee (tvay)
three	trois (trwah)	drie (dree)
four	quatre (kahtre)	vier (feer)
five	cinq (sank)	vijf (fife)
six	six (seess)	zes (zess)
seven	sept (set)	zeven (zayfen)
eight	huit (weet)	acht (aght)
nine	neuf (nuff)	negen (nayhgen)
ten	dix (deess)	tien (teen)
eleven	onze (onz)	elf (elf)
twelve	douze (dewze)	twaalf (tvahlf)
thirteen	treize (trayz)	dertien (dairteen)
fourteen	quatorze (katorz)	veertien (fairteen)
fifteen	quinze (canz)	vijftien (fifeteen)
sixteen	seize (sayz)	zestien (zessteen)
seventeen	dix-sept (deess-set)	zeventien (zayfenteen)
eighteen	dix-huit (deess-weet)	achttien (aghteen)
nineteen	dix-neuf (deez-nuf)	negentien (nayhgenteen)
twenty	vingt (vang)	twintig (tvintuhk)
twenty-one	vingt-et-un (vantay-ung)	een en twintig (ayn en tvintuhk)
twenty-two	vingt-deux (van-duhh)	twee en twintig (tvay en tvintuhk)
thirty	trente (trahnt)	dertig (dairtuhk)
forty	quarante (kahrante)	veertig (fairtuhk)
fifty	cinquante (sankahnt)	vijftig (fifetuhk)
sixty	soixante (swahsahnt)	zestig (zesstuhk)
seventy	* septante (septahnt)	zeventig (zayfentuhk)
eighty	quatre-vingt (kahtr-vang)	tachtig (tahgtuhk)
ninety	* nonante (nunahnt)	negentig (naygentuhk)
one hundred	cent (sahnt)	honderd (hondairt)
one hundred and ten	cent dix (sahnt deess)	honderd tien (hondairt teen)
two hundred	deux cents (dur sahnt)	tweehonderd (tvay hondairt)
one thousand	mille (meal)	duizend (doyzent)

* Belgicisms. In France, 70 and 90 are, respectively, soixante-dix (swahsahnt-deess) and quatre-vingt-dix (kahtr-van-deess).

INDEX

The letters H and R indicate hotel and restaurant listings

BELGIUM

LUXEMBOURG